DISCARD

A LIFE ON THE STAGE

Jacob Adler in Jacob Gordin's Elisha ben Avuya

A LIFE ON THE STAGE

A MEMOIR BY
JACOB ADLER

TRANSLATED, EDITED, AND WITH COMMENTARY
BY LULLA ROSENFELD

WITH AN INTRODUCTION BY STELLA ADLER

ALFRED A. KNOPF NEW YORK • 1999

This Is a Borzoi Book
Published by Alfred A. Knopf
Copyright © 1999 by the Estate of Lulla Rosenfeld
Introduction copyright © 1999 by Ellen Adler

www.randomhouse.com
Knopf, Borzoi Books, and the colophon are registered trademarks of Random House, Inc.

Library of Congress Cataloging-in-Publication Data
Adler, Jacob P., 1855–1926.
*A life on the stage / by Jacob Adler ; translated, edited, and
with commentary by Lulla Rosenfeld. — 1st ed.*
p.   cm.
Serialized 1916 to 1919 in the Yiddish newspaper Di Varhayt.
ISBN 0-679-41351-0
*1. Adler, Jacob P., 1855–1926.   2. Jewish actors — United States Biography.
3. Actors — United States Biography.   4. Theater, Yiddish — History.   I. Title.*
PN2287.A43A3 1999
792'.028'092 — dc21
{B}   99-31091 CIP

Manufactured in the United States of America
FIRST EDITION

To my beloved Netalia
—L.R.

CONTENTS

ACKNOWLEDGMENTS

The commentary is a relatively new form in American letters. There are few examples and those I found were not particularly congenial to my purposes. The memoirs of this actor are not only the record of the struggles, failures, and triumphs of an artist of the theater or of any other field; his life was a kind of adventure that took him across the backdrop of relatively large world events. Much of the material illuminates an era of Russian history, much of it is important in the development of Jewish history, and much of it plays a vital role in the theatrical history of our own country. The work became more complex the more I examined it.

A book like this could not have been written without the devoted help of a great many people. Among them I must single out first of all Elizabeth Schretzman, a beloved niece and lifelong friend whose devotion to my work can never be repaid, and who brought to all she did a quality of grace that can never be forgotten.

Anitra Pivnick, out of nothing more than pure friendship, took time from her own important pursuits to be at my side during a time of extreme pressure. Her assistance at this particular time cannot be overestimated.

Dena Levitt, a friend of many years' standing, also must have a place here. She never ceased to make me feel that I could overcome every obstacle. This faith of hers sustained me in hours when the sheer volume of the work ahead threatened to overwhelm me altogether.

For the Philadelphia chapter in the American section I am greatly indebted to Harry D. Boonin for the information he provided and the friendship he offered. His contribution to the book could never be replaced.

When I first embarked on the publication with my editor, Victoria Wilson, she asked me how much time I would need to complete the manuscript. Since I had already done, by far, the greatest part of it, I said that I would need six more months. She replied without hesitation, "I will give you a year." Sometime later she called and asked whether I had made any progress. I said I could send her the first introductory piece I had written in the hope that that would give her some idea of the direction I was taking. Her reply again was simply, "I trust you." This element of trust has been characteristic of our relationship from first to last. Victoria Wilson's respect for the writer, her passion for the written word, the brilliance of her own work, have been a revelation to me.

I am grateful, too, to Lee Buttala for his appreciation of the book and for his help and understanding throughout the publishing process.

I speak last of Josie Oppenheim, the daughter who has been my ally, my comrade in arms, and an invaluable consultant throughout these years of work. Time after time I have turned to her, knowing that her profound understanding of the work and her unfailing literary judgment would invariably bring me the solution I sought.

All these people have given me their time, their devotion, and their friendship. I am happy, at this time in my life, to express a small part of all I will always owe them.

INTRODUCTION

by Stella Adler

My first feeling of self, my first true consciousness, was not in a home, not in a room, but in a dressing room. A dressing room is not a room, it is something very different. Costumes hang on the wall. There is a large mirror. On a table in the corner one sees wigs, hairpieces, mustaches. But most important is the dressing table with its colored sticks of theatrical makeup.

Few people entered the dressing room. One almost did not dare to penetrate the loneliness there. The loneliness came from my father, putting on his makeup. There was a special quality in this choosing of his colors and placing them, like a painter, one next to the other, an almost religious sense of something being created.

I watched this creation. I watched a man change into another man.

Many of the characters he portrayed were European types not familiar to me. Dr. Goldenweiser, the leading figure in a play by Jacob Gordin, was one such portrayal. The aristocracy of this European doctor, his elegance, his behavior, were no part of the American world around me. Yet his bearing, his clothes, the dignity with which his hair was cut, the dignity with which his beard was cut, have remained among the strongest images of my life.

The courtroom scene of Shakespeare's *Merchant of Venice* was another lasting impression. As soon as the curtain rose, the inner meaning of the scene was revealed. The Venetians, richly dressed, possessed of all judicial and political power, stood closely grouped on one side of the stage. Isolated and alone, seated on two low steps, Shylock sharpened his knife against the sole of his shoes as he awaited the judgment of the court.

This sharpening of the knife had in it something theatrical, not altogether real. Shylock, as Adler portrayed him, was not the villain, but the hero of Shakespeare's play. He had no intention of taking from Antonio the murderous "pound of flesh"; he has brought his knife and scales from the court only to terrify and humiliate Antonio.

But Adler's Merchant, above all, was a man of power. When he was called before the Judge to give his testimony, one clearly saw the two powers living then in one community. Only as the trial proceeded, as Shylock began to understand that he had no legal rights in this court, no rights of any kind, did this sense of himself change. He lost power! When the verdict was pronounced, taking from him everything, taking even his religion, his strength left him. He crumbled and broke.

The Venetians, exulting at his defeat, now laid hands on him, brutally forcing him down to the earth. Chattering with fear, bent, stooped, he was an image of defenseless terror.

The scene was one of revolting oppression. But the injustice done to Shylock was not the center of Adler's idea. What he wanted to show was his grandeur. He threw off his fear. As the Venetians fell back, silent, he slowly rose again—and to those watching, all Judaism rose with him. Erect, with a backward glance of burning scorn for this court and its justice, in the full pride of his race, he slowly left the hall.

Adler's exit as Shylock has been described many times, a moment without words, where he summed up, together with his conception of the character, the whole meaning of his life and his theater.

From its inception this theater had been his ideal, his cause, his purpose in life. And from the first he envisioned it as equal in its art to the greatest.

Such lofty aims are not easily achieved, and the reality he encountered fell short of his dream. Conditions in Russia were uncertain, audiences small. Too many things worked against the great idea. The realities of survival, the pull of individual careers worked against it. Life itself worked against it. The Yiddish troupes existed at the whim of a hostile government. They were continually threatened, continually restricted, and finally they were outlawed. Part of a mass migration, the actors went into exile.

London was all-important in Adler's development as an actor. He writes of that city as the school that taught him his art. But the London years were tragically cut short, and in America he found a Yiddish theater sunk below even its first crude beginnings. Musical productions devoid of merit dominated the stage. The New York troupes were torn apart by senseless destructive competition. The audience was tiny; only a few very poor and unworldly people came. The Russian-Yiddish intelligentsia, already a force on the Lower East Side, took no interest in these performances on the Bowery.

But though the great idea was obscured and forgotten, it had not died. The vision of a great theater was still alive in Adler. He rebelled, took his own house, and against all advice, began putting on translations of European plays, the only actor to break with the musicals and rely entirely on the classics and contemporary drama.

"For to live forever with jest and song," he writes, "was hardly my idea. The time had to come when our theater would touch on the deeper side of life, when plays of a more serious kind would have a place on our stage. And this task of deepening our theater, of, so to speak, 'tragicizing' it, fell in large measure to me. Here I had to stand alone. Those who have grown into the old way, those to whom the old represents a spiritual as well as a material income, must oppose the man who brings the new. This is the fate of the innovator, the reformer."

In the face of opposition, Adler hung on, convinced there was a public in America for "better" theater. The Yiddish press supported him. The intelligentsia took notice. He found that his playwright, Jacob Gordin, and the overwhelming success of Gordin's *Yiddish King Lear* changed everything. With this first realistic play about modern Jewish life, the new Yiddish theater became a reality.

Overnight a mass audience was created, an audience of workers, intellectuals, Socialists, Zionists, men and women of every class, every shade of political opinion—a true theater of the people.

A great era began. Better audiences brought a rush of new and better playwrights. Revered authors of Yiddish literature began to write for the new stage. The comedies of Sholem Aleichem, the powerful dramas of Sholem Asch, were staged downtown, as were the plays of Tolstoy, Gorky, Ibsen, Strindberg, Shaw—a repertory superior to anything on the Broadway of that time.

The whole profession caught fire. Good theater apparently could "make it"! Everywhere new ambitions awoke. Every actor wanted to play Gordin. Every actor wanted to play the classics. And the people came. They had seen the best, and now would accept nothing less. Idealism, success, the competitive spirit—everything came together to form the new epoch. Adler, by his vision and will, had lifted a theater of song, dance, and entertainment to the heights of a world stage.

In the decades that followed he produced, directed, and appeared in an enormous number of plays, many of them world classics. Among these he is particularly remembered for Lessing's *Nathan the Wise,* Karl Gutzkow's *Uriel Acosta,* and for a memorable Iago, a role he played for a time with the German star Morris Morrison as Othello.

The plays of Tolstoy were a standard part of his repertory. Tolstoy's *The Living Corpse* was presented on his stage for the first time in America. Adler gave one of his greatest portrayals as Protosov, the lost aristocrat who turns away from his own world, his own class, preferring to live on as a "corpse."

In the last act of this play Protosov, soiled, unrecognizable, meets his wife in a courtroom. Seeing her again, Adler crossed the stage and, kneeling, kissed her long black skirt. His eyes silently asking forgiveness, he looked at her one last time, turned away—and shot himself. The critic Brooks Atkinson, who saw my mother and father in this play, described this moment as the greatest he had ever seen in the theater.

Tolstoy's *Resurrection,* dramatized by Gordin, established my mother, Sara Adler, as a star in her own right. In her shawl, her clothes, her walk, Sara brought all Russia onto the stage with her. The peasant girl seduced by the prince and pregnant with his child, the hardened prostitute condemned to hard labor—Sara had the power, the emotional range, to encompass all the aspects of the great role. The pregnant Katushka runs to the railroad station, but she is too late. The train and the prince are gone. In this moment of supreme agony, Sara ran across the stage and threw herself across the railroad tracks. In the prison scene she came before the prince half drunk, ready to entertain any gentleman who would pay for her company. Recognizing him, she turned from him with an indescribable movement of horror and negation.

Though trained in the school of realism, Sara's style was essentially classic, her movements on the stage always beautiful. At a banquet in her honor a fellow actor said, "You don't need to see Sara Adler act. You have only to see her rise from a chair!" Her voice was dramatic—passively dramatic, musical. She never broke her voice, never screamed in any play.

Sara's *Resurrection* was followed by another great performance, that of the simple Russian-Jewish housewife of Gordin's tragedy of immigrant life, *The Homeless.*

The productions downtown were now arousing the serious interest of a number of American critics and intellectuals. But while Adler acquired a larger fame through the great plays of Europe, it was Jacob Gordin who gave him his career, who in a sense created him, and it is with this playwright that Adler's name is most closely associated.

Gordin, idolized by the public, often caused controversy by his repeated attacks on the negative aspects of Jewish life. Over and over his plays spoke out against ignorance, brutality, bigotry, materialism. His *Sappho* is a daring plea for a woman's right to sexual freedom. In *Der Metureff* (*The Worthless One*) the life and work of a scientific genius is destroyed by the ignorance of a fanatical Jewish community.

In *Der Vilder Mensai* (*The Wild Man*), one of his strongest plays, a weak retarded child, victim of a brutal ignorant home, has grown up little better than an idiot. The father of this unfortunate has taken as his second wife a woman of the town. She brings her pimp with her, and between them the house is turned over to riots and drunken parties.

As the family goes to pieces nobody sees or understands that the "Wild Man," no longer a child, is madly in love with his stepmother. In a terrifying last scene he finds his release in the act of murder.

With only the woman awake in the sleeping house the sick boy enters. He sees his stepmother. He takes out the knife. She tries to escape. Her cries go unheard. He forces her down. The knife plunges. Holding it high over her body, he cries to his father in his mad triumph that he, like his father, is now married.

At this last moment of the play, Adler showed the orgasm of the afflicted boy. The action, extraordinarily daring for its time, would not have been permitted on any American stage. The Yiddish audience, frozen with pity and horror, saw only its terrible truth.

Coming immediately after the extraordinary success of *The Yiddish King Lear,* Adler's grotesque, pitiful "Wild Man" established him as the greatest star of the Yiddish theater.

Ten years later, in 1903, the role of Shylock brought him world recognition as one of the great actors of his time.

At the age of sixty, with his theatrical activity at its height, Adler agreed to write his memoirs. This history, published in a Yiddish newspaper, was read in large part by those who constituted his theater audience. It is, in fact, directly addressed to these devoted followers, who, he knew, would forgive him almost anything, and he conceals from them none of his youthful sins and follies. The loving son of a deeply Jewish home, it appears, has dangerous friends. He spends his nights drinking, carousing, and rioting through the town. Already there is an uncontrollable need for pleasure, for the company of women. And he confesses that even at the youthful age of sixteen, he had learned the way to every den of vice in the city.

He was saved from the "grave moral danger" of this moment by a new passionate interest in the Russian theater. His connection with that theater, the remarkable influences he acquired there, form an extremely important chapter of his youth. The standards set for him at that time remained with him throughout his life, and in that school he developed the theatrical judgment so valuable to him later.

Though the Yiddish theater disappointed him, he embraced it. He became an actor, took on the bohemianism so organic to the actor. But from the first he is set apart from the others by a higher aspiration. The young matinee idol, vain of his looks, burning for success, is all the while learning that art is not instinctive, that there is a form that must be studied, worked at, mastered.

Later we see him put away from himself all that is young. The reckless young actor, wasting his life in pursuit of every woman, every pleasure, is turning to his one passion—theater.

The man of sixty has remembered everything—the little provincial troupe of actors, the towns and villages they played, the jealousies and rivalries, the camaraderie and love. Through the life of one actor we see the story of a theater that survived poverty, persecution, and exile, a theater that, together with thousands of other refugees, crossed an ocean, entered America with them through Castle Garden, and, drawing strength from the soil of its new country, finally reached greatness.

It was a theater that had derived its style from the school of the new Russian realism. But though he had espoused it, there was in Adler a life force too strong to be contained in any school, even a great one. There was no truth for Adler in the ordinary, in what he calls the "flat imitation of reality." There was always something larger than life in his conception of the character, always something mysterious, something of the unknown, in the image he created on the stage.

The theater he built demanded extraordinary energy, demonic ambition, demonic will. It took from him the total of his life force, and in the end it took his health and the last drop of his strength.

It was the audience that repaid him. All that he gave, they gave back, in their gratitude, in their pride, in the triumph they felt in his triumph.

That was the Yiddish theater I remember, the theater of my youth. When the time came for me to spread my wings, to find my own way, it was perhaps this memory that made me hesitate, unsure of my path. For an aspiring young actress the road was clear; it led to Broadway. Yet I did not stay long on glamorous Broadway. It was somehow not the answer. I knew that in Russia, Stanislavsky had created a school for actors where new and revolutionary techniques were being explored. I wanted to know more about this new approach, this idea that, like a painter or a musician, there was a *course of action* for the actor, a *process* by which he could learn and develop his craft. I knew that a small experimental group had come together to study these new techniques, these new ideas. I joined them in this endeavor.

The group had come together in New York, where Richard Boleslavsky and Maria Ouspenskaya were examining and teaching these new techniques. I became part of this experimental workshop. It was in this little-known American Laboratory Theatre that I was thrown together with Lee Strasberg. Here, also, I met Harold Clurman. And when Clurman and Strasberg, together with others, formed the Group Theatre, I came in as one of its founding members.

Here in the Group I found what I had been searching for—a theater that had come together for something more meaningful than another Broadway hit. The plays of John Howard Lawson, the plays of Paul Green, the deeply moving plays of Clifford Odets, were chosen by the Group not because they would bring money into the box office, but because they had something to say about American life, something important that needed to be said.

My years in the Group were difficult. a time of pain as well as a time of growth. There were deep divisions, fundamental differences. But when the Group broke up, when the actors dispersed, I felt I had lost my home. My life now was Broadway, London, Hollywood—wherever the work took me.

The years that followed were productive years for me. I found myself as a director, and directed and staged some dozen Broadway and off-Broadway productions. I appeared in a number of plays; I made some movies. Most important, I began the teaching that was later to be the major work of my life.

But I can truthfully say it was only the Group that gave me again what I experienced in my youth—a vision beyond personal success. A conception of the actor's art as an expression of the highest human principles, the highest human aspirations.

These are the values I brought my students as a teacher. For me they can never change. Those principles, those aspirations, will always remain for me the best, the surest, the *only* way for the actor.

A Yiddish Theater?
How Did It Happen?

by Lulla Rosenfeld

Remembered today simply as an intimate part of the Jewish-American experience, the actual origins of the Yiddish theater are all but lost in time. This theater of the diaspora did not arise from the shtetl of Eastern Europe or the medieval Purim play, but out of the revolutionary upheavals of the eighteenth and nineteenth centuries. It had its birth in the idea of freedom.

No power, as we know, could withstand the force of this idea. All modern history begins with it. The changes it brought about could never be reversed. The old order never regained its hold on the minds of men. And life everywhere felt the shock of these events.

Jewish history reflects this turning point in a movement known as the Haskala (the Awakening). Like the much-admired American Constitution, this doctrine reconciled contradictory forces. Founded above all on reason, the Haskala still upheld faith. It called on the Jew to integrate, but not assimilate, to embrace the great Christian culture around him, yet still hold fast to his Jewish identity.

Education was the battle cry of this Jewish revolution. If the world would not break the wall of the ghetto from the outside, the Jew must break it from the inside. Education—*secular* education—was the tool that would break the wall. Free, no longer isolated, the Jew would take his place in science, in art, in political action, in every great endeavor of the time.

The foundations of this new Judaism were laid in the eighteenth century by the German philosopher Moses Mendelssohn. This renowned scholar died without ending the prejudice against his people.

His ideas, however, were carried on in the Society for Jewish Science and Culture founded by one of his daughters.

Allied now with the cause of Zionism, this society flourished for some years in the liberal Berlin of the 1820s. George Eliot wrote *Daniel Deronda* under its influence. Heinrich Heine acted for a time as its secretary. Outstanding liberals of the day espoused the Jewish cause. But the society, confined entirely to the brilliant Jewish salons of Berlin, had little or no effect on the ghettoized Jews it supposedly wanted to save. Dying of inanition, the Haskala journeyed eastward.

In Russia, Europe's bastion of reaction, the movement took on a new life and energy. Here, no unconverted Jew, however learned or gifted, could hope to enter Russia's academic or literary world. But unlike their German counterparts, these educated men had remained closer to their fellow Jews. To enlist them in the fight for liberation, poets and philosophers abandoned the Hebrew of the scholar and came forward as fighters for the despised "jargon"—the language of the people: Yiddish.

This ferment, this fight for the minds of the many, brought with it the idea of a Yiddish theater. To make such a theater a reality, a new political climate was needed. This was provided by the liberal reforms of Tsar Alexander II.

This ill-fated and now almost forgotten man came to the Russian throne in 1855. In that year his father, known to the people as "Nicholas the Flogger," suddenly and unexpectedly died. He left to his son the tail end of a ruinous war in the Crimea, a nation hated by all of Europe, and a liberal intelligentsia disgusted by Russian defeat.

In deference to his dead father, the new tsar continued the war for another six months—a delay that cost an additional eighty thousand Russian lives. In the end Sevastopol fell to the French, and the tsar had to sign the humiliating peace forced on him by the allies. To make up for it, he promised the nation reforms on every level of government.

The war once over, the tsar threw himself heart and soul into a program of change more far-reaching than anything in Russian history. In the first dazzling years of his reign he relaxed censorship, introduced a more tolerant regime in Catholic Poland, filled his cabinet with known liberals and "reds," and made sweeping reforms in the universities, the judicial system, and the army.

With all this in motion, the tsar in 1857 began his crowning effort: the long-overdue emancipation of the serfs, twenty-five million peasants who had lived for generations in conditions of inhuman servitude.

Throughout the country liberals foresaw a new epoch of freedom. These were Alexander's glory days. Wherever he went, huge crowds followed, cheering him. The radical writer Chernyshevsky compared him with Peter the Great. The revolutionary democrat Prince Peter Kropotkin wrote everywhere that all Russia was for emancipation and the tsar. And *Kolokol* (*The Bell*), Alexander Herzen's newspaper in exile, carried the famous article beginning with the words "Thou has conquered, O Galilean!"

Among the reforms of the new regime were certain laws affecting the Jews, the most oppressed of the Russian minorities. The special Jewish tax was revoked, Jewish travel restrictions were lightened. Jews were allowed into more of the trades and occupations. The doors of the universities opened to their sons and daughters.

Greatest among these dispensations, however, were the new conscription laws. Under Tsar Nicholas, Jewish boys were subject to army service at the age of twelve. When the twelve-year-olds were hidden, boys of nine and ten were taken in their place. Few of these children survived their first year of life in the army. The new tsar reduced the term of army service from twenty-five to sixteen years. He abolished altogether the juvenile recruitment of Jews.

All over the country, the children were sent home, by train and wagonload, to their villages and their parents. A cry of joy went up throughout the Pale of Settlement. And in every Jewish home in Russia Tsar Alexander's name was blessed by the Jewish people.

In 1855, the year of Tsar Alexander's coronation, a son, given the name Yankev (Jacob), was born to Feivel (Pavel) Abramovich Adler, a wheat merchant of the Ukraine, and his wife, Hessye. The less-heralded event took place in Odessa, a city known for its liberal traditions and cosmopolitan atmosphere.

Young Jacob Pavlovich, growing up in a great Russian city at a time of remarkable social and political change, seemed to accept the world around him as most people do—without thinking much about it. A desire for pleasure dominated his youth, and though he came of an educated family, he is not numbered among the Odessa intelligentsia. Nor was he of the *maskilim,* as the followers of the Haskala were called. Although the Haskala profoundly influenced all his generation—and indeed, every Jewish generation that followed it—he seems to have been as vaguely aware of it as of the air he breathed.

Of the Haskala as an organized system of ideas, he probably knew little or nothing. Yet it was he who, in another time and country, would build a theater that gave a struggling immigrant audience every great humanistic idea of the age, a theater where that "world idea" of the Haskala would find a platform and a voice.

The memoirs of Jacob Adler, translated here for the first time, were for some years a popular feature of the Socialist newspaper *Die Varheit* (*The Truth*), one of the many Yiddish newspapers published at that time in New York. These recollections, serialized from 1916 to 1919 and briefly resumed in 1925, cover the greater part of his personal and professional life—his beginnings in tsarist Russia, the struggles and achievements of the London years, and finally the migration of the actors to America, where the Yiddish theater was to have its greatest incarnation.

The prologue to Adler's memoirs appeared in *Die Varheit* on April 16, 1916.

A Life on the Stage

My life . . . what was it? To what can it be likened?

It is gone now, the thousand-headed monster whose din comes to me nightly through the thin wall of my dressing room—the monster that for forty years has dared me out into the arena, and whose noise, breathing, odor, have since boyhood unnerved me and sent a fever through my blood. It has departed, leaving only darkness and silence.

The applause is over. The curtain has come down for the last time, and to make sure it will not rise again, a wall of asbestos has descended. The theater is dark . . . only a single glare from the middle of the parquet throws a ghostly light over the loges, balcony, gallery. Something cold and infinitely menacing comes from those silent corners.

I stand in a darkened theater, a sixty-year-old actor with a face stripped of its makeup—that face with the dark circles under the eyes and the two long creases in the cheeks.

My life . . . what was it? To what can I liken it?

Once more I have won the battle. Once more the thousand-headed creature has been tamed, conquered. Once more it has laughed, wept, sobbed, shouted my name over and over until I showed myself, and the shouts turned into a sea of joyous faces and a hailstorm of applause. So many times this has happened, yet how one still longs for it, thirsts for it! And should the applause one night grow cooler by a thousandth, should I see one face without joy, one pair of hands not wildly applauding, I fall straightaway into melancholia, feel I am no longer needed, and turn away from the ungrateful public, asking myself bitterly what it is they want of me, the murderer, and what more I can give them.

Night after night it has been so. Forty years now it has been so.

My life . . . what was it? To what can I liken it? This time my own tragedy, not a tragedy I have learned. This time, my own *Faust*.

"Life's but a walking shadow," says Shakespeare's Macbeth, "a poor player that struts and frets his hour upon the stage and then is heard no more." A dark thought for every man, but darker still for the actor who has his true existence only in his everlasting duel with the public. For if every man's life is no more than a play, the actor's life is no more than a play within the play.

And what of all the rest? All that took place behind the scenes when he was a man like any other? Was all that, too, a show, an illusion, a tale "full of sound and fury, signifying nothing"?

What was it all for, then, and for what was it needed? What is it that flames up in me each night, dies down, and takes fire again on the morrow? What is it in *them* that catches that fire and burns with it so fiercely, with such joy?

No, my Shakespeare . . . For me, the Jew, your answer is not enough. My life has been no walking shadow, no brief moment. When I measure it with the measure of my feelings, it has been an eternity, an ocean.

Shall I recross the ocean to the far side?

Shall I revisit the graves of my old joys, my old woes?

Among those graves will I find my answer?

Something About My Family

It is a holiday, a festive gathering with many happy people around a great table. Out of that whole great joyous scene comes a face more full of light, more radiant, than all the shining candles. A woman beautiful as a picture, with beautiful, intelligent eyes and a wonderful smile. This is my mother, Hessye. At her side I see a man, short of stature, not at all handsome, but sympathetic and full of magnetism, for his face is clever, his personality lively and interesting. This is my father, Feivel (Pavel) Abramovich Adler.

Another memory—a less happy one. My parents are walking in the street, and I am walking behind them. No—I am not walking. I am being carried in the arms of our *meshuris*,* Elie. (Whether my father was rich at that time and could afford such a person, or whether his business required it, is lost now in the sea of forgetfulness. Enough that out of that sea has appeared the figure of Elie, our *meshuris*.)

This notable little procession is making its way from our house on Ekaterina Street to the great Richelefskaya.† Suddenly we hear screams from a house surrounded by a crowd. The screams are coming from the cellar. From the short answers of the onlookers my parents learn that a pair of horses have run over a child, a little boy, and killed him.

I hear this from my high seat in Elie's arms. Elie takes a notion to go into the cellar and see the dead child. I am carried into the cellar, see a bloodied little body, and hear the agonized shrieks of the family. We leave the cellar, and Elie and my parents do not stop warning me. "You see, Yankele, how careful you must be? And if you do not look after yourself, you too will be run over by horses and killed."

---

* A humble assistant used mostly for running errands.
† The main street of Odessa.

For a long time after that I lived in dread of all horses. Nothing, no dog, no devil, no corpse, terrified me as much as a harmless stationary horse. And whenever I passed that cellar on the way to the Richelefskaya I ran for my life, for it seemed to me I still heard the shrieks of that family overtaken by catastrophe.

In those days poor people moved often. I remember best a certain house in Market Street because of its unusually lively, populous courtyard. Although I was a *ben yochid*—an only son—I had no lack of playmates in this court, where a whole colony of little Jews and little Christians all played together.*

Apparently, as time went on I lost my fear of horses, for one day I saw a horse and wagon on the street, the carter some distance off, not thinking of his cart. Instantly I sprang into the wagon, grabbed the reins, and was off down the street at a mad gallop.

Why did I do such a thing? First of all, the ride itself—where is the little boy who could resist such a ride? Second—and this was the core of it—my desire (and there was a badness in it too) to play a trick on the carter, get the better of him. "Aha!" I said to myself. "You are not watching your cart? Now I have you!" I brought down the reins with all my might, the wagon tore down the street, and all this gave me terrific pleasure—a pleasure even stronger when I looked back and saw the carter running after me and shouting, a whole streetful of people beside him. The incident shows my wildness and recklessness as a child.

In the course of my life I have lived through three pogroms, the first of them in the years of my childhood in Odessa. As it happened, the synagogue and the Greek church were on the same street, and every year at Passover the Greeks beat up the Jews and robbed them.

This first "little pogrom" began with a fearful alarm. Screams filled the air. Jews ran by with torn bloody faces, a murderous mob after them. We were saved only because we lived in the house of Rollya the Greek. I watched it all in horror with my parents and others at the courtyard gate.

That year (it must have been about 1862), the Greeks committed

---

* Unlike Kiev, the capital of the Ukraine, Odessa had no ghetto. Jews in that city mingled freely with the Russians, Ukrainians, Poles, Greeks, Italian, French, and other nationalities that made up the population.

much robbery in Odessa. Jews were mauled and maimed, and one very poor man who sold lemons was beaten to death on the street.

For a long, long time the death of that very poor man was whispered and remembered in our home.

Police power in Russia went uncurbed even in the first liberal period of Alexander II's reign. The crimes committed during these riots had the tacit consent of the police, and the perpetrators were never brought to justice.

As it has now probably become clear, I was born into a simple, poor, Orthodox home. True, it was in the great city of Odessa, we mingled with Christians, and all around us Russian was spoken. Still, it was a Jewish home, and except for the Russian newspapers, Yiddish was our language.

Our family became more observant and pious when my grandfather, Reb Avremele Fridkus Adler, came to live with us. A handsome old Jew, always in a long coat, always with a book in his hand, he filled the house with cleanliness, belief, and peace. Not only my parents but the whole family revered him.

With my father often away on business and my mother occupied with household tasks and other cares, it was he who took me to school, taught me how to read, how to pray, how to make a blessing. He loved me very much, and sometimes when I had been up to mischief, it was the *zayde** who saved me some well-deserved blows. "Don't beat the child!" he would say. And he would take me away from my angry, excited father.

My grandmother was a fine old *Yidene.*† She had a shop where she sold remnants, but on Friday night she would lock up, come home with the keys around her waist, and make preparations for the Sabbath. Bathed and dressed in their best, she and my mother would set the heavy brass candlesticks on both sides of the great round table, and then stand together and bless the candles. And it was a picture for

* Yiddish for "grandfather."
† Yiddish for "old Jewish lady."

an artist to see these two beautiful women, one old, the other still young and blooming, each with a hand shielding her face, standing over the little tongues of flame and whispering something—something so quiet and secret that not a word could I hear, only a sigh and sometimes a tear that dropped to the pure white tablecloth.

With my grandmother I lived well. I spent hours rummaging about in her remnant shop, and as I grew older I was useful to her, too. Every year in August a fair was held in the suburb of Peresyp, and the old lady went there for her *galanteries:* scarves, kerchiefs, gloves, and other trifles of that kind. I would go with her to the fair and mark down her purchases and expenses. The whole great open-air tumult, the crowds, the chaffering, the delicious things to eat—all this delighted my childish heart, and in all the world I could imagine nothing finer than the fair at Peresyp.

Peresyp (pronounced Pere'sya), a popular beach resort near Odessa, was famous for its mineral springs and medicinal coastal lagoons, waters said to be efficacious in the treatment of rheumatism, gout, nervous afflictions, skin diseases, and respiratory ailments. Now called Louzanovka, this Odessa suburb may still be in use as a summer resort and health station.

In spite of our poverty, our house was a happy one. There were joyful holidays, lusty songs around the table, shining radiant faces.

The house was always full of people. On Friday night my father would come home from the synagogue bringing with him a poor man, a *maggid,** or perhaps a Jew from the Land of Israel. And he and this new friend would sit talking, talking, all through the night. The conversations in our house always came back to the plight of the Jew in Russia. On this subject my father needed no one's opinion. He was not a Jew who "hid behind the oven," but a man who read the Russian papers and took an interest in the great questions of the day.

---

* An itinerant speaker, a rabbi or layman, who traveled from town to town, often covering great distances. In remote rural areas the only news of the world was often brought by the *maggid.*

My father, like others in Odessa, dealt in wheat. He sometimes speculated, sometimes acted as a broker, but he seldom had luck either way. His intellectual gifts and his understanding of politics consoled him for his business failures. Men, and women too, liked to hear him talk, and perhaps because of this he sat more often in strange houses than in his own.

His nature was carefree, and he lived a carefree life. My mother's existence was very different. A daughter of the wealthy Halperins of Berdichev, her youth had held a tragic chapter. My father was not the first man she had married. She had divorced her first husband, and in so doing, lost the right to her child, a boy named Ephraim. If I were to make a guess I would say she met my father when some business matter took him to Berdichev, fell in love with him, and for his sake left her husband and her child.

She was a beautiful woman, tall, erect, with a wonderful but rather sad smile. She was well educated, read the Russian novels as well as the Yiddish novels becoming popular at this time. Fastidious, artistic, even theatrical, she was, most of all, outspoken. When my father brought home a new visitor she would immediately measure him with her great clever eyes and find out all his faults and failings. When in my bachelor days I began to associate with singers and actors my mother took alarm.

"Why are their faces so yellow?" she asked when I brought home these night birds of mine. "Why are their clothes so bedraggled? And where are their mustaches? They are actors? Clowns? And with this do they hope to earn bread for a wife?"

Poor Mother! Small pleasure she got from me, and not much more from my father. We were poor, pressed at times for the smallest sums. He was popular, out with his friends. She sat alone. More than once in her lonely moments I saw her brush away a silent tear.

In every family there is a king. In our family it was not my clever father, not my revered grandfather, but Aaron Trachtenberg, the renowned Uncle Arke who "kinged it" in Cambara's house on Market Street. He was the richest man in our family, but it was not in his wealth that his importance lay. He was a real Mohican, the patriarch, magnate, and ruler of us all.

I remember him as a fine man, tall, powerfully built, with a voice to command, eyes that ordered, and an open hand—in both meanings of the word! He was the judge and arbiter of the whole family. The whole world knew this. A daughter to marry and no dowry? Uncle Arke was called in. A father fallen into debt? A grandfather struck by misfortune? Everyone came to him, he took out his bundle, and all was made right. He was especially sought after in quarrels between man and wife, bride and groom. The women always brought him their problems. He settled all their differences, and his decision was final. If not—a *whack!* He stood for no nonsense.

A very interesting type, this Uncle Arke, and anyone interested in my life and career should make his acquaintance, for he is related to a figure I created on the stage, a figure that more than any other decided the course of my theatrical life. I refer to Jacob Gordin's *Yiddish King Lear.*

Some of you may recall my appearance in this play. My height and build were by nature like his. With the art of makeup, I made my face into his. For as soon as Gordin read me the play the image of Uncle Arke swam up from the depths of my consciousness.

Growing Up in Odessa

I have many memories of my school days, some beautiful, some ugly and brutal. Being a boy with a great leaning toward fun and mischief, I cannot boast of myself as a student. I had bad luck with my teachers, too, which made matters worse. Whenever by chance I had a teacher I liked, poverty began whistling in every corner of the house, and there was no way to pay for my studies.

My first taste of *chaider** was with a Reb Yokele, an angry rebbe who kept us in order with a threatening swish of the cat-o'-nine-tails. And he beat not only his students, but his own children and even his wife.

It was probably at this time that I acquired my lifelong disgust with the practice of beating children. I see the hateful picture yet: a child with his buttocks up, the pure white flesh cut through with long red stripes. And above him the torturer, gloating, degraded, his eyes and nose running, his face inflamed . . .

With Reb Yokele I learned the Five Books of Moses. I remember the long winter evenings, the guttering candle, the sweet night coming . . .

A year or so later I was in a *chaider* on Market Street. This teacher was a patriarchal Jew of about sixty, tall, proud, his hair combed straight back on a high broad forehead, a beard both black and gray, a pushed-out chest, a firm tread. His dress was fine and proper—a long mantle, spectacles, a cane—in a word, an important and arresting figure. He taught only ten children, probably because he liked teaching, for he was well off and did not need to teach at all.

* In *chaider* (Hebrew school) Jewish studies were taught along with a little grammar, geography, and mathematics.

With this rebbe I learned the Book of Joshua. For the first time I began to understand the greatness of our books. How I see it all still! The book on the table. The great black fiery letters. The word "Joshua." And opposite me at the table the beautiful proud serious rebbe. I hear his voice, his pure Yiddish speech as he explains. And again I see the ten-year-old boy, shaking back and forth, learning, learning and contented.

But what was the end of it? Poverty. The rebbe sent me home for money. I came back each time with the same story. There was no money. Until the day he grew disgusted and sent me away for good.

Since it was clear I had no bent for books, and my father was hard-pressed for money, he could see only one way—to get me into the Russian county school.

To get a boy into the county school was no great feat, since they took even a pauper's son as long as there was room. But my father wanted "connections"—someone who would see to it that I got special attention. He brought me to a teacher called Kenigshatz. He was to test me and then bring me into the school so that I would get some good out of it.

This Kenigshatz, a big drinker, duly examined me, and after painfully pinching my cheek, put me into the second class, though my knowledge prepared me only for the first. As soon as I was enrolled, the drunkard took me out of the second class, and put me into the third. Imagine my plight! I, the smallest boy in the class, am surrounded by big grown delinquents! I am given a book I do not begin to understand, cannot even get into my head. The teachers spit blood over me, insult me, dress me down. The big boys laugh at my ignorance with the usual cruelty of youth. And I—I don't know what they want. I only stand and blink.

But this was not the worst of it. Here in the Russian county school, the beating of children had something added. Modern pedagogy required that they be beaten not only with the cat-o'-nine-tails, but also with rulers. And this punishment, let me tell you, was a real Siberia. Beatings in this school were developed into a kind of art, with two teachers in particular as the artists. A shudder would come over us when we heard the howls of the children beaten by these men.

You can imagine how much I loved the county school, knowing what awaited me there. My greatest worry was not my lessons, but how to get my hands on a fiver. With a fiver I went to school happy—

without it, like a condemned man. The fiver was for the teacher. With it, you were beaten not on the naked skin, but on the pants.

I ask you, how long would it take before a clever boy would see his way? "Fool!" a voice said. "Have you no better use for your fiver?" With a fiver one could go around five times on the carousel, riding the back of a lion, a tiger, even a giraffe! One goes round and round to the sound of loud spirited music. All is lively, gay . . .

Short and sweet, I went more and more to the carousel, less and less to the school.

But the carousel was not all. This was fifty years ago, remember, and there was enough to see and to hear in those barbaric times.

Suddenly on the street one hears the fearful sound of military drums—a signal to one and all to come to the prison to see the flogging of a criminal.

For a small offense the prisoner was laid on the ground and beaten with a *nagaika,* a cat-o'-nine-tails that had been soaked in water. For more serious crimes a regular scaffold was erected, and the prisoner beaten so cruelly that his horrible screams and curses went out over the whole square, drowning out the drums.

It sometimes happened that a man of strong character would not give the officers the satisfaction of screaming when he was flogged. With every lash a shudder goes through him. He moans. Foam appears on his lips. The officers, excited by his silence, shout, "Harder! Stronger!" This goes on until the man faints, or—another tragedy—blood spurts from his body onto the scaffold.

For certain great crimes prisoners were branded on the forehead with a red-hot iron. The screams when the brand was placed on the flesh were like the howls of an animal being torn to pieces alive. The sound of it was enough to break the heart.

There were executions, too, of revolutionaries, arsonists, nihilists, and others guilty of crimes against the state. I vividly remember one case, widely spoken of in the city. A certain peasant had sold himself into the army in another man's place, as was often done in those days. This peasant, a man of gentle, placid nature, had fallen into trouble because he would not take the insults of his superiors. They stabbed him, tortured him, threw him into solitary confinement. All this he took in stony silence. Not content, these fine officers came every day to the prison barracks to further taunt their victim. One day, when an officer spat into his supper of grain, the prisoner threw the iron dish at his head.

He was tried for his crime, and received the death sentence.

As soon as I heard about it, I was off like a shot—to see. A large crowd had gathered at the barracks, stirring restlessly as they waited. Suddenly an excited buzz. Here he comes now, down Scizzor Street, an escort of soldiers around him. A tall handsome peasant with a broad Russian beard. As he was led to the scaffold a fearful howl broke out, and an old woman rushed out of the crowd, flinging herself on the condemned man in a frantic embrace. This was his mother, and a murmur of sympathy arose in the crowd.

For a short time the officers allowed the woman to embrace and kiss her son; then she was torn away and pushed back. Her howls died down into a continuous low moan.

The condemned man mounts higher and waits. Not a quiver, not a sign of fear; his face shows nothing but iron resolution. His eyes are bound. An officer gives the command. Rifles ring out with one report. The air rocks. The body sways, totters, and falls through a trap in the scaffold into the grave below, already prepared and waiting.

At once a little group of soldiers goes to work with spades, heaping earth on the grave until a high mound has grown over it. On this the soldiers sprang, leaping, stamping, dancing like devils, until the ground was leveled and no one could say which piece of earth was innocent and which had been so hideously violated.

I came away from these spectacles exhausted and sick. Often my parents did not believe the things I told them. There were times I came home in such hysterics that they grew alarmed for my health. "A blessing on him!" they scolded angrily. "Who told him to go?"

By 1867, when the twelve-year-old Adler witnessed these public scenes, the promise of Alexander II's reign had already given way to turmoil and division.

Liberal hopes received the first shock in 1861, with the much-awaited emancipation of the serfs. Five years of struggle with a hostile nobility had fatally weakened the tsar's great statute. No national law had emerged; every province had the right to make amendments. Worst of all, the tsar, fearing the whole statute would be defeated, had left the landowners in legal possession of the land. The peasants had the right to buy it, but nothing more.

Alexander II
of Russia

Though serfdom had been abolished, a crushing new economic servitude had replaced it. The angry nobles put such a price on their land that fifty years were needed to pay for it. And in return for this lifelong debt the peasants were given only the most inferior allotments. The poorest of them got "beggar's allotments," holdings too small and wretched even to sustain them. Many of them had been better off as serfs.

The peasants were bewildered by this outcome. A belief began to take form among them that this was not the real emancipation, that the tsar had been tricked, and the real emancipation was still to come. This idea took such hold that the tsar had to issue a manifesto instructing the peasants that they had been liberated, and were to expect no further liberation.

Widespread unrest followed this announcement. Revolt broke out in some provinces. There were acts of disobedience, and in the province of Bezdna thousands of unarmed peasants were shot down by government troops. Hundreds of men were killed that day by the tsar's infantry, and many more wounded.

The massacre at Bezdna set off a wave of student protests, the first in a long history of these demonstrations. In St. Petersburg, students and faculty members, marching from the courtyard of the university to the house of the curator, were forcibly stopped by the police. When they called a second meeting, three hundred students were thrown into the Peter and Paul Fortress. Students in Moscow immediately came out in sympathy, and riots followed in every university in the country.

The tsar, returning to the capital after an absence, felt the police had handled the matter clumsily. He ordered the arrested students released, with only the ringleaders to remain under police supervision.

Nevertheless, things had gone too far, and a show of authority was needed. The liberal minister of education was dismissed with the tsar's apology, and a rigid conservative appointed in his place.

The new minister discovered that every university in the country was a hotbed of subversive ideas. As a result of his report to the tsar, science was entirely cut out of the curriculum. Back to Latin, Greek, and mathematics! Professors who took part in the protests were summarily dismissed, and any attempt at student action met with police force, arrests, and mass expulsions.

The liberal nobility, shocked by open disorder on the streets, forgot their radical ideas and backed the government. Liberalism was out of favor, nationalism back in style. But radical dissent, abandoned by the aristocracy, now erupted underground—a new and dangerously destabilizing force.

As early as 1862 handbills and proclamations were on the streets calling for elected national and local assemblies, elected judges, the dissolution of monasteries, and the abolition of marriage. A smell of revolution had come into the air. Everyone in St. Petersburg expected an outbreak of some kind.

To make matters worse, a series of mysterious fires broke out, burning for weeks in both town and countryside. In St. Petersburg the blazes gutted two thousand buildings and, except for the accident of a windless day, would have destroyed the city.

Though they denied it, the revolutionaries were blamed for the fires. Public opinion turned against them, and the tsar's policy took a violent swing to the right. In 1863 a Polish insurrection was put down with a ferocity that horrified all Europe. Thousands of Polish nobles went into exile. Poles were forbidden to mourn their dead, forbidden to teach their language. At home, Russian and Polish students battled police together in the streets, blood was shed, and hundreds of people were rounded up in police raids. Liberal journalists were especially targeted, and in the hysteria of the moment, the radical writer and editor

Chernyshevsky, god of the Russian youth, was sentenced to fourteen years in the Siberian mines with lifelong exile to follow.

With the exile of Chernyshevsky, the tsarist government had created the great figure of the underground struggle. The organized movement that would bring armed revolution and the end of the Romanov line begins with this event.

In 1866 an expelled student named Karakazov, a son of the lesser nobility, fired openly at the tsar in the garden of the Winter Palace. A muzhik rushed forward and saved his life. Karakazov was hanged. But the following year, while the tsar was on a visit to Paris, an exiled Pole made another attempt on his life. The tsar behaved with admirable courage during both these incidents, but he was a man bewildered and increasingly angered by the forces against him.

Nevertheless, in 1869, at the urging of the liberals in his cabinet, Alexander granted amnesty to the exiled Russians and Polish students, restored some autonomy to the universities, and even reinstated a number of the suspended liberal newspapers.

Policy had once again veered to the left, and in official circles the tsar was criticized for a weakness that undermined authority. His new concessions were regarded as useless, since the old ones had accomplished nothing. The peasants still wanted the land. The radicals still wanted a constitution. The Poles still wanted independence. The tsar, giving up neither the old nor the new, had created a curious patchwork of liberal institutions functioning in the old barbaric Russia of Nicholas the Flogger. In the end he alienated both sides of the political spectrum. The nobility hated him for the loss of their privileges, the radicals for betraying the freedom he had promised.

But the tsar, hated by both the left and the right, was not hated by the people. In spite of political turmoil, the country had prospered under his rule. The decline of the landed nobility had given more power to the merchant class, a growing army of speculators and entrepreneurs now finding opportunities everywhere. New commercial activity and growth had encouraged foreign investment. Railroads were booming, a great new industry financed by a network of European credits. Peasants, leaving the land by the thousands, were forming the beginnings of a proletarian workforce. An early capitalist economy was emerging out of what had been a semifeudal, agricultural society.

Ordinary people do well at such times, and have few complaints.

They had a voice now in the all-class elective local assemblies (*zemstvo*) established by the tsar. Trial by jury, though novel, seemed to them fair and just. Universal conscription without regard to wealth or rank pleased them. Most Russians believed, as they always had, that the tsar knew what was best for them.

The Jews were especially loyal. The tsar had lightened their burdens, reached out to them—above all, saved their children. Adler all his life kept in his possession a picture of Alexander II and his empress. And through all the contradictions of that tragic reign, he revered the emperor who had protected and befriended his people.

By now the reader must have guessed that my days in the county school were numbered. I was soon sick of the beatings with the ruler, the stolen carousel rides, the fearful scenes I witnessed in my wanderings over the city. I finally confessed everything, told my father I could no longer bear it, pleaded, wept, until at last he freed me.

What came of all this was a bright spot in my childhood, a moment that has left with me a memory beautiful throughout my life. A private tutor appeared in our home, a Herr Mahler, who has remained one of the most beloved images of my childhood.

For the first time I was given knowledge in a human way, without shouting, without blows and brutal punishment. Herr Mahler taught me not like a teacher, but like an older comrade, and for this I loved him. I began to make progress, to learn, to enjoy learning, even to dream of putting on the uniform of a student and entering the Russian *gymnasia.**

These hopes all came to nothing. The wheel of my father's fortunes took another downward turn. The wonderful Mahler disappeared. And that was the end of Yankele's schooling.

Since it was high time I did something to earn my bread, I was sent to work in the textile factory of the Goldstein brothers. My education was over. The sum of my learning was a little arithmetic, some Russian grammar, and a few French phrases I used to shoot out like bullets whether they were in place or not. Further than this I was not destined to go.

.   .   .

---

* An eight-year course, equivalent to both high school and college.

In my thirteenth year our family suffered a misfortune. The *zayde,* who had loved me so much and had filled our home with such beautiful Jewish serenity, died. Of that wonderful personality, his singing, his studying, his knowledge and learning, remained only a little figure in a black shawl laid out on the floor with candles burning at his head and feet.

He had died on a Friday, and the word went from mouth to mouth: "A saint! A saint! Where else such a saint as Reb Avremele Adler? He will be a good petitioner for us in heaven!"

My thirteenth birthday fell a few weeks after his death, and my grandmother wailed all the way to the synagogue that her Avremele had not lived to see his beloved Yankele's Bar Mitzvah. My mother was also heavyhearted, my father off somewhere on business and the news he sent not heartening.

As I mounted the altar I heard my mother and grandmother weeping together in the gallery. I tried to recite the prayer from the Torah, but could not. The *shammos* whispered, prompting me, but my throat closed, tears gushed, and like a child, I sobbed aloud for my *zayde.*

A spoiled Bar Mitzvah.

I was working in these years at the textile factory of the Goldstein brothers. I had started there as very small fry indeed; I ran errands, was allowed to sell a few trifling items, and for this was paid five kopeks a day out of which I had to buy my lunch of bread, grits, and tea. But I did not stay on this lowest rung of the ladder. Since I wrote a good hand, could reckon a little, and the devil had still not taken me, I began to come up in the world. My employers took me into their books, my salary went up, and I soon had means to become a bit of a sport. I began to look around me and to take an interest in what was going on in the world.

What was going on was an epidemic a craze that had broken out like a form of madness. Boxing. No one in Odessa cared for anything else.

The scene of the new sport was the famous Moldovanka. And it was this sad hopeless Moldovanka that produced the new gladiators.

Moldovanka, a maze of unpaved squalid streets, was torn down in the Soviet era, but in its day the district had a certain fame. Like the rue de

Lappe in Paris or the old New York Bowery, the Moldovanka was gay. The sound of the accordion was heard there far into the night. People came to "see life," to get drunk in the taverns and brothels. Respectable Russians shunned this quarter, the haunt of prostitutes, derelicts, and thieves; but the upper classes were less squeamish. Aristocrats and people of wealth liked rubbing shoulders with the types in this dangerous quarter, and a late visit to the Moldovanka was a much-enjoyed feature of Odessa nightlife.

The craze for boxing had started with small boys, but in time this madness took in the whole city. The children were pushed aside and full-grown gladiators took their place with crowds of people applauding the winner.

Now I ask you, is my soul a raisin? A strong, well-grown boy of sixteen? And though I never dreamed then of being an actor, the applause of pretty women, the excitement of the crowd—all this was much to my taste. I threw off my jacket, turned up my sleeves, struck a heroic pose in my red Russian shirt—and into the battle! I was soon a popular boxer, greeted with applause and shouts of "Yankele Adler, *molodyets!* Yankele Adler, *nachinai.*"*

I would plunge into the fight, emerging sometimes with a bloody nose or a battered eye, but a "star" on the streets of the Moldovanka, and a hero to the street boys who tried to give me bribes to beat up some kid they had it in for.

My exploits in the prize ring did not last long. Not, heaven forbid, because I was conquered. No, no—not so easy as that to defeat me. Quite simply, boxing began to bore me. Having won all the laurels of this noble art, what more could it give?

I left the arena in my glory, but kept the inheritance it left me— fine new acquaintances. Sons of rich fathers, attorneys without diplomas, petty agents, middlemen, the very cream of Odessa society, were now my intimate companions.

My first wages at the Goldstein brothers' had been a fiver a day, but before long this went up to ten rubles a month. With this sum I could be a whole "cavalier."† I was no longer an apprentice, but a

---

* "Yankele Adler, good man! Yankele Adler, go to it!"
† In the colloquial parlance of the time, a gentleman of elegance and breeding.

white-collar worker, almost one of the intelligentsia. My new pals did not need to be ashamed of me. No longer did I live all day on bread, grits, and tea. I could fall into a tavern with my good brothers, and order a schnapps like any other young man of independent means.

I was tall, handsome, with fine new friends and money in my pockets. A desire awoke in my breast to live and have a time of it. Above all, it was the "soft battle" that drew me.

This interest did not lessen with time.

Since I was now a great personality, I became a member of the famous Odessa "pavement roamers." We were the young sports and toughs who at nightfall roamed the streets looking for a wedding, a brawl, excitement of any kind. Since the better streets of the city had recently been paved by the Italian architect Boffo, the Jewish community, with its usual indifference to foreign names, gave us the distinguished title of "Buff's Army."

The greatest pleasure of Buff's Army was dancing at strange weddings. As hungry wolves roam the woods for food, so we roamed the streets looking for these festive gatherings. And since such assemblages do not hide themselves but, on the contrary, let themselves be heard, we soon found them.

Once inside we would push aside the older people, grab the prettiest girls, and take them out on the floor in a polka, a mazurka, a quadrille. The girls pretended to be angry, but really they liked it, and the floor burned under our feet. The guests wanted to go on with the traditional Jewish dances, and fights often broke out with the younger men. On one of those nights the scandal rose to such heights that the police came in, and the whole gang of us spent the night in the lockup.

Through these fine romantic adventures I became a first-rate dancer, brilliant in the quadrille, heroic in the mazurka, glorious in the waltz, and a special virtuoso in the famous Parisian cancan. This *café chantant* dance had taken all Odessa by storm. I invented a finale on both hands and feet that made a terrific impression, and the girls especially swallowed me with their eyes.

Short and sweet, I was soon as famous for my dancing as for my boxing, and my fame spread ever wider over the whole young population of the city.

Bravo, Yankele Adler! First boxer, first cancan dancer of Odessa!

Dear friends, I fell. Step by step I sank lower and lower.

We Jews have a legend about *gilgulim.* The legend tells us that when a soul sins against itself, when it does not fulfill the great purpose for which it was created, it must live another life, and live it in a lower form. If the soul repents, it can rise again. If there is no repentance, it will fall and fall until it has reached the lowest depths.

It seems that in my youth I went through such *gilgulim.* My first sins were not so bad—nothing worse really than youthful high spirits. Perhaps if there had been better influences around me, they would not have amounted to much. No—my first true *gilgul* was that of the pleasure seeker, the idler, the frequenter of taverns. The second rung of my downfall was the Odessa sport, the young dandy of Buff's Army. Through my dark wanderings over the great city I fell into bad company, I became a boxer, a pugilist . . .

It is only now that I understand the critical nature of this period. For how far are nightly brawls, scandals with the police and arrests— how far is all this from an actual life of crime? Remember, I was only fifteen or sixteen at the time, a handsome boy, strong, daring, and with a fame, too, in low circles.

I had at this time left the textile factory and become a businessman, a *raznoschik.* In plain words, a custom peddler. Uncle Arke had started this way, and had ended by amassing a fortune. Now, in his older years, he gave over this side of his business to poorer relatives.

A *raznoschik* was simply a salesman who wandered around the city peddling his wares, a trade carried on in backyards and at backdoors. With his pack on his back the young peddler trudges around the bleakest, most out-of-the-way corners of the town. The character does not grow more disciplined through this work, for the customers are mostly servant girls, chambermaids, and such. As everyone knows, people very respectable in other circles grow remarkably free and easy in such company.

When his work is done, the peddler falls into a tavern— Olenikov's, or the Tsar's Medal. The great organ plays and excites his blood. Others entertain him with wine. And a longing awakes in the soul for empty pleasures, for the company of idle, empty people.

My life grew worse, my circle of merry companions larger, my nights with Buff's Army ever wilder and more dissolute.

I did not become altogether corrupt. The legend tells us that when the soul has reached the lowest point of all, it will begin to rise again.

Two angels saved me at that time. The first was my mother, whom I loved above every human being on earth. To spare her worry I put some limit on my dissipations, and managed at least to sleep every night under my own roof.

My second good angel, interestingly enough, was Uncle Arke. It was he who made me aware there were higher pleasures than running after girls and nightly escapades with merry companions.

A desire for higher things I had always had. As I grew older my wild life had dimmed these ambitions. It was Aaron Trachtenberg, my uncle, who reawakened them.

RUSSIAN THEATER IN THE YEARS
OF MY YOUTH

Aside from being a successful merchant and the king of our family, Uncle Arke was also a hot theater lover. He went two or three times a week to the Russian theater and was a tireless, devoted visitor of both the City Theater and the Mariinsky.

But Uncle Arke did not simply go to the theater. He loved it with all the fervor of the most youthful "patriot," as theater lovers were then called. Watching a play he would applaud, call out his favorites, and force his opinion on everyone around him. Coming home, he would again praise, criticize, and talk only of the theater.

Under his influence I was soon, like him, a burning "patriot." My favorites in the "City" were the famous Ivan Kozelsky and the beautiful Olga Glebova. I also acquired a great admiration for Miloslavsky, the City Theater's director. And all this gave me such pleasure that I remember this period as one of the most beautiful of my life.

I must make clear, however, that I was still a very undeveloped young man whose ideas of art were extremely limited. It was less Glebova's talent than her exceptional beauty that thrilled me. My enthusiasm for Ivan Kozelsky was less for his acting than for the rare perfection of his clothes. Most of all I marveled at his trousers. Father in heaven, how smooth they were, how perfect!

Now the buffet in the gallery of the "City" was owned by a certain Herr Aronowitz. This man had two daughters who presided over this little establishment, both of them beauties who drove all the young men up there crazy. They would leave the hall in the midst of the most famous scene, the greatest monologue, just to pay court to these two young ladies. I myself was much in love with the younger *M'amzelle.* And when she shyly confessed that she loved me too—who was then my equal in all Odessa?

This was my very first love—and how charming it was, and how proper! I spent whole evenings in the gallery helping my sweetheart serve the bonbons and sugared drinks she dispensed to her customers.

As it happened, this Fräulein Aronowitz was acquainted with Olga Glebova, the actress I admired. Knowing how much I wished it, she promised to introduce me. And before long, the meeting was arranged.

You can imagine with what thrilled emotion I stood before my adored idol. Apparently Glebova knew of my admiration and liked it, for she asked me then and there to be her *ataman*—the leader of her claque—an offer I immediately accepted.

Let me explain what was entailed in being the leader of a claque in those days. My good friend Mr. Harris has served many important functions in the Yiddish theater. But in his earlier years it was he who mastered the young "patriots" in the gallery, told them who should be greeted with bravos and who with a dead silence, which scenes needed applause, and how long the applause should last. All this gives "tone" in a theater, and belongs to the inmost secrets of theater politics—of which we will speak further.

Every actor or actress of that time had to have protection from the jealousy and even the plots of rival players. This was true not only of the Russian theater, but of every other theater as well.

The claque, an organized group paid for its applause, goes back to the seventeenth century, and in some cases existed even into the twentieth. It was made up for the most part of rough individuals of no known trade or profession, men living by their wits who cared little whom they served as long as they were paid.

Adler's "army" was not made up of such types, however, but rather of Odessa friends who, like himself, were devotees. Catching his fire for the actress he adored, these ardent young men would easily drown out the mechanical tributes of the professionals paid by her rival.

In those days two prima donnas queened it on the stage of the City Theater—the celebrated Olga Glebova and the equally famous Madame Kozlova. The bitterest rivalry existed between these actresses, and although their struggle was carried on within the bounds of decorum, all Odessa was aware of it.

Feeling on both sides ran high, and two parties formed in the gallery of the "City," the "Kozlovtsas" on one side, the "Glebovtsas" on the other. Finding I was in a war, I threw myself heart and soul into the battle.

I don't know exactly why I chose Glebova. I cannot truthfully say Kozlova was a worse actress. What I did know was that Glebova was a very beautiful woman, and I greeted her with stormy cries of bravo that rang through the theater. I was ready to die for her, to go through fire for her sake. She was my idol, and I was her knight.

Nightly then, like Hindenburg at his high observation post, I took my seat at the topmost point of the gallery. From that high place I could signal to the army scattered around me. And under my direction Glebova received such acclamations that her rival was quite crushed. The thunderous applause of our strong young hands rang throughout the theater, dwarfing the plaudits received by any other artist in the company.

It did not matter that people in the audience knew the secret of these ovations, that those in the know looked up from their seats in the pit growling, "Yankele Kulachnik* is at work tonight." Enthusiasm in the theater is catching, it runs from one to the other. The whole audience took fire from our applause and swelled it.

Madame Glebova was a generous woman; she appreciated my devotion. And so, with the grace and tact of a great lady, she would from time to time surprise me with a gift . . . usually a hundred-ruble note. Half of this I would divide honorably with my army. I spent most of the rest sending glorious bouquets over the footlights to my queen.

The City Theater of Adler's youth was not the imposing edifice standing in Odessa today, but a smaller theater, much loved by the public but destroyed by fire in 1880.

This older City Theater, built in 1809, played host at first only to visiting French and Italian troupes. Over the years the great Russian companies of Moscow and St. Petersburg also came and performed, and

* "Jacob the Fist," his nickname as a boxer.

by the time the sixteen-year-old Adler began haunting the gallery, the "City," with its own superb company, was recognized as one of Russia's great theaters, second only to the Mariinsky in St. Petersburg and the Maly Theater ("Small" Theater) in Moscow.

In 1872, having emerged from the iron censorship of Nicholas I, the theater in Russia was in a state of resurgence. Both the classical and contemporary plays of Germany and France were now produced, as well as Shakespeare revivals. Many Russian playwrights were writing in Adler's day, but the greatest by far was the brilliant Alexander Ostrovsky.

Unlike Gogol and other famous Russian writers, Ostrovsky wrote *only* for the stage. In the thirty years he dominated the scene he turned out over seventy theater pieces, not counting his opera librettos and collaborations with other writers. But Ostrovsky is best known for his brilliant satires on Russia's merchant class, a group he knew well since his father, a lawyer, had made a fortune representing them.

These comedies, astonishingly modern in tone, and built on character rather than plot, present a devastating portrait of Russia's rising bourgeoisie, a gallery of newly rich speculators, shopkeepers, tradesmen, and adventurers, all clawing their way to the top, aping the aristocracy, opposed to every liberal reform, though they themselves were mostly former serfs or the sons of serfs—bullying farmers embroiled in blackmail and fake bankruptcies, and children more greedy and heartless than their fathers.

Ostrovsky's first play, *It's a Family Affair,* was so savage an indictment of this class that Tsar Nicholas himself forbade its production, and Ostrovsky had to wait for the "thaw" of Alexander's reign before his plays could reach the stage.

Though the influence of Gogol is unmistakable, these comedies are really darker. The endings, in particular, are sometimes so chilling as to leave the reader more shaken than amused. But these brilliantly heightened rascals, bullies, schemers, and crooks were marvelous vehicles for the genius of the Russian actor, always at its most spectacular in character comedy.

While Ostrovsky would later be overshadowed by the greater plays of Tolstoy, Gorky, and Chekhov, his influence was a lasting one, and is felt even in the theater of our own time. His wide range of characters, all of equal importance, shifted the emphasis from the star to the ensemble, an idea later more fully realized in the Moscow Art Theatre. In 1923, when the world-famous company presented Ostrovsky's *Diary of a Scoundrel* in New York, the garrulous Kroutitzky, a relatively minor role, was played by Konstantin Stanislavsky.

Ostrovsky's social satire throws him into the camp of the "Realists," a school by then already gaining popularity in Russia. But the realism of the Russian theater (and later, of the Yiddish theater) must not be confused with the naturalistic tendency so widespread in our own time. The truth of human emotion was sought, rather than the realistic portrayal of daily behavior. Character and will were still seen as moving forces in human destiny. Heroes and heroines still rose to heights of nobility. It was a realism, in fact, still strongly influenced by the Romantic school that preceded it.

ODESSA NIGHTS

Nobody ever had so stormy a youth as I. I burned up the world! All Odessa was too small for me, and in my soul good and evil battled for supremacy.

During the day, true, I wandered around the outlying suburbs of the town with my pack of goods. But at night—ah, that was when life began!

At night the whole great city on the Black Sea tore as though out of a prison in search of pleasure. Drawn by the lights, the crowds, the noise, the people flowed out over the streets like a throng of pagan worshipers. And Yankele Adler, or, as he was now known, "Yankele Kulachnik," Jake the Fist, was part of that sinful procession.

For a merry life one needs money, and there were plenty of young charlatans among us with full pockets. Herschele Fetterman's mother was the greatest hatmaker in all Odessa. Dr. Scharfstein's son also had more than he could spend. Money there was, and to spare. More important, there were ways to spend it. Everything around us said, "Live!" And we lived!

I did not neglect my duties in the City Theater. I continued to rule over the beautiful Glebova's claque. But there were nights when Glebova did not play, nights when I was free to roam about with my comrades in out-of-the-way places that smacked of crime and strange doings.

In the Trushov district, on Belorskaya Street, a tavern was owned by a converted Jew who had done time in Siberia. Why was he sent to Siberia? "For not fasting and praying," people said.

The "Siberiac" had two daughters. The older one was a real churchgoer. She went to Mass every morning, abstained from milk and meat on fast days, and hated a Jew like a spider. But the magnet for Buff's Army was the younger daughter, Olga Petrovna.

It was this Olga Petrovna who drew us every night to the tavern and sent us home again with empty pockets. A devil of a girl, a beauty, and added to that, an accomplished cheat who knew how to rob her young guests of the last kopek they possessed.

The whole army was madly in love with this girl. We not only paid her shamelessly padded bills, but gave her presents besides—just for a word, a smile, a moment of her company.

And perhaps it was not so much her burning beauty as her interesting character that drew us to this girl. She kept strict accounts, and woe to the boy who did not pay—she would find him even under the earth! But if a boy had no money he was still a welcome guest; she gave him credit. And if he was really in trouble she would slip a bit of money into his pocket, even put him up for the night. But he had to behave himself. There could be no pleas, no demands. And if he tried anything rough he would get his bones broken by the whole crowd. There wasn't one of us who wouldn't have gone through fire and flame for her.

Like the others, I was madly in love with Olga Petrovna. As it happened, she was equally drawn to me. And there was danger in this, for it awoke the jealousy of Yankele Brainis, the wildest fellow in the bunch. One night, seeing her single me out with her attentions, the jealous boy threw a glass of wine into my eyes.

To console me, or perhaps to further awaken his jealousy, she took me to her room at the back of the tavern. There she helped me put myself to rights, scolding me at the same time for the company I kept. "You shouldn't be with these people," she said. "You are too fine."

After that I was less with the others, and more often with Olga Petrovna. We went about the city together, sat together in the park. Often she took me to hear court cases—trials for bankruptcy, theft, arson, murder. The sensational element of these trials had strong appeal for me. We would spend hours listening to the witnesses, the lawyers, and afterward talk over and analyze what we had heard. I came to respect her judgment, for she had a sharp, observant mind, and her opinion was always penetrating and original.

I came to see her in a new light, and the end of it was, I really fell in love with her. For the first time I experienced the pangs of jealousy, for I by no means had exclusive rights to her favors, and I suffered when she gave them to others.

This was my first real love affair, the first one that mattered, and one of the few that ended in a lasting friendship.

I was now at the threshold of my eighteenth year, and casting a glance back I see the changes in my life. I was a year older, and, it may be, also more mature. Whatever the reason, my wild impulses were beginning to die down. I became steadier, quieter, and, at the same time, deeper and more serious.

I gave up the custom peddling that had been such a harmful influence in my life and looked about for another means of a livelihood.

Among my wild companions at this time were several small writers, notaries, and journalists, as well as some unrecognized members of the bar known in Odessa as "hole-and-corner lawyers." Through these contacts I began to get work as a copyist, drawing up petitions and other official documents. Such papers had to be written by hand in those days, and it was essential they be written clearly and well. This was especially true of petitions, where one had to make the best possible impression on the highly placed person who was to grant the favor.

I began copying these documents for notaries and lawyers, sometimes drawing them up myself. It was through this work that I fell in with the Odessa lawyer Yisrol Rosenberg, with whom I was to live through much of my early theatrical life. I will have more to relate of him later. For the time it is enough that you remember the name Yisrol Rosenberg.

And now a weakness comes over me. I am coming to my first love and the most treasured memory of my youth. Esther Raizel was her name, and I write it with tears in my eyes. She was a child of eighteen, tall, slender, and so quiet, so gentle, that with one innocent, unthinking glance, she took my soul. Her eyes were blue with a very slight cast an added charm that somehow set off her lilylike innocence. Milk-white cheeks, blond hair, fresh lips, snowy, even little teeth—she was the classic Gretchen. Yet I swear it was not her beauty that drew my youthful heart. Before her, and after her too, I have known women more beautiful and more alluring. Some became my friends, some I loved after a fashion. But true love, love deep and pure, I gave only once, and only to Esther Raizel.

Dear soul, where are you now? Do you still live, or does the earth cover you? What would we feel if we were to meet again?

Her father, Reb Daniel Dovid, kept a tavern, and she and her sisters served the customers there. But you must not compare her with other such girls. "In the tavern, yet far from the tavern," says our poet Peretz. No trace of the tavern had touched her.

It was, besides, another kind of tavern. Her father, Reb Daniel Dovid, a man already in his eighties, sat all day in the backroom over his books. No man in Odessa had a finer name. His upright character and unstained honor were known to all.

I was drawn there, however, by nothing but the purity and sweetness of his daughter. I spent every night in the tavern, recklessly throwing my money about—as my Protosov throws his money to the beckoning gypsy girls who enchant him with their singing in Tolstoy's *The Living Corpse.*

Oh, the golden days when I strolled with Esther Raizel through the parks, the boulevards—the magic nights with her in the theater and afterward in some fine café or restaurant! We would come back so late to the tavern that her father already slept. Her mother and sisters would also leave us. And we would stay together until dawn, repeating over and over in the moonlit room our vows and our sighs of woe.

I now came home later than ever, and had to take the greatest care not to wake my parents.

One night we met with a misfortune. Her old father suddenly called out from his room. We held our breath. The old man came in, and in the stillness of night there was a terrible outcry. "My daughter a loose woman? My daughter receives lovers?"

He ordered me out, and I fled by the backdoor like a thief. The yard was full of angry dogs awakened by his shouts, and as I came out the whole pack fell on me. By a miracle a constable was passing or I would have been torn to pieces. With his help I was able to master the dogs. I had to deal with his suspicions afterward, but anything was better than dealing with dogs. I told him some story or other, and made my way home.

Now my real sufferings began. I was not allowed to see her again. Days I dwindled like a light. Nights I hung about the tavern like a shadow. God helped. Her little sister came one day and brought me a message. I may return. I need not fear. I will not be driven away. I understood. The mother missed the money I spent there.

The first person I encountered was the old man himself, reading his books in the doorway. "*Sholem aleichem,* Reb Dovid," I said in a low voice. He raised his head. I will never forget the look on his face. Hatred, protest, pleading—all were in that look. I went in to the others. Once again I was a friend and a guest. And I saw her again.

They would not let us marry. My wild reputation was in the way. My family background was also not pure enough for them.*

For two long years we met in this fashion, and the whole time I was between heaven and hell. With her life was a golden dream, without her an abyss of pain.

They sent her away finally to an uncle in Kherson. I was eaten up with loneliness, and at last I followed her.

Like something in a dream I remember the blue nights of that southern city, the pebbled paths of Potëmkin's Gardens . . .

The end was ugly. Ugly and sad. Not that anything ugly happened, God forbid. No—the end was ugly because *nothing* happened. Because there *was* no end.

If anyone had told me I could live without her I would have hurled the words back into his throat. Yet I not only lived, but sucked the honey of life without her. If anyone had said I could forget her, I would have torn out his eyes. Yet I forgot her.

Without a trace, my first and most beautiful love vanished, and was no more. I forgot her. She doubtless has long forgotten me. So it is that time makes us slaves and traitors to everything purest and best.

In the course of my life I have lived through three pogroms. The first, when the lemon peddler was beaten to death, I have already described. I was still a child, and remember only the screams and the faces of Jews running through the streets. The second of these events occurred in the years of my bachelorhood, in the city of my birth. I lived through it in my own body, my own heart, my own soul—lived through its fears, its horrors, and its heroism. It was a catastrophe that ruined my family, made ashes of my father's fortune, and left scars in all of us—scars that my mother and grandmother undoubtedly carried with them to the grave. Such things are not forgotten.

As always, it began at Passover. A black fog of terror hung over the city. Jews feared to leave their homes, and only the synagogues were full.

---

* Because Adler's father had married a divorced woman, the family lost its place in the priestly caste, the *kohanim*.

We were living at the time in Yuroshefsky's house on Market Street. With my father away on business, the household was composed of myself, my mother, my grandmother, and my sister Soore, still a child. As the only man in the house, I had to be the hero and protector.

I was afraid to see the terrible scenes enacted in the street, yet I felt an urge to go. Perhaps I had some thought of defending myself—I don't remember. But the women and the child clung to me in deadly fear, weeping and begging me not to leave them. Whether they feared for my life or were afraid to be alone I do not know.

Most of all, we trembled for my sister. She was now a girl of twelve, pretty, already well developed, and we knew better than to put our trust in the decency and humanity of the Russian beast. We decided we must send her to Uncle Arke's. But how to get her there? For one thing, I could not leave the women. For another, the courtyard gates were already locked. In the end I took her up to the attic, and from there carried her over the rooftops to Uncle Arke's house. Fortunately, it was not far.

I came back the same way and then went down into the courtyard with my brothers. Together we waited for the terror to strike, each of us determined to save what we could. With sinking hearts we waited for the inevitable, waited with fluttering hearts and dying hopes, listening for every sound like hunted beasts in their caves.

Suddenly it was upon us. Blows began at the courtyard gates, and with a frightful force, the mob burst in. The court was filled with a hideous tumult—a sound like the roar of lions and wolves who break from their cages and come out into freedom. Screams were heard, the cries of women and children, the crash of smashing doors, breaking windows, smashing furniture.

I ran up to the women, locked the door, tried to quiet their terror. Suddenly a thunder of footsteps. Fists began hammering at the door. Iron rods are wedged in, forcing it. A drunken rabble breaks in with wild triumph. Russians and Greeks, ragged, filthy, with rolled-up sleeves, hairy chests, bloodshot, burning eyes, faces blackened by smoke and stained with blood. *"Baie Zhidov! Lomai! Rozgromi!* Kill the Jews! Rob! Break!"

And with these inhuman cries, they began to rob and to break.

Through the years my father, who loved antiques, had collected some pieces of furniture that were the pride of our home. Against the wall of our best room was a tall beveled mirror, a treasured thing. A

Greek in a blood-spattered shirt took to this first with a raised club. My mother tried to stop him, and was brutally pushed to the opposite wall. A blow of the club. A yell from the mob, "Break!" The crystal splinters and smashes on the ground.

A carved sofa, a favorite of my grandfather's, was next. A wild-looking man, a derelict whose very look could frighten—more like a devil than a man—lifts the sofa and hurls it through the window. The old *buba* runs to save the loved piece. A push, a blow, her wig is torn from her head, showing the dark clipped hair beneath. A rivulet of blood falls from her nose to her jacket. I rush forward to protect my grandmother, and feel an avalanche of blows on my hands, my head, my back.

For a while the drunken beast raged, broke, robbed; at last it was satisfied. They went off, leaving us clinging to each other like survivors of a flood cast up on some ruined lost island.

This was not the worst. My father had at that time worked his way up to some extent. Unknown to us, he had a secret cache in the house of several thousand rubles. Either out of stinginess or some other reason, he told us nothing, but had hidden the money in the drawer of a seldom-used commode. None of us had any idea it existed.

Soon after the pogrom my father, to whom we had written everything, fell into the house more dead than alive. "The commode!" he called out. "Where is it?"

"Broken. In pieces."

"What was inside it? Is nothing left?"

"Nothing."

"Then we are poor in good earnest!" And the fifty-year-old Jew with a beard already gray broke down in his despair and sobbed like a child.

Those who know anything about the Yiddish theater are aware that it grew originally out of the Yiddish folk song. Concerning this interesting development I can speak from personal experience.

In the 1870s a new kind of entertainment sprang up in the wine cellars of Romania, Galicia, and South Russia. Folk songs and ballads grew popular with the people, and some of the wine cellar singers became famous.

I came upon the folksingers at the time of my youthful wanderings about the city. For the most part they were poor men who performed for the crowd and went around afterward with a plate. They

were of all sorts, all degrees of talent, but good or bad, ragged or elegant, crude or refined, I loved them. I recall old "Schmul with the
Hoarse Throat" as one of the best. When he sang of an old father
turned away by his children, grown men wept. And when the old man
threw back his head and snapped his fingers to a Chassidic *nigun,* the
snapping of his fingers rang out over the whole orchestra and had ten
thousand charms.

But greatest of all the folksingers was Yisrol Gradner, who was
already famous everywhere. Gradner did not demean himself by
going around with a plate; he had an assistant who performed this
task. He sat at a table with his friends like one of the guests, and got
up to sing only when the spirit moved him.

Gradner brought the whole thing closer to theater. He wore a different makeup and a different costume for each song, all to bring out
the character he was depicting, and the types he created were so realistic that at times the onlookers gasped. Once, I remember, in Kuk-
land's restaurant he built a real little stage with two doors and a
curtain. There he and his assistants, dressed as Chassidim, acted out
whole scenes in song and dance.

Some of the songs in the wine cellars were strongly nationalistic,
others simply moving and pathetic. Old Schmul's song about an old
father turned away by his children always had a very deep effect.

As it happened, this song had a great importance in my life, for
twenty years later, it was the memory of this song that made me put
on Gordin's *Yiddish King Lear,* the play that was the turning point of
my career.

The folksingers were among the deepest impressions of my youth.
I even wanted to be a folksinger. I could not succeed because I had no
voice. But I drew close to them, became their friend, their admirer,
their most ardent and devoted "patriot."

One of Gradner's sketches is described by the actor Reuben Weissman:
Three Chassidim argue, each claiming he has the best rabbi. Their
boasts grow more and more absurd. In the end it turns out they all have
the same rabbi. The three of them embrace, clap hands, and do a dance
together. Weissman tells us the audience went mad over it.

Gradner was born in Lithuania, but at sixteen he came to Berdichev
in southern Russia and got work there in a tobacco factory. He was

immediately popular with his mates, and on Friday nights, when work was over, we are told these young men turned the town upside down.

Because he had a good baritone voice, danced well, and had a personality full of charm, a friend persuaded him to sing in a tavern. The performance was such a success that he soon gave up the tobacco factory and began to travel about as a folksinger.

In Odessa Gradner was still known as "Srolikl Papirosnik" because of the cigarette (*papiros*) always in the corner of his lips. He dressed in European style: a short jacket, boots that squeaked, a cap flirtatiously tilted. Gradner was already famous throughout the Jewish communities of Russia, Galicia, and Romania, and later, when the Yiddish theater came into existence, he would be its first great star.

ROSENBERG: THE GREAT FRIEND OF MY YOUTH

The Yiddish theater in Russia was founded by an Odessa Jew named Yisrol Rosenberg. To him alone belongs the honor, not to Goldfaden or anyone else. He is dead now many years, and even when he lived the world knew little of him, but for those who loved him he can never die.

By profession he belonged to a class of men in Odessa known as "hole-and-corner lawyers." That is to say, he had not finished law school, had no diploma, no standing in court, but was allowed to represent clients in some cases—mostly petitions and other small matters.

We came together during my wild years in Buff's Army. Meeting up with a youngster always in need of money, ready for any kind of fun and not too particular about his company, Rosenberg immediately saw he could use me in his business.

Rosenberg's business . . . Shall I say what it really was? It is a shame and disgrace even to speak of it! But since I am now a historian, and bringing back a world long dead, I can tell the truth. Rosenberg's business was simply swindle. He was a faker.

But to say only this, to leave it there, would be unjust. True, Rosenberg did things that were bad. But when such things are done with charm, with brilliance, when they are done not with a bad purpose, but as a joke, a prank—when the trick is played to show off the brilliance of the trickster, and the victim is a bad person getting no more than he deserves—then the bad thing can take on ten thousand charms.

Here, for example, is one of Rosenberg's tricks. He and one of his "assistants" meet me one day on the street. "Yankele," Rosenberg says, "tonight I am going to get rich."

"How?" I ask.

"What do you care? Come tomorrow, and you'll find out."

This is how Rosenberg got rich. Since nothing in Odessa was hidden from him, he got wind that a man from Ochakhov (a town near Kherson) had come to town with a sizable sum of money with which he intended to buy counterfeit bills. The man was staying at a hotel near the police station.

Late that night Rosenberg, together with his "assistant," knock at the door. Rosenberg is in the uniform of a high-ranking officer. The assistant is dressed as a gendarme, the government cockade on his hat.

"You are so-and-so?" Rosenberg demands in official tones.

The man nods that he is.

"You are a resident of Ochakhov?"

"I am from Ochakhov." He is already chattering with fear.

"We have a report that you are a counterfeiter. Show your money."

The counterfeiter, more dead than alive, pulls out everything he has.

Rosenberg puts on a monocle, examines the bills. "You have nothing more than this?"

"Nothing, gracious Excellency. Only silver."

"Good. Our report was false. Your money is good." Rosenberg puts the assignats in an envelope, seals it, puts on an official-looking stamp, tells the counterfeiter to put his signature on the outside, and tells him to bring the envelope at nine the next morning to the police station.

"I will bring it," the man croaks out.

But Rosenberg seems to be thinking the matter over. "No—better give it to this officer." He hands the envelope to the assistant and says to the counterfeiter, "You may claim your money at the police station at nine tomorrow. At nine exactly. Do you hear? Not a moment later."

The man does not argue. The assistant puts the sealed envelope in his breast pocket, and the two "officers" depart.

The counterfeiter, needless to say, did not show up at the police station next morning, but made tracks out of Odessa long before daybreak.

I knew nothing of all this. I came to Rosenberg's office the next day to find a furious quarrel going on. The assistant was claiming he had done half the work, and was entitled to half the money. "Half the money!" Rosenberg repeated, outraged. "My plan! My idea! What did you contribute? The cockade?"

For a while they go at each other hot and heavy, and then turn to me. I must decide the matter. I come up with a decision: one third of the money to the assistant, two thirds to Rosenberg. And the two grown men, both of them fifteen years older than I, accept my judgment. They kiss, make up, and we all go to lunch at the Palais Royale. Since I have been the arbitrator, I, too, partake of the lordly lunch.

That's how it always was with Rosenberg. The money that came to him so easily slipped just as easily through his fingers again. A bachelor who lived in cafés and restaurants, he never ate alone, never went to the barber alone, never tried on a coat or a new pair of boots alone. A crowd was always around him, younger men for the fun and excitement he provided, older ones for some part of the money he seemed to pull out of the air.

Rosenberg, when I met him, was in his middle thirties, a man of medium height with a thin, small body, a small face, a wide mouth, a long nose, protruding teeth. His eyes were good. Big, smiling eyes. Long hands, long fingers. Always with gloves. Always a cigarette in the corner of his lips. Something was wrong with the way he spoke. Either because of a malocclusion or some form of mouth paralysis, his speech was sloppy. In his later years this grew worse.

Though he used his talents mostly for imposture and fakery, his ability was enormous. His memory was astonishing, he knew thousands of people in Odessa by name, there was no situation he could not get out of, and everything he touched turned to money. I have always believed that if he had put his mind to some better use—to books, say, or to science—the world would have rung with his name and he would have been immortal.

I was sixteen or seventeen when I met him—a time when I easily fell under anyone's influence. Imagine how a boy with so little understanding of the world would feel about such a person! His cleverness amazed me; I couldn't get over it. I was soon his secretary, his clerk, his assistant, and received for my services a bone. "A boy, a child!" Rosenberg said. "What does he need?"

I was so inexperienced and gullible that for a long time I had no idea what he was up to. By the time I knew the truth, it was too late. I could not live without Rosenberg. One look from him held me captive.

One day on the street I ran into him with a villainous-looking man beside him. His face lit up as he caught sight of me. "Alexei Alexeyevich!" he cried. "Thank God. I have been looking for you all day!" To his companion in a low voice: "Give him money. Quick! Everything you have!" He is already in the man's pockets as he speaks. "Remember, Alexei Alexeyevich!" he says to me. "Help us! Save us!" He gives me the money, but somehow only the coins are in my possession, the assignats remain in his own fingers. Sleight of hand. The man bows low in gratitude and Rosenberg takes him off, turning to blow back kisses through the air. I stand there with a foolish face and an open mouth. I understand nothing.

The man, a known thief and horse thief, had been sentenced to two years. Rosenberg told him the sentence would be reversed if he bribed the secretary of the court.

After this I begged Rosenberg to leave me out of his masquerades. The heart could stop from such adventures.

I was afraid to become involved with him, afraid to be his tool. But I could not do without him. I was like a homeless child who meets up with an experienced tramp. Under that fatherly eye I felt nothing could happen to me. Knowing I was afraid to perjure myself he never brought me to court. He loved me and, in his own way, protected me.

When the Russo-Turkish conflict began in 1877 thousands of small merchants, agents, and middlemen ran to Romania to make money from the war. Rosenberg, like others, went to Bucharest to make his fortune. He did not get rich in Romania, but he met Avrom Goldfaden, saw the Yiddish theater as it came out of the egg, and brought it back with him to Russia.

"For Fatherland and Tsar!"

The War of 1877

The Russo-Turkish War, which brought prosperity to Romania, also gave the Jewish people a theater.

In Romania the poet Goldfaden was thrown together with the folksinger Yisrol Gradner. These two, in turn, were thrown together with a whole crew of agents and contractors, all in a strange land, bored to death, rolling in money, and looking for ways to spend it. From this mishmash of history, war, the desire to make money, and the great universal urge to pleasure, the Yiddish theater swam out.

To comprehend how this wonder took place, one must first have some idea of this particular noisy, lively, stormy moment in Russian history.

In 1877 war was declared. Mobilization began and the streets of Odessa resounded with the feet of marching men. Rousing military music could be heard everywhere, and the city was caught up in wild patriotic excitement.

Every day fresh bulletins were posted, and the public crowded around, devouring the news. Great fear when we learned our men had crossed the Danube into Turkish-held territory. Wild rejoicing when our secret treaty with Romania was revealed, and we knew the two armies were joined.

The Russian commissariat was stationed in Jassy,* and soon all Odessa was empty. Every flour merchant, every speculator in hay, in wood, in foodstuffs—everyone was off to Romania to make money.

* A town on the Romanian border with direct rail connections to Odessa.

And in fact these men came back after the war, built houses for themselves, and lived like rich men. Throughout the war money flowed like water.

In the midst of this excitement, a proclamation. All men of twenty-one were drafted. Having been born in 1855, I was among them.

You can imagine what went on in my family. My father never stopped sighing and moaning. My mother tore her hair. My eleven-year-old sister lay in bed with a bandage around her forehead. All day relatives came, wailing that Yankele must go into the army and be killed. Only Yankele was happy. Go to war, see the world, shoot Turks—what could be better? That the Turks might shoot me? That never entered my mind.

The family soon discovered that under Alexander II no man could buy a "substitute." Every man must serve. But is there a situation where some clever person cannot be found? Through the beautiful convert, Olga Petrovna, whose uncle was a doctor in the army, things were managed. If a sum of money changed hands I would not go as an ordinary soldier of the line, but as a *sanitar*—an assistant in the medical corps of the Red Cross.

And so, instead of going to the front, I enrolled in a government school where I learned my new duties. I spent about two months at this task, and enjoyed it. The work interested me, and I very soon mastered the entire Torah of the *sanitar.*

And so, when my audience sees me portray a doctor in a play—say in Gordin's *True Power,* they do not see before them a mere actor, indifferent to whether he is wielding a scepter or a scalpel. No, no! It is not only an actor they see, but a bit of a doctor too—a man who served Alexander II in the Army Medical Corps during the Russo-Turkish War of 1877, and received from him a gold medal for outstanding achievement!

This war with Turkey, the third in Russian history, began with an uprising against Turkish rule in Bosnia and Herzogovina. The rebellion spread. A Bulgarian insurrection was savagely repressed, and throughout Europe a cry of atrocity went up. In Russia anger rose to fever pitch. A Christian people under the Turkish yoke! A *Slav* people!

Alexander, for his part, viewed this Balkan crisis with extreme caution. He had no desire to risk another Crimea. He needed time to consolidate his reforms. He did not want war, and went so far as to caution the Bulgarians against "premature action" against the Turks. But powerful forces were working against him.

Pan-Slav sentiment, always strong in Russia, was calling for the union of all Slav peoples under the Russian crown. A growing capitalist class, itching for conquest, was already putting in bids for concessions in oil, sulfur, fisheries, salt mines. The military was especially eager for action; younger officers were hungry for glory and promotion. Under it all the old forbidden dream: Constantinople and the great waterway of the Mediterranean.

The burning interest of the day was Serbia, where strong nationalist feeling favored all-out war. Russian sympathies reached a pitch in May of 1876 with the arrival in St. Petersburg of Milan, the Serbian prince. The prince was hoping for Russia's assistance in the event of war, but the tsar was either characteristically ambiguous, or his answer was easily misinterpreted by a visitor with pronounced opposite interests.

The prince went back to Serbia with no direct assurance of help, but highly placed Pan-Slav forces intrigued to mislead him. Deliberately falsified messages were sent to the Serb court, and in the summer of 1876 Serbia and Montenegro, firmly convinced of Russian support, declared war on the Ottoman Empire.

In Russia wild excitement greeted the news. Thousands of volunteers left for the Serb front. A Slav Benevolent Society sprang into existence. Huge sums for Bulgarian relief were donated in churches. Society ladies took up collections on trams and on street corners. All upper-class Russia was in the grip of Pan-Slav hysteria.

Young Alexander, the heir apparent, always opposed to his father, had placed himself at the head of this movement. The empress, an unhappy lady much under the influence of her confessor, also devoted herself heart and soul to the relief of her fellow Slavs. And though the tsar opposed Pan-Slavism as a dangerous delusion, he did nothing to check it.

In a last effort to avert the crisis, the sultan was offered a compromise. Russia would not intervene in the war if the persecution of Christians in the Balkans ceased. The message was ignored, in itself an insult that could not be overlooked. The tsar was losing prestige every day by his hesitation, and on April 9, 1877, against his will, against his better judgment, he declared a war practically forced on him by popular opinion.

On a clear sparkling day in 1877 I marched off to war. About a thousand men went that day, all parading from the Tsaronsky Barracks to the depot. The march was in three contingents—first the raw recruits, then the volunteers, and last the *sanitars,* the men of the medical corps. Military bands played rousing music all the way, the whole city came out to cheer, and ladies on balconies threw flowers and presents to the marching men below. The families of the soldiers walked beside them—whole little crowds of friends, neighbors, sweethearts, and wives, keeping pace along the sidewalks, calling out messages and waving good-byes.

I strode proudly along with my own contingent. The whole affair pleased me. Not only was my whole family there, but all the friends and all the sweethearts too, of that happy youthful time. I liked being the hero of the occasion. But when I saw tears in the eyes of a beautiful blonde, Masha Kornblut, who was then very close to me—when I saw my mother weeping, and that Masha, too, lifted a snowy handkerchief to her lovely blue eyes—I forgot my heroism and began to weep myself. It was only by recollecting my position and the seriousness of the occasion that I was able to master my weakness.

At the depot the soldiers boarded the train, crowding at the windows, shouting last good-byes, waving handkerchiefs. I myself could hardly wait to be off. I had a moment of terrible fear only when the train began to move. Through the window I saw my mother's upturned face, white, despairing, and over all the din, the music, the shouting, heard her last heart-rending "Oh, my Yankele! Oh, my Yankele!" At that moment I realized I was going to war and might never come back.

How does the saying go? "Man proposes, God disposes." My heroism and my mother's sorrow were equally vain. We detrained that night in the border town of Bender. And there I was destined to remain.

This is what happened. After a night in the Bender barracks we lined up at the station next morning for inspection. A general with a black beard looked us over, his glance fell on me, and I was called out of the ranks. I was told to remain on one side while the others got back on the train. The train pulled out. I stood there bewildered, angry, insulted. What did it mean? Everyone has gone to war and only I am left behind? Is something wrong with me? What is the reason for this?

I learned the answer later. The general who had beckoned me out of the ranks was none other than the famous Prince Meshersky. I had been left behind not because he found fault with me, but on the contrary, because I pleased him.

It seemed a military hospital for Russian wounded and Turkish prisoners had just been built in this town by some rich German colonists who lived there. These Germans were very patriotic. They believed ardently in the war, and their wives and daughters were not only willing but honored to serve as volunteer nurses of the sick.

Naturally these wealthy people knew they must supplement their numbers with nurses and assistants better trained than themselves. They also wished these nurses and assistants to be young, strong, intelligent, and presentable. Since I seemed to fit these requirements—at any rate Prince Meshersky thought so—it was my fate to remain in Bender.

I was so angry I would not have cared if the whole thing had gone to the devil. Who could have imagined such a dull, flat end to it all? I wanted to be at the front, in the thick of the battle. Instead I was to sit in a godforsaken border town! Instead of heroic encounters with Turks I had been left behind—with Germans!

It seems whatever is ordained by the Highest cannot be bad. In spite of my disappointment, the adventures and dangers for which my young soul thirsted were not entirely lacking in the Bender hospital.

I soon found I had fallen into a fairly good situation. The wives and daughters of the German colonists were pretty, and I soon felt quite at home with them. Nothing but German was spoken in the halls and dining rooms, for no matter how great their Russian patriotism, their German patriotism was greater still. But to speak German was no hardship for me. Where is there a Jew who does not reckon himself a bit of a German? Especially a Jew with the name Adler, and an ancestry going back to Germany.

It may be that my familiarity with their language made these ladies treat me with such kindness. Whatever the reason, I began to enjoy myself in Bender. In fact, I ended by having such a good time that I forgot about the war.

My first assignment was night duty in the sick ward, a task I shared with a young and lovely German daughter. Try to picture the scene: A long room on the second floor of the hospital. Two long rows of beds in which lay the soldiers seriously ill, most of them with typhus. It is late—after midnight. Outside a leaden sky and a downpour of rain. An icy wind whistles over the half-empty square on which the hospital stands. The rain, driven by repeated gusts, beats harder against the shuttered windows. Black and white shadows play on the wall. It is dark; only a guttering candle on the table gives a glimmering, flickering light. Nothing is heard but from time to time a half-choked snore from one of the sick and dying. Someone turns restlessly. Another utters a word or two—a half thought murmured in sleep or in delirium.

If it was a scene of horror even for me, how much more for the young German girl? It goes without saying that we stayed as close as possible. To while away the hours we whispered tales about our lives, all in the lovely language of the Rhine. Often we whispered in this way until our eyes grew dim and we slept, one head near the other on the table, our sound young breath mingling with that of the sick.

Sometimes the nights passed quietly, but there were times when disturbances woke us. On one of those nights a Turkish prisoner suddenly sat up in bed. Before either of us could move, he sprang across the room and began climbing out the window.

Instantly I ran, caught at his nightshirt, and began begging him not to jump. "Turk! Turk!" I pleaded. "Where are you going?" I tried to hold him, but the fever gave him superhuman strength. "You will fall and be killed, devil take you!" I cried desperately. He shouts at me in Turkish, which I understand like the dead. I answer him also in Turkish—that is, in plain Yiddish together with whatever gibberish comes into my mind. And this went on until we both realized the best language is that of push and pull, I pulling him by the collar and he pushing, mostly with his feet, in my stomach. He was already halfway out the window! I put forth all my strength to hold him back. The German girl helped a little with her hands and even more with her German shrieks. Between us we dragged our Turk from the window, put him forcibly into his bed, and bound him down with towels. When all was safe my companion collapsed, half fainting, against my shoulder. *"Ach, Herr Adler!"* she breathed. "All this has so frightened me!"

It was through such nights and such dangers that Matilda and I became friends. I knew her only as Matilda, and since it is a pleasure to remember her, I will try to describe her here.

She was a typical German girl, no more than eighteen, tall and slender with golden braids. Her pretty round cheeks were pink and white, and her eyes under the long blond lashes blue as the sea. She was intelligent too, well versed in her German literary classics, but with all that, lively, gay, affectionate, and naïve and simple as a child.

The worst several hours of my military service—truly the worst of all my youth—I lived through with Matilda. It was a bitterly cold night in late fall. An angry wind tore at the windows. The streets of Bender were drowned in rain and every dog in the city kept wake that night with a melancholy howling.

Matilda and I were on duty in the tent that now served as the typhus ward. We had long since gone the rounds, giving our patients their medicines and offering them whatever relief or refreshment they were allowed.

For one man, a Russian with the name Lopatin, no medicine had been prescribed, since it was unlikely he would live through the night. This Lopatin lay in a high fever, and in his delirium continually talked at the top of his voice. He was convinced a dog was playing around him, and kept looking for it everywhere, under the bed, under his pillow. Terrible as it was to see the dying man, we could not help laughing at the gay, lively way he clicked his tongue to this invisible dog.

It was very late. The tent was dark except for one small lamp on our table. Separated from the sick by a Spanish wall, Matilda and I whispered together, pausing from time to time when the rain beat with special force against the windows. At last we could no longer fight our drowsiness, our heads fell forward, and we slept.

Some instinct woke me an hour later. I looked at the clock. One in the morning. Matilda slept, her childish shoulders resting on the table, her blond hair tousled. I went quickly through the rows of beds. My heart seemed to stop. The dying Lopatin. He is gone! I make a search. He is not to be found. I wake Matilda and tell her. She throws on a shawl, I put on a coat, take a lantern, and we hurry outside.

We are now in the great silent court where a new hospital wing is being built. It is a scene so dismal that the flesh creeps at the very memory. The wind howled, the rain beat down. We search here, there, peering into every corner, venturing as far as the gate, dogs howling after us all the while. *"Ach, Herr Adler!"* she exclaimed. *"Ich muss laufen. Das ist ein schauderliches Ungluck. Das vert mich nicht fergeben vehren. Ich muss fortlaufen."**

"Good," I said. "Let us run away together. But where shall we go? I will be a deserter. Money too will be needed."

"Then we must look again," Matilda said desperately.

This time I left her, took my lantern, and went outside alone.

The court was divided in two by a long broad trench that had been dug as the foundation for the new hospital wing. On the other side of this trench was a great empty stall. Here the mattresses of the dead were thrown before being disinfected and disposed of. Perhaps the madman is hiding in this stall? I must go over the ditch, and into the pest hole.

In daylight and in dry weather this would have been easy, for a board had been laid across the ditch. Now, however, the ditch was full of water, the board swimming in the middle. But what will a person not do when he is desperate! In my coat, the lantern in my hand, I threw myself onto the board—swam, slid, pushed, until I got to the other side.

I now come to the pest stall. My eyes eat into the mountains of infected bedding. By the weak light of my lamp I see two rolling eyes in a corner. It is he. Lopatin. He is half naked, covered from head to foot with dirt and mud. He calls out hoarsely in Russian, "Go away! An officer is over there watching." I fall on him, seize him, drag him. He does not resist, pleads only not to be beaten. I drag him to the trench, sit him on the board, throw myself on it, hold him tight, push with my feet, and with God's help somehow get him to the other side.

"Matilda!" I call. "He is here. Lopatin. I've got him."

Matilda came running. We both gazed in horror. The dying man looked as though he had been dragged out of a swamp. Before we took him back into the ward we had to get him clean.

I carried him into the wash house, and we undressed him mother naked. Matilda brought water, towels, fresh clothing. We prepared a bath, placed him in it. There was no warm water, but we could not

---

* Ach, Herr Adler! I must flee! This is a frightful misfortune. I will not be forgiven for it. I must flee!"

think of that. There must be no sign that he had been outside the tent. Matilda bathed him, and I poured bucket after bucket of ice-cold water over his body. We dressed him in fresh linen, and only after all this put him back in his bed. He was chattering so with cold that the whole bed shook. We were afraid he would fall out of it and to prevent this threw ourselves on top of him. We remained there until at last he stopped shivering and fell asleep.

Matilda burst into tears. We both breathed free for the first time, and in our relief, threw our arms around each other and kissed.

The following morning the doctor came to make his morning rounds. Matilda and I, as always, accompanied him. When he came to Lopatin our hearts pounded as though we were his murderers. The doctor looked at him, felt his pulse, and seemed perplexed. He took his temperature, looked at him again, then turned to us, saying, "How did he sleep last night?"

"Very quietly, Herr Doktor," I answer.

"Remarkable!" the doctor said. "His temperature is normal. His pulse is normal. He is better. Much, much better!"

Astonishing to say, Lopatin lived. Our fearful midnight search and our buckets of icy water had brought a dying man back to life!

My four months in Bender were filled not only with Turks, Russians, and Germans, but also with Jews—and with their daughters!

I don't know why, but in those years Bender was a city full of established Jewish families. This community was greatly concerned that their sick and wounded receive kosher food, and that those who died receive proper burial. In these matters they could work only through a Jewish *sanitar.*

Because of this I was on cordial terms with the most pious and respected Jews of the town. I stood near their pew in the synagogue on the Sabbath, and sometimes was even asked to recite a chapter— a sign of special respect. I was also an honored guest in their homes— and these houses were full of beautiful Jewish girls!

I had long ago outgrown my shyness with the fair sex. I was lucky enough to find favor in the eyes of women. My position as *sanitar—* only one rung beneath that of doctor—gave me an added prestige in the eyes of these Bender girls. And all this led to such delightful youthful romances that the horrors of the war and the hospital were completely drowned out.

As everyone knows, the paternal home under the watchful eyes of father and mother is no place for youthful love. My Bender idylls were played out on porches, in courtyards, and in little backstreets where I and my lady love often waded ankle deep in mud. The romances of Bender always mingle in my mind with the memory of its incessant rain. But love sweetens everything, even muddy clothes and dirty boots.

The happiness of those Bender nights! Dear God above, the happiness! May they not be reckoned against me; I will have so much less of paradise!

My most serious love in Bender was the daughter of a rich Chassidic merchant. Pessye was her name, a modest child religiously raised. Hair in braids. Long brows. Long dark eyes. But how those eyes had looked at me the day I told her I loved her!

What does our playwright Chekhov say? "Everything the rich man will give the actor. Applause, honor—but not his daughter in marriage." Though I was not yet an actor, it must be the pious Jew saw in my face the traces of a licentious past. I was a welcome guest in his home; I had an honored place at his table. But if he had known of my secret meetings with his daughter a terrible storm would have broken.

In the midst of all this, a new order from the tsar. The recruits of the 1855 cohort were suddenly recalled from duty. I was ordered home.

I should have been the happiest of men. Instead, my heart was torn to pieces. God above, why have you given the human being so soft a nature? No matter how terrible a place may be—be it a prison, a madhouse—if we have stayed there long, the heart clings to it.

I parted with the soldiers in the typhus ward, and my heart ached to leave them. Jew and Christian alike, they had grown dear to me. I had read the papers to them, written letters home for them. It seemed to me so wrong that they must remain here on their bed of pain while I went back with my healthy young body into the beautiful world.

I parted with the golden-haired Matilda, and my heart wept to see her sweet face and her laughing sea-blue eyes. Yet I spoke of the parting lightly, almost with a jest. I saw her pretty pink cheeks turn red, then pale as ashes. Her eyes turned steely and then overflowed. For a moment I feared a terrible outburst. But no! Her strong cold German blood won the mastery. A quick look about the tent. Others are present. Patients. Officers. She smiles. She is calm. She accepts it, she forgives me.

"Adieu, liebe Matilda."

"Adieu, liebe Yakob."

It was over.

It went harder with the innocent Pessye. So hard it is painful now to remember it. Pessye, sweet Pessye. A quiet obedient girl, her father knew nothing of our love, or how much she risked for my sake.

I still had something of the ways of Buff's Army about me. With the first light of morning I was at the gate before her house. I kept a little whistle around my throat. On this I gave the low prearranged signal. At the sound this obedient Jewish daughter would spring from her bed, steal out of her parents' home and meet me at the gate. I threw my military cloak around her shoulders, and the two of us were off together in the first misty light—through rain, through snow. All this she did for my caresses and my words of love. And now she stood before me and heard her death sentence. I am leaving. It is over.

Her face turned white. Her hands burned as with fever. How can I be leaving? Was she to remain here then, without me? "Take me with you to Odessa," she whispered. "We will be married there."

Money? She brushed away the word. What is money? Why speak of money with love, happiness, everything holy at stake. She runs to her father's strongbox. Her fingers know the combination. One quick turn. The safe is open.

I fell back, reeling. Pack on pack of red and blue assignats! Diamonds—pearls—jeweled watches—gold and silver beakers—golden candelabra. And this good Jewish daughter told me to take whatever I wished—to take it all.

I gazed, hypnotized. Thoughts of gold and crime were whirling in my brain. Theft. Unlawful happiness. Arrest. Prison. But wait! We will already be married. Her father will not harm his child. He will be forced to forgive me, to take me back as his son. I will have sweet Pessye, be the husband of the dearest truest girl in the world, be the son-in-law of the rich Chassidic Jew. I will quiet my driving blood, tear myself away from bad companions.

What was it that held me back? First, the thought of my freedom, my wild, roving bachelorhood. And then, to exchange my glorious Odessa for dull, muddy, sleepy Bender? Never again to see the beautiful cheat, Olga Petrovna? Never again to see *Rosenberg*? Take the lusty young Yakob, chop off his head, and on that chopped-off head place a yarmelke?

I told her I could not marry without my parents. I would have to speak to them first. And strange to say, I was not lying. To this day I marvel that she, an innocent girl, was prepared to deceive her parents and run away with me, while I—the impure libertine—hung back like a naïve boy, unable to take such a step without the approval of father and mother.

I swore I would come back to her, swore I would see to our life together. I fell on her bosom and wept, mingling my tears with hers. And I went away and forgot the innocent Pessye, as I have forgotten so many others, and as so many others have forgotten me.

For in this terrible world of ours only one thing is sure—that everything ends.

Lebewohl, Bender. *Lebewohl,* blond romantic German girls. And you, dark-eyed and deeply lovable Jewish daughters, *Lebewohl!* Farewell! Of the whole experience, the mobilization, the hospital, the golden Bender nights, nothing remained but a wilted flower and a small gold medal: FOR LOYAL SERVICE TO THE TSAR.

The Odessa Attractions:
Pleasure and Malaise

What chiefly drew me back to the city of my birth was my desire to enjoy its pleasures. To come back from the war with a medal for heroism! What a furor I will make in my soldier's uniform and the Red Cross on my breast! What a sensation I will make among the girls who know me, and even among those who do not know me! How the boys of Buff's Army will listen, open-mouthed, to my stories about the war. I had a furious need to enjoy all this in the city so important to me—Odessa.

In addition I was really aching to be home. I missed my genial and always interesting father, my adored mother, the little sister who had wept for me in my absence.

The day finally arrived. I was back in the arms of father, mother, little sister—together again with my family, my friends, with the whole happy company. And having greeted all those closest to me, I was off to show myself to the world.

With great parade I sought out other recently discharged soldiers, gave them the war news, answered their questions. I called on certain officials too, hinting quite openly, though with a certain tact, that my heroism should be suitably rewarded. To speak plainly, I was hoping for a post suitable to such a fine person as I had become—a position, it is understood, that would be well paid and not demand too much work.

Since I had an excellent recommendation from Prince Meshersky, friends advised me to apply for a place on a newspaper, either the important *Novy Telegraf,* or the somewhat smaller *Odessa Messenger.*

There was not much chance on the *Novy Telegraf.* Azmirov, the editor, was well known for his slander and hatred of all Jews. I applied instead to the *Odessa Messenger,* and was taken on as a distributor. My duties were to see that the paper was delivered, by railway or by the mails, to the cities of the south.

It was a fine job, and a pleasant one. The whole staff of the paper was made up of outspoken liberals who accepted me in the most friendly way. Still, it did not please me. My work began at six in the morning! How could I go to work at six when I had gone to bed at three? How could I go to bed at ten, when it was only then my real life began? My life in the wine cellars, in Falconi's Pastry Shop, at the glorious Palais Royale! It was fine, gentlemanly work. It gave me prestige, importance, but once again, it was not for me.

The truth was, something was missing, something without which I was a bird without wings, a bear without a master.

Rosenberg was missing.

I began to live, as the saying goes, "as one lives in Odessa." That is, a life where one could ask for nothing more. True, I had to rise too early, but for the rest I could not complain. I had money, I had charm in the eyes of women, and I had the most irreplaceable of all treasures—I was young.

To understand my existence at that time you would have to see me as I walked to my newspaper office in the early-morning light. I am dressed like a dandy, and everything about me seems to sing. My handsome new coat with coattails from the waist. My high silk hat, my gloves, my beautifully tied cravat, my lacquered shoes. Even my elegant cane, which I swing gaily from side to side, seems to sing in my hand. I am making my way through Spiridonov Street to Pochtover. The whole world is quiet at this hour. The sidewalks are lined with acacia trees with their soft fresh perfume. Birds flutter about the branches and leaves, and their sweet twittering fills the air. The eyes grow drunk with the beauty they see, the breast expands, and the heart expands, too. It was spring, and beautiful is the spring in that glorious city on the Black Sea, even more beautiful to me after a year in muddy, rainy Bender.

High on a cliff on the northwest coast of the Black Sea, Odessa had all the power and splendor of a great European metropolis, together with the ideal climate of a pleasure resort. Youngest of Russian cities, it was built by Catherine the Great after the victory over the Turks in 1792.

The empress had acquired a territory with a long history of wars and invasions. The Greeks were on this coast at the dawn of antiquity; Odessa derives its name from Odessos, an ancient outpost left by this people on the cliff above the sea where the city now stands.

But whatever commerce and civilization the Greeks may have brought was wiped out in the raids and incursions of later ages. The region was overrun by Roman legions in the first century A.D. The Goths invaded it from the West in the third century, and wave after wave of marauding Huns came from the East in the fourth century.

The centuries of peace that followed were ended by the oncoming hordes of Genghis Khan. These Tatar horsemen swooped down on Russia through Central Asia and Siberia and descended on the coast, cut Russia off from the sea, and decimated the Slavic peoples living there.

A remnant of these people, however, fled inland and survived. They settled in the region between the Dnieper and the Danube, built townships there (some of them existing to this day), and traded peaceably with the old Kingdom of Rus. After the historic defeat of the Tatars in 1380, the Slavonic people, now divided into Great Russians, Ukrainians, and Byelorussians, came back to the northwest Black Sea coast, and some of them settled again on the cliff above the sea. The half-legendary Odessos was long forgotten. The steep cliff dwelling and the beach below exists in an old Polish ship's document as the Tatar village of Hadji Bei.

In 1475 the Ottoman Turks, spreading Islam by fire and sword, sailed up the coast, enslaved the remaining Tatars, set up a fortress at Hadji Bei, and from there exercised total control over the Black Sea and the Mediterranean. With Constantinople under Turkish siege, Poland and Hungary both on their knees, and all Russia under tribute, this empire was now one of the wealthiest and most powerful in the world.

The Russo-Turkish wars of the eighteenth century, all fought against Turkish domination, culminated in 1791 in a great Russian victory. For a long time Ottoman power was broken. General Alexander Suvorov tore down the Turkish fortress at Hadji Bei and, finding that the harbor would provide excellent shelter for the Russian fleet in wartime and commercial shipping in times of peace, he advised Catherine to make use of the site as a Russian port and naval base.

The empress, acting on his advice, spared no effort or expense to make her new city as beautiful as any she possessed.

The first piles of the port were sunk on September 2, 1794 (old calendar), and work on the city itself began soon after. Of the two previ-

Primorsky Park, Odessa
Odessa's medieval Belgorod Dnestrovsky Fortress

ously used names the empress chose the Greek Odessos, requesting it be given the feminine gender, Odessa. But though the old Tatar name was discarded, something of the wild freedom of those days was felt for hundreds of years in the steppe lands of this region.

Planned by Russia's best architects, the city was built to follow the natural terrain, with the boulevards and thoroughfares of the summit descending in regular terraces to the bay below. The famous Potëmkin Stairway was added in 1866, but work on the heights went on throughout the initial period. Parks and boulevards were laid out. Tree-lined streets appeared. Splendid public buildings arose. Hotels, shops, and restaurants opened their doors. And from the first, aristocrats and people of wealth came, drawn by the spectacular setting and the many pleasures of this new "Paris by the Sea." Homes were built for these people on the most beautiful streets, many of them mansions in the classic Italian style. And as the beach resorts of Langeron, Fontaine, and Arkady sprang up along the bay, Odessa's residents built villas too, and summer homes.

But people of a different sort were also coming, from every part of Russia and from other lands as well, men and women of every nationality, every trade and occupation. And they also settled in Odessa, the poorer ones on the outlying unfinished streets, the poorest of all in the gullies leading down to the beach.

Great Russians, Little Russians, and Byelorussians made up the bulk of this population, but many Greeks, Poles, Germans, Italians, and French came, many Albanians, Moldavians, Armenians, Tatars, and Bulgarians fleeing from the Turks. And, migrating by the hundreds from their villages and towns in hopes of a better life, the Jews also came. And it was these people, with their skills, trades, and professions, who mingled, worked, traded, and together, created the city.

In the first year, the population had tripled, and by midcentury Odessa was Russia's third-largest city, its chief center of grain export, and the true capital of the Ukraine.*

But from its inception, a passionate interest in the things of the mind shaped the life of this city. Before Odessa had a theater, French and Italian troupes performed in the open squares. The opening of the university in 1866 was one of the greatest events of its history. In the

---

* This rapid progress was due to the closeness of three navigable rivers, the Dnieper, the Dniester, and the Danube, as well as to the unusual depth of Odessa Bay. With the short winters and long, hot summers of this region, these waters rarely froze, making shipping to Europe and countries of the Mediterranean possible all year round.

publication of books and magazines it surpassed even Moscow and St. Petersburg. By the 1880s it was one of the country's great cultural centers, with a museum of fine arts, a university and medical school, a famous astronomical observatory, a public library (one of Russia's first), a conservatory of music, and two superb theaters, both regarded as among the best.

But over and beyond all this, Odessa was the country's great southern seaport. This fact dominated its commerce, its pleasures, and the outlook of its people.

The sea, it is said, brings thoughts of freedom, and the Odessans have always been a special breed, more "Western" in their thinking, more open to new ideas, than their fellow Russians in Kiev and Moscow. From the beginning a tradition of liberal and radical thought marks out this city among the rest. It had a part in the Decembrist uprising of 1825, and it would play a crucial role in the revolutionary era still to come.

I had chosen a good time to return to the city of my birth. The war was still on, and all Odessa throbbed with life. Wine cellars and *cafés chantants* did not close before dawn, and both theaters were packed every night. I could see my onetime favorite, Kozelsky. I could visit my idol, the beautiful Olga Glebova. Her dressing room backstage was always open now to her old *ataman*. My circle had grown, with new friends always ready to laugh at my humorous stories of the war. I could lunch at the glorious Falconi's, dine at the imperial Palais Royale.

And yet, there was an emptiness. Something was lacking. I was restless, ill at ease, blindly seeking a place where my soul could find peace. I longed for a friend to whom I could tell my dreams, my vague longings. I tried to confide in my parents, but got no sympathy. Perhaps they were right. In my dreams at this time there was much that was trivial—even impure.

One day as I sat in the editorial office of the *Odessa Messenger* reading about the war, my attention was caught by a notice. Reading it, my heart began to beat fast, the blood rushed to my head, and I sprang to my feet. Plainly, in black and white, I read that in Bucharest, Romania, a company of actors was playing Yiddish theater.

I looked again. No, I have not dreamed it. Yiddish theater! The language is Yiddish, the plays Yiddish, the actors Yiddish. I read further. The troupe is under the directorship of the poet Avrom Goldfaden. And listed among the actors I see two names: the student Jacob Spivakovsky, and—God above—the Odessa attorney Yisrol Rosenberg!

Then he has risen from the dead, my Rosenberg! He lives! He has swum back into my life. And in what a new and interesting form! Rosenberg an actor? A *Yiddish* actor?

Spivakovsky I knew well. A young man of a wealthy Odessa family, handsome as a picture, who, in addition to an academic education, had acquired polish during long periods spent abroad. He acted with talent and taste in Russian amateur theatricals, and was sought after in the most aristocratic Russian homes, where, it was said, he recited the poetry of Pushkin with something close to genius.

Adler also took part in some of these amateur theatricals, but apparently showed no talent as an actor, and had success only in a comedy role.

It may seem surprising that a boy of my kind should have as a friend such a person as Spivakovsky—a student, one of the intelligentsia. I must explain that before I left for the army I had come under new and better influences. This was thanks to my old friend, Olga Petrovna.

Yes, thanks to that same devil of a girl, whom I think of now as a sort of feminine Jekyll and Hyde! In her father's tavern she was a true girl of the Trushov district, onto every trick of her trade. But what a change when you sat with her in the theater, or walked with her on the boulevard! In what a different light she showed herself! Another person. Well read. Even idealistic. More, she had secret ties with nihilists, and helped to distribute their propaganda! Once she let me read one of their pamphlets and I marveled that people dared write such things in Russia.

At the time I speak of, the best homes of Odessa were meeting places of the underground. Olga Petrovna had entrée to these circles, where she was much valued for her daring and intelligence. Through her I met young people passionately absorbed in literature and social questions. I rarely took part in their discussions, but they made a deep impression on me and played no small part in lifting my entire spiritual condition. It was in these homes that I met Fräulein Sophia Oberlander, the idealistic young woman I later married. And there also I met Spivakovsky.

You can imagine, then, how great was my excitement to find him listed among the Yiddish artists in Bucharest, how great my astonishment at the whole thing. From joy I became another person. A new soul came into me. Gone, my vague longings, my melancholia and malaise! I had a goal, a purpose in life. I was determined to bring the Yiddish theater to Odessa!

Without delay I spread the news among everyone I knew, making clear how remarkable, how important it was. My audience caught fire, and together we worked so well that the existence of the Yiddish theater was known in homes we ourselves could not have entered.

I had some influence on the *Odessa Messenger.* I arranged for a second article on the theater in Bucharest to appear. Because of this, a notice even came out in the anti-Semitic *Novy Telegraf.* Finally, after endless effort, I discovered Rosenberg's whereabouts. I wrote to him. He answered. A lively correspondence sprang up between us. I assured him a Yiddish theater would have success in Odessa. I was certain of this, and one way or another, I was determined to bring it about.

The Yiddish theater, now a reality in Romania, had almost come into existence a number of times before.

As far back as 1598, comedies in a Dutch Yiddish dialect were performed in the ghetto of Amsterdam. The manuscript of a Purim play actually found its way into print in the early eighteenth century, but the play itself is lost. The coarseness of the text shocked the cultured Frankfurt Jews, and all the copies were burned.

Over the years Yiddish performances, some of them drawing great crowds, sporadically took place in Holland, Germany, Poland, and Russia. All of them were stopped by civil authorities, alarmed that so many Christians came, or by active opposition from within the Jewish community. The rabbinate tolerated theatricals only on Purim, the one day of Jewish carnival. Not until the nineteenth century, with religious authority breaking down everywhere, could such a theater take root as an accepted part of Jewish life.

The modern Yiddish theater was created by the popular poet Avrom Goldfaden, a man whose talents, temperament, and education uniquely equipped him for this task.

Born in 1840, the son of a watchmaker, in Old Constantin, Russia, Goldfaden began composing songs at the age of eight, and was known to the town as "little Avrom the merrymaker." He had no formal musical training and all his life composed in a notation of his own devising.

When the Crimean War broke out, his father, fearing the thirteen-year-old boy would be conscripted, enrolled him in the rabbinical school in Zhitomer. Students in these schools were exempt from army service, but the father was much criticized in the Jewish community. The rabbinical schools had been established by Nicholas I in opposition to the Jewish *chaider* and *yeshiva*. Their real purpose was to bring Jewish students into the Greek Orthodox church.

Conversions, however, were few, and since the crown schools, in addition to Jewish studies, provided an excellent modern education, Jewish scholars of advanced views took every opportunity to become teachers.

These men, on fire with Haskala, ran these schools on extremely liberal lines. Dances, masked balls, and visits to the theater were organized with the aim of bringing Jewish youth into contact with the modern world.

His teachers placed great hopes on the talented Goldfaden. They let him off on hard subjects, encouraged his musical gifts, his talent for verse, and fostered his love of Yiddish, a language these men had taken up as their cause.

Two great events took place during Goldfaden's school years. Through the efforts of his teachers, two of his songs were published in *Sunrise,* a Yiddish magazine published abroad. Folksingers coming into Zhitomer heard of these songs and asked him for others. The young composer obliged, and these men carried his songs to other towns, where they were instantly popular with the people. His talents as a composer and folk poet were becoming known while he was still a student.

In this last year another important event occurred: a school production of Dr. Solmon Ettinger's *Serkele.** Written in 1825 in the first surge

* A diminutive, not necessarily affectionate, of the name Sarah.

*Avrom Goldfaden,
1877*

of the Haskala, this comedy-melodrama was actually the first Yiddish play of modern times.

Goldfaden not only took the leading feminine role, but rehearsed and coached the other students, took charge of scenery and costumes, and, without previous experience, seemed instinctively to grasp every element needed for a theatrical production. The performance created a furor in Zhitomer, and all the *maskilim* in the town came to see it.

His studies over in 1858, Goldfaden left for Odessa. Wires had been pulled to get him a teaching post there at the government rabbinical school.

He soon felt at home in Odessa. A reputation for brilliance had preceded him. He was taken up in the best circles. His job at the school was easy, entailing only a few hours a week. For the rest he roamed around town with the novelist Yoel Linetzky, went to the theater every night, and came home in a coach at four in the morning, waking everyone in the neighborhood with his noise.

During his stay in Odessa Goldfaden brought out two poetry collections. The first attracted little attention. The second, *Dus Pintale Yid*, created a storm of enthusiasm. These were the first popular verses to emphasize the joy of the Jew in his traditions rather than his sufferings. *Dus Pintale Yid* made Goldfaden famous, and the title, summing up all the traits of character and mind that make up the "Jewishness of the Jew," became a permanent part of the language.

The collection must also be noted for the author's first attempt at the dramatic form: the full-length play, *Auntie Sosya,* a comedy later performed many times.

Goldfaden had settled down by now, and married Paulina, daughter of the philosopher Mordecai Werbel. Since in spite of his fame the poet was still poor, he swallowed his pride and with the help of his father-in-law, opened a hat store.

This business did well as long as his admirers gave him merchandise on credit, but by the end of the year Goldfaden was bankrupt. Besieged by creditors, he fled the city and, soon after, left for foreign parts.

He studied medicine in Munich, but soon gave it up and went on to Lemberg (Lvov). Here he ran into Linetzky again, and the two men got out a journal they called *Yisrolik,* a magazine aimed at purifying the Yiddish language. But the magazine had no success, the two men quarreled, and Goldfaden left for Leipzig.

In that city he heard the operas of Verdi, Meyerbeer, and Fromentol-Élie Halévy, saw the great Italian actor Tommaso Salvini in *Othello,* but still had no luck as a journalist.

In the fall of 1876 he was in Bukovina, Bessarabia. He was making another try at journalism with the *Bukovina Yiddish Weekly,* when a letter came from Jassy, a town on the Romanian border. The cultural society Lebanon was willing to pay his expenses if he came to Jassy and brought out his journal there.

Two days later, Goldfaden was on the train that took him over the Romanian border. He found all the *maskilim* in Jassy gathered at the station to greet him.

Goldfaden had come to Romania hoping to found a journal. He was destined instead to create a theater.

As it happened, the folksinger Gradner was in Jassy, performing nightly in an open-air garden. The two men were thrown together. Gradner, unknown to himself, was already as much an actor as a singer, and Goldfaden, struck by his dramatic effects, conceived the idea of a Yiddish theater. "The idea came to me of combining my songs with prose in a theater piece," he writes. "I forgot about the journal. Yiddish theater became my dream."

Gradner, immediately on fire, rounded up some young people willing to take part in the venture, among them one Socher Goldstein, a seventeen-year-old apprentice to a saddle maker. This boy worked in the evening as Gradner's assistant, and had ambitions to be a folksinger.

He was extremely tall and lanky, but Goldfaden thought he might play girls. The others, he said, were fit to come on only as extras.

He had already set to work on a two-act play around a simple plot line. The dialogue was mostly improvised. The actors were *told* when to kiss and when to quarrel. The songs and dances were the main thing. Goldfaden threw in a few of his old songs, wrote one or two new ones, and turned out some sort of playlet on the age-old theme of the love triangle.

The piece was performed twice with moderate success in October of 1876 and was never repeated. Goldfaden recalls it as a "nonsensical hodgepodge," but he had written it as an experiment, a test to see whether the thing could be done at all. And in spite of its weakness, the little play had held up. That was enough.

With the end of the holidays, cold weather set in. Performances in the garden came to an end, and Goldfaden set out for the town of Batushan. He took with him Gradner, Socher Goldstein, two or three folksingers, and a bookbinder named Schwartz. Money for the trip was supplied by Lebanon.

In Batushan the little troupe found the newspapers full of the Bulgarian rebellion, and everyone talking about the coming Russo-Turkish war. With war fever already in the air, Goldfaden wrote *Recruits,* a comic operetta about the woes of a raw soldier in the army—a theme still successful in our own time.

Recruits drew good audiences in Batushan, but after Goldfaden paid for the hall and the musicians, nothing remained for the actors. One by one the men who had started with him turned back. Finally, only Goldfaden, Gradner, and Socher Goldstein remained.

They played the Romanian provinces all that winter, arousing great excitement and curiosity, but rarely clearing a profit. If not for the generosity of Lebanon the three of them might not have survived the hardships of that winter.

In February, just before Purim, they came to the town of Galatz, Romania. Here a branch of Lebanon existed, and they got their first real welcome. A temporary stage was built for them at the Hotel Sager, and they were housed, for once, in decent, comfortable quarters.

In Galatz a historic event occurred: the first appearance of a woman on the Yiddish stage. A sixteen-year-old seamstress, Soore Siegel, a girl known to the town as "the songbird" because of her remarkable voice, drew Goldfaden's interest. He had a new operetta, *The Intrigue,* his most ambitious effort so far. He wanted to make a splash in Galatz, and this girl would give him the sensational element he needed. He put forth all his charm, and the girl's mother, overawed by his great name, finally consented.

Goldfaden had tried before to bring a woman into the troupe, but had always failed. No respectable Jewish girl would show herself on a stage, and to bring a woman of loose character before a Jewish public would have risked very great scandal.

These taboos, however, were beginning to lose their power. Goldfaden wrote in two easy songs for the new actress, one of them his own, the other borrowed from the popular operetta *The Daughter of Hell.* The girl got through better than expected and, as Goldfaden had foreseen, was received with resounding applause.

The Intrigue was Goldfaden's first real success. It was praised in the Galatz papers, and Romanian actors came back afterward with compliments for the whole cast.

The girl, however, was not allowed to appear again. Her mother had taken fright and in spite of the daughter's tears and hysterics, withdrew her from the cast. The troupe had to move on without her.

In spite of this setback, things were clearly looking up. Goldfaden, encouraged by success, went off to see what he could do in Bucharest.

There he was able to get only one performance at the Jignitza Theater, but he found a man named Lazare who had a hall in the Jewish quarter. This Lazare put up the money that brought the actors to the capital.

In Bucharest the troupe acquired three new members, all young men who sang in the choir of the famous Bucharest cantor, Israel Kupfer. These singers, all trained in the Bucharest conservatory, picked up a little extra money whenever the French opera came to town. They were also in great demand at weddings and other Jewish festivities, where they jested, danced, and were generally known for their liveliness. All of them were young, musically gifted, and dying to be actors. Laiser Zuckerman sang a bass aria from *Lucia,* and was engaged on the spot. Moishe Silberman, though somewhat wooden, was handsome and had a good voice. He too passed with flying colors. Siegmund Mogulesko, the seventeen-year-old leader of the chorus, was known to all Bucharest. The wealthiest Jews of the city came every Saturday night to the cantor's home just to hear Mogulesko imitate the great Romanian comedi-

The Yiddish actors Sophia and Socher Goldstein, Russia, 1877

ans. Fragile, not much bigger than a child, Mogulesko had inborn comic genius and was musical to his fingertips. Goldfaden immediately knew he had made an important find.

A fourth candidate, Abba Schoengold, failed to get an offer. This young singer, the handsomest of the four and with much the best voice, desperately wanted to be an actor. Unfortunately, he assumed an air of disdain for the whole proceeding. Goldfaden did not like him, and he was turned away, the only one of his friends to lose his chance.

With three new actors, Lazare's hall began to draw a small but steady audience. To keep them coming back Goldfaden had to constantly turn out new plays, new operettas, new songs, new couplets for the *divertissements* between the acts. In addition he had to bribe officials, handle business problems, rehearse the actors, jump in, like as not, and play a part himself, and when called out by the public, appear before the curtain with a speech or recitation. He did not like this last duty, feeling he was not talented enough. "I stood on the stage, spoke casually, jested with the public," he writes. "But business problems were overwhelming me. Backstage there was disorder, things not going as they should. Just then the public would call me out. I would come before them in a bad mood, with an angry face."

And in fact Goldfaden's public appearances went badly in spite of his fame. High-handed and with a violent temper, he was revered by the actors but not loved. He thought of the theater as his sole creation and in his harsher moments did not hesitate to tell them all they were nobodies made great only by his talents.

In April 1877, Russia declared war on the Ottoman Empire, Russian troops crossed the Danube, and Bucharest filled up with contractors, middlemen, and agents. All Odessa seemed to be in Romania, making deals with the Russian commissariat, and Goldfaden discovered it was "raining gold."

Overnight, admission to Lazare's hall jumped from eight to twenty francs. Yiddish theater in Bucharest had suddenly caught on. The wealthy Jews of the city came. Scholars and intellectuals came. Even Romanian officers came. They liked the comic antics, the songs, the dances. And the beards and long coats of the Jews on the stage gave them all a hearty laugh too.

With success, the troupe expanded. Spivakovsky, in Bucharest as a war correspondent, came into the company as a leading man. Rosenberg

Earliest known photograph of Siegmund Mogulesko, 1878

forgot his deals with the Russian commissariat and became instead a comedian. And Goldfaden soon acquired not one but two prima donnas, the sisters Margaretta and Annetta Schwartz, both with trained voices, both beauties, and both absolutely respectable.

That season all Bucharest was laughing at the comedy hit *Vladutzul Momei (Mama's Boy)*. On Mogulesko's advice, Goldfaden took this play, turned the hero into a petulant little *chosid* made some other adaptations to Jewish life, and turned out his first smash hit, *Shmendrick.*

So great was Mogulesko's success as the spoiled, foolish Shmendrick that Gradner grew sick with jealousy. To pacify him, Goldfaden wrote a two-act piece, *The Desolate Isle.* Gradner played the lost mad "European," Annetta Schwartz sang the role of Regina. Mogulesko had a comedy scene with a song and dance as "a little Black Boy." Gradner was forgotten. The audience wanted no one but Mogulesko. They brought him back to the stage twenty times.

This had such an effect on the emotional Gradner that he left the company and went back to Jassy. There he took in the folksinger Moishe Finkel, found a woman named Rosa Friedman, made her into a character actress, gathered up a few amateurs, and formed a company of his own.

Goldfaden, shocked by the loss of such an important star, soon consoled himself. Mogulesko's success was so great that Gradner was not even missed. *Shmendrick* had a triumphant run at the Jignitza, and when the theater closed down for repairs, the company went into the Pomul Verde (Green Garden), a café where the owner broke a wall to build them a stage.

Yiddish theater was the rage of the Bucharest season. The actors played four times a week, and according to the Romanian journalist Shigorin, hundreds of people were turned away every night, many not Jews.

This was the heyday of the Yiddish theater in Romania, the theater that so astonished Adler, and that he was now determined to bring to Odessa.

HOPES, PLANS, AND DREAMS

While I was corresponding with Rosenberg an event of importance happened. I moved up in the world. I became a government official. An official of a kind no Jew in Russia had ever been before.

I had quickly tired of my job on the newspaper. And was it a business for me, I ask you, to get up at five in the morning—I, who was used to carousing half the night with my good companions and sleeping half the day away afterward? I began to look around for something better.

It was a good moment. The war had ended with victory for the fatherland. A patriotic wave swept through the country and it was a good time for heroes. One recommendation I already had from Prince Meshersky, general of the Russian Army and head of the Bender military hospital. I got a second recommendation from Avrom Markovich Brodsky,* a member of the city *duma*, or council. With these highly placed patrons I became an official in the Department of Weights and Measures.

Every morning, then, at a certain hour, the government cockade on my hat and a police captain at my side, I made my appearance in the marketplace. This brought a loud murmur of fear from the men in the stalls and the women with their baskets. A furious stir began. One hid his weights, another buried his measures. But I was not to be fooled! I weighed and I measured, and I made out my reports. I went about it with a will. They felt my hand. They trembled. Still, I was not altogether hard. If it was a poor woman I forgave a first transgression and even a second.

---

* A brandy and sugar magnate, also involved in the building of the Russian railroad. Brodsky was so wealthy and influential, he was known as the Jewish tsar.

But after a short time I noticed that the Russian policeman was better to the Jews than I was! At times he even took me aside and told me to be a good fellow and tear up some report I was making. At first this puzzled me, but the little smile on his lips soon cleared up the mystery. Knowing the ropes better than I, the Russian officer had come to terms with the shopkeepers. Discovering I was a young lord who took no bribes, they were giving him money to put in a good word for them!

The new official finally learned to take his job less seriously. My Russian policeman had become most friendly. He often borrowed money from me until the twentieth of the month, the day police were paid. We usually had a glass of wine together when our duties were over. Various officials greeted me with respect every morning. The police master himself bowed when our paths crossed. In short, I was getting to be quite a personage in police circles.

The appointment of Adler to an actual government position, though unusual, was not out of line with the times. While for the majority of Jews life remained much the same under Alexander, there were some who rose to prominence. It was not unknown in the southern provinces for an influential Jew to win a seat, even an official seat, on Alexander's elective town councils. A few Jewish lawyers made reputations in the new liberal courts. Some Jews even made fortunes in railroads, though it must be said these were already men of great wealth who had always enjoyed absolute freedom in Russia.

It must be understood, however, that these meteoric rises occurred for the most part in the cities. To the mass of Jews scattered throughout the towns and villages of the Pale, the great changes of the new reign often penetrated only as distant cloudy rumors. In these tiny self-contained *shtetlach,* the days and years went by much as they had for generations. Surrounded by forces that might turn hostile at any moment, these people expected little from any Russian tsar. They wanted to live as Jews and raise their children as Jews. For the rest, their lives focused on survival.

Although my official position brought me both money and prestige, I now thought day and night of one thing, Rosenberg! Not only

I, but my whole circle was on fire to know more about this Yiddish theater he was bringing from Romania.

Night after night we met in the wine cellars where folksingers performed, as though we knew in our hearts that out of these same cellars the Yiddish theater would rise.

A Yiddish theater! How wonderful, how good! We spent whole nights talking about it, giving full rein to our imagination. I myself expected something high, almost holy. No small thing, this theater born under the cannon of Plevna!* All the thunder of the war would be in it. It would be full of Jewish heroism, Jewish suffering, and heart-lifting Hebrew melody and dance.

Night after night we met at Akiva's Restaurant on Rivnoya Street, never guessing that in this very room where we sat and dreamed of it, the first Yiddish performances in Russia would take place.

In the meantime, Akiva's was our bourse, our news depot. One night Rosenberg's young wife ran in to tell us he was actually on his way. (Just before leaving Odessa, Rosenberg, old bachelor that he was, had married.) Another night it was Fuchs, Rosenberg's new father-in-law, with word that Spivakovsky was also coming. A third night some boon companion arrived with news that Rosenberg was bringing all Goldfaden's plays.

The great day finally came. Rosenberg and Spivakovsky were on their way, and we gathered at the railway station to meet them.

Such a meeting takes place only once in a hundred years. First, who was there. Spivakovsky's aristocratic family arrived in their carriage. Then Rosenberg's old parents, humble Orthodox Jews of the old style, with his sister and his new young wife—both soberly dressed, good Jewish women. Next, my own followers, fine young sports and dandies who spent their nights carousing and creating scandals around the town. With them certain ladies over whose pedigree and occupation a light veil of discretion must be drawn. Last of all, mixing with the others, the folksingers, looking like small-town fiddlers, hangers-on at some poor synagogue, or beggars altogether.

---

* Plevna, in Bulgaria, was taken by the Russians after a 143-day siege by the Turks. It was celebrated as a great victory in a war that gave the Russians little else to celebrate. Russia got back a part of Bessarabia lost in the Crimean War. Having won a victory at Plevna, they made the most of it.

But the meeting itself was very touching. Kisses and embraces. Rosenberg's parents wept for joy, and we, his good brothers, watched, grinning with pleasure. At the same time we felt a bit queer. Our glances held a certain unease, even a hint of mockery. Inside ourselves we shrugged. Rosenberg and Spivakovsky—they were the same, yet not the same. Rosenberg, who always wore the mustaches and side-whiskers proper for an Odessa lawyer, was now completely clean-shaven. Not a hair on his face—a regular priest! Spivakovsky, too, who took such pride in his elegant little mustaches, was clean-shaven. And the two of them were alike as two drops of water, both in black winged capes, high hats, dangling pince-nez, gloves, spats, lacquered boots—a pair of barons!

We gazed at them, astonished and curious. But we were surrounded by too many people and with no time for questions. We agreed to meet the next day at the Palais Royale, and the two heroes were carried off by their families.

I went home, on fire with curiosity, bewilderment—and unimaginable hopes.

ROSENBERG: ACTOR AND IMPRESARIO

Next day, punctually on the hour, our little group came together at the Palais Royale to make plans for the conquest of Odessa. A remarkable assemblage we were, with Rosenberg, our chieftain and sage, reading us the law: the untold wealth and glory of the Yiddish theater in Romania.

Looking back on that scene now I realize what a genius comedian he was, and how brilliantly he played his role. But we saw nothing of this at the time. His careless manner and lordly air threw dust in our eyes.

"Thousands in Romania!" he exclaimed. "Right, Spivakovsky?"

"*Da, da,*" Spivakovsky assented.

"The greatest millionaires came. The king and queen of Romania came! Right, Spivakovsky?"

"*Da, da.*" Spivakovsky was not so used to lying. He got red at times.

Rosenberg talked money in francs, showed his Romanian coins, and threw in a Romanian phrase at every opportunity. All in all he had not been in Romania long, and had taken away as much of the language as a very small bird could carry away on its beak. As we found out later, he often made the most laughable mistakes. But these Romanian expressions were his background, the local color, so to speak, of the canvas he was painting. "Yankele, you will play lovers," he said to me. "I will make you great. Look at Spivakovsky! All Romania rings with his name." He turned to him. "So, *domnelli!*" he cried. "Give us the monologue from *Recruits*!"

"Bravo!" we all shout. We are applauding already. But Spivakovsky begged off. "Let's only get a permit from the government," Rosenberg said. "But Adler is a whole official now. He has the police master in his pocket and will arrange everything."

From the Palais Royale we went to Falconi's Pastry Shop, where Rosenberg ordered coffee and *pirozhnoye,* pastries. After bragging a little more he went on to anecdotes, and finally he told such stories of the theater in Romania that we held our sides laughing. Falconi's was an open-air restaurant, and such cannonades of laughter shot from our table that strangers gathered around us, also laughing.

In the midst of all this Rosenberg took me aside. "Yankele, I need money," he said. "Things are going well with you, so share with a brother, eh?" The mask dropped, his eyes confessed the truth. "You think we did well there, in Romania? We hungered, brother! We hungered, Spivakovsky and I."

He quickly gave me the story. Goldfaden saw that he and Spivakovsky were capable, that they had talent. He insulted them, hounded them, made their life a hell. What to do? They got together and formed a troupe of their own. For a time they were successful. They had plays and they had money. "The plays we still have," Rosenberg said, "but money goes fast."

He was already in my pockets as he spoke, and as always, his fingers were extremely nimble in these operations. Half of what he found he gave back to me. Calling Spivakovsky, he divided the rest with him, saying tersely, "Partners are partners!"

With money in his pockets, Rosenberg was gay again. We parted, he making his farewells in Romanian, the rest of us in Russian.

I could not shut my eyes that night. I was already imagining myself as Hamlet, as Chlestakov in Gogol's *Revizor.** In Russian it was all so magnificent, but how would it sound in Yiddish? And I, who had only finished the second class of the county school, I who had publicly boxed for money in the Moldovanka—how could I be an artist, an actor?

True, I had rubbed shoulders with Russian actors by now. I knew many of them for big drinkers, big cardplayers, big woman chasers. Still, their manners! Their clothes alone! They are gentlemen, cultivated, they know literature. And I who had spent my nights carousing around the town with Buff's Army—how could I be Hamlet?

Sleep came at last, but it was a broken sleep that brought no rest.

* *The Inspector General.*

Rosenberg and Spivakovsky, breaking away from Goldfaden, had formed only one of a half dozen Yiddish troupes at that time giving performances in Romania.

The new era had begun with Gradner's defection to Jassy. Gradner had not only formed a rival company there; he had also found a rival playwright. Joseph Lateiner, one of the Jassy *maskilim,* was inspired by Goldfaden to try his own hand as a dramatist. Taking as a starting point a humorous German story, *Nathan Schlemiehl,* Lateiner wrote in a speech or two against fanaticism, threw in a reference to a current quarrel among the Jassy Jews, and turned out a comedy he called *The Two Schmil Schmelkes.* Since the play had some success, he wrote another, then a third, and soon he discovered he could turn out plays, one after the other, like yard goods.

It was now open war. Gradner wrote to every actor in Bucharest, promising each of them more money and more recognition of his talent than he would ever receive from Avrom Goldfaden.

The promise of recognition went deep. Actors had feared that without Goldfaden they would have no livelihood. Now they saw the beginnings of an open field.

Socher Goldstein was the first to desert. Others followed him. Finally, Mogulesko himself declared for freedom and left for Jassy. He and Gradner had a talk. They agreed that Goldfaden was the real enemy, and Mogulesko came into Gradner's troupe as his partner.

Gradner had triumphed, but it was a triumph that already held the seeds of his destruction. Mogulesko was fast becoming a legend in the Jewish world of Romania. Jews who had never seen him spoke of him as part of their life. He had only to appear for the whole house to rock with laughter, crash with applause.

All this was death to Gradner. Not long before he had been the first and greatest actor of the Yiddish theater; he now was taking second place in his own troupe. There were violent explosions, and finally Gradner took his wife (now his prima donna), and together with Moishe Finkel, Rosa Friedman, and one or two others, went out with his own troupe into the Romanian provinces. The company in Jassy immediately reorganized as "The Mogulesko Troupe."

With three companies in the field, actors began wandering freely from one to the other. A number of them, however, returned to Bucharest.

For all his troubles, Goldfaden came through with two more smash successes; *Breindele Cossack* and *The Witch of Batushan,* a play that would be performed successfully in the Yiddish theater for some fifty years.

On March 4, 1878, the Russo-Turkish War ended with Russia victorious. The business of the Russian commissariat, the army supply department, was over. One by one the contractors, middlemen, and agents who had swarmed into Romania packed up and went home.

The war had brought prosperity to the Yiddish theater, and with the end of the war, it vanished. The big audiences of Bucharest and Jassy were in the main made up of Russian Jews doing business with the Army Supply Department. Now only the original small audience remained: simple people, most of them poor, many illiterate.

Goldfaden managed to hang on in Bucharest, but in the provinces, where conditions had never been the best, things were now wretched indeed. Actors who had known luxury in the war years now got a taste of starvation.

Gradner lost heart and took ship with his wife for Constantinople. Turned down by Goldfaden, Schoengold toured the sticks with yet another playwright named Hurvitz. Mogulesko and three other actors formed a quartet and went about singing for their livelihood under the open sky. Since his colleagues could not bring themselves to take the collection, it was Mogulesko who went around with the plate.

Rosenberg and Spivakovsky, trying to make it on their own, were soon in a desperate situation. Their troupe had scattered, and Rosenberg was ready to snatch at any straw in the flood. Adler's letter was the straw. Romania was played out, Russia the only chance. Putting together whatever money they could, he and Spivakovsky took the train back to Odessa.

The Yiddish theater came with them.

Rosenberg did things cleverly. Since he needed money, he rounded up the *podradchike,* the Odessa middlemen and contractors he had known in Romania. These people had supported Goldfaden in Bucharest. They had come back to Odessa rich from the war, and Rosenberg wanted to win them over.

He threw a party in their honor, an amusing affair in the upper room of a restaurant. Musicians played, wine flowed, and the table groaned with food. Rosenberg took out his merchandise. Not plays.

In those days nobody knew of such things. He *told* the subject, the content, sang bits of the songs, described scenes, told stories—what can I say? We laughed until we were sick, and it was very gay.

Meanwhile the folksingers entertained. They were for the most part men with unprepossessing faces and bedraggled clothing. Yet, since these were the first Yiddish actors in Russia, let us give them the attention they deserve.

Old "Schmul with the Hoarse Throat" was their leader and the best of them. He did not have a good voice, but his face was fine, even beautiful.

Next, Boris "Budgoy," real name Holtzerman. Not a pleasant or sympathetic personality. Face and voice of a Barrabas. Big dog's lips. A short body. A big stomach. Hairy hands. But good with the plate. You had to give or be insulted.

Laizer Duke. Tall, thin, a bony face. A strong voice, but sang off-key and danced clumsily. Still, when he put on a long coat and a Chassidic *shtreimel,* he could be entertaining.

Aaron Schrage—another type entirely. Tall, smooth-spoken, and dressed well, but did not have a fine manner. He told loose stories, and ran after girls.

While the folksingers performed, Rosenberg, sotto voce, assigned to each of them his rightful profession. This one, he said, should make boots, that one raise potatoes. All the same, he said, they would do. Take off their beards, dress them in frock coats and high hats, put gold spectacles on them, and no one would know them for the same men.

Throughout the evening Spivakovsky sat quiet, reserved—a real young Salvini.* Though I laughed at Rosenberg's stories until my sides ached, I was always aware of his more reserved bearing. I told myself that someday I too would be like him, quiet, proud, and fine.

The evening came to an end with Spivakovsky's Russian poetry. The guests departed. Rosenberg, Spivakovsky, and I, along with the musicians and folksingers, went off to a tavern to talk and make plans for the future.

It was very late, but we were all night birds accustomed to staying up twenty-four hours at a stretch. Rosenberg, in an excited state, kept speaking to Spivakovsky in Romanian. I found out later he was cursing us. Having thoroughly cursed us all, he turned to the folksingers.

* The renowned Italian actor Tommaso Salvini (1829–1915).

"All right, you mangy, poverty-stricken dogs!" he began. "How long will you sing in the wine cellars and go around afterward like beggars with a plate? Don't you see, don't you feel, how your sun is rising? I tell you, you won't need to go around with a plate. I tell you, people will bring you armfuls of money. Yes, they will give it to you before they even see what you look like! Take Moishe Finkel, who once sang in the cellars like you. Look at him today. See what the Yiddish theater did for him. He is a king! No mustaches! A high hat! No longer the same Moishele. An artist! You will be artists too, all of you. Never mind! There is enough material in you, enough talent." Turning to me he said, "And you too, Yankele, you will be an actor. You will be with me. I feel it."

The folksingers were dazzled. "Is it true, Yankele?" they asked me. "Will you really become an actor?"

"Yes, of course. Of course. I am certain of it." I was not certain at all, but Rosenberg threw me a glance, and I caught my cue.

Day had come in the meantime. It was time to break up. We decided to come together that evening to make practical plans.

Happiest of all were the folksingers. If Rosenberg had ordered them to shave off their beards and mustaches they would have done it for him there in the middle of the street.

When things go well they go well from every side. The following evening Alexander Oberlander, an attorney involved in our enterprise, came with great news. We have a prima donna! His sister, Sophia (Sonya) Solomonova, a young woman respected in the best circles of the city, had agreed to join us.

Rosenberg, too, had news. He produced a photograph. A beauty with marvelous red-gold hair. "The real goods!" he exclaimed with satisfaction. The young lady, Masha Moskovich, had also agreed to join.

It was, in fact, a night of surprises, for our little army grew in size with every hour! We acquired not only Miss Moskovich, but her brother, too, a young engineer, and after him three young men from the choir of Cantor Blumenthal.

The singers were not as convinced as the others. They were more inclined to wait and see. But they were impressed by Spivakovsky, who was one of the intelligentsia, and who looked like a prince without his mustaches. They were also interested in my involvement. I was not of the intelligentsia, but I was known to be clever and to have

Jacob Adler, during his early days as an actor, Russia, ca. 1879–80

a good understanding of the theater. Oberlander heard one of them saying, "If Adler goes in, we will too."

After several of these meetings, the task of getting together a troupe began. In this process I was to play no small part. While as an actor I was still a beginner, an experiment yet to be made, as a connoisseur of theater I had something to contribute. Both Rosenberg and Spivakovsky knew this, and made use of it. You must remember that in the course of my year in the gallery of the City Theater, I had become familiar with almost every play in the repertoire, including many of the classics. I had a good knowledge of the popular tragedies of Shakespeare. I was acquainted with Schiller, with Goethe's *Faust,* with Gutzkow's *Uriel Acosta,* and with many of the operas.

I had learned to trust my critical powers too, for my opinion had importance not only to my army in the gallery, but also to the actors. It was the actors, in fact, on whom it worked with special force, for both Odessa newspapers invariably followed my verdict. Even Azmirov of the *Novy Telegraf,* a known anti-Semite, concurred with my opinion. The younger actors in particular searched my face when I passed, worried over the impression they had made. Happy the actress to whom I said, "Bravo! Splendid!" She was in seventh heaven. Woe to her whose glance I avoided, passing with bent head to hide my verdict. She knew she would get bad reviews!

Rosenberg was aware of all this. Both in the organizing of his actors and the preparations for the first performance, he took counsel not only with Spivakovsky, but with me. Because of this I can say I am older by several weeks as a director than as an actor.

With the spring of 1877 came the fatal moment when I stood on the threshold of a life in the theater. Yes, fatal—for there is seldom a way back. The actor does not swim with the stream. He burns his bridges, parts with family and friends, enters a world of gypsies, vagabonds, people of questionable morality. A certain fear surrounds him, as though he had joined a secret order. This has not altogether changed even today. Imagine, then, how strong it was some forty years ago.

We got together with the folksingers one day in a tavern, and Rosenberg began trying them out, teaching them the songs and explaining the stage business. But the coarse appearance of the players, their beards, their bedraggled clothing, kept interfering with his inspiration. "Devil take it, it's no good!" he broke out. "You look like chimney sweeps, not actors! I need human beings. Do you understand? Go and make yourselves into human beings!"

And he began to make them into human beings. Beards, mustaches, fell to the ground in snips. Off came the short coats, the low hats, the deep boots. With his magic wand and his last few *groschen*, Rosenberg worked a transformation. In frock coats with narrow trousers, high silk hats, white shirts, and black flowing ties, the folksingers looked like Englishmen, Frenchmen, or better still, the upper-class Romanians who were now Rosenberg's ideal.

And so, before the comedy on the stage, we had a comedy of our own. We are living now in another time, another world. It is hard today to understand how the heart of a simple Jew wept to part with his beard. It was painful to see them come together again. Shaven Jews! Chins, cheeks, mouths, never seen before! They laughed, but their laughter was hollow, hysterical, more like the squealing of a chicken being slaughtered. Each one joked bitterly at the other, each looking miserably at his reflection in the tavern mirror and feeling unhappily with his hands for the beard that no longer existed.

I laughed at them. I had no beard, and my little mustaches were only recent citizens on my face. I thought I looked well.

The folksingers had never been afraid before, but this was no cellar performance. It was in a real theater on a real stage. I laughed at their fears, but when I remembered that I myself would have to face an audience my heart pounded. Suppose I lost my courage, became too frightened to say my lines? Suppose my parents came? Suppose my *uncle* came!

I breathed freely only when I learned I would take no part in the first performance. God be thanked, I would not be on the stage, but in the audience!

Our first performance was to take place in Akiva's restaurant, on Rivnoya Street, and the day came when we gathered there for our first rehearsal. We were all in a holiday mood, full of hope. Not only the actors were present in force, but also the *podradchike*, businessmen who had all been in Romania and couldn't wait to see a little Yiddish theater. Rosenberg too was full of joy. He felt his moment had come, and in my eyes he grew that day.

It was a summery June morning, and a whole crowd of girls, women, and children gathered at the open window, laughing and applauding. Everyone asked for a song, a dance.

"*Domnelli, gospoda!*" said Rosenberg. "Gentlemen! We are no wine cellar entertainers, no folksingers and clowns. You will have to pay money to see us. We are actors—artists!" He began an excited speech about the triumphs of the Yiddish theater in Romania. The high commissioner of the Russian Army had come! The king and queen of Romania had come! He began reeling off names. Annetta Schwartz. Madame Sophia Goldstein, the beauty of the world. Moishe Teich. The great comedian, Laizer Zuckerman. (All the *podradchike* had spoken of Zuckerman, and I was curious to see him.) Last of all he spoke of Mogulesko, whom he described as handsome, young, a great singer, a marvelous dancer, and a genius.

Rosenberg concluded his speech at the window by saying, "Yes, the actors in Romania were great, but they will never be as great as we. And therefore we will create a theater for the Jews of Russia—and right here in Odessa!"

A storm of applause at the open window. The *podradchike* bought tickets on the spot at five and ten rubles apiece. Rosenberg was actively engaged in shoving this shower of rubles into his pockets. But it would be wrong to say he cared only for the money. From happiness he became good to the whole world. He told the chorus to give the onlookers the song from *Breindele Cossack,* he himself did his scene as Yankev the Drunk, and then he told Spivakovsky to give the monologue from *Recruits.*

Joyous bravos at the open window. Impossible to describe the enthusiasm of both onlookers and invited guests. The *podradchike* ordered tables to be brought in, they were set with food and wine, and everyone ate, drank, sang, danced, kissed, embraced.

But in the midst of this celebration the door was flung open, and a policeman entered, measuring us all with his eyes.

"*Chto sobranye?*" he demanded, looking us over. "What's going on here?"

We were all frightened to death. Rosenberg, always a coward in these situations, whispered, "Adler—well?" Since I am the great official it was up to me to smooth this over.

I saw something had to be done so that the Yiddish theater would not die in the belly of its mother before it was born. I explained to the officer that we were actors, come together to rehearse a play that would be given on these premises.

He was writing every word I said in a notebook, and things looked bad. We were silent as he left. But he did not leave alone.

Akiva went with him. He came back, a broad smile on his lips. Money had changed hands. All was well again.

With this incident the onlookers at the window had melted away like a flock of frightened birds. Soon the guests, too, took their departure, and only the actors remained.

Now Rosenberg showed himself in a new light, that of the good benevolent boss. Holding high his new rubles he called out, "Who needs money to make the Sabbath?"

Who needed? Everyone needed! And Rosenberg gave to each according to his need. "Was it the truth?" he exclaimed, radiant with happiness. "They gave us money even before they saw us! That's theater!"

Among the early actors mentioned by Adler, the greatest, without question, was Mogulesko. Like Chaplin he was master of both laughter and tears, and again, as with Chaplin, both the simplest audience and the most demanding critic were captured by his art.

Adler describes him as the only genius in the Yiddish theater. Later, in the United States, the writer and journalist Abraham Cahan, too, was dazzled. Cahan saw Mogulesko for the first time in a melodrama by N. M. Sheikevitch in which he played three parts, a young criminal of the Odessa street, an old soldier destroyed by drink, and, in the last act, a comical gossipy old matchmaking woman. "His personality was as marvelous as his art," Cahan wrote. "His talent and charm lit that foolish play with rays of divine fire. From that time on, I was his most ardent 'patriot'!"

In America Mogulesko performed memorably in many of Gordin's plays, but actually, he preferred the early operettas, finding more room there for song, dance, and improvised comic effects.

In both Russia and America he was loved by a public that found in his indomitable "little Jew" a figure that supremely expressed their struggle and their will to survive.

Mogulesko has a place among the greats of the Yiddish theater, but other early actors also went on to stardom. Annetta Schwartz, one of the two sisters who sang in Bucharest with Goldfaden, married Moishe Finkel and came with him to America in 1886. She starred under his direction for a few years, but went back to Europe when the marriage ended in divorce. She is mentioned only in the bitter reminiscences of Bessie Thomashefsky (wife of Boris Thomashefsky), who resented her as a rival.

Finkel acquired extraordinary power in America, where he was known for a long time as the tsar of the Yiddish theater. His fortunes declined when the early operettas of Moshe Hurvitz and Joseph Lateiner lost their popularity. In 1904, after severe blows to both his personal and professional life, he committed suicide.

Sophia Goldstein, praised for her beauty by Rosenberg, was the stage name of the sixteen-year-old seamstress, Soore, whom Rosenberg had left behind in Galatz. Consumed with ambition, this girl had never forgotten her one night on the stage. A year after her one brief appearance, she freed herself from the control of her parents by marrying the eighteen-year-old Socher Goldstein, and as his wife joined the Gradner-Mogulesko troupe in Jassy. Because Gradner found the name Soore too prosaic for the stage, he billed her as Sophia Goldstein.

She rose to importance in 1881, when she starred in a Yiddish troupe that took over the Odessa Mariinsky Theater. When she came to America in 1884, she was a famous star. Socher Goldstein had died of tuberculosis in Europe, and in America she married the actor Max Karb.

Sophia Karb had great success for many years as Thomashefsky's prima donna, but died of pneumonia in 1904, her untimely end deeply mourned by the Yiddish public.

Laizer Zuckerman, who came over with Goldfaden, was an immediate favorite in America, and danced well into his seventh decade.

Moishe Teich began his acting career with Hurvitz. He later entered Goldfaden's troupe as a tragedian, but did not gain prominence.

THE GREAT NIGHT:
AN ECHO OF MY YOUTH

The first performance—the night is burned into my heart with letters of fire. The memory of it will die only when my eyes have closed for the last time.

A platform had been built, and Akiva put up a calico curtain that did not roll up, but came together in the middle. Evening fell. The lamps were lit. Inside the hall a Yom Kippur feeling, joyful, yet deeply serious. The families of the actors and folksingers were in the hall, everyone dressed as though for a wedding. Rosenberg's family sat in the front row, their faces tense, expectant. But the seriousness on the face of Rosenberg's old father cannot even be described. Only my family was absent. I had not yet dared tell them I had bound up my fate with the actors.

Although I was not on stage that night I had spells of fear, turned hot and cold, and went continually from the hall to the actors backstage. I watched them as they put on their makeup, caught snatches of their talk, caught the mood, the tension. An unseen force seemed to lift me high—very high. A spirit of prophecy came into me. My eyes opened. I saw the future. It was not a vision, not even clear as a thought. It was no more than a momentary feeling—a flash. But I knew that from this poor hall, from these smeared, frightened faces, a great theater would rise, that in time to come this scene would be recorded in festive fiery words as the beginning of a rich and wonderful epoch.

Oh, how I hear them still, the voices of those still living and those long, long dead! I see their faces again. I breathe that air again. Time rolls off my white head, off my shoulders, off my soul. I am young again, a boy of twenty-one again.

Dear God, how great is the power of memory! Among all your

gifts what can compare with the miracle of once again finding one's youth—if only for a moment, a breath of time, as a faraway echo.

If in the audience it was Yom Kippur that night, backstage it was Judgment Day. Not only fear, but an almost religious awe was on every face. Every actor knew that not only he himself but the Yiddish theater would be judged that night. All of them, even the coarsest, knew they were taking part in a historic moment, and on every face was a determination not to fail, a determination that the beginning should "take."

Before the curtain went up Rosenberg spoke to me. He told me that the first time he went on in Goldfaden's theater he went to a ritual bath and prayed. "Nobody saw my tears," he said. "Only myself and my God." I confess I had a terrible moment of doubt. Rosenberg? The skeptic, the jokester? Was he laughing at me? But no—great tears were in his eyes. "No, Yankele," he said as though guessing my thought. "This is no longer the old Rosenberg before you. When I go on the stage, no matter how foolish the play, I remember Avrom Goldfaden wrote it, and every word becomes holy to me. I will go hungry, I will lose all, but never will I stain the name of my theater!

"Look at Spivakovsky!" Rosenberg went on. "He has given up cigarettes, given up new clothes! He spends his days reading German books, learning about the theater, learning about the drama—all to make himself a worthy pioneer. And you too, Yankele," said Rosenberg, concluding his remarkable address. "You too, if you mean to be an actor—a *Yiddish* actor—will have to do the same. Remember, we live at a time when Jews are being persecuted. A crisis is coming in Jewish life. Young people who adored everything Russian are turning back to their own language, their own traditions. See who is here tonight!" He led me to a peephole in the curtain. "Cantor Blumenthal, beloved throughout the Jewish world! Werbel, the philosopher, the giant of our generation! And where have they come to see us? Here, in the hall of a restaurant!"

He let me go. I was shivering from head to foot. I gazed at the actors. They were now in their costume and makeup, one as a *chosid*—another, a merchant—another, a scandal mongerer. Spivakovsky paced up and down like a lion in a cage, declaiming his lines. Often he wept.

A strange sensation came over me, a quicksilver feeling in my bones. I felt a desire to *play*—to be on the stage. Without willing it, my feet moved. I stole away to a corner where there was a mirror, and began to "act." I looked into the glass, showed fear, anger, pride. I gesticulated, spoke lines. Words came to me from I don't know where. Whole speeches issued from my lips. I forgot where I was, forgot my surroundings. I "played." I was in a role.

Suddenly music, ending with a crash of cymbals. A nervous bell. The curtain parted. The play began.

The program that night consisted of two vaudevilles followed by the Goldfaden operetta, *Recruits*. The opening sketch I hardly recall. The second piece was just as slight. The usual business of love. The parents are against the marriage. The lovers decide to elope. The matchmaker gives away their secret. Tears—the parents give their blessing—a song, a dance—the curtain falls.

The two-act operetta *Recruits* was the important part of the evening. A Jewish student (Spivakovsky) is recruited into the army. He parts with his fellow students, swearing loyalty to his country and his tsar. (The Yiddish intelligentsia were very patriotic in those first days after the war.) Standing guard, the new recruit sings a duet with a Russian army officer. "Who goes there?" the recruit asks. The officer responds with the password: *"One of your own."* After a few songs the recruit's parents come to the army camp to see him. They do not know the password, and the son almost shoots his parents. Just in time he recognizes they are truly "his own."

This was the serious moment of the operetta. The fun of the piece was provided by the comedy recruit enacted by Rosenberg. Spivakovsky played with feeling, wept with real tears, sang charmingly, and was warmly applauded. Between the acts the folksingers entertained.

Rosenberg played three parts that night, but although he wore in each a different costume and a different wig, he was the same in all three. He was applauded, but probably less for his talents than as the director and entrepreneur of the evening.

All three plays were performed with spirit, and the right energy and gusto. The audience loved it all, laughed at the jokes and the nonsense, and applauded everything. This was not surprising. Aside from the invited guests, they were for the most part simple people, neighbors from the nearby streets or relatives of the folksingers.

The curtain came together for the last time and the invited guests came backstage with compliments and words of encouragement. Even the sternest critic admitted that a beginning had been made, and that it had "looked like theater."

Tables were brought back into the hall, and a royal party took place. Rosenberg and Spivakovsky made speeches, and we all ate, drank, and celebrated.

Two beautiful and highly respected ladies were among our guests that night: Fräulein Sonya Oberlander, sister of the lawyer, and Fräulein Masha Moskovich. Both these ladies had consented to enter the troupe, but only if we performed in a proper theater or hall. Rosenberg trembled over these two young women; he did not want to lose them. Since I was the cavalier, he begged me to make sure they were entertained and happy. Needless to say, I did my best.

Of the two, I was more strongly drawn to Sonya Oberlander, a young woman already known to me. We had met in the homes to which Olga Petrovna had introduced me, homes where the best of Odessa's young intellectuals came together.

Although we were on purely formal terms in those circles, it appeared now that Fräulein Oberlander had noticed and liked me. I myself had never dreamed of anything but the greatest respect. But that night in Akiva's restaurant, we drew closer, we became truly friendly and—why deny it?—we fell in love.

When we parted that night I thought only of the bouquet, the present, I would give Sonya Oberlander when she made her debut in our theater—our troupe!

My Uncle's Verdict

In a short time we had a theater! No more cellars, no more restaurants. A real stage, like the Russians! We rented the Remesleni Club, a hall where a German society gave theatrical performances. The Remesleni had everything needed in a theater—even loges. Here Rosenberg set to work on a new play, the Goldfaden comedy *Granny and Her Granddaughter.* A new star, the folksinger Weinstein, shaved off his beard in order to play the Granny. The Granddaughter, another triumph for Rosenberg, would be played by Masha Moskovich, an actress he had already publicized very widely.

Fräulein Moskovich was a young girl well known in respectable Odessa circles. She was lovely to look at, had a pretty little voice, and, added to these attractions, was much run after by young people. From all this Rosenberg concluded, this was a prima donna who would "draw."

I saw with bitterness that my own name did not appear on the poster. The role of the lover, Leon, had gone to Spivakovsky. I was out in the cold.

The whole thing began to rankle. Rosenberg had promised this role to me. I had already sacrificed my pretty little mustaches. All my friends were asking when they were to see me on the stage.

Rosenberg tried to appease me. I was not to worry, he said, I will soon play. An opportunity will show itself. Things may turn around. Instead of Weinstein, he—Rosenberg—will play the Granny, in which case I will play Leon.

What could I do? Rosenberg had me in his power. I could not take a stand against him, for by now I was drawn to the stage as to a magnet and the desire for theater sat in my soul like an evil spirit. And what would I gain if I quarreled with Rosenberg and lost this new, interesting world? The delay, after all, was in a sense welcome—it gave me time before I showed myself as an actor to my family.

Well, finally it came. Our first night at the Remesleni. Very early a large crowd gathered in front of the hall, everyone impatient, everyone anxious to get in as soon as possible. Women chattered, men shouted; there was such an uproar it sounded like the marketplace. Everyone was crowding around the box office, trying to get their tickets.

The hall inside, with a balcony and seats for about eight hundred people, was run in the German fashion. Waiters with big bellies and red necks ran about with mugs of beer and German sausage. But under their breath these waiters continually muttered curses and insults. Some of them pushed the people back with open hatred—hatred because they were Jews.

Jews of a certainty there were, and of all kinds. Young Jews and old Jews. Ragged kids from Buff's Army, and fine Jews in high silk hats. Middlemen and contractors rich from the war, and their wives with diamonds on their thick fingers. Merchants and shopkeepers, who knew me as an official of the Department of Weights and Measures. They bow to me from the boxes, they wave. Among them is my policeman, the companion of my rounds in the marketplace. He smiles at me, he beams, I have grown greater in his eyes.

But I am hardly aware of all this. I was on fire for the play to begin. For I wanted finally to reach a decision about this Yiddish theater that had torn its way with such strength into my young life. And the rest of the audience, too, would decide tonight whether this new theater was worth something or not.

For you must know that after the brief success of the first evening the opinion of the Odessa public was divided, with no one overly enthused. People like myself who had seen theater were, truth to tell, dissatisfied. From the intelligentsia came an angry murmur that the Yiddish theater laughed at Jews, and was an insult to the Jewish people. As for the "man on the street," the all-powerful, kingly Moishe*—he had as yet not spoken.

The program began with two curtain-raisers, Rosenberg playing the comic roles. Watching him I decided that once again he had created nothing new. His was the kind of art we call plagiarism, that is,

---

* Yiddish actors referred to the public by this intimate name, a diminutive of the name Moses.

it consisted almost solely in the slavish imitation of life. He had chosen as his models two well-known characters of the Odessa street, a half-crazy boy in an army coat called "Shloimke Meow" because of his crazy fear of cats, and in the second piece, another familiar of the street, an eccentric beggar known as "Yossele Sausage."

That he did this well I must allow. In his movements, his bearing, his makeup, Rosenberg was both these characters to the life. But to copy a human being, to imitate his look, walk, speech—all without bringing to it something of your own, without breathing into it a soul—cannot be called acting.

I pause on this because it is a type of acting still seen on our stage. There is no nourishment in such art, and actually, it had no great success with the public that night. They were restless, in suspense for the main thing—the two-act operetta. Don't forget this was the first play with a real prima donna, the first time in Russia that a woman would appear on the Yiddish stage.

Since the play that night prepared a way for our theater in Russia, it deserves to be recorded. I set it down, then, as well as memory serves me.

The curtain rose on the "Granny"—the new star, Weinstein. In addition to an excellent makeup, the folksinger possessed an undeniable power of mime; it was impossible to say it was not a woman on the stage. He acted well, bore himself well—one would have sworn he had been an old Yiddish *buba* from the day he was born!

But I cannot say the folksinger was altogether convincing. His gestures were exaggerated, the whole conception overheightened. Still he made a good impression, and prepared the audience for the masterstroke—the entrance of the granddaughter.

Make a path, my friends! All honor to the first actress of the Yiddish theater in Russia! On the stage was seen the noble face, the milk-white arms, the slender form, of Masha Moskovich.

What was it that stirred in the hearts of those Jewish men and women on that long-ago night? Perhaps simply the freshness and charm of a young girl. Perhaps the knowledge, the instinct, that with the appearance of a woman, the Yiddish theater had become a reality.

The acclamation that greeted her rose to a height seldom equaled in the theater. The hall rang with bravos. Many in the audience rose.

The girl herself played like a child. She was frightened. All the same, it was clear she would be a favorite, and that the warm reception that night would not be her last. And when she sang, "Granny,

Granny, he is in my heart," and then, with a charming bow to the audience, disappeared, she was called back two, three, even four times.

The climax, the great moment was over, but enough remained. Spivakovsky made his entrance as Leon, and his handsome appearance and aristocratic bearing made a splendid impression. Gold-rimmed spectacles gave him added charm, and when he and Masha sang their duet together the audience overwhelmed them with applause and for a long time simply did not let them go.

At the close of the play Rosenberg came out before the curtain in a frock coat and received a truly warm ovation for his personal achievement, and for the theater he had given the Odessa Jews.

The audience left happy, and the invited guests came back with compliments and praise. Even the sternest critics admitted that the matter looked serious, that Yiddish theater was not a dream, not child's play, but a possibility beginning to be realized.

As always the evening ended with an intimate supper in the buffet of the Remesleni. Full of joy, we feasted, drank toasts, listened to speeches.

Happiest of all was I. For all through the joyful banquet I had at my side my adored, my idolized Sonichka Oberlander.

With pomp and parade Rosenberg now played his trump card. Goldfaden's *Shmendrick.** No one-actor, this, no two-act operetta, but a real full-length play with the best actors he had. And so sure was he of success, he announced it for three nights running: Friday, Saturday, and Sunday!

No small thing, this *Shmendrick*! The very name was enough to throw the world into convulsions of laughter. It called to mind a small-town booby, a ridiculous young *shlimazl,* a young fool. And what they do to him! They lead him by the nose, fool him, change his bride! But I have no need to describe our classic Shmendrick who has "shmendricked" about us these forty years and more. Infants in their cradle know him. Imagine then, how it was at the cradle of that infant, the Yiddish theater.

* This was Goldfaden's adaptation of the Romanian comedy *Vladutzul Momei (Mama's Youngest).* Now lost, it was hugely successful in the Yiddish theater for some forty years. To this day *Shmendrick,* a term of affectionate derision, is in use among Jews (and even non-Jews), who are entirely unaware it was once the title of a play.

We threw ourselves into the production—above all, into the cast-ing of the main role. There were candidates, and to spare, but out-standing among them was the charming seventeen-year-old singer, Yankele Katzman. In his appearance, his bearing, his whole personal-ity, Katzman was perfect for the role. Rosenberg took in his first entrance, saw his first stance, heard his first lines, and at once knew he had his actor.

What was it in this play that made Rosenberg so sure of success? True, the name itself had in it something indescribably Yiddish, clownish, small-townish—something that called up whole moun-tains of mockery and fun. But this was not the real guarantee. The fact is, the very word *"shmendrick"* had already woven itself into the lan-guage as one of its most characteristic expressions. Contractors and middlemen from Romania came back with *"shmendrick"* on their lips, and it spread through Odessa like wildfire. People blessed each other with *"shmendrick,"* cursed each other with *"shmendrick."* The word could be stretched in every direction, it was so broad, so elastic. It was at once a term of affection and a term of derision. Women said to each other, "Have you seen my *shmendrick?"* adding, "And where is your *shmendrick?"* Going the rounds with my policeman I would hear the shopkeepers calling, "Quick! Hide the weights, the *shmendricks* are coming!" A sneeze was a *shmendrick.* A ruble was a *shmendrick.* One merchant said to the other, "Here are the goods—where are the *shmendricks?"*

As for me, I walked about with my head full of the songs, the scenes, most of all, full of talented young Yankele Katzman as he sang and played the role. I was so excited it was some time before I realized Rosenberg had once again given me nothing to play.

This time I was really offended. I had gotten a strong hint from him that I was slated to play the lover, and my vanity was much tick-led at the idea of playing love scenes with Masha Moskovich. Now once again Spivakovsky got the role, and I was out. This time it was too much. I withdrew entirely, angry at everyone.

But angry or not, I had to see *Shmendrick.* Since I wanted no favors, I took my six *shmendricks* and bought my six tickets. I was taking my parents, my little sister, Tante Hanna, and Uncle Arke.

A great deal hinged on their opinion that night, for the family knew now that I wanted to be an actor, and they were not happy about it. I wanted them to change their mind, to approve of my decision and respect it. Most important was the judgment of Uncle Arke. He, the connoisseur, the theater man, would now see for himself what the Yiddish theater was, and what it could do.

The Remesleni was packed, the women in white shawls, many of the men in high hats. I myself had bought a high hat for this occasion— the first I had ever worn. I was vastly pleased with myself, and kept looking into every mirror I passed. My mother could not take her admiring eyes off me. Even Uncle Arke said I looked handsome. Only the little sister laughed at me and said I looked like Shmendrick.

We took our seats. The curtain rose. The play began. I now had a double task: to watch the performance, and at the same time watch the effect on my family. For whether or not I became an actor depended very much on how they felt tonight.

The curtain rose on a *chosid* (a young student of the Talmud) in low shoes, white stockings, and a long coat. Rosenberg. Beside him an old Yiddish wife. The folksinger, Weinstein. A quarrelsome dialogue begins. Husband and wife quarrel, insult each other, spring at each other like enraged barnyard fowl. The audience laughed. I laughed with them, but kept an eye on my family. Tante Hanna and my little sister enjoyed it all, they clapped at everything. My parents? My uncle? A first pang. Not a muscle in their faces moved. They were not only not laughing, they did not understand why I was laughing.

The play continued. Shmendrick himself appeared. He made the wildest gestures, performed the craziest antics. The audience broke continually into applause, beside themselves with pleasure. I glanced at my three critics. Again, they were stony-faced, immovable. My heart began to pound. "They don't think it's good," a voice in me said. "They don't like it."

The first act ended. The aisles filled up with men, women, children. A din, a deafening chatter. Uncle Arke turned to me with a smile. "Well, Yankele? What do you say? Is this theater? No, no, my child, this is a circus! I am ashamed for the Germans! And in this dark swamp you want to make your life?"

My father shook his head mournfully. My mother sighed, even more sorrowful. She even wanted to leave the hall, but at this moment the curtain rose again, and she remained seated.

The play went on. Foolery. More foolery. Uncle Arke, less patient, began to make remarks under his breath. "See for yourself, Yankele," said the connoisseur, the theater man. "Is there a crumb of truth in all of this? It's supposed to be taking place in Romania. Is there one drop of Romanian atmosphere?"

I sat like a dead man. Every drop of desire to be an actor had left me. Suddenly my eye fell on my policeman, my fellow official, now such a devotee of Yiddish theater. He is shaking with laughter. But he does not always laugh where he should. Perhaps it is not a laugh of pleasure at all, but the coarse idiotic laughter of hateful mockery. The thought was terrible. I did not like the way he looked at me. I was sure that when we met in the morning he would not greet me, as always, with "Good morning, Yakob Pavlovich," but with a hateful, laughing "Good morning, Shmendrick!"

The third act began. The wedding scene offended Uncle Arke; it seemed to him a caricature, a mockery of the Jewish wedding cere- mony. The play finally came to an end with Shmendrick's discovery that they had changed his bride, and his famous demand that he be given "*both* brides." Everyone laughed. My sister and Tante Hanna clapped and did not want to go home. The audience could not stop applauding. The very air rang with "*Shmendrick*." Only my parents and my uncle remained sunk in gloom.

I made my way home that night with a bowed head. Fallen was I in my own eyes, for fallen was that which had been great in my eyes! I crept into bed, but could not sleep. One thought hammered over and over in my brain: "It's not the real thing. It's not theater. It's not for me."

SONYA OBERLANDER,
MY THEATER MAGNET

Icome now to a great event in my life, my engagement to Sonya Oberlander. This moment, of such importance to every human being, was doubly important to me, for this event changed forever the whole direction of my life.

You must know that after seeing *Shmendrick* my parents both pleaded with me not to ruin my future by sinking into the mud of Yiddish theater. Perhaps these warnings would not have greatly influenced me. I was young, of an age when one does not trouble about the future. Nor was I put off by the coarseness of what I had seen. I had mingled in low circles, and had a strong stomach. But with the judgment of my uncle the scales fell from my eyes. I saw the crudity, the falseness, the absence of anything serious, anything fine. If I did not listen to the ill opinion of my uncle, to my father's disapproval, or my mother's tears, it is Sonya Oberlander I must thank for it.

Sonya Oberlander, elegant beautiful daughter of an assimilated family, mother of Rivka, the child we lost in London, mother of Abram, the son with me still. She is dead now many years and the grass has many times grown green on her grave, yet I still think of her when I am troubled.

When we first came together she was an idealistic girl who had finished the *gymnasia,* and was a *coursiste,** at the university. She had a thorough knowledge of our Russian literature, spoke French and German as well as Russian, and from early youth had taken a deep and passionate interest in the theater.

Like all the best young people of that day, she was involved in the nihilist movement. She worked for the underground, receiving

* A young woman taking postgraduate courses at the university.

brochures and proclamations which she distributed among her fellow students and friends. I originally met her, in fact, in the homes where these young people gathered, homes to which my good friend Olga Petrovna had given me entry.

I myself took little part in the discussions in these circles, but I was on firm ground when the talk turned on the theater, which it often did. I knew the plays of Ostrovsky and other Russian playwrights, was well grounded in the popular tragedies of Shakespeare and other classical works. Because of this I occasionally allowed myself a word, and at times even a longer opinion. Though we rarely spoke, Fräulein Oberlander made an impression on me, and, as it later turned out, I on her as well. When her brother was drawn into the Yiddish theater, this acquaintance between us was renewed. That was when Sonya met me again, and when my respect for her developed first into a deep interest and then a truly serious love.

A beautiful and romantic love it was, as always when the lover looks up to his beloved. Sonya was very different from the women I had known, and very different was the way I tried to win her. I was used to girls of quite another sort, and had to be careful of everything I said, everything I did. Yet this lack of freedom was never unpleasant to me. There were times when I sat beside her for hours, happy just to be in her presence. Impure as I was, my love raised me in my own eyes, restored my almost lost sense of shame.

For truly I was ashamed before Sonya, ashamed of my ignorance, my lack of education. True, I was no longer the ignorant boy who had trudged about the city with a pack on his back. I had read a good deal since then, had come to know people, and to move in better circles. But a systematic education was entirely lacking.

It was to Sonya I confided both my longing and my disappointment in the Yiddish theater. One day I told her I had reached a decision. The Yiddish theater was not for me. I was leaving it.

At these words something both terrible and wonderful happened. Sonya's pale face grew even paler, her great clever eyes widened. In a small, frightened voice she said it was only because of me she had ever gone near Rosenberg or his theater.

In that one moment I passed from the depths of dejection to the heights of joy. My friends, it was May, and everything around me was bathed in radiance, everything sang of youth and hope. Until now I had not seen it; it had not existed for me. Now, in a moment, spring with all its ecstasy and perfume rushed into my soul. I felt once again that I was young, that the whole world was young—that for me, for all the world, life still held all its hope, all its beauty, all its joy.

There began for me a beautiful, a heavenly time. The streets of the city were fragrant with opening blossoms, and the whole world was dressing itself in green. Soft winds blew, white cloudlets floated in the heavens, and from the shore one heard the secret sighing of the sea.

In this green holiday of a newly awakened life I strolled the city with my beautiful, my adored Sonya Oberlander. As to a good friend, I told her all my heart. I loved the Yiddish theater, I told her. I wanted to give it my life. But what kind of theater was it? Everything I had seen was coarse, raw, tasteless. To bind myself forever to this falseness, these clown's masks, these idiot antics?

That is how, in our long walks through Odessa, I waged war on myself, tortured myself, and unburdened my heart. And it is remarkable how clearly she understood even then, this daughter of an assimilated family from the Courland.* At a moment when our young people were mad for everything Russian, everything European, Sonya took the poor Yiddish theater under her wing.

She spoke to me of the Greeks, how they smeared their mouths with grape juice, rode about in wagons, played under the empty sky, and yet from this beginning made their great art. She spoke of Shakespeare's day. No scenery. Nothing but a shield with a word on it. No actresses. Juliet, Ophelia, Cordelia—all played by boys because no decent woman would demean herself by standing on a stage. She spoke of Molière's time, when actors traveled the countryside like vagabonds, and were reduced to stealing a chicken for their supper. These first actors played on boards, and begged for pennies afterward. When there were not enough players they put a hat on a stool and spoke their lines to that. And yet the French theater rose to the heights on which it now stands. And today, Sonya said—when we have Hugo's *Hernani,* Gogol's *Revizor,* when we have a *Faust,* a *Wallenstein,* when France has given the world such immortals as Rachel and Bernhardt; Germany, such giants as Possart, Barney, and Sonnenthal; when America has produced the genius of Booth, Italy the giant Salvini—what is the place of the theater today? Kings value it as their highest pleasure. Millionaires and aristocrats pay fortunes just to have

* A Baltic province, now Latvia.

Sonya Oberlander Adler (stagename: Sonya Michelson)

a box at the play. Young intellectuals wait hours in the cold, in the rain, stand outside all night, just to drink in the art of some great actors, some world-famed actress. And if from these lowly beginnings, these theaters rose to such loftiness and beauty, why cannot our Yiddish theater rise equally high?

There is no way to describe what Sonya's words meant to me. They were a revelation, a message from the divine intelligence. A heaven opened before my eyes. Long after my doubts were overcome I returned again and again to this theme, only to hear her speak again. We talked of nothing else all that day, and returning to her home, took up the subject again.

Sonya's brother and father also came to the defense of the Yiddish theater. Her brother said it was a sin for an intelligent human being to speak against it. "We must be pioneers," he said. "We must fight for the future of the Yiddish stage." And old Oberlander, the assimilated Courlander, raised his fists to heaven and in his half-German Yiddish cried, "My child, no hard word! If I were to meet Goldfaden, I would go down on my knees before him. He has given our people a theater! You are young, you do not understand what it means for the simple Jew, who knows no other language, to have a theater."

My doubts were vanquished. I was conquered. I swore that where

Sonya went, there I would go also. If she was willing to follow the Yiddish theater, I, too, would give it my life.

Poor Yiddish theater. Poor Yankele. How goes the old song? "Two corpses went dancing." But I embraced the Yiddish theater. I took it to my heart. And there it would remain forever—forever.

Sonya made her debut in our next production, *Breindele Cossack,* the premiere once again at the Remesleni.

Breindele is a woman who victimizes men and drives five husbands to suicide. The sixth husband, Guberman, is to be the hero who will conquer the terrible woman. But man plans and God laughs. Guberman also ends as her victim.

This, in brief, was the plot. Naturally, since the play was written by Goldfaden, it was filled with songs, dances, comedy scenes, and a number of minor characters.

Rosenberg gave the whole production serious attention and provided it with excellent scenery and costumes, and the audience was surprised at curtain rise by a rich and tasteful set.

Since this was the first play with a woman in the leading role, the main interest, of course, was the prima donna. First, she was new, while all the others had already been seen. Second, it was understood that Sonya Michelson was really Sonya Oberlander, a personage respected in the best circles of Odessa.

As Breindele, Sonya wore a ball gown, spoke in a commanding tone, and played with passion and dramatic power. On the stage, a Yiddish Lady Macbeth. Though she was an absolute beginner, the new actress showed a rich and flexible talent. Every flicker of her sensitive face revealed her feelings.

In spite of Sonya's thankless role the audience gave her a full measure of acclaim. This is in contrast to the present day, when an actress playing a role of this kind is hissed. The audience of that time understood they must separate the actor from the character, and Sonya was greeted with applause, and hot cries of "Bravo!" She received many bouquets, among them my own. I had made sure that the prettiest roses came from me, and that both her name and mine were large on the streamers.

Sonya, tactful in her great success, thanked the audience with blown kisses, the first of them to me. This was all I needed to complete my happiness.

The two of us were now more united than ever. I saw very well that while Sonya held other admirers at a distance, she was close to me. She allowed me to kiss her hand, a liberty she permitted no one else. I must mention that Sonya was extremely reserved and proud and did not allow her hand even to be pressed by just anyone at all.

Since she wished to draw me into the theater, Sonya took it upon herself to speak for me. And thanks to her position—Rosenberg's first prima donna in such a dearth of actresses—she succeeded.

I was to make my debut as Guberman in *Breindele Cossack.* I cannot say Spivakovsky liked it, but he had to give in. Sonya had an important voice in the troupe. After the furor she had created as Breindele she had become a leading force, the first feminine star of Rosenberg's company.

My heart began to beat hard with the thought that any time now I would have to make my first appearance on the stage.

STRATEGIC RETREAT:
WE PLAY IN KHERSON

One fine morning, in the midst of everything, a catastrophe. Word that Avrom Goldfaden and his troupe had left Romania, and were even now on their way to Odessa.

To what can I compare the effect of this news? If America today should hear that, out of a clear blue sky, England, armed to the teeth, was advancing on her shores, the bewilderment, the shock, the disbelief, would not be greater. Who? Why? From where? We could not make ourselves believe it.

This is what happened. Enemies of Rosenberg and Spivakovsky had written to the "real" director, that is, to Goldfaden, telling him of our success in Odessa—a success we had achieved with his, Goldfaden's, plays. And these people had worked so shrewdly that by the time we found out Goldfaden was coming, everything was in place for his arrival.

Since in early spring both Russian theaters were occupied, our enemies had rented the Remesleni Club. They had cut the ground from under our feet. We were without a stage.

What does one do in such a case? What does one even begin to do? After the first panic, a hailstorm began of opinions and advice. Some of the actors felt Rosenberg should pay no attention to Goldfaden, but remain in Odessa and compete with him. "Why should we run away?" they argued. "Who is he, this Goldfaden, that we must make way for him?"

Rosenberg, however, was too clever to be misled. He decided on a retreat, but a strategic retreat that would allow us to hold our ground. With Goldfaden in Odessa we would have to withdraw. But not too far. Only to the nearby provincial towns. To make sure of success there, Rosenberg thought up one of his brilliantly scoundrelish schemes. Striking his forehead with his palm, he suddenly cried, "Wait! They have a Goldfaden? We also have a Goldfaden!"

Not far from Odessa Goldfaden had a brother called Naphtali, a watchmaker by profession. Rosenberg hit on the idea of taking this brother into the troupe. Thus we could also call ourselves "the Goldfaden Company."

Our next step was to send out what Americans call an "advance agent" (we called it a "lookout man")—someone who would research the situation in the towns near Odessa, find out the best place to run up our flag, and dig our trenches.

Our "lookout man" was Alexander Oberlander. We gave him a sum of money, a trunk full of posters—and quick march into the field!

In a few days we received the telegram of a victorious General: "Kherson is taken!"*

This city, as it happened, had a fortress, and one can only imagine what trouble would come of such a telegram today! At that time, however, we rejoiced, celebrated, and prepared to set sail for Kherson.

Before we left, however, a prompter had to be found. Until now Rosenberg had prompted, another actor replacing him when he was on the stage. But we were taking ourselves into strange territory, and could not be so loose in our arrangements. A prompter was definitely needed.

God in His heaven who sends the drinker his wine and the spinner his wool, sent us our man. It happened that one Avrom Zetzer, a prompter in Goldfaden's company, had just returned from Romania.

I cannot say Zetzer was the ideal prompter. He had lost two of his upper teeth, so that when he prompted, a great deal of whistling and hissing was heard, but very few words. But he was a learned man, versed in Sheikevitch's novels and the writings of Linetzki, and in those years that made him a treasure. Zetzer became our prompter, and the troupe was richer by a new member.

Next we needed an orchestra leader. The same story. In a great city like Odessa something can always be done, but where to turn in a wilderness?

Once again God smiled on us. He sent us Zorach Vinyavich, a vir-

* A town at the mouth of the Dnieper River, a boat ride of about fifty miles east of Odessa.

tuoso, an artist who, by a stroke of luck, happened to love the Yiddish actors. Perhaps affection alone would not have brought him into the troupe, but he also had a daughter of sixteen, pretty, intelligent, and dying to be on the stage.

Rosenberg rejoiced. He now had a prompter, a conductor, and three actresses—Sonya, Masha Moskovich, and now, little Bettye Vinyavich. The young girl was to make her debut as Shmendrick's changed "bride." True, she had not a word to say, since the bride did nothing but hold a kerchief before her face. But the new actress was as happy with her mute role as Sarah Bernhardt with the longest, most fiery monologue.

One fine morning our field marshal gave the signal with a roll of the drums, and we set off. I asked for a leave of absence from the Department of Weights and Measures, and together with the other actors, boarded the steamship *Jason*.

I think I will remember that trip even when I am in the other world. A strong wind blew, the boat trembled and rocked, and not less wild was the rocking and trembling of my heart. I was seasick, which was bad, and soul-sick, which was worse. True, my uncle and parents would not be there to see my debut. But how will I face an audience? How speak my lines in a house full of people, all of them looking at me? Will I be able to play at all? Will I fail, disgrace myself, fall through altogether?

Everyone else was talking, laughing. Rosenberg and Spivakovsky went into the buffet, drank, stood treat to the others. Only I lay in my corner like a man already dead.

God knows what the end would have been if not for my sweet friend, my Sonya. She did not forsake me. She told me my nervousness was the best possible sign. "It shows you feel your responsibility," she said, "that you are not a frivolous person, but a serious man, an artist!" She told me the tortures she had lived through in the *gymnasia* when she had taken part in school performances. She recounted episodes in the lives of famous actors. She strengthened my belief in myself, taught me to trust my powers. And because of her friendship and her understanding words I took courage and grew calmer.

We drew near the end of our journey. The whistle blew. A voice called out, "Kherson!" The Dnieper grows very narrow at this point. Spring was already in full leaf, and Kherson greeted us with its flowers and trees. On the pier a crowd of people, beautifully dressed, the women in flowered summer dresses, the men in high silk hats. The

Jason drew in to the shore. A hurrah came from the pier. And a band struck up in honor of the Yiddish actors.

Kherson, we discovered, had no theater. Our performance was to take place in a storehouse, a granary. As a theater it had two qualifications. It was big, and it was empty. The owner, one Lipitz Beygun, had cleared it of grain, oats, and hay, brought in benches, built a stage for us, hung a curtain, and imported good scenery from Spain. He had done all this not for money, but for love of art. A tall stern man with a red face and a red beard, he looked more like a Russian than a Jew. He had done his twenty-five years in the army, and for this service was allowed to own his land.

Since I knew the town well (I had been there several times), I acted as guide to the others. Like a general I led the way, pointing out with my stick the most interesting streets, shops, and markets.

We stopped often to take in the sights, but for all of us the most beautiful sight was the Russian posters announcing that on such-and-such a night *The Witch* by Avrom Goldfaden would be performed with Rosenberg as the Witch,* Masha Moskovich as Mirel, and Yakob Pavlovich Adler as the First Lover, Marcus.

The night before the opening I tossed and turned until dawn, tortured by my doubts and fears. Suppose I failed miserably, disgraced myself? How would I look my fellow actors in the face? What would I say to my old teacher, Rosenberg? Above all, what would I say to my idolized Sonya, who believed in me, who had insisted I must be beside her when she played Breindele?

The terrible night passed. A leaden-footed day also crept away. The sun sank beneath the river. Night. I am in my dressing room. All around me noise, confusion, haste. I am in my makeup, in my costume. A rap at the door. "Adler! Adler!" It is time.

As I took my position in the wings an interesting little ceremony took place. Rosenberg had once seen a Russian director make the sign of the cross over an actor making his first appearance. He gave me a Jewish version of this blessing, a hand stretched over my head in the sign of the *kohanim,* and the words "May God lift up His countenance upon you. May God give you His light!"

---

* The role of the Witch was originally performed by Gradner, and after that was traditionally played by a man. In the Yiddish Art Theatre production of 1925, Maurice Schwartz played the Witch.

Onstage it was the birthday celebration of Mirel, my beloved. The guests call me joyously through the garden. "Marcus! Marcus!" I heard the cue through the roaring in my ears.

Once as a boy I saw a peasant leap from a high raft into a stormy, angry sea. The peasant came to the edge of the raft, hesitated, then crossed himself and plunged. I am no peasant and I did not cross myself, but like him I hesitated, and then plunged—onto the stage, and into my life!

People who train wild beasts—bears, lions, tigers—say that everything depends on the first encounter. If the man can call up in himself a feeling so sharp, so stern, that it strikes fear into the beast, he remains forever its master.

Something of the same kind occurs between the artist and his public. It is a struggle, a fight. For at the beginning the public does not want to give in, does not want to recognize the power of the actor. The public is critical, and looks only for faults. But if the actor can *surprise* the audience in some way, take it by storm, hypnotize it— then it is vanquished.

I knew by instinct as I made my entrance that this was the critical moment. A pause to measure each other like opponents in a duel, and then I heard it, that for which the actor longs all his life, his lullaby, his Kaddish, his dirge—the first, the eternal, the sound of applause.

I grew hot and cold at the sound. I knew I had conquered. My glance, my manner, my bearing, had made an impression. The world, as personified by the Jews of Kherson, had become aware of me. A flame was kindled inside me. And triumphantly, without fear, I shot out my first lines.

I cannot ascribe my success that night to any talent I possessed at that time. I had to work many years before I perfected and purified my talent. My success was due to my youth, my appearance, my strongly developed individualism, and my determination to make a place for myself in the world.

The first-act curtain fell on prolonged applause. The actors crowded around, congratulating me. Rosenberg, all smiles, told me I was a marvel, a real beauty! But more than the applause, more than all the praise of my fellow actors, was the glance of one pair of eyes— a glance that flooded me with an ocean of joy and courage.

Sonya did not play that night. It may be that the role of the gentle Mirel did not suit her. It may be because at this moment when I was risking my entire artistic life, she felt one pair of eyes should watch over me with love.

She sat in the first row with the family of Lipitz Beygun. Her eyes burned me, but with a good, a blessed fire. And over all the applause I heard her ringing "Bravo, Adler! *Prevoshchodno!* Excellent!"

It was a good, a happy debut. Rosenberg and Spivakovsky no longer doubted, and after that I played continually.

I had a more critical test coming in *Breindele Cossack.* Guberman was a really big part, calling on the actor to show love, hate, wildness, jealousy, character weakness. There was also a "dream picture" where Guberman appears as an old man, feeble and pitiful. I wanted to make this transition effectively.

Again I had a success, a better, truer success than the first. Best of all were the love scenes between Guberman and Breindele—that is to say, between Sonya and myself. Rarely have scenes of this kind been played with such fire as those between us that night.

My performance was appreciated by the audience. More important, I myself knew it had value. With this my fate was sealed.

The anchor is pulled up, the wind fills the sails. The ship moves out, out, there is no longer a return.

On the red or dead! I was an actor.

News of Goldfaden
and Our Guilty Longings

With the success of *Breindele Cossack,* the company gave itself to a life of pleasure. We ate, drank, and spent our days strolling Potëmkin's Gardens, at that time a famous feature of Kherson. Rosenberg played the clown and kept us all laughing. His jokes were not always fit for delicate ears, but he found ways to get rid of the ladies of the troupe.

In those days a statue of Catherine the Great adorned the center of this park. Anecdotes about the tsarina and her many lovers are known to all, but never were there such stories as Rosenberg's, and never were they so masterfully told. We rolled on the ground, roared so with laughter that strangers gathered around us also laughing, and I marveled at my friend anew.

Everywhere we were pointed out as the *Evraiski aktiori,* the Yiddish actors. People stared, some with wonder, some with mockery, even fear. One day a peasant spat at the sight of us. We felt no anger, for there was no hatred in it. A man sees the devil, he does what he can to defend himself.

The streets of the town were drowned in sunflower seeds. Couples walked in Potëmkin's Gardens, courted, flirted, and spat seeds. For years afterward any mention of the great tsarina brought back to me the streets, the alleys, the people of Kherson.

Such perfect days could not last forever. Before a week had passed a telegram came. Goldfaden was in Odessa! Hundreds of people had met him at the station, and he and his troupe were already installed at the Remesleni.

How ungrateful is the human heart! What did we need? We played, we had success, recognition. Now I heard Goldfaden was in

Odessa. *My* Odessa. And a traitorous voice whispered, "If it must be Yiddish theater, let it be the real thing. To him! To him! To Goldfaden!"

My guilty longing was mirrored in every face, even Sonya's. Rosenberg, who saw everything, began a propaganda. Have anything to do with Goldfaden? An actor would have to be a madman! Money? Not a *groschen.* Recognition, honor? Never! Nothing for Goldfaden!

Seeing this had no effect, Rosenberg tried another tack. "Go to him," he advised us, laughing. "I won't be angry. I prefer it. After that you'll appreciate a director like me. You'll come back to me for life!"

Seeing this also did not work, his real feelings broke out. "What magic do you think he possesses, this Goldfaden?" he passionately asked. "Who do you think he has in this great Romanian troupe of his? We are a hundred times better than the lot of them!"

He spoke with true insulted pride, and at that moment I respected him. But the spark in his soul soon went out. Once more he was the mountebank, the clown. He began to cut capers, to swear we would all go to China, play *Shmendrick* in pigtails . . . One fine day we packed up, bag and baggage, and steamed back to Odessa on the same *Jason* that had taken us to Kherson.

For me it was not a trip; I flew back on wings! I was bringing with me a valise full of reviews, posters, articles in which my name was mentioned.

As soon as I threw open the door I cried out, "Mama, congratulate me! I have passed my examination. I am an actor, an artist!"

Instead of joy I saw only a cold face full of bitter reproach.

Without speaking, my mother handed me a letter from the Department of Weights and Measures. I had overstayed my leave and been dismissed. Now it was my turn to be silent.

"And what will be now?" my mother asked, shedding tears. "A small thing to have been a government official! To take such a position and destroy it! You have killed yourself with your own hands. And for what? To be a buffoon, a clown!"

I tried to make her understand. I told her what it was to have a passion that gnaws at the heart, that can take away health and even life. I described what it was to stand on the stage, the fever that burns in the soul, the wild rush of the blood. I told her my need for applause, a need that was like a sickness. I swore to her that others give me courage, that I hoped someday to stand with the greatest. My tongue grew wings. I found words to express it all, to make it all live for her. And remarkable to say, the old-fashioned woman who knew so little of theater understood. Perhaps it is true that words from the heart go to the heart. My mother grew calmer, dried her tears, and found refuge from her fears in her son's dreams of the future.

Once again at peace with the world, I put on my best and went off to Falconi's. There I found everyone already gathered, all talking about Goldfaden and the sensation his arrival had made. Everyone was on fire to meet him, everyone was insisting Rosenberg must arrange it. As soon as possible! Tomorrow!

Rosenberg sat the whole time as though on hot coals, refused to open his mouth, and continually shook his head in stubborn refusal. I saw this was something more than fear of losing his troupe, even more than our insulting ingratitude. I finally asked him what was wrong. Always openhearted as a child, he came out with it.

"No, Yankele, I will not see Avrom," he said. "He insulted me in a way I can never forgive. I have a bitter heart against him." At last we had the story.

After breaking away and forming a troupe of his own, Rosenberg had come to Goldfaden at the Jignitza Theater in Bucharest. "I came to him with the best feelings, with reverence in my heart," Rosenberg said. "I held out my hand to him in friendship. But he did not take my hand. Instead he said, 'So it is you, the Odessa dog who has stolen my plays!' And before the entire troupe, he struck me across the face. I almost fell to the ground with shame. I found my way into the corridor, and wept there two hours without stopping. Now he is in Odessa. This is my city, here I could pay him back. But he is Goldfaden. I revere him. I will not harm a hair of his head. But go to him? See him again? Never!"

We were silent, but our need to see Goldfaden still burned.

The following day we were all at the Remesleni Club. We did not meet Goldfaden there, but the two troupes met for the first time— the Romanians on one side, the Russians on the other.

The meeting that meant so much to us meant less than nothing to the Romanians. Goldfaden's actors looked on us as a giant looks on a child. I admit I was overawed by their *chic,* their fashionable dress and bearing. The men were all in elegant summer attire with light surtouts, light winged capes, embroidered Romanian shirts. They sported gold pince-nez on heavy gold chains, carried handsome walking sticks. The very air around them seemed to say, "Hey, there! Do you know who you are looking at? We are from foreign parts!"

Actually, their dress set them apart not only from other human beings, but even from other actors. The Russian artists of the City Theater and the Mariinsky wore sober black suits, black ties, black cravats; compared to the Romanians they looked like deacons, Protestant ministers. But in those years I did not look for substance, either in people or in life. Only the highly colored, the ostentatious, excited my imagination.

Highest and haughtiest of the Romanians was the former folksinger Maurice Finkel, now Goldfaden's director and manager. Finkel's handsome face let the whole world know he was there. He wore his high hat as though for spite, and his mouth opened so rarely, one felt words would have to be begged before he would utter them. His word, in fact, was feared, for whatever Finkel decreed was done. All business with Goldfaden had to go through him.

Exactly the opposite of Finkel was the comedian and dancer, Laiser Zuckerman. Slender, lively, of mercurial temperament, Zuckerman was fond of drink and was often found in low company. His agile body was never still, and his feet seemed to move by themselves, as though with quicksilver. I was told Goldfaden and his wife loved him like a son and he was even mentioned in their will.

It was a comedy to see Finkel and Zuckerman together. Zuckerman was all laughter. Finkel never so much as smiled. Finkel's eyes said, "Careful, rabble! Remember who I am!" Zuckerman's eyes said, "Brother, let's have a dance and be merry!" Finkel looked down on the world from the top of a high mountain. Zuckerman stayed at the foot of the mountain playing with puppies, kittens, and children. Naturally, I preferred Zuckerman.

As everyone knows, actors are a gregarious lot. The two troupes soon began to mingle. The actresses, especially, soon were so close one would think they had played on the same boards since childhood. They were always together, drinking their sweet drinks and chattering like a flock of nightingales.

Outstanding among these ladies were the sisters Margaretta and Annetta Schwartz. Both these actresses wore dresses made in Paris, and not even the wealthiest ladies in Odessa had such dresses. On the street, they both wore white mantles, large white hats, and parasols set with false stones that glittered as they walked, attracting all eyes to them.

These new acquaintances only whetted our desire for a meeting with Goldfaden. Such a thing was not easy to arrange, for the father of the Yiddish theater was as difficult to approach as an emperor in those days. A sponsor was necessary, a sort of protector.

With this in mind we sought out an interesting Jew by the name of Fischandler, one of the wealthy men who had financed Goldfaden's return to Odessa. Fischandler knew my father. In addition he knew me as a connoisseur of the Russian theater. He agreed to introduce us, but only at the proper moment.

Sonya and I waited, restless and impatient. All our talk now centered on the coming meeting. What would the great man look like? How would he receive us? What kind of person was he? And though we did not say so, we were both hoping beyond hope to find favor in his eyes, to remain in Odessa, and to become part of his troupe.

GOLDFADEN'S COURT

Those of you who knew Goldfaden in his last years in America saw only a broken man, old, poor, and forgotten. We live today in skeptical times, times when everything is habitually belittled, habitually torn down. It is almost impossible in these days to understand the tremendous role he once played—especially in 1878, after his enormous success in Romania.

Like a king or a great Jew—Goldfaden was both—he had his court, a place where he was surrounded by something akin to adoration. And one spring day, with the touch of Fischandler's magic wand, the doors of this "court," that is to say, Goldfaden's rooms on Preobrazhensky Street, opened for us.

We found ourselves in an elegant anteroom where a number of people were already gathered. A well-dressed, well-fed crowd, most of them actors and actresses already known to us, the men smoking cigars or cigarettes and everyone very much at home. Tea and cakes had been laid out on a table, and the buzz of voices and tinkle of spoons made a pleasing music that spoke of a busy kitchen and an easy life.

Sonya and I, somewhat confused, seated ourselves to one side and looked about us. Lithographs or photographs of Yiddish actors were not the custom, and we had no idea what Goldfaden looked like. We fixed our gaze in turn on all the more serious and intelligent faces. At last, in a whisper, I asked Fischandler to point him out. He replied that Goldfaden was still in his inner office, but would soon appear.

I waited, tense with expectation, feeling I would soon be in the presence of an exalted being, a kind of rabbi.

Twice in my life I had seen Alexander II, once at a midnight Mass in the Odessa cathedral, and again at Yalta, when I had been part of a multitude gathered to honor his entrance into the city. On that occasion I stood so close to him I could see the wrinkled skin on his hands and the iron rings on his fingers. Both times I felt love for my emperor, the friend of my people. The same feeling welled up in me now, but this time with something added. For the tsar had not inspired in me the deeper, *Yiddish* reverence.

The moment came. The door opened. Goldfaden entered. We all sprang to our feet. The men whipped off their hats. And I saw him. A handsome figure of a man, tall and imposing, with a tiny pointed beard and a mustache that he occasionally twirled as he spoke. His face was serious, but the seriousness struck a false note—it did not go with his laughing eyes. He wore a Romanian costume—a blue Hungarian uniform with Brandenburg epaulettes, an embroidered hat with a tassel. I remember thinking that these people were all mad for Romania.

His eyes went quickly around the room, passing over Sonya and me as strangers, but lighting with pleasure on Fischandler, whom, in fact, he embraced. Looking back on it now, my main reaction was disappointment. This was neither a great man nor a great Jew, but a man of the world, a bon vivant.

Fischandler, as good as his word, introduced us at the first opportunity. Goldfaden was a cavalier. Sonya pleased him. He took her pretty little chin in his hand, a compliment she did not encourage; she remarked in Russian, the aristocratic language, that Herr Goldfaden was "friendly to ladies." Goldfaden saw that his familiarity was out of place, apologized, and turned to the others. He quickly got rid of those he did not know and, after a fleeting glance at me, suddenly called out, "Rosenberg!"

To my astonishment, Rosenberg trotted out of the inner room. Knowing this was the day we were to meet Goldfaden, he had gotten there first to bar the way! He greeted us with some embarrassment, praised us to Goldfaden, but added with a nervous laugh, "They are mine, Herr Goldfaden. Don't take them away from me!"

After some talk Goldfaden introduced us to his tragedian, Moishe Teich. I was curious to meet this actor who was stone deaf but had never been known to miss his cue. He was thirty-five or forty years old, short of stature, bald, with an ugly face but fine eyes. He was wearing a suit too big for him, shoes too big for him, torn gloves, and a handkerchief none too clean.

"A great talent as you see him," Goldfaden remarked with an unpleasant laugh. "Catches his cues as a dog catches fleas."

Since Teich heard nothing he continued to smile.

"A tragic figure!" Sonya murmured with pity. She asked Goldfaden if Teich had no wife to look after him.

"He is married, but stingy," Goldfaden replied.

He indulged in several other humorous remarks at the expense of his chief tragedian. But Sonya, whose womanly nature was higher than this, drew up a chair near the deaf actor, managed to engage him in conversation, and when the time came to part, shook his hand with unaffected warmth and respect.

We left, particularly pleased that Goldfaden had invited us to the Remesleni that night.

The play that night was *Neither This, That, nor Kukerikoo.* The old theme of the imposter. Molière has a peasant who becomes a gentleman, Shakespeare a lackey who becomes a lord. Goldfaden devised a cobbler who becomes a rabbi. This thin idea had been dressed with so much stolen music that it was shameful to hear. But like everything Goldfaden wrote, the play itself was interesting. Spivakovsky played the *maskil,* the modern enlightened man, and among the others his playing shone like a diamond in the dark. Finkel portrayed the moonstruck old *maggid,* and that he played excellently need not be said. The reader surely remembers how sharply and well this actor brought out a deeply Yiddish type.

The full title of this early comedy is *Neither This, That, nor Kukerikoo or The Struggle of Culture with Fanaticism.* The play itself is lost, but the subtitle indicates a serious theme within an amusing, nonsensical plot. For all the singing, dancing, and fun, the audience was being led in a certain direction.

The fight against the forces of fundamentalism would be dramatized in the Yiddish theater for forty years, the hero battling, sometimes to the death, for progress and enlightenment, while his enemy, usually of the older generation, stoops even to dishonor in the service of his bigoted faith.

This emphasis on education, progress, enlightenment, is found nowhere else in the popular comedy and melodrama of the nineteenth century. It is special to the Yiddish theater, which was, even from the beginning, a theater of ideas.

A few nights after *Neither This, That, nor Kukerikoo* we saw Goldfaden's *Todros, Blos* (*Todros, Blow!*). Again, I was not particularly impressed. A foolish comedy from the German. A young man lives beyond his means, gets into debt and gives his servant Todros a trumpet, telling him to blow whenever his creditors come around.

With *Todros, Blos* I felt the Yiddish theater had taken another downward step. Why, if we must steal, I asked myself, must it always be something old and stale? Gogol's *Inspector General* is also about a young man with debts. Jews as well as Russians run to see it whenever it is played. Why not translate the Gogol play for the Yiddish audience? Instead, Goldfaden toured all Russia with *Todros, Blos,* and everywhere it was not worth the air he blew.

With the coming of summer the Yiddish theater took itself to Liman, a summer resort on the Black Sea. Goldfaden rented a dacha for the summer, and the actors sat around his table, happy Chassidim around their kindly rabbi.

Sonya and I came every day by train and in the evening went home again. It was a worrisome expense, but Liman drew us like a magnet.

Life there centered on the beach. We bathed in the sea, wandered on the sand, regaled ourselves with food and drink, and spent happy hours rowing on the nearby coastal salt lakes. Rosenberg, chief funmaker, saw to it that things stayed lively. Under his direction we played endless jokes on the Romanians, jokes they always repaid in kind.

Amid pranks and horseplay, worries about money, and plans for the future, the summer passed. The managers donned their high hats, their winged capes, and went back to Odessa. The theatrical wheel began to turn and the city was full of theater news.

Our own hopes were doomed to disappointment. Only Spivakovsky was engaged for the coming season. As for the rest of us, poor devils, Goldfaden put his brother at the head of our troupe, and sent us out into the provinces again.

Rosenberg clapped me on the shoulder and told me to buck up. "Courage, brother!" he exclaimed in Russian. "Things will yet come right!" And in fact I plucked up some spirit. Here Rosenberg had just lost everything, and still he was gay!

With Tulya Goldfaden our new head and captain, we were off again. The first stop, Kishinev. Spirits lifted at the prospect. A new city! Why not have a look?

KISHINEV REVELS

It was a three-hour trip by rail, and we arrived at nightfall. Perhaps it was the end of summer that depressed us, for we found the atmosphere rather gloomy. Actually, it was a city like any other and livelier than most, but lively in a peculiar way, for whatever differs from our own little dung heap must at first seem peculiar.

We walked around for an hour or two, taking in the town. The streets, lit by moonlight and gas lamps, were crowded with all sorts of people—Jews, Bessarabians in colorful dress, workingmen on an outing with their girls, young sports seeking an evening of pleasure, and, as in Kherson, many officials and soldiers. Officers strode by, dazzling the girls with their uniforms. *Coursistes* with short hair* strolled arm in arm, and everywhere you saw native Moldavians, dark, charming, but coarsely dressed and coarse-spoken.

We all wanted to try the famous Bessarabian wine, poured here in such abundance, and so, on that evening thirty-eight years ago, we fell into a Kishinev restaurant. You must know the restaurants of this city were famous in those days.

This one was packed to the doors, every table crowded with individuals, most of them frankly of the third class, and all of them noisily enjoying themselves.

It does not take long for such a lusty crowd to make friends. They soon found out we were actors, singers, and from then on we were welcomed with enthusiasm. In no time at all, then were our blood brothers. They joined our tables, they swore eternal friendship, they vied with each other in doing us honor. And in the center of it all, catching the best and most flattering compliments, Tulya Goldfaden.

Tulya took his new position very seriously. He was never seen now

* Short hair suggests revolutionary leanings.

but in a white waistcoat and flowing cravat, and he received the attentions of these new friends with all the dignity befitting the head of the troupe.

On the other side of the table Rosenberg also was trying to look puffed up and proud. He continually shrugged in a refined way as if to say, "Why do you look at him? I am the real director!" In vain! The white waistcoat carried the day. I could not resist slipping in a needling word. "Hey, Yisrolik!" I called across the table with a tongue already loosened by wine. "This isn't Odessa or Bucharest, eh? Gone now, all those good times!"

"Wait, Yankele," Rosenberg answered, sad but self-possessed. "Let them only see me on the stage. Then they will know who is an eagle and who is a mouse."

And in fact he was right. When we began to play, Rosenberg had an enormous success with the Kishinev audience.

We stayed on in that restaurant all through the night. We partook of the famous Bessarabian-Romanian *machlis,* those strongly peppered dishes of which all Romanian patriots are so proud, the smoked meats, also highly peppered, the true Romanian *mommeligge,* cut with a thread, for God forbid a knife should touch it. Our new friends drink with us. They pour glass after glass. Their faces grow red as beets. And since it has gone so far, their feet, too, take wings. They begin to dance, to stamp, to sing. They dance first in twos, then others join. They turn and turn again, they make a ring, they dance a hora. And they stamp in the Romanian style, and they shout in the Romanian style. More dancers join the circle. They push the tables back. The whole group begins to weave in and out, to cut such extraordinary figures that it all tears through me like gunpowder exploding in my veins. I forget that I am an engaged man, forget that I am wearing a high silk hat, that I am an actor, a leading man. The wild blood of the old Odessa "Yankele Kulachnik" awakens in me. I have a mad desire to show these Moldavians what dancing is, a Russian dance on hands and knees, like the cancan I performed when, together with my companions, I used to storm the taverns of the Moldovanka.

I want to throw myself into the whirling circle. But I feel a glance. I feel an eye. My beloved is present. My wings falter. I sink back, sigh, and apply myself to my glass, reflecting that the ladies are a good and lovely company, but when it comes to having a time for oneself, it is better to leave them at home.

In the meantime it was growing late. We parted at last with our new friends and walked back to our hotel. I say walked, but my feet were finding their own queer way. There was a roaring in my head. I talked a good deal of foolishness. I kissed everyone. I laughed at everything, and very loudly. Alexander Oberlander urged me several times in a whisper to control myself. He finally turned to his sister, saying, "Well, Sonya? Do you not blush for the boy?"

But at just that point something happened that did a great deal to sober me. Sonya refused my arm and took that of Tulya Goldfaden. All the blood rushed to my head. I lunged forward, wanting to throw his coarse arm off her. I restrained myself in time, and no one noticed the gesture or the jealousy it betrayed. Only Rosenberg, that scoundrel, saw everything.

I went up to my room in the hotel, and as soon as I closed the door, looked in the mirror. My clothing was in disarray, my eyes glistening, my face aflame. But a good-looking boy, devil take the lot of them!

My blood was boiling in my veins. Sleep was out of the question. I left the hotel and took myself wherever my eyes led me.

I had long ago lost my innocence—the good companions of my youth had seen to that. By the time I was sixteen I knew the way to every nest of vice in Odessa, those places where one found enchanted princesses who were dressed in silk and who spoke with a sugary refinement. The wild youth had his loves there. And if the princess of his choice accepted the attentions of another, it was right and proper to smash mirrors, overturn furniture, make the greatest scandal. The young man had experienced these rages even when the princess of his choice was by no means the most beautiful girl in the place—yes, even when he was seriously in love, and about to take on the responsibilities of marriage.

Coming out of the hotel that night, my heart still gnawed by jealousy, my head still swimming, I found myself in the marketplace. Here I encountered an individual well known in the city, who offered to take me under his guidance. For a moment I wavered and then, with drunken decision, followed him.

Again music and wild carousing. Again enchanted princesses, again respectable young men of good family. Although nobody knew me I was ashamed and remained near the door. Suddenly a song! Loud voices in another room. I follow the voices. God in heaven! Mine! Rosenberg. Others. I am surrounded, greeted with shrieks of joy.

"*Molodyets!* Very good! Well done!" Rosenberg whispers in my ear. "That is how it should be. Always the man. Honor to your bride, yes. But apron strings? Never!"

Suddenly I see that *he* is here too. My fledgling, Yankele Katzman. The gentlest, the youngest! We fell into each other's arms, embraced, wept. But in these places people soon grow impatient with sentimental scenes. They part us, urge us to drink again.

A wild and ugly night. Brandy. Wine. More wine. More brandy. On and on until white daylight came through the windows. At last Rosenberg, who never got drunk no matter how much he drank, called out, "Enough, charlatans! Home! Remember, we play on Sunday. It does no harm to have a time for ourselves, but gentlemen we must be!" And calling a loud "Good night!" he left, singing a Russian song.

I woke next morning wishing the night could have lasted forever, so that none of us would have to look the others in the face. The reaction was terrible. How ugly it had been, how hateful the finery of those painted girls next to the straightforward Sonya, the serious young student and revolutionary.

Later that day I sat with Sonya on the boulevard. I led the conversation to our future, I spoke of an eternal bond. I was humble, deferential, like all guilty lovers. But the clever, cool Sonya said only, "*Posmotrit.* We will see." After a silence she said, "You are too much Don Juan, Yakob. I am not sure I trust your character."

I had no answer. Truly, what could I have said?

Our first performance was scheduled for Sunday. Very early that morning a low voice woke me. Rosenberg was bending over my bed. "Adler! Adler!" I heard him say. "Look into the court!" I sprang out of bed, more dead than alive, and ran to the window. The entire court below was covered with sleeping men, women, and children. I was seized by a terrible fear. But Rosenberg reassured me. No, it was not a pogrom, not a Cossack raid. The people below had slept all night on the bare ground so as to be sure of tickets to our performance that night.

Rosenberg had tears in his eyes. "You see, Yankele?" he murmured. "You see a love, a gratitude? And all for Yiddish theater! Did you and I ever dream of Yiddish theater, brother?"

The other actors crept in, one by one, some in coats, some wrapped in blankets or shawls. Many of them brushed tears from their eyes as they saw that picture in the court.

It is a picture that still lives for me in all its details as though it were yesterday. A thousand times in my moments of doubt I have called it to mind, and a thousand times it has given me strength. Great God, when my end draws near, with my last breath, before my eyes close forever—let me see that picture one last time.

In this mood of repentance, of inner humility and trembling, we appeared that night before the thrilled Kishinev Jews. We had a house packed to the doors, and the excitement was so great one could have cut it with a knife. Everyone in the troupe wanted to do his best, and we were rewarded with grateful and warm applause.

Grossman's theater, where we played, was part of the hotel. Although small, it had a good stage, an auditorium with red velvet seats, a balcony, and even loges. Since in those days it was the only theater in the city, we alternated with a Russian troupe from Odessa.

The leading tragedian of the Russian troupe was Ivan Nikolayevich Kitin, a great actor but a great drunkard. One night, watching backstage, I saw him so drunk he could hardly stand on his feet, so drunk he could barely be understood when he spoke. Nevertheless, he put on his makeup without even looking into the mirror, and when called for his entrance, stood up like another man. He played magnificently, made a marvelous exit, then fell, weeping, into the stage manager's arms, beat his breast, swore he would never drink again, and made his way with a bowed head to his dressing room. The stage manager told me the same scene took place every night.

We stayed four weeks in Kishinev, and during that time the prosperous, easygoing city showered us with money. It was a free life and we could ask for nothing better. There were no rehearsals, we played old plays. Our whole stay there was one unbroken vacation.

In addition to my other bad habits I now acquired a new one. Cards. Until now this esteemed and popular art had been unknown to me. The favorite game of the troupe was oke, a game of three cards with the high card winning. I soon caught the fever.

As a player I was not very outstanding. I lacked the true gambling spirit. I grew hot, I burned, but I did not risk much. I had only one desire, to win . . . and always lost. I swore each time I would never gamble again, for truth to tell, I could not afford even the sums I risked. The managers had agreed to pay me two hundred rubles a month, but I rarely got more than fifty, sometimes no more than twenty.

Under Tulya Goldfaden the troupe had been reorganized on a crass business basis. No more communistic "shares," no more idealistic comradeship. There were moments I wanted to throw over the whole thing, pack up, and go home. This was not the theater I had dreamed of. Managers and stars alike spent their time in low places, with people of bad character. The Kishinev police had fallen in love with us, and not only the petty police, but high-ranking officers as well. Every night as the performance ended the snorting of their horses could be heard outside the theater. As soon as the curtain fell they swarmed backstage, and a wild masquerade began. The officers flung their brass-buttoned uniforms to the actors, while they gleefully got themselves up as rabbis, Chassidim, village fools. All of them fought for Katzman's costume. Katzman himself was thrown into a general's coat and set up on a horse. And in this fashion, his head fuddled by wine, the eighteen-year-old boy rode over the streets of Kishinev, looking for the first time truly like a *shmendrick*. And every night we rioted and caroused in this way along with the petty police and the Cossack night patrol, stopping everywhere to drink and make merry. Others joined our revels. Women became our followers. And there seemed no way out of this, even had we wished it.

I looked for my earlier self, but could no longer find it. I cannot pretend I had been a saint, but my follies until now had been those of a young man, a boy who might still hope to do better. Now I was being drawn night after night into the lowest kind of company.

How long does it take, after all, to fall into bad ways? I soon learned to make my way home at daybreak with an unsteady step, to sleep half the day away, to receive love letters . . .

In the new career to which I had so long aspired I had as yet shown no great marvels, but I was already "a real actor."

One incident in Kishinev has been omitted. Shortly before the troupe left the city a friend asked Adler, as a favor, to see a young man in the town, a David Kessler, who had ambitions as an actor. Adler agreed to look him over. The meeting was arranged for the following day.

Kessler was the son of an innkeeper, a dour, angry man with little money and a houseful of children to feed. Since the eldest son had no bent for learning, he had been sent out to earn his living as a peddler. He was soon a familiar figure on the Kishinev streets, nicknamed

"David with his *kobze*" because instead of shouting his wares he sang them, accompanying himself on this instrument, a primitive guitar of sorts. Coming home after work, Kessler would relate the scenes he had witnessed on the street, sometimes acting out, with a deep curse, some incident of falseness or brutality.

One day posters went up in the Jewish taverns and restaurants of Kishinev announcing a performance by the tragedian Abba Schoengold in a play by the world-renowned dramatist Professor Moishe Isaac Halevy-Hurvitz.

This Halevy-Hurvitz, a former convert and missionary, had declared himself a Jew again after the success of Goldfaden in Bucharest. When Goldfaden refused a play he wrote, he left the city and toured the Romanian provinces with a troupe of his own.

Abba Schoengold was the young singer who had failed his audition with Goldfaden in Galatz. Taking the only chance left to him, Schoengold had joined the wandering troupe of the self-styled Professor Halevy-Hurvitz.

Kessler had laughed at the wild exaggerations of the poster, but out of curiosity, he had gone to see the play. He came away in a daze. He could think of nothing but Abba Schoengold, his voice, his cloak, the romantic spell of his presence. The thought came into his head that he, too, like Abba Schoengold, would be an actor.

The sixteen-year-old Kessler went home, cleaned out an empty stable, hammered together a stage with his own hands and, gathering some young people of the neighborhood, began putting on "plays." He had no text, no book, did not know such things existed. He simply strung together whatever he remembered of Abba Schoengold's scenes and speeches.

A few people came and went away, laughing. His father, enraged at his craziness, threatened to put him out of the house. But an educated man named Geller saw flashes of talent in the wild "acting" of this young Kessler. Geller, a medical student, had once tried his hand at a comedy called *Mechtze the Matchmaker*. Before leaving for Paris, where he completed his medical studies, he gave Kessler the manuscript.

Kessler took the dramatic lead, gave the comedy lead to a boy named Leon Nadolsky, and put the play on in Moser's hall, a room where weddings and other Jewish festivities took place. Hardly anyone came, but a man with a hall in Dubasori, a town across the river, liked the play, and Kessler gave two more performances of Geller's comedy there.

When Rosenberg's troupe came into Kishinev, Kessler began hanging around the stage door. He had not enough nerve to speak to anyone, and finally asked a friend who knew Adler to speak for him.

The meeting took place at the gate of the New Market. Arriving at the appointed hour, Adler saw a powerfully built, roughly dressed young man of about eighteen, with the neck and shoulders of a bull and an angry, scowling face.

The impression was not promising, but since Kessler claimed some acting experience, Adler told him to come to the theater the next day and show what he could do.

He appeared the following morning, and went through the dramatic scene of his "success." The actors roared with laughter, and one of them, a wag, kept stealing up behind the tragic hero and giving him a playful rap on the head. The second time this occurred, Kessler caught him by the collar and said pleasantly, "One more such trick, my friend, and you will have cause to remember me." He got through the rest of the scene without interruption.

Since he had a good voice, Rosenberg would have taken him on as an extra, but as events fell out, the troupe left Kishinev without him. A storm had broken out in Kessler's home, such an outcry from his father that he should go off to be a beggar, a clown, an organ grinder, that the young man was forced to let the troupe leave without him.

Three years later a small wandering company of Yiddish actors came into Kishinev. When they left the town, Kessler and Leon Nadolsky left with them.

Kessler and Nadolsky spent three years with this troupe, enduring great hunger and want, until finally, Kessler's luck turned and better days came, for both men.

Kessler died in 1920, one of the immortals of the Yiddish theater. Nadolsky survived to celebrate his fifty-year jubilee on the Yiddish stage. He never rose to leading roles; he was an actor among many. But he remained with Kessler and had a place in Kessler's theater as long as Kessler lived.

After our Kishinev success, I entered my birthplace for the first time like a conqueror. My mother and sister met me at the station with happy tears in their eyes. News of my triumphs had come home before me. The ne'er-do-well who had dragged himself around with other do-nothings was now an actor, a talent who had carved out a career for himself.

Everyone in Odessa looked on me as an actor now. My father, once so pessimistic, went about with my reviews in his pocket, and at every opportunity read them aloud to anyone who would listen.

We had returned to get instructions from Finkel as to the next leg of our tour. Meanwhile we looked around to see what was going on. There was enough to see. Goldfaden was at the height of his power. He stood so high these days you needed a ladder to look at him.

At the Remesleni the very air resounded with *Neither This, That, nor Kukerikoo.* Goldfaden himself led the dance of the Chassidim, though he looked more like a university professor or a French diplomat. He bathed in bouquets and honors, and the troupe bathed in applause.

The heavenly rays of Goldfaden fell on his troupe as well. And why deny it, we envied them. We were "the Provincial Troupe." They were the "Goldfaden Academic Society." They were soon to play in the great Mariinsky Theater! We hardly existed in Odessa, and walked around as though we were shadows.

"So, Yankele," Rosenberg sighed after one particularly mediocre effect, "aren't they the bottom of the barrel? But let it go. Luck is everything."

In the winter of 1879 the Odessa Mariinsky in effect became a Yiddish theater—a change brought about by financial considerations.

The Jews, in spite of rabbinical disapproval, have always been inveterate playgoers, and from the beginning both the City Theater and the Mariinsky had relied heavily on their support. A part of this audience had been lost to Rosenberg's theater. With the runaway success of Goldfaden, the Jewish public had deserted the two theaters in overwhelming numbers.

The state-subsidized City Theater could weather the drop in attendance, but the owner of the Mariinsky, unable to take such losses, dispensed with his Russian company and threw open his stage to the popular Goldfaden troupe.

The enormous popularity of Yiddish theater would, in fact, soon be a threat to a number of Russian and German troupes in the southern

Ukraine. Later this would also occur on the Lower East Side of New York. In 1885 we find the National, an American vaudeville house, switching over entirely to the growing Jewish audience. In the next ten years a dozen theaters on the Lower East Side would follow the National's example.

While we waited for our instructions, December came with its snows and storms. White streets, white roofs. Finkel finally worked out the details of our tour, and the throw of the dice fell on Yelizavet-grad.* This was our first really big city. An overnight trip, the longest yet. The thought of it excited me. Travel, see the world—why not?

All eyes were on us as we trooped through the train. All of us were young, handsome, lively, all in coats with huge Kamchatka fur collars, our traveling bags dashingly slung over our shoulders. My Sonya is always at my side. We read together—newspapers, journals. She and her brother discuss literature and social questions. I could not take part in these discussions, I knew too little. But I was proud that my Sonya, my bride, discoursed on such subjects.

There were as yet no Pullmans on Russian trains. We slept as we could with a fist for a pillow, and awoke to a gray snowy Russian dawn. Yelizavetgrad. We got off the train feeling unwashed and unprayed, for in those years the Yiddish actors, good Chassidic Jews, still said a prayer every morning.

The sight of Yelizavetgrad, beautiful and stately, sent our spirits soaring. We went down the street shouting, "We will take her! We will conquer!" Everyone turned to look at us. Our high hats caused a particular sensation, for this type of headgear had never been seen in this city.

Since the only theater here was occupied by a Russian opera company, we played in an officer's club on the main boulevard. A small and inconvenient stage, but for our poor plays, it would do.

Shmendrick, as usual, was our first offering. It was followed by others as light and as lacking in any real content. These comedies, filled out with foolish couplets, had a sensational success in Yelizavet-

---

* Present-day Kirovograd, in the Ukraine.

grad. They gave me, however, almost nothing to do. I played small parts and often did not play at all.

I already knew the taste of jealousy, but this was something new. My beloved this time was not a woman, but a shadowy, thousand-headed being—a kind of Sphinx. My beloved, in fact, was none other than the public—that same public that had applauded me in Kherson and Kishinev, and that now gave its love and applause to others. And in what? In comedies and farces without value, without meaning!

Not that I was entirely without consolation in this carnival of clowning and horseplay. For if I had no success on the stage I had more than my share in another arena. That short time in Yelizavetgrad was the very button, the very flower, of my pursuit of feminine charm. If the critics of Yelizavetgrad did not love me, the young people adored me like a god. Among these young folk I had become what we now call "a matinee idol." And with greatest impatience, with most languishing love, they waited for me to show myself in my true, radiant image—as Guberman in *Breindele Cossack.*

To deserve this worship I had to conduct myself as befits a god. This I accomplished chiefly by my dress. Try to imagine a handsome young actor in a smashing costume complete with glistening gloves and a graceful walking stick. Picture him with a light springing step, a conquering glance, a courtly bearing, and a condescending smile. Imagine all this and you will have some idea, if not of the roles I played on the stage, at least of those I played before the mirror and before the eyes of my admirers.

Although it was winter I always appeared now in a white cravat. Whether this was the mode or I wanted to be original I no longer remember, but I spent hours fashioning these cravats out of the finest lace. But more than anything I liked my hair, which I wore in a lock over my brow, a lock that lightly and graciously waved about with every movement of my head.

This lock exerted a kind of magnetic spell on my feminine admirers. The more impassioned ones not only caressed it, but in an excess of endearment actually tugged and pulled at it so as to cause pain. In vain I begged them to stop. I had to endure it or avoid their company.

Seeing what a treasure I had in this lock I naturally spared neither time nor money to preserve its beauty. Long hours before the mirror it cost me, as well as the most expensive perfume and the finest almond oil. Well, only once is one young, and only once so divinely empty!

Interesting, as always, was the attitude of Sonya. She, so affectionate, so endearing, took no notice of my glory, never spoke of it either to praise or to criticize. She simply smiled. Her attitude seemed to say, "Yakob likes all this. His friends like it. Why not? Why should I trouble myself that he devotes himself to empty trifles?"

Although the circle of my adorers grew larger and larger, I felt I had not truly earned their adoration. Until now, I told them, they had seen nothing. I had not yet truly played, what you call playing. Soon they will see me as Guberman in *Dreindele Cossuck*. Then they will know me in my glory.

At last the play was announced, and you can imagine with what fire the news spread, what expectation it kindled. In short, the whole city was waiting.

But more than the whole city, *I* was waiting. For in spite of my success with the *mam'zelles* of Yelizavetgrad, I was not so intoxicated as to forget that the critics in this city had so far treated me like a stepchild. This, I told myself, was because I had played only small parts. But wait. Now they would see me in a real role, and if they were not swept off their feet, their criticism was not worth the paper on which it was written.

At last the great night came. A packed house. Hundreds of young people, all beautifully dressed, all with such excited young faces and each fluttering happy little hearts. I play. Applause rings out after every scene. Bravos storm the house. Every curtain stronger than the one before. The audience carries the theater. My name is called, shouted. The stage is covered with flowers, strewn with laurels, my dressing room crowded with visitors. A crowd waits outside the theater to give me more ovations, more applause, and congratulations.

A party afterward in a restaurant. Joy, gaiety, compliments. I came home late to my hotel room. I was on fire to see the morning paper, to read my review. I waited all night without closing an eye, continually running to the window to see whether it was not already day, whether the boys were not already running about and calling out their newspapers.

At last I hear it—a voice shouting, *"Yelizavetgradskaya Novosty!"* I rushed down into the street, seized a copy of the paper, and ran back to my room. I tore open the paper. No review. I turn the pages, strain my eyes, turn again. Nothing. No review.

I sat at the window a long time as the sky slowly grew lighter. I was too stunned to think. I sat beaten, motionless. A deathly weariness reminded me I had not slept all night. I told myself the critic must have decided to wait before writing his review, or perhaps had written it too late for the press. Quieting myself a little with this thought, I lay down on my bed. My last thought was that I must go to the Voronsky Club. The actors gathered there every day, and the critic of the *Novosty* was always on hand. There I would learn the reason for this.

This critic, a Jew called Lerner, was a red-haired man with a pair of fiery penetrating little red eyes. He had taken an interest in our troupe, often came to our rehearsals, and was friendly with all, especially with Rosenberg, whom, in fact, he mentioned more often than others. He did not seem ill-disposed toward me, but I noticed that his glance, when it fell on me, held a certain irony. I am not sure whether this bore more on my talent or on my well-tended pompadour, but these looks of his were more than I could endure. I had been counting on *Breindele Cossack* to remove his doubts.

As soon as I woke that morning I hurried to the club. Lerner had not yet shown himself, but the actors were already gathered, everyone talking about last night's play and wondering why there was no review.

Suddenly the door opened and Herr Lerner appeared. He smiled, greeted us, but shook hands with no one. This was not his usual custom, which in itself made us uneasy.

Rosenberg soon found his tongue. He began asking Lerner's opinion of last night's play, and in particular, of his own performance. Lerner's long face grew even longer. His smile died. With a glance that lingered particularly on me, and in the dry tone of a pedagogue, he said, "*Gospoda,* gentlemen, I must inform you that your play not only convinced me that the dramatist should be severely criticized for having written such a piece, but that every one of you, with the single exception of Fräulein Michelson,* should be castigated for such playing as I saw last night."

At this my heart began to hammer. Even Rosenberg turned pale. Lerner proceeded to take the play apart, and to mercilessly flay each of us in turn. We had all looked only for how foolish we could make ourselves, not one of us had shown a serious attitude to his role. We had not even made use of the small talent we possessed, if indeed we did

---

* Sonya used the stage name Sonya Michelson.

possess it. "And don't tell me in a melodrama everything is allowed," Lerner said. "Even in a melodrama one can, and should, portray a human being. You are clowns, not actors, and Rosenberg the worst of all. Study. Learn. I will not come again until I am told you deserve to be reviewed." And with a terse *"Tsum Wiedersehen"*—"Until we meet again"—he was off.

Now there was total silence. None of us had courage even to look at the others. Slowly, silently, the actors began dispersing until only a few remained.

"Well, Adler, I am sorry for you," Rosenberg said. "You thought your pompadour and your victories over the *mam'zelles* made you into a talent, a genius. No, Yankele! The applause has fooled you. The bravos are empty. The smiles of pretty girls are the flash of a false diamond. You have no right to these honors you have not earned. Study, observe life. Learn and remember well what Lerner has just said. He is a severe, but a wise critic."

I broke out in a sweat at these words, and Rosenberg suddenly burst into laughter. Again the clown, the mountebank came out in him. He began to prance madly about the stage. "To hell!" he said recklessly. "The public wants to laugh! Let them laugh! And call me what you will!" And with that he went off.

I sat heavily on a bench. This was the first real blow of my young life, the moment when I judged myself. "Let them laugh," Rosenberg had said. But bitter was the sound of that laughter. No! To be a clown was not my idea. If it was to be acting, let it be the real thing. Had I until now done anything worth doing? Yes, I had had some success, but not from my art; it had come from my appearance, my high hat, my dandyish airs. Away with all that! Enough of the fake. Let's be an actor.

I took myself to the barber, and emerged from his hands with no more hair on my head than is worn by ordinary mortals. My high hat, my white cravat, my elegant little stick were next to go, and with them went all my carefree, youthful gaiety. I slid through the streets like a shadow, with a haggard face, avoiding everyone. No one so sad as a sad clown. Who wants to be his friend?

Finally I made up my mind to go to the person who had so grimly pulled me from my pedestal. If Lerner could destroy, he must also be able to build. He had said I must learn. Good! Let him teach me.

Lerner, critic of the Yelizavetgrad paper, was a cultured man who lived with his family in a quiet, well-regulated home. He and his wife received me in very friendly fashion, and after my first visit I was often invited. Some fine things came of this, for the Lerners drew me into their circle, and through them I met all the serious intellectuals of the city. These people held the Yiddish theater in high regard. Not in its present state, of course. In its possibilities. They gave me courage to remain on the stage, and to win a place there as an actor.

One morning as we sat over breakfast Spivakovsky suddenly fell in among us. A black cat had run between him and Goldfaden. He had come back to the troupe.

He was as attractive and handsome as ever, and greeted us with his usual exuberant "*Zarastvuytye, tovarishchi!* Hello, comrades!" Everyone was overjoyed to see him. Only I felt a blow at the heart. Spivakovsky and I both played romantic leads. We were rivals. His reappearance could bode only ill for me.

My fears were soon confirmed. A new poster of *Breindele Cossack* went up with Spivakovsky announced as Guberman.

My feelings were hidden from no one. There was no way I could hide them. It was as though someone had taken a great whip and in the middle of the marketplace, before everyone's eyes, had struck me with it across the face.

As their only prima donna Sonya had some power with the management. I had never made use of it before, feeling instinctively that it was not right, not fine, to use my closeness to a woman. Now I threw away my pride and for the first time begged her to intercede, plead for me, if all else failed, refuse to play with Spivakovsky.

But the clever, coolheaded Sonya saw the matter quite differently. Such a demand, she said, would make it appear that Spivakovsky was better in the role, and that I played only through her protection. True, Lerner had not been pleased with my Guberman, but Spivakovsky's, Sonya insisted, would please him even less.

Her words did not quiet me. The closer it came to that cursed performance, the more my torment grew. At the opening I went to the theater, but not into the hall. Instead I paced up and down a corridor where some Russian officers were playing cards. I strained my ears, listening with sick attention to every sound from the stage.

Suddenly as I listened I heard a great rush of applause. Spivakovsky had made his entrance. I felt a lurch of the heart and went into hysterics. Oberlander had to get me out of the hall, take me to the hotel, and put me to bed. I lay there in a high fever.

At midnight four visitors arrived: Sonya, Rosenberg, Tulya Gold-faden, and Spivakovsky. Spivakovsky himself gave me the news that he had failed as Guberman, flopped completely. The others confirmed it, and Sonya reminded me that she had known it all along.

This had such an effect on me that my fever went down and I was well again. And my friends shared my happiness. A remarkable thing. All of them—Rosenberg, Tulya Goldfaden, and Spivakovsky him-self—rejoiced at their own downfall!

I needed only one thing more—Lerner's review. But how to live through the night? How to live until morning when the newspapers came out? My friends understood and waited with me. The cold dark winter hours passed gaily until, with the first gray daylight, we heard the newsboys below the window. Just as I had that other morning, I ran down into the street. But what a difference this time! Splashed half across the page I read the blessed words, SPIVAKOVSKY'S FAILURE.

The critic took the entire performance apart, showing, scene by scene, how much better my performance had been. True, he said I was still young, not yet fully developed (oh, excellent critic, oh, knowl-edgeable critic!), but my interpretation, he wrote, my whole approach to the role, was the more artistic of the two.

My friends congratulated me. And Spivakovsky, truly the best of men, gave me back the role with his own hands, swearing he never would have taken it had he known it would give me the slightest pain. And I? May the goddess of art forgive me, I rejoiced in his mis-fortune.

Fate decreed that my life should be strangely bound up with the life of Yisrol Gradner. I knew him first as a folksinger in the wine cellars of my youth. Though he himself did not know what theater was, he brought a kind of theater to these cellars.

I lost track of him during the years of the Russo-Turkish War. When I heard of him next it was as the first and greatest actor of the Yiddish theater in Romania.

I ask myself now why this rarely gifted human being was so soon withered on the branch. What broke him so early? Why so soon fallen from his height while others, less gifted, made their way to the top. Was it blind fate? Some may say so. The truth is sadder. It was human envy, human badness, that pushed this actor down. Intrigue pushed him out of the first troupe in Romania. He wandered with a troupe of

his own, suffered, came to Odessa, made up his quarrel with Goldfaden, and was taken back into his company. His success was enormous until, once again, intrigue and politics began, and Gradner,
who should have been the crown of our theater, was again shamefully
pushed out.

It was during our last days in Yelizavetgrad that he appeared—no
longer as great as formerly, but still one of the great stars—and asked
to be taken into our troupe. We were thrilled. Who had not heard of
Gradner, the actor who had created plays, created characters, who,
together with Goldfaden, had actually created our stage!

But as it turned out, it was no easy task to get Gradner into the
troupe. We met with strong opposition from Rosenberg, who saw
him as a rival. Gradner, like Rosenberg, was a character actor and
comedian. In addition he was a fine singer, while Rosenberg was weak
in this regard. Also, together with Gradner came his wife Annetta, an
actress with the seventh degree of charm, and a marvelous singer
besides. And what could Rosenberg do, stick that he was, against
these two?

Feeling instinctively that here was a martyr of art, I took up arms
for him. Spivakovsky joined me, Sonya followed, and to our surprise,
Tulya Goldfaden came in on our side. Through our efforts, Gradner
was not only engaged, but even got a contract and an advance. Soon
after, his wife joined us.

If there are angels among us on earth one of them was Annetta
Gradner. She was from Kremenchuk, the daughter of a bootmaker, a
poor girl but honorably raised. Gradner met her during his wandering years as a folksinger. He fell in love with her voice, married her,
and when the Yiddish theater had its birth in Romania, Annetta was
its first prima donna. Audiences idolized her. From childhood she
possessed a sweet voice, not strong but melodious—a voice "with
tears in it." There was always something sweetly sad in her singing—
even her gay songs tore at your heart.

People intrigued, tried to come between husband and wife.
Impossible. Annetta was true, even when he was poor and alone.

Although not yet the mere shadow of himself he became in his
later years, Gradner, when he came to us, was already on the downward path. Here is a sketch of him as I recall him at this period. A
man in his middle thirties, of medium height, with an oval face, long
hair, and something of the poet about his brow. He was gallant in his

dress, careful of any speck on his black coat, his black hat. His speech differed from ours. He was a Lithuanian by birth, at that time the only Lithuanian in the Yiddish theater. Knowing that his dialect created a dissonance, he affected a Germanized speech on the stage. And though he probably did not think much of our abilities, he was merry during his short time with us and behaved like a colleague.

One day he was off—gone his own way. But we were to meet again, and at a critical moment in both our lives.

WINTER IN YELIZAVETGRAD —
MY DOWNFALL

Although we spent only four months in Yelizavetgrad, I can say
I lived through more in that city than in all other places put
together.

The last event occurred just before we left. This was a strike organized by myself against our troika of directors—a strike in which I
was betrayed in an ugly way, in which I lost everything and went
through the most terrible ordeal of my life.

It came about in winter, and winter it was also in my heart. I was a
fallen giant. Rosenberg and Tulya Goldfaden had treated me with
care when I was their only romantic lead. With Spivakovsky's return,
I felt the bitter difference. Before I had almost been a codirector. Now
I was shut out of their councils. I had grown cheap in their eyes. That
meant I was paid less, and sometimes not paid at all. I who had
thrown about my rubles now had to watch my kopeks. My clothes
grew shabby, and I had no money for new ones. I began to feel like a
pauper.

Because Sonya had to support her parents, she was paid more regularly, but Katzman, Oberlander, and others too got the same treatment. Our weekly wages now depended entirely on how much went
into the pocket of Tulya Goldfaden.

The managers tried to quiet us with diplomacy, flattery, and
delays. "Wait!" they told us. "Soon we will go on to Kremenchuk.*
The Jews there have never seen Yiddish theater. We will make fortunes, and everyone will be happy."

Finally we grew tired of these empty promises, and I organized a
revolt.

* On the Dnieper River, in the Ukraine.

Strikes were at that time unknown among actors. I did not even know the word. Nevertheless I worked matters out exactly as one organizes a strike. I began to propagandize Sonya and her brother as well as Katzman, who was always under my influence. Others in the cast were also interested. It was easy enough to fan their anger, and we decided on an ultimatum. The managers would give in to our demands, or we would not set foot on the stage.

All this was resolved in a secret meeting in my hotel room. We made out a list of our demands, and set out for Kremenchuk, our declaration of war in our pockets.

In Kremenchuk, an ugly but lively city, we held another meeting, pledging that none of us would make a separate agreement with the managers. All for one, and one for all. No separate peace. We felt we could not lose, for posters were already up announcing *Shmendrick,* and Katzman, who had the leading part, was with us. With this trump card in our hands we sent Oberlander to the managers with our demands.

He came back pale as a ghost. The managers had refused to hear him out.

A dialogue followed, rapid as balls flying between juggling clowns.

"What do you mean they refused to hear you out? How will they play tonight?"

"They say they will play."

"But how? How will they play?"

"They say they will play without us."

This was impossible to understand. We decided they must be relying on fresh actors from Odessa, semiamateurs probably, untried and unrehearsed. Arrogance in the theater was no less in those days than now. The people were looked upon as fools, and if actors were lacking, one played with logs. But apparently this was not the case. As time went by, it was clear they had sent for no one.

The day of the performance came. It cannot be, I argued. How can they possibly give the audience *Shmendrick* when Katzman, who *is* Shmendrick, is with us?

We waited together in the hotel, but evening fell, and still we were not called. Finally we sent Oberlander to the theater. We were sure he would tell us the performance had caused a scandal, perhaps even a riot, that the audience had hooted and jeered, even that at the last minute the program had been changed.

At twelve midnight Oberlander came back, more dead than alive. Rosenberg had played Shmendrick. His success had been fantastic. The audience had carried him on their shoulders.

Soon after this crushing news, the three directors came back in triumph to the hotel. They assembled in their room, broad and proud. We cowered in our corner. They spoke in loud, assured voices, we in halting, broken whispers. The very air between the two rooms was full of hatred and contempt, the contempt of the conqueror for the beaten and trampled enemy.

From time to time words reached our ears, poisoned words, full of hatred and scorn. "Who needs them? Let them go!" My blood boiled for vengeance, my eyes, like knives, tried to bore through the walls. I wanted to speak to Spivakovsky, knowing he was the best of them. But he did not appear. He avoids me. He is with them.

The only one to cross into the enemy regions was Oberlander. He left each time as our ambassador, but returned each time as their messenger. With a face white as the wall he finally brought back a demand that his sister "speak with the managers. They have something they want to say to her." My heart told me this was not a good omen. I protested sharply that Sonya was not to go! Everything in the open! No secrets! If they had something to say, let them say it before us all.

I already felt that Oberlander had gone over, betrayed us, and my suspicion soon proved correct. Seeing that Sonya remained with me, he came out with the truth. "Sonya!" he cried in a terrible voice. "Our parents must have bread! They give you money! Go to them!"

Sonya's face turned ashen. I lunged at Oberlander with a raised fist, and in a voice not my own cried, "Traitor! Not enough you have sold us? Now you sell her too?"

Sonya, tears in her eyes, began to plead with me. "Yashenka, let me talk to them. What harm can it do? I will make everything right. You can see for yourself they have beaten us."

"How have they beaten us?" I denied it, hot with rage. "How long can it go on, an old man playing a boy, a child! No, he won't be able to do it. They will drive him off the stage, that charlatan, that scoundrel."

But Sonya tore away and with desperate decision crossed the hall and went through that other door. Two of the strikers followed her.

Now only Yankele Katzman remained. The boy sat with me, shivering like a leaf. What would happen to him now? He had been pushed off his little throne. A star no longer. A nothing, a nobody. Yet he stayed, and even tried to reassure me. "I am not going," he said. "I am with you." In those years he still used the formal "*Du*" when he spoke to me.

The two of us sat like people already buried. Laughter came from the other room, singing, the sound of corks popping. They were drinking champagne in there. Waiters hurried with red faces from the buffet and wine cellar, bringing wine, food. Honey draws flies. The city has its share of idlers, flatterers, good brothers. Hearing of these merry doings, they come to be close to the winners, to add their stab at the losers. They throw us glances full of mockery, they laugh among themselves at our downfall.

Now Rosenberg shows himself in the hall. He laughs. An ugly laugh. His eyes pierce the depths of my soul. I see that it has happened—the worst betrayal of all. I sprang up like lion, ran to the door and banged on it with my fists.

"Sonya!" I shouted, "Sonichka!"

I did not care if I caused a scandal, and pounded like a madman. Sonya was silent. It was Spivakovsky who opened the door. He looked at me with bloodshot eyes, tried to say something, and with drunken laughter closed the door again.

I banged again. "I want to see Sonya!" I shouted. "I am going away. I want to say good-bye."

This time Oberlander opened the door. Also drunk. "You are going?" he asked with a jeer. "Go in good health. Father, mother, brother, mean more to her than your love!" With a sneer he shut the door. And though I pounded it did not open again.

Exhausted, I went back to my corner. My clothes in disarray, dazed and hopeless, I sat by the window.

Suddenly, stealthily, the door opened. Surrounded by the others, Sonya came out. They were taking her to her room. Perhaps she had not courage enough to go alone, or it may be they were afraid she would talk with me and I would win her over. She did not look in my direction. She was weeping.

I sprang up and rushed toward her, calling her name. She did not answer, did not look at me. It was clear now. She was with them. They led her quickly out of the hall and up the stairs. I heard the door shut, then the grating sound of the lock. Then silence.

Katzman, weary, had gone off to bed. I was alone now, and I sobbed aloud in my pain. It was over. There would be no marriage.

Before this we had been unable to live an hour without looking into each other's eyes. I had prepared everything for the wedding, taken the most beautiful bridal rooms. Now it was finished. How can I go back to Odessa, lowered, mocked, and insulted? How can I show my face again to the world?

And I will not be with her again. Never. I will never see her again.

They played a whole week without us—that is, without me and Yankele Katzman. We could do nothing but be eaten up with envy and remorse. A thousand times a day my heart almost gave way, seeing how Sonya had gone over to my enemies. As far as I could see she had forgotten my existence.

I would have gone back to Odessa. But how? Katzman and I had barely a *groschen* between us. Katzman pawned two rings, then, with heartache, parted with a medallion with his mother's picture. This gave us money enough to stay alive and pay for our rooms at the hotel.

Heavy and long the dark days drew out. I lay in my corner, a snake drinking my blood. When I left my room I pinched my cheeks to give them color; I did not want my enemies to see how pale, how beaten I was. I played a part, acted carefree, laughed—all this until I could close my door, drop the mask, and give way to frightful weeping. Only one who has greatly loved and whose beloved has died can understand the loneliness and desolation of those days.

To make it worse, my enemies had never been more gay. They lived, laughed, enjoyed themselves, and it seemed all to torture me. The more I tasted gall, the greater the impetus and abandonment with which they gave themselves to pleasure.

Dead winter came on. The great lake of Kremenchuk lay frozen. A sleigh-riding party to a nearby town was organized.

I watched it all, hidden by the bushes at the edge of the lake. My Sonya laughs as they hand her into the sleigh. One arranges her fur, another covers her feet. How charmingly she accepts their attention! The sleigh bells ring out gaily. The whips whistle. The horses fly over the ice like eagles. And I watched it all, out there in the biting cold. They were driving, I dragged myself on foot. They were in gay company. I rotted in my isolation. They shouted boisterously in their gaiety. I suffocated in my silence.

It seemed to me that Sonya saw me. Yes. She saw me. But false heart of a woman, she turned away, she pretended not to see me. Wild rage came into my heart. Thoughts of revenge burned in my brain. I will do some terrible thing, I told myself, I will punish them, harm them. Then, with inner weeping, no—better to harm myself. A hole in the ice. A short note. Finished. No more Adler. Let them see what they have done to me!

And the snowstorm wailed about me. And the frozen weeds by the lake wept with me. Alone, like a madman, I raced along the side of the lake. The snow drove blindingly into my face, the wind blew through my thin worn fur.

I grew quieter at last, went back to the hotel, set myself to rights, and went to call on a friend named Zemlinsky. There I learned that the troupe was going on to Yekaterinoslav. Lordly covered sledges have already been ordered for the trip, a long and costly outing of several days. My Sonya will enjoy herself, give herself to pleasure.

And so it was. Next morning great covered sledges with sleigh bells and handsome horses drew up in the courtyard of the hotel. Everyone crowded around the sledges, everyone was joyous. My Sonya is wrapped in a fur, a red scarf at her throat. Her face is rosy. She shines. She laughs as she mounts the sledge. No—she doesn't even know I am alive. Adieu! You are leaving me. Good. Good.

But my cup was still not full. I had not yet drunk the last drop of poison. As they were leaving I saw Rosenberg take Yankele Katzman aside. He talks to him, he reasons with him. And it works. I see that it works. He wins the boy over. You too lost, my last friend, my Shmendrick? Now I am truly alone.

The boy runs gaily to the shops in the courtyard, back to the sledges again. His eyes are shining with joy. A fur hat is on his head, a red scarf at his throat. He catches my glance. In his face is a weak attempt to explain, to justify himself.

I wanted to feel anger, but could not. Would it help me if the boy dragged himself after me to Odessa? How could I ask him to throw away his happiness, put out his own sun? From an unknown Odessa kid he had become a favorite, a star. Girls waited for him outside the theater, threw him kisses, sent him notes. Was he to lose all this? Again to be lonely, again forgotten? For what? For friendship? No! I forgave him, but my own heart was not lighter. Now I was in truth alone.

Only one thing still interested me. Among all these once good friends was there not one who would look at me with loyalty, sympathy? Some were embarrassed, some showed a trace of guilt. All avoided my glance. I saw no sign of friendship, no sign even of pity. Bad a person asks for pity! But to be alone is worse.

But wait! There was one exception! Long live the heart of a woman! Young Bettye Vinyavich, daughter of our orchestra leader, a child sometimes allowed to say a line or so on the stage, she, little Bettye, wept for me. Each time our eyes met, hers overflowed with tears.

Poor little Bettye. She loved me, as everyone knew, but stifled her feelings, knowing I was engaged to Sonya. A good child, she tried to be happy in our joy.

Suddenly I noticed something strange. Rosenberg stood far from the sledges and looked at me with a frightened face. What does it mean? His eyes are fixed on me. I did not wish to speak to him, and turned into the hotel. He followed at a distance, evidently afraid to come closer.

It was the prompter, Zetzer, who caught up with me in the corridor. In spite of his missing front teeth he was this time extraordinarily clear. "*Gospodin* Adler, allow me a few words. I have just spoken to the managers. They wish to be reconciled."

Although in my heart I wanted very much to be reconciled, I replied curtly, "No!" However, realizing this would accomplish only what it had in my childhood when my stamping foot and my "No" earned me nothing better than to go to bed without supper, I asked him to repeat the message. He did so, and I muttered angrily, "*Khorosho!* Very well!"

Zetzer, happy, hurried away. I went to my room but left the door open. Almost immediately Zetzer entered, and on his heels, Rosenberg. Our glances met. Rosenberg broke into a sob, turned his face to the wall, and wept.

Although I was moved I remained outwardly cold. Zetzer had tears in his eyes. "*Gospodin* Adler!" he exclaimed, with reproach. He went no further, but the look on his face said, "Have you no heart?"

Since I still did not answer, Rosenberg began "acting." Coming to me and taking my hand he said sadly, "Yankele, you are going back to Odessa? Go in good health. If you should see my wife or my sisters, greet them for me."

I did not like this at all. Here I thought Rosenberg would fall at my feet, beg my forgiveness, and instead he was saying good-bye! I found my tongue and began to curse him. "Where am I to go, damn your soul—and with what? You scoundrel, you charlatan! You give parties, drink, enjoy yourself, spend money like water. You have not even paid me my wages! You have stolen my friends, stolen my sweetheart. And now, robbed, naked, I am to go?"

"I don't tell you to go," Rosenberg protested pathetically. "For my part you are welcome to stay!" But the mention of Sonya had given him the opening he needed. He began to pour fire and brimstone on her and all women. "Your sweetheart, did you say? Didn't you see how she threw you over, how she laughed at you? My heart bled to see it. Not once did she say a good word for you, not once defended you! You showed your love, behaved respectably, showed you could be faithful. She laughed in your face, sent you to the devil. Three hundred rubles, Yankele—two 'Katerinas'—meant more to her than all your love." And he went on and on, pouring out scorn and filth, and ended on a note of reckless gaiety, "Come, fool! Come with us to Yekaterinoslav. We are driving in covered sledges. In every village, at every inn, we will stop and have a time of it. Time enough to rot in a hole. Now let's live! We are taking the Kremenchuk musicians with us, we'll be merry all the way." He cracked an imaginary whip. "Hey—off the road! Odessans are on their way! Yakob Pavlovich Adler is on his way!"

I had only one thought. Sonya. She had thrown me over. Well and good. In Yekaterinoslav, a gay town, I would find a bride prettier than she, richer, and even better educated. I would marry her, make myself into a developed artist. And I pictured how she would burst with regret, how it would torture her. "Good!" I finally said. "I will go."

Rosenberg's face lit up with joy. Zetzer began dancing around the room. Rosenberg ran off, saying, "I will bring you money. A hundred-ruble note, Yankele, and let it be in a good hour!"

He came back with the note, which he pressed into my hand, and a red scarf, which he himself tied around my throat.

A cheer went up as we came out into the court, a joy like the joy of a great happy family going to a wedding. "Yankele is coming. Yankele is coming." The word flew from one to the other. Rosenberg could not do enough for me. He made sure my sledge was fitted out with everything needful—warm robes, brandy, hampers of food.

I was concerned only not to travel in the same sledge as Sonya. "God forbid!" he answered, and then, with a wink, "Don't worry. I have given you a better companion. Bettye Vinyavich will go with you. She will console you."

Everyone was joyful, gay, everyone making preparations. Sonya remained hidden in her sledge and did not show herself.

All was merry as we started on our journey. I alone remained dark as though on my way to a funeral. The sledges began to move. The bells rang out. The whips snapped. The snow glided under the runners of the sleighs, and from all the shops in the Jewish quarter men and women ran out to wave good-bye. "Come back, Shmendrick!" they called to us with laughter and love. "Sweet Shmendrick ours, come back soon!"

THE MIRROR ON THE WALL

I sank back in my sledge. As Rosenberg had promised, I had been provided with company in the person of little Bettye Vinyavich. Traveling with us also was her father, our *Kappelmeister* (orchestra leader), Zorach Vinyavich, who was already drawing a whole feast out of a hamper. A glass of spirits brought me a little to myself. The snowy fields and forests glided by. I thought of Sonya, so near me on the road. Between us now there was an abyss. Who knew if I would ever be near her again. There was a terrible ache in my heart.

We glided on in a deep silence. It grew darker. The movement of the sledge had already lulled Vinyavich, and he slept. Bettye gazed at me with her tender innocent girl's eyes. I caressed her hair, but my thoughts were with the other—the false one.

Morning came, and we stopped in the court of an inn along the road. I smoothed out my wrinkled clothes, put on a gay face, and went into the inn.

Traveling in a light sledge with four horses, the managers were already seated around a table on which a brass samovar was humming. Everyone looked refreshed, in high spirits. Sonya, too, seemed rested, and her delicate intelligent face had for me at that moment the seventh degree of charm.

A chorus of welcome went up as I entered, but I seated myself at a small table apart from the others, took a Russian book from my pocket, and began to read. From time to time the others tried to break the barrier, but I turned my back, and held them off. Let them suffer a little longer.

From time to time I glanced surreptitiously at Sonya. Not directly. Through a little mirror on the wall. Twice our eyes met in this mirror. After this we constantly exchanged glances, and each time her eyes lit with a fire I mistook for hatred. I misunderstood. It was not anger in her eyes, but the frightful struggle going on within her. It would have lifted the burden from my heart if I had knelt before her and kissed her hand, but I would not give in. When we left the inn we had not exchanged even a greeting.

It was a two-day journey, and the second day not as easy as the first. A bad frost delayed us. Vinyavich and I had to get out and push together through the snow.

At dusk we drove into Verach-Dneprovsk, and stopped at a *kretchma,* an inn, along the road. Hot dishes were set out for us on the big table in the main room. We ate, drank, everyone was gay and my own spirits rose. It seemed to me my love for Sonya was over. My heart no longer beat quickly when my glance fell on her. I laughed, told jokes. And remarkable! The easier I grew, the more agitated and uneasy she became. Everything she did betrayed her nervousness. She rose from the table, went into the kitchen, came out with dishes, and began serving everyone—me, with special attention. She poured raspberry juice into my tea, set whatever I lacked before me. This transformation of Sonya into a serving girl was astonishing, but I answered her attentions with cold silence and pushed away everything she set before me. She saw it well. Her face flamed, her hands trembled. She mastered herself, and with a bitter sarcastic smile, turned away. She began to laugh and talk with the others. I saw she had put me out of her mind, forgotten me.

How strange is the human being! A moment ago I had told myself she meant nothing to me. And now, because she turned away, because she ignored me, because she laughed with others, I felt my life was over and I had lost her forever.

The last day of the trip was hard for everyone, but hardest for me. Sonya had apparently forgotten I ever lived. She went off in the light sledge with Rosenberg, Spivakovsky, and Tulya Goldfaden, went off with a ringing triumphant laugh—a laugh like a death stab.

To make it worse, Bettye constantly talked of nothing but Sonya and Spivakovsky. They are always together, Bettye said. Sonya smiles on him, they laugh together, talk together. And without ceasing she gave me a hundred instances of Sonya's falseness with Spivakovsky. I could not bear to hear her, and it ended with my detesting her. She would do better to be silent, I thought. I would love her better.

I continually thought of Sonya in the sledge with Tulya Goldfaden and Spivakovsky, and the coarsest, most hateful pictures came before me. There was wild rage in my heart, a desire for revenge. Like all young men of my immoral nature, I meant to get this revenge by sinning. As soon as we got to Yekaterinoslav, I told myself I would go out into the city, I would find a brothel, and there, where so many bitter hearts find consolation, I would find mine.

We drove into Yekaterinoslav well after midnight, waking every dog in the town as we passed. It was much too late for the revenge I had planned. The whole town slept, and only Lutzki's Hotel was lit for our arrival.

Inside a whole company had gathered to meet us. Herr Lutzki, the greatest theater lover in the town, presented us to the others, all theater "patriots," some rich and influential, others simply young people eager to help in some way. All around the room were huge ovens which the servants continually fed with great bundles of straw. And though half the night was over, a long table had been set with an array of steaming dishes.

The warmth, the friendly atmosphere, meant nothing to me. The presence of Sonya stabbed me like a knife. It was torture to sit at the table. Finding an appropriate moment I withdrew, went to my room at the back of the hotel, threw myself on the bed, and, exhausted, sank into sleep.

It was not my destiny to rest that night. I had no sooner dozed off than I felt a kiss. Waking, I saw Sonya bending over me. There was a smile on her face, and she was calling my name in a low and loving voice.

My first impression was that it must be a dream. But the image did not disappear. It was really she bending over me, and I saw that her eyes were wet.

Perhaps I wanted to play the proud knight, or it may be that I did not take thought of what I was doing. Whatever the reason, I pushed her away with a gesture of contempt and said, "Leave me! I no longer know you!"

"Listen to me, Yashenka," Sonya said, trying to explain. "Listen, and you will understand everything."

But I was not to be moved, and from my heart tore out the hateful words, "Away from me, slut!"

It was as though a storm burst. Sonya's face flamed. Her eyes grew bloodshot and seemed to start from her head. "I a slut—I?" she stammered. I saw her hand go up, and then felt a stinging slap. Having avenged herself, Sonya fell into a chair and went into hysterics. And so violent was the outbreak of this controlled woman that it roused half the hotel. Frightened people appeared on the stair, asking each other what had happened.

Oberlander was the first to rush into the room. Seeing the state of his sister, he sprang at me like a tiger, crying, "What have you done to her?" Spivakovsky followed, exclaiming, "She came to reconcile, and this is how it ends!"

Only then did I realize what I had done. "Sonya," I stammered, "Sonya, forgive me!" But there was no longer anyone to hear my words. Sonya had gone into convulsions. Alternately weeping and laughing, she was carried up the stairs to her room.

I remained where I was, feeling terrible remorse. I had trampled the feelings of a gentle soul, and my coarseness lowered me in my own eyes.

From above I could still hear Sonya's hysterical cries. Oberlander, with bitter reproach, now told me a very different story than the one I had heard from Rosenberg. Sonya, said Oberlander, had all this time played a double game.

The managers, Oberlander said, wanted Sonya, but not me. Sonya pretended to go along with them, made them believe all would be as they wished. Her strategy was to put them at their ease, make them trust her. Then in Yekaterinoslav, a town too distant for them to get an actor to replace me, she would work things out so that I got back my position in the company. This was what she tried to tell me when I so brutally drove her away.

I paced the room when Oberlander left. Sleep was impossible. I left the hotel. It was almost daylight now, only the last few lamps still burning on the streets. There was not a soul to be seen but a heavily coated *gardavoy* ending his nightly rounds. Once a merry party drove past in a sled, singing a last hoarse song and emptying the last drops of whiskey from their flasks. I crossed a square, came to Lutzki's theater, saw my name large on the posters, and in the midst of my great sorrow, rejoiced.

The sky grew lighter. Around the marketplace great wagons began rolling in, bringing produce from the country. Huge gray dogs sat on top of the wagons, protecting them. From every side church bells began to ring, calling good Christians to morning Mass.

I went back to the hotel. The night porter was wakened by my footsteps and, kind man, brought me tea and a bagel. I drank the tea, read the Russian papers, and reading, dozed off.

I awoke in full morning, the hotel buzzing with activity. Tulya Goldfaden and Rosenberg were both seated in armchairs opposite me. "So it's peace, eh?" Rosenberg said with a bestial smile. "Fool that you are, I wanted to save you from the woman."

His words were like a poisoned stab. I made no answer. I loathed him. Hearing Spivakovsky's voice on the stair I got up and went to my room. To see him now? The intriguer who had tried to rob me of Sonya, rob me of my place in the troupe? No, that would be too much!

I lay on my bed, thinking. How much trouble and shame I would have spared myself if in my young arrogance I had not insulted her! I decided on a letter. It must be in Russian, of course, but how to address her. My dearest? Not right. Best beloved? Also wrong. I wrote and tore, wrote and tore. But suddenly a thought. Suppose her brother had lied? If Sonya truly loved me would she not have found a way to tell me so in those terrible days of my ordeal? Why tie my fate to her? Should I not make use of this quarrel to finish with her for good?

"To the devil with it!" I suddenly said aloud. "It's now or never!" And without giving myself time to think I went to Sonya's room with gritted teeth and clenched fists and knocked at her door.

"*Vykhoditye*—come in," Sonya called in her ringing voice. I pushed open the door and remained, with a classically foolish face, on the threshold. The room was full of people. Her brother, Rosenberg, Spivakovsky, and two people I did not know. A gentleman holding out a box of diamonds for Sonya's inspection, and a gallant young man in a military coat.

Sonya saw my predicament, but remaining cool, presented me to the two strangers, a Dr. Kollomayetzov and a Herr Granovsky. I mumbled out my respects, inwardly cursing the lot of them. Under cover of the polite talk Rosenberg told me pleasantly that I was to play the lover that night. I said coldly, "Spivakovsky is here. Let him play it."

"Why Spivakovsky?" Rosenberg said, taken aback.

"Because that is what I prefer."

Even though my name was on the poster I was as angry as seven devils, and it was my caprice to refuse.

Spivakovsky, always clever, sensed the possibility of a scandal. He rose and withdrew.

My angry reply had put an end to Rosenberg's lighthearted mood. With a more sober face he also left.

The conversation began to languish. Herr Granovsky realized this was not the moment to sell his diamonds, and gathering them up, made his farewells. Even the elegant young doctor finally understood he was in the way. Declaring we would meet that night in the theater, he, too, bent over Sonya's hand and was gone.

As soon as the door was closed with nobody there but her brother, Sonya threw herself on my neck and began to sob. In a tumult of feeling Alexander Oberlander exclaimed, "Then go to her, in the devil's name!" and ran out of the room.

It was as though a mountain of ice melted in my heart. I clasped her in my arms, pressed her, shouted something, mumbled something, talked whatever came into my head, acting, yet not acting. Tears poured from my eyes, and the more I wept, the easier and happier grew my heart. Sonya the whole time caressed my hair, kissed me, and never stopped murmuring, "*Mili,* dear, Yashenka—you suffered, yes? You didn't understand. If not for what I did they would have parted us."

Now she told me the story I had heard from her brother, but told it so I could have no more doubts.

To leave the troupe, Sonya explained, was impossible because of the need of her parents. To leave me—their wish—was also out of the question. And so she was forced to play a role. She tried to catch my eye, to signal me in some way, but I was like a wolf, she said, buried in my pride. To approach me, even to send me a letter, was too full of danger. If I knew the true facts I would be so angry it would be impossible to control me. There was only one way, to pretend she cared nothing for me, and even hated me.

Spivakovsky wanted to marry her and make her one of the managers. She pretended to agree even with this. But once the managers were convinced of her indifference to me, she continually argued that I was an experienced actor whom they would not easily replace, and should absolutely be taken back into the troupe. And she persevered in this until she got her way.

There was nothing but truth in her beautiful eyes, a truth that could not be mistaken. I begged her forgiveness. I swore that never again would any misunderstanding arise between us. To make sure of it I proposed that we wait no longer, but immediately sign the marriage contract. Happy as a child, she agreed.

Wild with happiness, we decided to spend the day together. "No more 'Sonya'!" I cried in my enchantment. "My bride!" "No more

'Yakob'!" she answered in the same tone. "My husband!" I helped her on with her cloak, her furs. We entered the warm sledge. I held her close in my arms, and with the gay ringing of sleigh bells, we drove together through Yekaterinoslav.

That night the sidewalks outside the theater were thick with people, the theater corridor was crowded, and our cashier was sweating hard. The parterre was already sold out, always the sign of a good town.

Backstage a chorus of *Mazel tov*'s rang out. The last to greet me was Yankele Katzman. I gave him my hand, reading in his eyes that he repented and was happy in my happiness.

The performance that night was carried through with spirit. Sonya and I, especially, played "with fire." When Sonya sang, "Dear one—beloved—" and pressed me to her heart, many in the audience noticed we were inspired by more than a stage love. When the curtain fell we both received ovations. Flowers were sent up to the stage, among them a bouquet from Spivakovsky with one word on the card—"Forgive!" This moved me so that after the performance I called the whole troupe onto the stage and embraced them all, Spivakovsky included. How does one say? If it is to be peace, let it be peace with all.

The whole troupe celebrated afterward, and that night Sonya and I signed the marriage agreement. Telegrams came from both our families. Happier than Oberlander was only one person, the bridegroom himself, who, as hero of the occasion, celebrated and danced less like a groom than like a wild being half out of his senses with joy.

Soon after our engagement in Yekaterinoslav the troupe left for Poltava. In that city we did so well that Tulya Goldfaden urged us to delay no further, but to marry. He was, of course, thinking less of our happiness than of the interest such an event would excite in the theater world.

Couples were often married on the stage in our theater, the ceremony sometimes even woven into the play itself. Tulya did not propose anything as crass as that, but wanted to invite some of the city's important people to the wedding. But there Sonya put her foot down. "Yakob and I will play no comedy on our wedding day!" she said. And from this she would not budge. She agreed to marry in Vassilyevsky's hall, where we played, but insisted nobody be present but the actors and our close friends.

As the day drew near I grew more and more gloomy. I did not want to marry without my parents, but did not say so for fear the others would laugh at me. I went about melancholy, lost, and looked at everyone with helpless eyes as if to say, "It is fated—do with me as you will."

It was not that my love for Sonya had changed. Just the opposite. It was something deeper and more tragic, a matter of conscience. I feared the serious step I was taking. I felt the proud, pure girl deserved a better fate than to be my wife. I saw it all, my reckless past, my wild adventures and wild loves, the sordid recklessness of the life I had lived.

The day before the wedding I decided there was only one way. I must tell Sonya everything. Then let her do as she judged best.

I went to her room with a trembling heart. She had laid out her wedding dress on the bed, and the sight of it was agony. I poured out everything, leaving nothing out, not even the worst nights. I called in her brother as my witness. I told them both I had a bad heart and would not live long. I believed this myself.

The clever, strong Sonya laughed at the whole thing. The sins I had committed did not frighten her, the filth I spoke of did not touch her with the lightest stain. My bad heart also made no impression. She took it all with a laugh and her usual "*Nis trashno!* Not so terrible! I have studied you well, Yakob," she said. "I know you, and I know your heart is mine. If it is sick, we will cure it. As for your sins, your confession will be my guarantee." She caressed my cheeks. "Never mind, Yasha," she went on with a touch of sadness. "You will forget all that. You will make yourself into a fine man, and you will be a great artist." And with a change of mood, she suddenly threw me backward on the bed, and with a hysterical laugh, wrapped me in the dress.

News of the wedding soon traveled over all Poltava. When the day came a gendarme had to be posted at the door of Vassilyevsky's hall, the theater was so jammed with "witnesses."

I went about in a trance. I don't remember how I got to the theater. Somebody led me, took me, sat me down. I felt like a ghost that had nothing to do with the living world. I knew I was in a frock coat, that I arrived in a carriage, that as I arrived another carriage drove up, that a little door opened, and that a slender woman in a white dress and a white veil alighted and disappeared into the hall.

Somebody led me onto the stage. I saw people, saw the wedding canopy. I was told to come in on my right foot. I came in on my left foot. I broke into a loud sob as I was led under the canopy. They circled me seven times. I said what was needful, broke the glass. And through the whole ceremony I wept.

Sonya kept whispering, asking me what was wrong. I did not know myself. I knew only that if my father and mother had been there, if Uncle Arke and Aunt Hanna and the little sister had been there, my heart would not have been so heavy.

The wedding was over. A feast followed. That too at last was over. Like something bewitched in a fairy tale, the wedding hall was once again a theater, the platform once again a stage, and Sonya and myself again two lovers in a play.

The performance was our wedding gift—that is, the profit was ours. The Poltava theatergoers, knowing this, had packed the theater in a holiday mood, and money flowed from every side.

The whole troupe was in a state of joy. Rosenberg in his comedy role kept putting in improvised jokes about the bride and groom. Spivakovsky danced with his new Dulcinea, Charlotta Spinner. Zorach Vinyavich led the orchestra heroically. Little Bettye kissed Sonya and smiled. The whole troupe rejoiced. Happiest of all were Oberlander and Tulya Goldfaden, who danced behind the scenes with linked hands.

And as in a dream I realized it was done. Sonya and I were joined forever—man and wife.

YIDDISH THEATER IN THE *PROVINTZ*

We did well in Poltava, but immediately after our marriage the police turned hostile, and we could not play. Rather than take a chance in another city, Rosenberg decided on a tour of the *shtetlach*—little Jewish towns and villages far from the central authorities and relatively safe.

Sonya and I spent the first week of our honeymoon in the town of Kabalyak. A dreary place. A call to prayers at five every morning, the Jewish streets steeped in mud, the faces gloomy. We lost money there and went on to Smila in the government district of Kiev. Smila, however, was not Kabalyak. A whole epoch of Yiddish theater is bound up with Smila, as you will see.

We got there on the eve of Rosh Hashonah. Every fish was shivering in the water, and every Jew shivering in the synagogue. But how does the saying go? If it is narrow, one must squeeze. Since there was not even a hall in the town, we set up our stage in a garden—better said, in an open space between trees.

As luck would have it, it rained all through the first performance. It rained on the stage, and on the audience. The wind howled like ten thousand cats. Yellow leaves flew in our faces and into our beards. But the Jews came. All Smila came to see *Shmendrick*. They came in their long coats and under umbrellas. They laughed, they roared, they stamped their feet, and to us actors, Smila was a big town!

In the midst of this success an order from Goldfaden. The whole troupe was to return to Odessa to play at the Mariinsky Theater. Sonya and I were overjoyed. We will be in our beloved Odessa, play in the world-famous Mariinsky! Our parents will rejoice with us in our marriage. To say nothing of our new honor and fame! For remember, we had been nothing when we left—mere beginners, and hardly that.

We were returning as experienced actors with a slew of roles already played. The whole prospect seemed dazzling.

All this changed when Rosenberg began taking apart the situation. Rosenberg had good reason to distrust Goldfaden. Experiences in Romania were burned into his memory. He had other fears too. An emperor in the provinces, in Odessa he would compete with comedians like Zuckerman and Moishe Teich. He had only one hope—to organize a rebellion.

He began with me and Sonya. "Money you must have, no?" he said. "But Goldfaden does not like to pay. You think you will make more with him? You will make less! As for roles, parts, forget such ideas. Your roles, Adler, he will give to Spivakovsky, Sonya's will go to his Odessa favorites."

Seeing we were listening very seriously, Rosenberg pressed on. "Goldfaden has put Tulya at our head, given him all power here. But what do we need Tulya for? Does he play? Does he help? He is nothing but a burden on us. Let him go to his brother in Odessa. For our part we will go on to Rostov, Kharkov, Kiev—why not Petersburg? Who can tell in these times?"

Sonya and I saw a great vista opening before us. We decided we must speak to Tulya, and speak plainly.

The talk took place soon after. Tulya entered, seated himself, but remained silent. At last, trying an old joke, I said, "An angel is flying overhead." The silence broken, the following exchange took place.

TULYA: All must go.

ROSENBERG: This is not Romania. Here we are not paid in fish scales. Here we are used to taking in thousands of rubles.

ADLER: How much money did he send, and how much will Sonya and I be paid?

TULYA: He sent no money. All must go.

SONYA (*hotly*): Not I. And not Yakob! What is this? Maybe in Romania things were done this way. In Russia one comes to artists with an advance, with contracts. This way? With nothing? No one is going!

TULYA (*woodenly*): All must go.

It was his last word. He left for Odessa that night.

Most of the troupe left with him. We were like survivors after a fire. Fishkind was the only real actor we had. Rosenberg had held him with the role of Hotzmach in *The Witch.* He also hid his coat.

We remained with the mere skeleton of a troupe. Oberlander was only half an actor, since as a rule he traveled ahead of us. What to do? We had no father in this play, no mother in that. Even for *The Two Kuni Lemels* we needed a girl who could sing. Where to find one? Rosenberg, with all this on his mind, walked the streets of Smila begging God to send him a prima donna.

God, who listened to the prayers of Abraham, did not forsake Rosenberg. Passing along the street he heard a girl singing at a window, the song a mixture of Russian and Yiddish, the voice strong, fresh, fiery. He stood listening with an open mouth, and then turned into the house.

Why draw out the story? He brought us the happy news that he had found a prima donna. Sure enough, she appeared next morning. We looked her over, heard her sing, and knew immediately that Rosenberg had made no mistake. A devil of a girl, young, full of temperament. A strong fresh voice, good diction. Just as she stood, you could put her on the stage!

She went on that night in the role of Carlina, sang a little, played a little, and so got through her baptism of fire. Rosenberg had cut her part to almost nothing. Not wanting to use her own name, she was billed as Keni Sonyes—a little later, as Keni Liptzin. Yes, my friends! The same Keni Liptzin who today is one of our greatest stars. It was in Smila that Rosenberg discovered her, and that her career began.

With two actresses we felt we had a troupe again. Rosenberg was as happy as a boy, and with new courage, we moved on.

We played next in Spolya. This town belonged to the famous Count Abaza, none other than the minister of the tsar's possessions. We were a little nervous, since the great man was at that moment vacationing there. But things turned out well. The count's steward, a Jew named Charnivolsky, had the management of the entire town in his hands. We were met at the station by a pair of his carriages, and an invitation to stay with him throughout our visit. You may be sure we did not refuse.

Charnivolsky, we soon discovered, lived in a small palace, and the man himself had me in his spell from his warm *"Sholem aleichem."* He had seen us play in Poltava, and he praised the whole troupe, who he said were bringing enlightenment to the people.

Spolya had no theater, no club, not even a hall. Oberlander, our advance man, had felt there was no possibility at all. It was Charnivolsky who had persuaded him to stay, assuring him we would have everything we needed.

He was as good as his word. He had cleared out a storehouse, built us a stage with a rich curtain, laid carpets on the floor, hung mirrors on the walls, placed lusters and candelabra everywhere, and created a marvelous hall. Furniture was brought from the minister's own home, a splendid velvet couch for the count and his family, another for his own.

In this wonderful setting we played *Breindele Cossack,* and all Spolya turned out to see us. Count Abaza sat in the first row with his children, all in white with fur mantles. Charnivolsky, with his wife and children, sat in the second row. The orchestra struck up a rousing overture, and the play began.

You would have to see it to believe the joy, the enthusiasm. Jew and non-Jew, simple folk and cultivated connoisseurs, all applauded with shouts of "Bravo!" After every act Abaza himself came backstage with compliments for me, for Sonya, and for Rosenberg, who created a real furor that night in the role of Yankel Schweig (Yankel Say-Nothing). The catchword "Yankel Schweig" was on all lips, and the audience left, still laughing. The minister and his family were pleased, and we had a hint from Charnivolsky that if we went to Petersburg, the count would put in a good word for us in the very highest circles.

The presence of this minister at a Yiddish performance, as well as the wide authority he gave his Jewish steward, reflect the liberal tendency of Alexander's Russia even during times of reaction.

One of the outstanding liberals of the day, Abaza gained a dominant influence in the 1880s, but his attempt to bring about a constitutional monarchy was cut short by the tsar's assassination in 1881.

Novomirgorod. Why is this town like no other to me? The very name brings to mind something beautiful, white, pure as childhood—more than this, the consciousness of something great, something that transformed my life and elevated it.

In this town a gathering took place at the home of one Dovid Liebovitzky. All the intelligentsia were there, and one felt immediately the Russianized spirit. Our troupe, however, were for the most part simple Jews who spoke no Russian, and of Russian intellectual life had no notion at all. At last someone proposed that we speak Yiddish. This was accepted with such a cry of *"Razgavo!* Yiddish!" that it was a pleasure to hear.

Present on that occasion was a young *gymnazistka* called Itta, a girl with beautiful eyes and the seventh degree of charm. This girl persuaded me, against my will, to sing Goldfaden's "Arise, My People." Because of her eyes I melted and gave the song.

I might have forgotten that long-ago afternoon, but years later the writer Herr Gershoy, Jacob Gordin's intimate friend, told me, in Gordin's presence, that he had been among the guests that day. And he reminded me of the young *gymnazistka,* and how, to please her, I sang the famous song.

As we talked, recalling Novomirgorod, a deep sigh came from Gordin's breast, and his eyes filled with tears. Though I did not know it, we were speaking of his birthplace.

Since then, whenever that name is uttered, two images rise as if out of a deep chasm. I see the church, the marketplace, the beautiful Itta—God knows where she is now. And clearer, more full of light than all, I see the great departed playwright, his majestic face sad, his wonderful compelling eyes full of tears.

"If I forget thee, O Novomirgorod!"

We moved on through the vast Russian countryside. Spolya, Zlatapolya, Novomirgorod, Bogoslav—little lost hamlets where Jews sometimes lived out their lives knowing nothing of the world but what they heard from some traveling *maggid.* The people were small-town types, fascinating, unforgettable. In some of these villages the coming of actors was the greatest event anyone could remember.

No railroad lines passed through these regions and we had to travel from town to town in wagons. I remember well the long rocky road in the oxen wagon with the actors, the *Komediantchikis.* When it rained great puddles formed in the road, and the jolting numbed the very soul.

But we had marvelous days. Fall days in the Ukraine, a many-colored, ever-changing panorama. On one side blackish forests. On the other gold wheat fields. Now and then tobacco fields, their saffron leaves shimmering in the sun. And everywhere orchards, the wonderful orchards of the Ukraine. Red apples, golden pears, blue plums, red grapes, watermelons—the small, blue, round, delicious watermelons of the south. We used to get out of the wagon just to drink it all in, wondering at God's gifts.

In Zlatapolya we had not even a tavern where we could play. We had to put on our performances in the stable of an inn, but a stable as large as a city street with gates at both ends. Here one Semyon Semyonov, a peasant carpenter, built us the stage on which we played. But "play" is not the word for it. For no troupe in the world ever played as we played in Zlatapolya! Our theater there cannot be compared even to the ancient amphitheater, for there they had an audience only on one side while we also had an audience overhead—and an audience not only of human beings, but of poultry, roosters, hens!

The roof of the stable was loosely clapped together and very old, with plentiful holes and cracks between the slats. Well, these Zlatapolya folk, who either knew nothing of tickets or had no money to buy them, stole up to this roof. There, by looking down through the cracks, they could see the play. Since this was also the hen roost, they had a whole collection of fowl as their neighbors.

And so, standing onstage, the hero, looking upward at the heavens, sang sentimentally and with feeling the famous "Birds in the heavens, tell me I pray, where is my beloved?" But instead of the off-stage singing of the birds, I was answered with a cackling, a quacking. Looking up I saw hens and roosters, peaceful and philosophical, and beside them faces—beards. The sight enraged me. Murderers! For nothing do they want our blood? Instead of the song I sent aloft a curse and the query, "You up there! Are you too sick to buy tickets?" My anger was in vain. I saw clearly if I made one move against them there would be such a cackling and crowing I would have to run for my life. What could I do? I remained silent, and to my relief the cackling quieted down. But not for long. As the song ended and applause broke out, the chickens lost their philosophical indifference and began fluttering, flying, and making such an outcry, we thought the roof would cave in and bury us all. We went on with the play, but the worst was yet to come. At the most intense moment, with the Witch about to work her fearful magic, at that exact moment evening fell, and the birds began such a "kukerikoo" that the clamor went over the whole theater, making an effect no opera could duplicate or wish for.

If it had been any other audience we might have saved the situation, but everyone in Zlatapolya knew about the hen roost. A laugh went up. A laugh, did I say? A howl. Nothing helped. No dramatics, no music from the orchestra—the performance ended in hooting and howling. To this day when any of us meets a friend or a landsman from Zlatapolya, we are not greeted with "*Sholem aleichem,*" or "God save," as is proper among Jews, but with "Kukerikoo" and "Bababa!"

Somewhere along our tour we lost Alexander Oberlander. He had gone ahead to Brest Litovsk, but could not get a theater there because it was Lent. We had no word for weeks, but finally a letter came from the town of Brisk. Oberlander was settled in Brisk not only for the season, but for life. He had met the Masha he was going to marry, and the troupe saw him no more. We had lost our advance man, an important part of our company. But we rejoiced in his happiness. Heaven sent help in the form of one Cheikel Bain. This little Odessa businessman, with a stammer and a bad asthmatic cough, was none other than one of the two Goldstein brothers who had once given me a first leg up in the world. Cheikel had given up the textile business for the new and lucrative Yiddish theater. He came into our company now as our manager, advance agent, and general good angel.

To avoid army service the Goldstein brothers had apparently sought out two men of the same family who were willing, for a sum of money, to take their place. Since this was done by an exchange of names, they were no longer the Goldstein brothers, but Cheikel and Laibel Bain.

The buying of "substitutes" was not allowed under Alexander II's reign, but the practice was in time resumed.

With Cheikel as our new entrepreneur, we went on to Pereyaslav in the district of Kiev. The same Pereyaslav where our radiant, our great Sholem Aleichem first saw the beautiful day.

The days in Pereyaslav are among the happiest I can remember.

Why? I do not know. It was a town much like the others. Churches. Small houses. Gardens covered with snow. The Jews affable, friendly. The older people would gather around us, asking if truly there were wagons that went without horses. When we told them the locomotives ran on the power of steam they were struck with awe at "God's wonders"!

Our great friend in Pereyaslav was the postmaster, Herr Aaronson. This was a magnate in the true sense of the word. Tall, handsome, a strong, fine figure, a blond beard barely silvered with gray, a soft voice, an aristocratic yet cordial manner. Aaronson had great influence with the liberal governor-general of Kiev. In fact it was through him we were permitted to play.

Although the theater in Pereyaslav was small, it was a real theater, and we had full houses night after night. The audience was simple, naïve. There was no criticism, no assessment of our worth, but in no other town did we have such respect as in Pereyaslav. Jews took off their hats when we passed in the street. When we protested that we were in no way above them, they answered with great seriousness, "Don't say that! If you can show such things, Jewish children that you are, every honor is due you!"

"Yashenka," Sonya said, impressed, "we are teaching people, educating them."

Our stay in Pereyaslav was a quiet and happy one. The respect of the townsfolk and our friendship with Aaronson gave us a sense of worth. There was a feeling of peace, a quiet happiness. We forgot we were living in Russia. A hateful incident was to wake us from our dreams.

Like all Russian towns Pereyaslav had an *ispravnik*—a head constable. Naturally we had to deal with this man, for where is there a person in Russia who has no dealings with the police? We had to have his permission to play, and could not even put up our posters without his signature.

Well, this coarse officer used to walk into the theater in the middle of the performance, jingling his spurs and making a racket with his companions and underlings. He did not seat himself as others did, but stood waiting for me to make my entrance. As soon as I appeared he would call out in a loud voice, "Very good! Fine! I like it." And turning to the audience he would bawl out, "So, Jews, you like it? Is it good?" Turning to the stage again he would shout, "Bring the posters, Adler. Don't be afraid. I will sign them." I was apparently his favorite and was always sent to his office for the signature. Apparently this swinish individual felt he was doing us a great favor by his behavior in the theater.

One day we were sitting at cards; the door opened and a policeman walked in, a man who stood guard in the *ispravnik*'s office. We knew at once there would be trouble. The man was drunk and looked insolently at the women. Coming up to our table he said roughly, "Who is the boss here?" a question we heard with a shock at the heart. The actors pointed to Rosenberg, but he, always a coward in these situations, murmured under his breath, "Not me. Let Yankele answer."

I asked the man what he wanted, and he disclosed the reason for his visit. His *barin,* his lord, is giving a party that night. He wants us to send two of our women, the youngest and prettiest we have. Apparently this official of Alexander II took us for white slavers, and our theater for a traveling bordello!

My knees gave way under me, and I had to catch at the wall so as not to fall. All the blood in my body rushed to my head. I shouted in a voice I did not know—the voice of a man calling out of a nightmare, "Tell your master he is an ignoramus and a lout."

Hearing this, the policeman left the hotel. Nobody spoke, and I also said nothing. The blood was boiling in my veins. We played no more that night, our gaiety was as though wiped away with a sweep of a hand. We separated in silence, each to his own bed.

Next morning the posters had to be signed, and as always, it was I who had to bring them. I found the *ispravnik* lolling about in his office, his messenger of the night before also present. The *ispravnik* glanced at me indifferently and said to his man, "Why didn't you use your stick on him?" Turning back to me he said deliberately, "Do you think we don't know that your theater is a blind, and your real business is with Jewish prostitutes?" And he said, to my face, that he had seen Sonya in a Kiev bordello.

With this everything seemed to sway before my eyes. My head grew so hot that my hair seemed to be on fire, and my eyes were starting from their sockets. I saw before me the Moldovanka in Odessa, saw "Yankele Kulachnik" standing ready for battle, and I lunged toward the *ispravnik* with a fist raised to kill. Startled, he ran into his private office and locked the door. The frightened clerks advised me in whispers to get help from the postmaster, Aaronson.

I ran back through the streets like a madman and did not stop until I got to the inn. Falling into a chair, I told the others what had happened. In consternation they ran to find the postmaster. Aaronson was with us in minutes. He listened, grew red with anger, and exclaimed, "To the governor, I will take the *ispravnik* to court. He will remember me!"

Not a half hour had passed before the *ispravnik,* in a pitiable state, ran into the hall, stammering, "Alexander Isakovich! You are telegraphing the governor?" They withdrew to another room, and we heard Aaronson's angry words: "You have insulted artists! You will pay for it!" After more words which we could not make out, Aaronson called me in. Before I had crossed the threshold the *ispravnik* caught my hand and stammered out, "*Prostitye!* Forgive me!" With this he crept out and was gone. And for a long time his terrified, despairing voice did not stop ringing in my ears.

Cheikel Bain stammered out, "To l-l-ive through such things!" Rosenberg clasped his head in his hands and wept like a child.

We were no sooner finished with the *ispravnik* than a telegram came from Goldfaden demanding a thousand rubles in royalties and threatening us with the authorities if we performed his plays without paying him. Since we had no other plays, this meant we could not perform at all. We were really frightened, for if Goldfaden carried out his threat we knew the *ispravnik* could take his revenge!

Someone had to go to Kiev and talk to Goldfaden. Since Rosenberg refused this commission, it fell to me. And since Goldfaden was known to be partial to beautiful women, Sonya came with me.

We traveled by the postmaster's diligence, a closed carriage with two fiery horses. At our first stop we were joined by a Russian officer, an affable man who readily fell into conversation with us. Finding that Sonya spoke French, he soon passed over into that tongue while I, being weak in the language of Boulanger, nodded off and dozed. I woke with a start to hear a terrible snorting of horses and the cry of "*Volpi! Volpi!* Wolves!"

I started up, and moved by an overpowering curiosity, leaned out the carriage window. Where were they, then, the wolves? I saw only a pack of dogs circling around us with open jaws and glittering little eyes. "My gun! My gun! Away!" the officer cried. The coachman whipped up his horses, and as we all gave a great shout, he drove straight through the pack. They turned off, scattered. Then I saw they were no dogs. They were thin as rails, their eyes shot red sparks, the fur on some of their backs was half torn off, hanging in strips. They had let us through, but their glittering eyes never left us.

For years after, when I cried out in my sleep Sonya would wake me, whispering, "What is it Yacob? The wolves again?"

After three days of travel we arrived in Kiev. This is a city divided in two. On one side live the Gentiles, on the other, the Jews. Some of these are shop owners, prosperous and doing well, others desperately poor. How is it they live in this holy city where Jews are not allowed? "They pay," was the answer.

We found Goldfaden at his hotel. He was unchanged—the same aristocratic appearance, the same handsome face. He greeted us courteously, was hospitable in his manner and welcomed us to his table, where we met his sister Zhenya. And I saw once again that marvel that had so bewitched me in Odessa, that even now made me forget my wife, forget Goldfaden, forget the terrible situation of our troupe—forget the whole purpose for which I had come.

Zhenya was famous as the most beautiful Jewish girl in Russia. Such a glorious apparition God can create only once. A body and face white as alabaster, full eyes of a dark lustrous brown, pure pearly little teeth, a proud little golden head, rounded shoulders, a symmetrical breast, and a smile, a manner, like that of a princess. The beauty had one defect, known only to those closest to her. The heavenly Zhenya had no eyebrows—not even a sign of them. Taking a hint from the actors, she drew them in with burnt out matches, so that to the unaccustomed eye their absence was not observed.

I sat through the breakfast like a man bewitched, but coming to myself, I opened up the matter on which I had come.

In one moment the friendliness, the *politesse,* vanished as though it had never been. Goldfaden jumped as though a snake had bitten him. I heard a torrent of dark angry words. "Don't talk to me of business!" he shouted. "You will have no business. Robbers that you are! I sit here tormenting myself for a livelihood while you laugh and stuff yourselves with money?" Never had I seen him so wild, so angered. I would never have imagined that he, the man I looked up to with such reverence, could show such a frightful rage. I listened to him like a man who is being beaten. But even in my defeated state I felt that such insult and anger we did not deserve.

"Pan Goldfaden," I began, "we love and revere you, but you do us an injustice. I admit that in fifteen days out of the month we have our fill of food. But the other fifteen—either we fast or fall into debt to restaurateurs who pursue us from town to town."

Goldfaden did not even hear me. His eyes now fell on Sonya—on the watch and medallion on her breast, the bracelets on her wrist, the rings on her fingers. They were set with stones that were truly not very costly, but once again anger rushed to his aristocratic face. "And these?" he demanded. "Where have these jewels come from? From my work, my talent, my plays!"

"You are wrong, Herr Goldfaden," Sonya said agitatedly. "You are wrong. These are presents given to me by people who admired my playing and wished to give me some pleasure in return."

"They are mine just the same!" Goldfaden exclaimed, a little more restrained, but still angry enough. "It is because of my work that you have them. My wife should wear them, not you. My sister, a marriageable girl, should wear them!"

Sonya was silent, very pale. Then, quietly, she took off the bracelets, the rings, even the medallion from her breast. "You are right, Herr Goldfaden," she said in a low voice. "They belong to you. I owe them to your work, your talent, your plays."

Goldfaden was moved. "You, Adler, you and Rosenberg are my children," he said in quieter tones. "For you I am willing to suffer wrong. But who is this Cheikel Bain? What have I to do with him, or with these coarse folksingers who live from my suffering, my labor?" But Sonya's words had softened him, and little by little he resumed his role of elegant cavalier. He complimented Sonya on her beauty and tact, and gave me a brotherly wink as if to say I had caught myself a truly charming wife. He expressed regret that he had not been at our wedding, and said he would make up for it now. Inscribing a photograph of himself with the words, "Wishing you a long and happy life," he signed it and, with a flourish, gave it to Sonya.

"And here I have a telegram with good news for you," he said gaily. "Your troupe has left Pereyaslav and is on the way to Chernigov, where they have a permit to play. Go! Make money! I will come to Chernigov and have a reckoning with your stammering entrepreneur."

Later, as we were taking our departure, Goldfaden told us a secret. He was taking his troupe to Petersburg! "And if you are good children," he said with a smile, "I will take you with me."

This, for us, was like a bolt of lightning. To play in Petersburg!

The Mother of Russia, the city of cities! We were still in a dream as we left him. But we could not help a last look to where Sonya's poor jewels still lay in a little heap, sadly twinkling away.

Soon after our return, with God's help, we left Pereyaslav for Chernigov. Cheikel had at last gotten a permit for us there. We breathed a sigh of relief. We were out of the provinces at last.

THE TROUPE BREAKS UP:
DESTINY TAKES A HAND

We shared the theater in Chernigov with a Russian company. Unlike the actors in Kishinev, there was no resentment on the part of the Russian artists, even when our performances robbed them of part of their audience. Their impresario, Cherkassov, assured us we would do well, and promised to bring the governor to one of our plays. "My theater is supported by Jews," Cherkassov told us. "Yiddish theater is a phenomenon, a remarkable development."

Business in Chernigov was middling. As they say in the provinces, bread there was, but without a spoon. But rather than drag ourselves to other towns with who knows what luck, we stayed where we were.

As usual at such times, we passed the time in parties and amusements. And it was simply as one of these amusements that Sonya and I appeared on the Russian stage. Cherkassov had arranged this; he wanted to take us away from Rosenberg and make us into Russian actors. His troupe was giving an evening in his honor, the classic Pushkin drama, *Boris Godounov.* Cherkassov drew us into this performance as a test.

We were thrilled by the challenge. The rehearsals went well, and Cherkassov put up posters everywhere reading, "For the First Time the Famous Adlers in Russian!"

All the Jews in the town came to the performance, and as Cherkassov had hoped, he had a packed house. The play went beautifully, and after the third act Cherkassov took us out before the curtain and presented us to the public as "two great Russian artists." Over the storm of applause, we heard one voice. Cheikel Bain had risen out of his seat, shouting, "Over my d-d-dead body!"

The actors were divided about Cherkassov's offer, and the whole company cooked like a kettle. Some thought we should accept, others were against it. It was Sonya who made the final decision. "We are pioneers of the Yiddish theater!" she said to me. "As long as Jews are happy to see us, we must be the standard bearer of Yiddish art."

The actors were proud of our decision, and our life together became closer and more loving than ever before.

One day as we sat around the table, intimately chatting and jesting, Goldfaden fell in on us. We sprang up and greeted our "rabbi" with a glad "Hurrah!" Only Cheikel Bain looked gloomy and, aside to me, muttered, "Not for any good has he come."

He was right. As soon as Goldfaden seated himself he launched into a tirade against the troupe, who he said lived by exploiting his labor and talent. "You eat, drink, and make parties," he exclaimed wrathfully. "And *torsky*? Royalties? Don't tell me your business is bad. If it were ten times worse something should still be set aside for the creator, the composer to whom you owe everything! Why speak only of creating, composing? Have you forgotten what it is to play Yiddish theater in Russia? Have you forgotten the money I must find, the bribes for every official down to the pettiest? All this you take for granted? You know very well you are living on what is mine, on my money!"

I must confess I felt very bad hearing Goldfaden's bitter words. It seemed to me he was too hard, too severe, that he asked too much of the poor devils who sat there so beaten, so punished. But many years have passed since that day and I have since then filled many roles in the theater, not only that of first artist, but also that of director and, yes, entrepreneur. And what our troupe did to Goldfaden many actors have since done to me. I have my own bitter complaints very similar to his, and I see the matter differently than I did that day.

But to return to Chernigov. Little by little Goldfaden quieted down, satisfied with the effect of his anger. But since he still did not want to make friends, he began to torment Cheikel Bain. This he did with a jest, but the kind of jest that destroys. As it happened, Cheikel had large ears. Goldfaden amused himself by making fun of them. "Where could he have gotten such ears?" he asked me in a whisper heard by all. "Did he bring them with him? Could he have grown them here in the Yiddish theater?"

I tried to tell him that aside from his ears Cheikel was the best of men, the most goodhearted, that he had put much of his own money into the troupe. "I don't deny it," Goldfaden answered, "but tell the truth, Adler, how does a Jew allow himself to wear such ears?"

Poor Cheikel. At times Goldfaden seemed to forget his ears, but he always came back to them. Cheikel grew more and more pale. He wanted to break out against his tormentor, answer him. But he remembered that one defect would not save him from another. If he answered he would stammer, giving Goldfaden more reason for laughter. In this way the cruel scene played itself out until Cheikel pledged that within a certain time Goldfaden would get his money.

At dinner that night Goldfaden played out a singular comedy. He let it be known that he had a permit for St. Petersburg. He was taking his company there, and was looking for new actors.

This was a bolt of lightning. To play in St. Petersburg! The Mother of Russia, the city of cities! Everyone was breathless. As though coming to a decision, Goldfaden suddenly said, "I am not going to St. Petersburg without Rosenberg!"

Rosenberg could hardly believe his ears. Goldfaden had never thought much of him—and now this? His joy was embarrassing to see. Before the words were fairly out, his face lit up, his long nose turned red, and a foolish smile appeared on his lips. "Will you come then?" Goldfaden demanded, pressing him. "Will you leave the others?"

"A fish swims for deeper water—a man runs to better money," was the impudent reply.

This was more than Cheikel could bear. He forgot that he stammered, forgot that Goldfaden would laugh at him. He shrieked in a tone that cut us all to the heart, "False s-s-serpent! We have gone with you over half Russia! Now this? You desert us?" And rising, he left the table. Keni Liptzin burst into tears. The other women followed, and most of the men too.

Goldfaden sat unmoved. "And so it goes, Adler!" he said carelessly. "Rosenberg does not refuse. What does he say? 'A fish swims for deeper, a man runs to better.' So goes the world. Everyone for himself." He turned to the others, and passing over only Sonya and me, asked each actor in turn if he would come to Petersburg. Not one of them refused. They could not hide their joy, and why deny it, it gave me pain.

Happiest of all was Rosenberg. He walked about in a state of elation, kept transferring his hands from one set of pockets to another and could not help showing his joy. At the same time he was ashamed and could not meet my eyes. The others, too, knew they were doing something not right, not fine; and the victims still before them! Sonya and I withdrew early and went to our room.

We sat there sad and disheartened. We were being left behind, the only ones not needed. And what could we do alone? It was a bad business. It hurt. It hurt badly.

Suddenly, as we spoke in low cheerless tones, a door in the room opened. As in a melodrama, it was a side door, a door we had not even noticed. And with a secretive air, again like an actor in a melodrama, Goldfaden entered. He brought with him a great sheet of foolscap covered with signatures. He shook this before me, saying, "You see? All have signed. All!"

It was too much. I could not hide my bitterness, and came out with "Herr Goldfaden! This is the second time you have broken up the life of our troupe—once before in Smila, and now again! You seem to take pleasure in destroying what we have built."

But my words stopped midway, for Goldfaden's head was slowly shaking from side to side. "Adler, it was a *chantage*," he said. "A hoax. It was perhaps not fine, it may perhaps be criticized, but I had no other way. If I had gone about it directly, asked you to leave the troupe, you would have refused, out of loyalty to Rosenberg. Now I have shown you how little he or the others deserve your loyalty. I went through this comedy for one reason—to have your consent." He tapped the paper in his hand. "They have all signed. Only the stammerer refused. If you want to take him with you, well and good. I need no one else, only you and Madame Adler."

I heard this with a rush of contradictory feelings. Restored pride. Anger at others who so lightheartedly would have left us alone. Pity, too, at the thought of the trick that had been played on them. Stronger than all, the sense that for Sonya and me a great world was opening.

Late as it was, I sent for a samovar, and we three sat down to talk, a scene I recalled later like something in a dream. At times I felt stifled, the room seemed too small. At times I rose and paced the floor like a lion in a cage. I was torn between joy and doubt.

At last every detail had been settled, and the moment had come for a yes or a no. I turned to Sonya, relying as always on her womanly heart. After reflecting, she decided. "We go, Yakob!" she said. "We are betraying no one. Rosenberg and the others have betrayed themselves. No conscience qualms, Yakob. No remorse. We leave! Sign!"

I signed, and Sonya after me. It was done. Goldfaden rose with the air of a general who has won a great battle.

An hour later, in the first faint daylight, a covered sleigh drew up at the hotel door. Porters carried out our trunks and boxes and stowed them in the sleigh. I wrote two letters, one to Rosenberg repaying him for his treachery, the other to Cheikel asking his forgiveness, but congratulating him that he still "kept shop."

A last look at the hotel where we had all lived through so much. A last glance at Chernigov. Then into the sleigh, and off. Farther! Farther! Life calls! Our sleigh flew over the snow-covered road. Swifter still, on the wings of the electric telegraph, Goldfaden's message: "Adler and Michelson make their debut in *The Capricious Daughter.* Make arrangements."

The trip ended at Tannenberg, where Goldfaden's troupe were now awaiting his return. We learned now that it was here and not in Petersburg that Sonya and I were to make our debut. But Goldfaden assured us our stay would be short, and that Petersburg already beckoned.

We opened in *The Capricious Daughter,* a melodrama most likely from the German. Goldfaden, to test my powers, had chosen this play because of the strong role of the father. He was not disappointed. The public received us with enthusiasm. Many waited outside and gave us an ovation when we left the theater. Goldfaden was already dreaming of glory in Petersburg. But destiny was about to take a hand. A whole world would soon be overturned, and our little theater world with it.

Our final performance in Tannenberg was *Shulamith.* Sonya and I did not take part in this piece but were watching in the audience. It was the last day of February 1881.

The first-act curtain went up, but immediately came down again. The audience was silent, mystified. Sonya and I supposed some mishap backstage. But the curtain did not go up again. Instead a Russian officer came out. With an ashen face he announced that black tragedy had descended over the land, and that our beloved tsar, Alexander II, had been assassinated by criminals.

In one instant the scene changed to one of horror and panic.

Women screamed. Some fainted. Hysterical cries broke out every-where, and deathly fear was on every face.

Outside the theater church bells continually tolled as though for a burial, and mounted Cossacks rode about through the streets, driving everyone off.

It was with great trouble and danger that we got back to our hotel where in frightened whispers, we were told what had happened. Long, long into the night we spoke of this great and terrible event.

With the first sign of daylight police began distributing circulars throughout the city, ordering all, according to his faith, to swear allegiance to Tsar Alexander III.

Throughout the day masses of people assembled in church and synagogue, taking the oath of allegiance.

In official circles the tsar's death by violence had long been regarded as almost inevitable. His reign had been marked by repeated attempts on his life. His popularity had reached a low point after the Russo-Turkish War. Though he had opposed the war, he was blamed for its failures. The incompetence and corruption of the Russian forces were again an open secret. A profound dissatisfaction stirred the country, a feeling that things could not go on this way.

Demands for a National Assembly were now heard not only from liberals, but from many of the nobility, who believed a constitutional government would give them more power. Some of the *zemstvo,* or local assembly, leaders even wanted to achieve it by negotiating with moderate members of the underground.

Dissident action grew very bold in this atmosphere. There were nihilists who successfully resisted arrest with pistol and dagger, and a cavalry officer by the name of Kravchinsky shot down and killed the chief of police in broad daylight in the center of St. Petersburg. Kravchinsky escaped to London, where, under the pseudonym "Stepnyak," he lived to write his memoirs, a widely read account of the criminal abuse of police power rampant in this period.

During the uproar over these events, a Jewish student named Soloviev, acting on his own initiative, publicly fired five times at Alexander II in the garden of the Winter Palace. Once again, the tsar survived. All five shots missed their target.

A major crackdown followed. Twelve revolutionary leaders were publicly hanged. Hundreds of students were rounded up, tortured, sent into exile. Floggings and public executions became common occurrences. No one, high or low, was safe from the dreaded midnight knock that signaled a night raid of the police.

Though these measures were detested by all, they appeared to take effect. All underground activity came to a sudden stop. A deceptive calm reigned.

Actually, a crisis had developed, a split in the revolutionary ranks. Those who still put their faith in the effectiveness of propaganda rallied around Plekhanov's peaceful "Black Partition" party. Those convinced that only violence could bring down the regime closed ranks in the terrorist Narodnaya Volya ("the People's Will"), a party aimed at social change through prison raids, sabotage, and assassinations. At the head of this organization was the brilliant, fearless Alexander Mikhailov.

In September of 1879 the executive committee of Narodnaya Volya formally condemned Alexander Romanov to death. The "sentence" was later rescinded on condition that he form a Constituent Assembly. When the tsar ignored these pronouncements, the terrorists concentrated on one objective: his death.

Two attempts were made to blow up his train, one on his return from a trip to the Crimea, another just outside the Moscow station. Both attempts failed.

In the winter of 1880 a master carpenter by the name of Khalturin obtained employment in the Winter Palace. Khalturin was a member of Narodnaya Volya. For several weeks he smuggled explosives into the palace, and on the evening of February 17, 1880, a violent explosion demolished the dining room. Forty Finnish guards in the room below were killed or wounded. The tsar again remained unharmed. He had lingered in the corridor talking to the newly crowned king of Bulgaria.

It was the sixth attempt on his life, and it was received with almost total indifference. Official hopes had for a long time centered on Alexander's son, the tsarevich. Little was expected of the emperor, who now gave most of his time to bear hunting or the gaming table. His policy shifts had destroyed confidence on both sides. And a prolonged affair with Catherine Dolgorukaya, a maid of honor to the empress, did little to raise his prestige. The tsar was forty-seven and Catherine eighteen when the affair began, and the difference in age was much talked about. A discreet arrangement would have been accepted, but the tsar lived openly with this girl as his mistress. She gave birth to a son in 1871, and two more children followed. With the tsar's aging wife already ill it was feared he would marry Catherine and secure her coronation. The young tsarevich saw his succession threatened, and there were violent altercations between father and son.

In June of 1880 the empress breathed her last, hearing as she died the children of her husband's mistress playing in the rooms below. Forty days later, the minimum interim allowed by the church, Alexander made Catherine his morganatic wife. At the end of the year, he raised her to the rank of Princess Yurievskaya, a family name of the Romanovs, the first step, many feared, to making her empress.

This, in fact, was now the tsar's most ardent wish. Every consideration took second place to his overriding desire for personal happiness. The imperial meals took place in a heavy silence and with the heir apparent conspicuously absent, but the fifty-three-year-old tsar, already a grandfather, behaved with his wife like a lover of eighteen. His infatuation actually hastened his death, for he dismissed a capable minister of police who had criticized his marriage to Catherine, and replaced him with an inexperienced man entirely unfit for the position.

The tsar was now surrounded only by his hunting companions and a few die-hard liberals like Abaza. The Conservatives gathered around the young tsarevich, but the liberals kept their hold on the tsar through Catherine.

Under her influence, policy again shifted to the left. A number of prisoners were pardoned, some of the more flagrant police abuses were checked, certain oppressive taxes revoked. Abaza, now minister of defense, pressed hard for the last great concession, the creation of a National Assembly, but the tsar would not take this final step. "You probably think I refuse to give up power out of petty vanity and ambition," he told these friends. "I assure you that is not the case. I would sign a constitution today, but I know that tomorrow, given a constitution, Russia will fall to pieces." History has yet to prove him wrong.

Nevertheless, after turning down two proposals in this direction as "disguised blueprints for a constitutional monarchy," the tsar gave a half-consent to a newly created "Supreme Commission." This proposal, curiously combining liberals and conservatives in an effort to conciliate both, would have allowed elected representatives from each province to have a voice in the drafting of new laws. Though a far more radical step than both the others, the tsar did not veto it. Abaza had persuaded

Catherine that this concession would reconcile at least a part of the population to her coming coronation.

While the tsar was weighing the pros and cons of the all-powerful Supreme Commission, the revolutionaries, their time running out, were making a last grand plan for his assassination. A decision to run a shaft full of explosives through one of the city's principal streets was abandoned, since the blast would have killed innocent people. Instead, four of the terrorists volunteered to throw individual bombs.

This plan was reaching the final stage when Andrey Zheliabov, the leader of Narodnaya Volya, was caught and arrested. His place was taken by Sophia Perovskaya, his fellow revolutionary and common-law wife.

On the last day of February 1881, the tsar left the palace for his weekly inspection of the guards. He always left for this duty by one route and returned, as a precaution, by another. His wife, apprehensive, begged him not to go, but the minister of police assured him that both streets had been closed to the public. Actually, this order had been given, but not carried out.

In some way the conspirators learned that the tsar's return that day would take him through Catherine Street, along a canal of the same name. Sophia Perovskaya, acting as lookout, walked up and down this quiet thoroughfare. As the royal sledge entered, she gave a prearranged signal.

The first bomb was thrown by Rysakov, a student who had been expelled from the university. The explosion wounded two of the Cossack escorts and spattered the horses with blood. Against his driver's advice, the tsar came out of the sledge to speak to the wounded men. A bystander asked if he was hurt. "No, thank God," he answered. Echoing "Thank God?" the Polish student Hrinwiecki hurled a second bomb. This exploded at the tsar's feet, shattering both his legs. As the tsar's brother Michael came galloping up, Alexander whispered only, "Home to the palace—to die."

He was carried back in his brother's arms, and died before nightfall. He had that morning signed the document that might have paved the way for Russia's first constitutional government.

The funeral was hasty, the conventions barely observed. The German ambassador, asked why he showed so little grief at the loss of so close a friend, replied, "We have already mourned him."

For a time a few frightened people brought flowers to the spot where he fell. Many of them wept. Many in the country mourned him.

But the court, spared the coronation of his wife, rejoiced. The country was now in the hands of Alexander III, an archconservative who had long hated his father's reforms and could be trusted speedily to dismantle and destroy them.

On March 1, the day after the assassination, the period of mourning began. It would be observed until Easter. A long period of mourning, without theater, without money, and full of dark foreboding. St. Petersburg was out of the question now. We could not play even in Tannenberg.

My Sonya's jewels soon found their way to the pawnshop, where they prepared a path for her winter coat. My own coat went the same way. Passover was drawing near and the weather was warmer, but we still shivered a bit when the wind blew.

We met the beautiful Passover without joy, with heavy hearts. Our brothers and sisters of the stage were taken in at strange tables like poor people. Sonya and I were not even that lucky. We celebrated the holiday with a meal of matzo and potatoes.

Right after Passover, hungry and downcast, we paid a visit to Goldfaden's hotel. We found his rooms crowded with people, mostly actors, everyone talking in low voices about the assassination. Sophia Perovskaya and Zheliabov were on all lips, their names whispered with a certain sympathy and respect. Hessye Helfman was also mentioned, everyone marveling that a young Jewish girl should have found courage to perform such a deed.

These revolutionaries were all under sentence of death. Rysakov, the student who had thrown the first bomb, was caught immediately after the assassination; he turned informer and implicated the others.

Zheliabov had been arrested several days earlier. Learning in prison that Rysakov had turned traitor, Zheliabov revealed it was he who had organized and led the entire conspiracy.

Sophia Perovskaya might have saved herself had she left the city, but she refused to go. Half mad with grief, this daughter of General Perovsky, a close confidant of Nicholas II, spent her days devising wild, unreal schemes for Zheliabov's escape. A fellow conspirator, out of pity, remained with her. Both were recognized as they walked on the Nevsky Prospect, and both would hang with the others.

The Jewish girl, Hessye Helfman, had not taken part in the assassination. She was sentenced as part of the government plan to link the assassination with the Jews.

Count Tolstoy sent a letter with a strongly worded plea for clemency. The newly crowned Alexander III remained unmoved. Asked by his ministers about the request the tsar replied, "Have no fear. They will all hang."

Sophia Perovskaya spent her last night writing a letter to her mother.

Rysakov failed to save himself by giving away the others, and went to his death with those he had betrayed.

As talk of these events finally died down, Goldfaden invited us to take tea with him. At this the bitterness in Sonya's heart exploded. She got to her feet indignantly, crying "Tea! We have had nothing else all through the holidays—" Lapsing nervously into French, she exclaimed, "Three days we have not eaten!" And taking out a handkerchief, she dashed angry tears from her eyes.

I needed nothing more. I began to blubber aloud as I know how, and the whole hungry crew followed my example. From Passover it became Tisha Bov.*

Goldfaden turned pale, took us all in with one glance, then rang for the waiter and told him to bring everyone whatever they wished. "Is it my fault?" he demanded with a certain defensiveness. "Am I a prophet? I also have nothing, but I am an entrepreneur, an impresario, they give me credit! To go hungry? Fools that you are! The world has everything. One must take!" In a lower voice and with pain he exclaimed, "Yes, when people are hungry, they take! That is why the nihilists have brought down the Russian tsar, showing the world in this way that the present regime cannot continue!"

Waiters brought in a table. Dishes of every kind were brought in, and we ate. Ate? We fell on the food like hungry animals. Better said, like hungry actors!

* A day of fasting and penitence.

"Petersburg is finished, children," Goldfaden informed us in a melancholy voice. "We must look for bread where we can find it." Taking out a telegram he outlined a tour of Minsk, Vitebsk, and some Lithuanian cities. And Goldfaden consoled us. "Never mind, children," he cried. "They haven't beaten us yet. Lift your heads. We will still see better days!"

Lithuania: Stardom and Starvation

Right after Passover, the mourning period for the tsar over, we left Tannenberg for Minsk. But we did not leave without pomp and parade. We had an escort! The restaurateurs and innkeepers who had fed and housed us in Tannenberg now had only one hope, to be paid out of what we earned in Minsk. We were their living collateral, and they had to follow wherever we led.

Once on the train, our creditors found themselves beaten with two whips. We had paid them nothing for the meals we ate in Tannenberg; now they also had to feed us on the train. There was no way out. Goldfaden had found money for our tickets but not for our food on the way. As a result, these people stuck to us like glue, and watched every morsel we put in our mouths.

When we begged Goldfaden to give us an advance so we could eat in peace, his answer was "Debts, my friends! Debts! These people are strangers. They come first."

I don't say he was wrong, but if we were talking of debts, we also had something to say. We owed, true enough, but we too were owed, and by none other than Goldfaden. None of us had received a penny for the Tannenberg performances. Not that Goldfaden could be blamed for it—the assassination of Alexander II had transferred all debts to the great Book of Death.

In Minsk we fell into the hotel of "Shmaye the Minsker." The restaurateur took in not only us, but our creditors too. He had offered to feed everyone, and in addition, to pay all expenses for the theater. As a consequence, his pocket every day grew emptier and lighter. Scenery? Shmaye. Costumes? Shmaye. Posters? Shmaye. And Shmaye paid not on percent like here in America, but in hard money. Once he had begun there was no help for it. He could only be repaid out of our performances.

Poor Shmaye! The actors took up all his tables, and his regular customers had to eat standing. Worse, word got around that you could eat at Shmaye's for nothing, and such crowds came that he began to see black ruin staring him in the face.

As money began coming in the actors began to murmur. Time we had a corner we could call our own, time we got out of Shmaye's debt and knew where we were in the world. But it was always the same answer: "Wait, children. Wait! Not so quick. The creditors come first."

Thank God, our followers finally began to leave. We ceased being collateral, we became human beings again, and Goldfaden began to pay us. But not in wages. In "marks." That was our system in Europe, and in America too, until the Hebrew Actors Union changed it. Every actor, according to his standing in the troupe, got his "mark," a share of the company's total earnings.

This seemed to mean that all were equal. But what was the end of it? The impresario took his lion's share, the stars got their big bear's share. The smallest, poor devils, got *seckka*—a mash of straw, hay, and oats that left the belly swollen and the mouth dry.

To say I was opposed to this system would be too much. What did I care? I was young, in love, a rising star. Who thought about money? For me it was enough that Sonya and I got more than the others. It was May. Minsk was beautiful, and on the great St. Francis Street everything shone as in a polished mirror. The city was lively, not depressed by the assassination.

Best of all were the audiences. The most serious Jews of Minsk came to the theater. In spite of their well-known reserve these Lithuanians were warm enough when something really interested them. The actors they liked they received with applause, flowers, ovations. I promised myself that when I had become an artist in my own eyes, I would come back and play for this more discriminating public.

As always when things went well, we began to make up parties and celebrations. One of these festivities took place when Madame Goldfaden joined us, and with her the goddess, Zhenya, Goldfaden's sister.

Zhenya's arrival caused a sensation. All over Minsk word traveled that Goldfaden's troupe was richer by a prima donna of unbelievable beauty. The young *Litvakkes* were jumping out of their skins to see her. Being so beautiful, she would doubtless play like a Sarah Bernhardt, a Rachel. And since she was such a great actress she must also sing like a bird, a nightingale, a Patti! In short, there was such a rush for tickets you could not squeeze a pin into the theater.

The audience sat on hot coals. They could not wait for this marvel to appear and for her glorious trills to be carried to them. But the heavenly Zhenya's beauty did not project. The audience saw only an actress, certainly not plain, but hardly a great beauty, and with only the usual voice of the usual Yiddish prima donna.

The audience left sad and disenchanted. The great new sensation was Goldfaden's sister—and there it ended.

After Minsk we passed some interesting days in Bobruisk, a town famous for its walled fortress. This was a whole hidden city of bridges, gates, underground passages, and dungeons—a buried forbidden world with its own secret laws and dark mysteries.

The military atmosphere was felt throughout the town. Soldiers and army officers high and low seemed to spend most of their time strolling around in search of amusement. In fact our public in Bobruisk was made up largely of these Russian army men who brought a noisy unbridled mood into the theater with their hot cries of "Bravo!" and their extravagant compliments and bouquets for our ladies. For the men in the troupe they cared less, and this was especially clear when they were drunk.

Our next stop was Vitebsk. Here, immediately on our arrival, a new order came from the management. No more "commune." No more living at one hotel and eating at one table. Everyone was to fend for himself, and those who found it hard were free to go. The sea is wide with room for all. Let him swim who can. If some cannot—well, it is still the sea.

Very downcast, very sad at heart we were at this. No matter how hard it had been in Tannenberg, we had still been one family. Now a wall came up between ourselves and the management.

Our little pack of *Kommedianten* drove to the splendid hotel in the center of Vitebsk, but only the managers went through the door. The rest of us, poor devils, remained on the cold pavement. We might have been ugly sacks of rags the servants had flung from those high windows onto the street below.

A ring began to form around us, curious and not too respectful, people sensing our outcast condition. We looked at each other, a long, long chapter in our eyes.

Time to think of where to go, where to find a corner. Slowly we began to disperse, one to a friend in the city, one to some poor inn. In less time than it takes to tell, our little group was no more.

Some stranger in the crowd advised me to look for quarters in the German section, a suburb called Yeloni Sod (Birch Garden). How far was this Birch Garden? Very far. To walk was not possible. I hailed the first *drozhky*,* our luggage was thrown on, and the wheels began rattling over the cobblestone streets.

My sad thoughts kept time with their rhythm. So many years to have lived together in good times and bad, and now, alone! Sonya, too, had tears in her eyes. There she was beside me, my Sonya, so delicate, so fine. She had trusted me with her whole life, and what kind of life had I given her? Perhaps she now regrets everything, everything. I drowsed over my heavy thoughts. Suddenly Sonya woke me. Yeloni Sod. We had arrived.

We played in Vitebsk in this same Birch Garden. Poor gardens we thought them. No flowers, no fountains, a few small trees, some tufts of grass here and there, a broken picket fence, and behind a fenced-off enclosure, a stage lit by gas lamps. This was our theater.

But we began to play, we soon were giving performances almost every night, and Yiddish theater was the talk of Vitebsk. The most prominent people came to the theater, and Sonya and I received much honor. There were full houses, ovations, but Goldfaden still had the usual excuse—debts. Sonya and I had long known the whistling of poverty, but now it came to our door and began whistling on notes! Our German innkeeper did not press us, but with every meal served us our growing bill.

What to do? Sonya and I agreed to eat as little as possible. But what good was that? One cannot, after all, fast to the end. Rent, as everybody knows, must also be paid. Every day Sonya looked more weak and pale, and my choler rose. What sort of life was this? On the stage a king, at home a belly swollen with hunger! I began to agitate among my colleagues.

The management does nothing. They do not work, do not bring in the public, yet they live like lords and bathe in glory and gold. And we, who work every night, who support the theater with our blood, our nerves, what is our reward? Hunger! Beggary!

* A light, horse-drawn carriage for public hire.

You can imagine with what fire I propagandized my colleagues, and I doubt whether today's "walking delegates" could do it better.

My heat was contagious. Our forces grew from day to day. The other side, of course, was not silent. They saw what I was doing. Word was spread about that I was a dangerous agitator, a limb that must be severed from the parent body.

I didn't give a damn. I went on, since I was paid nothing. I refused to play.

Every night I came to the open-air theater, spoke to the people, and demanded justice. And my words were not in vain, for the public loved me and took my side. Goldfaden, beside himself with rage, gave orders that since I paid no admission and was no longer part of the company, I would not be allowed into the theater. Air and wind! Children of Israel thought it the greatest honor to pay for our tickets. And when Sonya and I showed ourselves in the garden, the public gave us ovations.

Finally we held a meeting and worked out our demands. First, Sonya and I must be taken back into the company. Second, half the weekly intake from now on must go to the actors. The other half we gladly give to payment of the troupe's debts. A committee was chosen to bring these demands to the management.

The management, however, was prepared. They knew our every move, for they already had their spies among us. Five of these provocateurs were in our strike committee, and it goes without saying that we had welcomed these people with the greatest joy and trust. Since the story is not a pretty one, and some of these heroes are still in our midst, it is best they remain nameless.

And so it began. Messages back and forth—but no result. One by one Goldfaden bought the strikers off, one with a promise, one with a pair of his old pants, one with a smile from the heavenly Zhenya, the least important with some smart fatherly blows about the ears. "Hey, there, nobody that you are! I have made you great, and you go with my enemies?" And so it went until there was nobody left but myself and one or two others. The troupe played every night. I dragged myself around the German quarter, raging, defeated, and alone.

Sonya was in a delicate condition. I was soon to be a father. I racked my brain and the thought came to me: "I will go to court. Let the law decide." It was my last resort, my only salvation.

My German innkeeper approved. *"Ja, gehen sie in Gericht,"* he agreed. Go to court. He promised to help, to appear for me as a witness. More important, he once again gave us credit.

God above, how great is Your mercy!

On the advice of our innkeeper, Sonya and I had an informal meeting with a justice of the peace. We laid out our grievances. Thus and so. Goldfaden had taken us away from our troupe, promising us worlds. Now we were demanding at least a part of what we were owed—enough to pay our debts and go back to our families.

The justice was a dignified old *goy*. He reminded us that we are not ordinary people, but artists who should settle our affairs without ugliness or scandal. To this we agreed, and Goldfaden was summoned to an official hearing that night.

The reform spirit of the sixties and seventies left its deepest imprint on the courts. The magistrates of the lower "peace courts," in particular, were confirmed liberals who bent over backward in their verdicts for the poor and underprivileged.

Goldfaden came to the hearing with a fire-breathing attorney and a whole pack of "witnesses." The attorney denied everything. Sonya and I, he declared, had been paid in every city including Vitebsk, and it was simply caprice on my part to make this shameful accusation. He described me to the judge as a known agitator, a troublemaker, the kind of man, in fact, who would best be escorted out of the city by the police. "If the authorities here allow him to remain, well and good," the attorney said. "The managers are too noble to insist. But as for money—nothing whatever is owed him."

Hearing such words as these, all control left me. I began to shout so loud that even the dignified old justice could not stop me. Everything came out in a torrent, and with my last breath I demanded that the attorney bring the company books and let the judge see for himself whether Sonya and I had ever received so much as one broken pfennig!

The attorney declared there were no books.

"No books?" the judge exclaimed in surprise. "I do not believe you. The smallest business, the poorest shop, keeps a record of its profits and losses. Your denial alone strikes me as most suspicious." Ordering another hearing next day, he closed the session.

The following morning we assembled again. Goldfaden came without books, and lost the case.

The verdict of the court was as follows: Jakob Pavlovich Adler and his wife, known as Sonya Michelson, would receive from Goldfaden three hundred rubles apiece, this being the largest sum in the power of the lower court. And Goldfaden was issued an injunction not to leave Vitebsk until he had discharged the debt.

The white-haired old justice detained me after the others had left. Apparently he was sorry for all I had gone through, for he quietly pressed a twenty-five-ruble note into my hand—a piece of human kindness that all but unmanned me.

How be an *afikorus** and not believe in God when in one instant the Highest One can turn everything from happiness to misery and back to happiness again! Only yesterday, who was my equal in misfortune? I had left the court penniless, friendless, accused of a serious crime. And today? In the flash of an eye, twenty-five rubles in my pocket, my case again strong as iron, my enemy standing before the judge with an ugly stain on his honor, and those who egged him on crestfallen, all their plans overturned.

With joy I ran to tell Sonya the news and found her talking with the German innkeeper. We gave him twenty rubles on account and decided to spend the other five on pleasure, for we could not remember our last happy day.

The two of us ran out to the meadow above Birch Garden, ran uphill and down like children, flung ourselves down on the grass, watched the ants at work, and finally went to take tea in an open-air restaurant near the theater. The air was fresh and fragrant. Birds hopped about on our table. But suddenly we look up. Who is approaching, and with such serious, important faces? Goldfaden. Several important-looking townsmen. Also, a Christian. They take a large table and talk among themselves, ignoring us.

But how long can they keep it up? The Christian, who turns out to be a Vitebsk lawyer, takes me aside and asks me if I understand the meaning of this assemblage. I make no response. Seeing he does not

* Epicurean—that is, a freethinker.

have the key to my heart, the Christian calls over two of the Jewish townsmen. They put the matter to me, first in a highfalutin way, then with anger, and finally with flattery. In brief, they do not want this shame on their city. Arrests? Siberia? Surely not. And turning once again to threats—anyone who tries to do harm will have something to remember.

"We want nothing," I answered. "We have asked nothing. We wish to go home. We have left our troupe who are now like sheep without a shepherd." And I showed them letters from Rosenberg in the town of Nezhin* urging me to come, letters saying that his troupe is soon going to St. Petersburg, that the wealthy people there have covered the troupe with gold, that he himself is covered with diamonds, that the great Jews of Nezhin are coming to greet me with a military band, and no honor will be lacking. "Instead of this I sit here in Vitebsk, falsely accused, swindled, and now a threat to put us out of the city with a police escort? Is this human?"

The townsmen, more conciliatory, agreed that some wrong had been done to me. Goldfaden, the townsmen now said, had only wanted to frighten me, and would never have carried out this threat. As for the money, they had only one answer. The theater was drowning in debts. "What is to be done?" they said. "We are, after all, still Jews in this world."

I knew this was true and remained silent for a moment. Then I came up with an idea. A benefit. No—two benefits. One for me, one for Sonya. On this there was an agreement, and Goldfaden and I shook hands.

The news must have slid down the hill over Yeloni Sod and blown like a wind through every house in the city, for by sundown that day all Vitebsk knew that Adler and Goldfaden had made friends. The garden was packed to the doors that night, and Goldfaden and I came out together to joyful shouts of *"Sholem!"* and *"Mazel tov!"*

The two benefits were played in the same holiday mood, Goldfaden's debts were paid by the Vitebsk public, and with kisses all around, with bad feeling toward none, Sonya and I boarded the train.

---

* Near Chernigov, in the northern Ukraine.

Rosenberg's Theater in Nezhin

We traveled in some style, for if we were to be met by a military band we could not arrive like beggars. I had a new coat with a wing collar, a high hat, a cane with a beautiful ivory handle. And Sonya, too, was richly attired. Her jewelry had been redeemed, she had a fine velvet cloak, a many-colored umbrella in the latest Paris style. And both of us had the joy of knowing that, folded away in a handsome leather *porte-monnaie,* we still had crackling new bills in high denominations.

As the train neared Nezhin I suggested we put on our cloaks and prepare ourselves, for it seemed to me I already heard the military band. "I believe I hear the drum," I said. "Do you hear it, Sonichka?"

"No, Yakobchik, I hear nothing."

"The trumpet too," I insisted, listening. "Don't you hear it, love?"

"No, *dorogoi,* I hear nothing. I don't hear very well."

A little surprised by Sonya's sudden deafness, I stuck my head out the window. Telegraph poles. Buildings, the kind one sees near a railway station. No sign of a crowd or celebration. "*Nichevo!* Nothing!" I muttered like a real Russian. "They will still come."

"Nezhin!" The conductors shouted together, shooting it out as from a gun. Sonya and I grabbed our luggage and sprang down from the train. I look here. I look there. A sickness and a darkness on Rosenberg's head! A military band? Wealthy townsmen? Not even a dog from the troupe was there! Nobody but the stationmaster, a few Christians, and a gendarme with a feather in his hat.

Wishing fervently that seven devils might enter not only Rosenberg but also his father's father, I took an ordinary *drozhky* and told the driver to take us to Shimen Kaplan's hotel on Commercia Street.

There we found only a small sleeping chamber had been prepared for us. With this we had the privilege of warming ourselves in the main room, where four windows looked out on the city prison.

After a miserable wait we finally heard voices at the door. A moment later Rosenberg entered, followed by Cheikel Bain. A long silence followed.

"Well, Yisrolik," I finally said. "I have come to organize you and take you to St. Petersburg."

"Yankele, I fooled you, got you here by a trick," Rosenberg admitted with shame.

"As long as you have come," I said with a sigh.

After a glass of wine and a bite of food I suggested we take a look at the theater, for Sonya and I were to give our first performance the following night.

The walk took us past all the Jewish shops of the town. But Rosenberg did not walk beside us. He followed a few steps behind, rolling his eyes and gesticulating with such a caricature of respect and awe that on both sides of the street people came out to stare. "Did I tell you?" he kept saying in a whisper heard by all. "Did you ever in your life see such great people?" Sonya and I didn't know where to look in our embarrassment.

We walk, we walk. Yards. Small stores. Small houses. Soon we had reached the outskirts of the town. I stopped and looked around, bewildered. Where was the theater?

After a silence I said, "Then where are we to play?"

With shame Rosenberg pointed across a field. "Behind those trees, Yankele, we have put up a tent. Like the gypsies. That is our theater."

Seeing how I took this, Rosenberg broke out again with passionate pride. "And even here the greatest millionaires came! And they will come again—yes, if they die for it! To see you—and not the theater!"

"Yeh, yeh, Yankele," Cheikel put in. "As true as I am a Jew, they will c-c-come."

I could not help being touched by their belief. Holding out both hands I said, "Then take me to my theater!"

We came back that night to see the play. The tent was pitched among some trees in a kind of yard, and lit inside by candles and lanterns. In the center of the tent was a makeshift stage clapped together with boards. A little box for the prompter. So? What more do we need?

A few people were scattered here and there. Mostly empty benches. We had come late, and the play was already in progress. On the stage a young woman in the last stage of pregnancy . . . the ingenue. The stage was laid with straw, and from time to time she bent, plucked up a straw, and sang from Goldfaden's *Bar Kochba:*

> So long as it grows
> The grass is young.

And each time she bent, she came closer to her confinement. Thirty-five years have gone by since that night, but never again have I seen such a play—or such an ingenue.

Rosenberg had miscalculated. Our arrival made no great difference at the box office. Summer was coming. People of means were going to their dachas in the country. Those who remained were not hurrying out to Rosenberg's tent. What was to be done? We rehearsed, we played, broke ourselves, but everything was slow, lifeless, cold. A bad world! Does not care for poor people. Are wood and bricks the theater? Does scenery alone impart the aesthetic thrill?

Spivakovsky had gone to Berdichev to get help, but day after day went by without word, and we were falling more and more into debt at our inn. Shimen Kaplan was an easygoing old fellow, but his wife screamed that unless we paid up she would call the police and seize our possessions. Sonya and I trembled for the five hundred rubles hidden away in our trunk. Rosenberg would not care if I lost the last I had in the world. He would shrug and say, "Why should you have if I don't have?"

I reasoned with the Kaplans, told them we were not thieves, were not leaving, made them understand they would get nothing at all if they prevented us from playing. In the end I gave them 150 rubles on account and my sworn word that as soon as we got out of Nezhin we would send the rest. They finally agreed. What else could they do?

Just as things looked blackest a letter finally came from Spivakovsky. A letter? A miracle! Everything was settled. We have a theater in Lodz, and he had found a man with money. God has sent him a watchmaker, one Schneiderman by name, who will lay out whatever is needed for our trip to Lodz and our expenses there. The watchmaker asks in return only a certain percentage of our profits.

Alexander III and Tsarina Maria Feodor-ovna of Russia

Hearing such words as these, we were greatly rejoiced. God, we said, had taken pity on us. We all sat down, one with the stub of a pencil, one on the back of an envelope, and began adding up our debts, our bills, working out how much to ask of the watchmaker. Cheikel reckoned, reckoned, and at last muttered, "A thousander this Schneiderman will have to *schneider* in! A thousander or nothing!"

"Only a thousander?" My artistic soul was offended. "For a mere thousander are we so many comedians, tragedians, prima donnas, singers, and even an entrepreneur?"

Everyone was crowding around Cheikel, everyone wanted to know whether his own bills, his own debts, were in the reckoning.

"All in the r-r-reckoning," Cheikel stammered happily.

We were on fire. We wanted to pack up, to go! But not so fast. We still had much to live through in Nezhin before we were again on our way.

This was the famous year 1881, remember, the year Tsar Alexander II was assassinated, and his son, Alexander III, mounted the Russian throne. It was in the summer of that year that the pogroms began. They had already broken out in Kiev, in other cities of the south, and now, day by day, the danger came closer to Nezhin.

In the Jewish quarter one felt an unnatural calm, the deadly calm of the forest before the hurricane. Everyone was waiting for the terror to strike. And at nightfall of a certain day the dreaded word came: "They are here." All the shops near the railway station had been ransacked, smashed, and destroyed.

That night people locked themselves in their homes. No one came in or out, and no sound, no voice, was heard. The night passed in silence, a night without sleep. When the sun came up the Jews of Nezhin were on their feet, waiting for whatever the day would bring.

Anti-Jewish riots were breaking out all through southern Russia at this time. Provocateurs from St. Petersburg would come into a town by train, inflame the most ignorant part of the population with stories of Jewish wealth, and, having started the pogrom, disappear again. It was an open secret that these men had ties with the St. Petersburg police, and acted with their connivance.

In Berdichev the Jews surrounded the station and prevented the rioters from getting off the train. In Odessa Jewish and Russian students fought them together through the streets. The police themselves dispersed them in some cities. The authorities allowed the pogroms, but also feared them. Anger against the Jews could easily turn against the nobility and the rich. The government would allow the riots to rage a day or two, until they got too dangerous, and then send in the cavalry to put them down and restore order.

It began as we sat together at breakfast. A long shrill whistling outside the window, then running footsteps, shouting voices, the sound of glass smashing, the dull thud of doors splintering, and the wild inhuman cry, *"Baie Zhidov!* Kill the Jews!"

We sprang to our feet, fear on all our faces as though written there with chalk. The four daughters of the innkeeper set up a wail, terrified for their old parents. In the end the Kaplans carried their valuables to the ice house, where they buried everything and finally hid themselves, too, under the straw.

Just as we were, still in our shirtsleeves, we went out into the street, driven by an overwhelming need to *see*. Every house on the street was surrounded by murderers. While those outside smashed windows and tore down doors, others hurled furniture and household gear through the windows into the street. A whole featherbed, ripped and in pieces, sailed out, whitening the air as it fell like a strange summer snow. From the high window of another house a piano crashed to the ground and lay there, its strings sending up a hum like the groan of all humanity. The alarm bell continually tolled as though for a fire. And the wild mob met each ripped featherbed, each smashed, shattered piece of furniture with wild laughter and drunken screams of joy. While the men tore down doors, walls, and roofs, their wives and children hunted through the destruction, thrusting into great sacks everything that in their eyes had value.

The Kaplans had been right to hide themselves. Nobody was spared, neither young nor old. Jews ran by without hats, with bloody faces, half-torn-out beards, and were beaten anew as they ran. Soldiers and policemen stood by and watched, and those who ran to them for help were beaten back with the flat of their rifles into the carnage. And so it went from morning to noon in the Jewish quarter of Nezhin.

The worst destruction took place in the synagogue and houses of study, where the mob took an especially murderous pleasure in defiling the scrolls of the Torah. They ripped whole pages out of these scrolls, ran out with them to the screaming mob outside, hurled them into the gutter, stepped on them, danced on them. Jews running for their lives stopped at the sight, pain in their faces. Many tried to save what was left. As the mob rushed on they crept out of hiding places, picked the pages out of the gutter, kissed them, wept over them.

Suddenly, as we stood with bursting hearts, we were surrounded by a gang of the ruffians. "And who is this bunch here?" the leader demanded. "Jewish mugs, are they?" another asked with a ferocious laugh. A third was already screaming, *"Baie Zhidov!"*

Rosenberg's quick wits were all that saved us. *"Oui, oui!"* he cried with a gay laugh. Pointing to us, he exclaimed several times in a foreign-sounding Russian, *"Françuski aktiori!* French actors!" To us, in quick Yiddish, he whispered, "Jews! Speak French!" And he went on bowing and laughing, continually crying in a shrill voice, "*Je vous pris! Merci! Au revoir! Bonjour!*"

We all fell into his tone and began babbling whatever French-sounding gibberish came into our heads. The leader eyed us suspiciously, but Rosenberg pointed to Sonya, who began rattling madly away in real French. In the end the mob believed us and went off.

Moments later a carriage drove up, and a tall elegant gentleman sprang out. It was Spivakovsky. "Fools!" he cried. "To the station! Save yourselves!"

It was good advice, but he had brought no money and I was the only one in the troupe who could help. I knew at such a time it must be "commune"—that I must save the others, and if I had forgotten my duty, my Sonya was there to remind us. "Yakob, this is a moment we must share and share alike," she whispered. "These were our friends in the good times. We must not desert them now."

The three hundred fifty rubles came out of their hiding place. We packed whatever we could. I took a carriage for ten rubles, everyone piled in, and we drove to the station.

Some things in life can never be forgotten. Thirty-seven years have gone by, but that short trip is with me still as though it were yesterday.

The way to the station lay over a broad, peaceful highway lined on both sides with gardens, flowers, and trees. And amid this freshness, this idyllic beauty, a mass of people were fleeing for their lives. Crazy-looking people with ashen faces, torn coats, bandaged arms, bandaged heads. Some were limping, some stumbling, some ran in terror at every sound, fearful the killers were still at their heels. Many were in ragged, bloody clothing. Many had children in their arms, and these bowed low before any official, any decent Russian as long as he was not one of the murderers, and begged for the lives of these children.

Shame rose in all of us. Shame for our shaven faces, our fine actors' clothes. Flashing before us was the scene not an hour past when we all had stood, babbling dog-French, denying our people, denying our language. By what right had we saved ourselves? Why should we be spared the fate of these, the beaten, the humiliated, the driven, the slapped? We all felt the same; none of us could look the others in the eyes.

We had barely alighted when Sonya gave a cry of horror. Our conductor, Zorach Vinyavich, and his daughter, Bettye. We had left them behind, forgotten them!

For one terrible moment we hesitated. To go back into that carnage? "Back! Back!" Sonya screamed hysterically. The pregnant
woman sprang into a carriage. I sprang in after, Spivakovsky after me,
and after him, that cynic, libertine, but good Jew and good brother,
Rosenberg.

We found the Vinyaviches, father and daughter, hiding in the cellar of their inn. The young girl flew like a bird into Sonya's arms,
weeping for joy. She thought we had all been killed.

As we rode back through the town my blood ran cold at the scenes
we saw. Every Jewish house and store in the marketplace had been
smashed, wrecked, and gutted. Wine was running through the gut-
ters, broken bottles lay on the streets, and a drunken, riotous crowd
was carrying off bolts of satin, velvet, lace.

At a crossing a Russian officer with a group of soldiers was trying
to bring this mob to their senses. He ordered them to disperse. They
answered with jeers, insults, curses. He repeated his order, and with
mounting anger threatened to fire. A howl went up from the crowd.
Bottles flew murderously through the air. "For the accursed Jews you
will shed Christian blood?" the women screamed. Enraged, the mob
advanced. The soldiers retreated, their guns at the ready. A sharp
command. Rifles rang out. Shrieks tore the air. Dead and wounded
dropped to the ground. Near our carriage a well-known notary fell,
shot to death—an innocent bystander.

No way to describe the roar that now came from the mob. Like the
barbarian hordes of old, like a wave driven by the fiercest hurricane,
they hurled themselves at the soldiers. The men closed ranks, preparing to fire again. The mob wavered, full of rage, but uncertain. The
threat of more gunfire quelled them. Somehow the crisis passed. They
began slowly to disperse, some bearing away the wounded and dead,
others carrying off the spoils of their crimes.

Months later I read in the *Gazette* that a Russian officer was sentenced to eight years' hard labor for actions during the riots at
Nezhin. It was undoubtedly the same man.

At the station the situation was now worse, with newcomers continually adding to the already dangerous press of people. Fortunately
the stationmaster was a good man who allowed all to enter. But a
rumor had started that the killers were on their way to the station,
and the people were milling around in great confusion.

With our actors' faces and fine clothes many of these people mistook us for Christians, lords of the earth. Old men bowed low,

crying—a cry from the grave—"Save us, great *barin.* Save us from death." Women snatched our hands, kissed them, pushed their children forward, told the children to beg for their lives.

How shall I tell what we felt at that moment? The heart gave way as in a mighty torrent of tears and blood. Christians? Lords of the earth? The tears in our eyes were our answer. The tall aristocratic Spivakovsky sobbed, emptied his pockets. We all did the same. The women kissed the children, fell on the necks of the other women, and we all wept together.

The stationmaster was determined to defend his ground. With the help of some of the younger men he attached a rubber pipe to a locomotive. "Let them come," he said. "We'll burn their eyes out!" We ourselves organized a collection to provide the neediest with train tickets. But suddenly, all in a moment, the clamor around us died away. A low wail passed over the crowd, and voices cried, "The rabbi! Woe to us all, our great rabbi!"

Instinctively, like a soldier before his general, I drew myself up to my full height. In the doorway of the station stood the Good Jew of Nezhin.

He was tall, frail, very old. A silken, godly face. A high beautiful forehead. Great eyes staring into the distance beneath thick, milk-white brows. His family, perhaps twenty in number, stood around him, the children dressed like princes and princesses, his wife, the *rebbetzen,* old, wasted, but still with the ghostly remains of once-great beauty.

Without a sound the crowd parted, making a path. The rabbi seemed to wake from a dream. His great staring eyes filled with tears. His family, too, clung to each other, their heads lowered. Not a sigh, not a moan was heard. It might have been Rosh Hashanah when the prayer is ended and the congregation waits, without drawing a breath, for the sound of the shofar.

The stationmaster gave orders to his people, and the rabbi and his family were led to a separate chamber. Men were posted outside the door and no one was allowed to enter, though many tried to do so, we actors among them. Only Rosenberg found a way. I don't know what he said to the stationmaster, but he was allowed to enter, and we followed him. I could not help wondering what idea was in his mind.

The rabbi had seated himself. Water was brought to him. After washing his hands he turned to us and waited.

"Rabbi," Rosenberg began with a tremor, "we are Jewish children. We comfort the people, teach them, give them courage to bear their burdens. We were in your city many weeks, and we were loved. We too have our followers."

"Ah, yes," the rabbi finally said in a gentle, quavering voice. "You are the theater people. I have heard of you."

"Rabbi, though we are actors we are not frivolous folk," Rosenberg said, going on with an effort. "Our parents are good pious Jews, and we too are respected." He pointed to Sonya. "That lady, Frau Adler, finished the *gymnasia*."

The rabbi waited, attentive.

"Rabbi, we are leaving your city now," Rosenberg said. His voice faltered and two tears rolled down his cheeks. "Rabbi," he said. "Give us your blessing on our way."

We were not destined to have the rabbi's blessing. At that moment a shout went up, and everyone rushed out to the platform. It was not a murderous assault on the station. It was the train, sighted as it came down the tracks. Everyone stampeded forward to board it. A frightful moment. Fortunately no one was trampled.

It was not a journey, but a flight, a wild rout. Children wailed, old people moaned, the sick nursed their wounds, women wept. A Jewish poet has described these "trains of living sorrows," trains "driven by sighs." If we wanted to forget the horrors we had seen, we could not. We were taking them with us.

An hour later, through the train window, we saw cavalry galloping toward Nezhin. Another hour and we were in Berdichev.

We did not come to Berdichev to play, but to meet with our new financier, the watchmaker. Herr Schneiderman arrived that evening, bringing with him a pack of bills as well as contracts full of his conditions. The conditions were really not that bad. The worst was his insistence that he sit in the box office and take the biggest share of the profits until he got back his investment. After some wrangling we agreed. He and Spivakovsky took the train that same night for Lodz, and three days later sent word they had the Victoria Theater.

All in all we spent about a week in Berdichev. Remembering that my mother's family lived there I paid a visit to the relatives about whom I had heard so much in my childhood. But I did not tell the aristocratic Halperins I was an actor, dancer, trickster. These stern Chassidic Jews, masters of great factories and mills, would have looked on me as a disgrace.

The trip to Berdichev had taken us south, and traveling north again to Lodz, our train stopped at Nezhin. As the conductors called out that name our carefree mood was wiped away as with a hand. We sat in silence.

Since the train made a two-hour stop at the station we got out and walked into the town. Nezhin was like a city that had been bombarded. Soldiers with rifles posted at the corners, mounted hussars driving away anyone who loitered. The Jewish quarter empty, deserted, houses and stores smashed in, ransacked, a few people wandering about like ghosts in a cemetery.

We looked up the friends we could find, and exchanged some quiet words with them. What was there to say? We parted in silence and, with heavy hearts, boarded our train again.

My First Great Role: Uriel Acosta

Lodz! Then as now the great Polish-German-Yiddish city was a world unto itself, a town of many factories, hub and center of the silk-weaving trade. People here worked by the clock as they do in America, and there was a tremendous commotion at noon every day as, by the hundreds, they rushed out of the factories and swarmed into restaurants and cafés.

But the city itself was elegant; in the better parts of town one saw only the "clean public." I liked the parks, the stone vases everywhere, the outdoor cafés like those in Paris, the trees. The women were beautiful, the men dressed with elegance and dash. In a word, Lodz was much to my taste.

Russian was rarely heard up here. The official class in Lodz all spoke German. Even our posters came out in German. The actors cut their German names out of the posters and pasted them on their doors. Rosenberg clowned in German, everyone bought German coats, German high hats. We forgot our recent troubles and felt like millionaires.

We would have been happy to stay on all winter, but Spivakovsky wanted Warsaw. He had already played there, he was a favorite there, and Spivakovsky was our commander. Whatever he said was the law.

I am writing, of course, of a day gone by—a youth gone by. Now word comes from London that the old Spivakovsky is ill, penniless—his family has to go for help to strangers. Is this the end of an artist of our stage? See then the end of Spivakovsky, one of the finest artists of our stage!

Things went well at the Victoria Theater in Lodz. Business was good, and much money ran through the thick fingers of Herr Schneiderman. In time he took his departure, satisfied, and we were on our own again. We had good audiences, Rosenberg and Spivakovsky dipped into the till as into their own pocket, and Cheikel went out to conquer other towns.

As the family party grew smaller, the celebrations grew gayer. And it was here in Lodz that the greatest event of my youthful career took place, my debut in *Uriel Acosta.*

It was early fall of 1882, and the newspapers were full of the Odessa lawyer, Osip Mikhailovich Lerner.

Yes, the same Lerner, once a *maskil,** who later died a convert and a Gentile, leaving behind him a book vilifying and denouncing his people.

But in 1881 this same Lerner took over the famous Mariinsky Theater of Odessa, and had a great success there with both Yiddish and Russian critics.

Although there were many fine Yiddish writers at this time, they did not occupy themselves with writing for the theater. After putting on plays by the novelist Sheikevitch and the publicist Lilienblum, Lerner turned to the world drama. He realized, however, that the greatest play would have no meaning to his audience if it did not have some content relating it to Jewish life. To show the Jewish public such a play would never do. The ordinary Jew would not understand why he should interest himself in such things, and the intellectual would rake him over the coals for neglecting the basic purpose of such a theater in the first place. It was only later, in America, that our audience accepted the classics on their own terms.

Lerner found a compromise. From the German repertoire he chose Karl Gutzkow's *Uriel Acosta* and from the French, Scribe's *La Juive.* Both were on Jewish subjects, and both were in the repertoire of every important European stage of the time.

Goldfaden, competing with Lerner at the Remesleni, found these triumphs hard to swallow. He put on his own production of *Acosta,* and in his overriding need to get the better of his rival, he inserted songs into the text as well.

And so, at just this time, there were two *Acosta*s in Odessa. It was fated, however, that there be a third. Rosenberg declared that he too would have an *Acosta,* and one that would put both the others to shame!

And without losing a day, he set to work.

* A follower of the Haskala movement, the Jewish Enlightenment.

Rosenberg worked with feverish haste, and I too burned with the same fire. No small thing, *Uriel Acosta*! A classic drama, a truly great role! All my ambition flared. Good! I told myself. Time to throw away the ABCs. Time to forget the *chaider* and go on to Commentaries!

I threw myself into the work. I encouraged Rosenberg, woke his energy, his ambition. A hundred times I read and reread the translation, compared it with the Russian text. My soul was full of Uriel. My blood pulsed with his speeches. My heart pounded with his monologue. And within me hope warred ceaselessly with self-doubt. Did I truly dare to play Uriel? My God, where to find certainty, where to find one scintilla of faith, one scintilla of belief in oneself!

My *yaitzer horre* [the lower nature of man] of the bad, small Odessa time said, "Not for you, Yankele! Better men than you will play Uriel." My *yaitzer tov* [man's higher nature] answered, "The world is a battlefield. Fight for your place or remain forever in your corner." But although this soul struggle went on a hundred times a day, no hint of it crossed my lips.

And now all this was done. The play was ready. Rosenberg gave out the parts. I was given the role of Da Sylva. Spivakovsky would play Uriel.

I smiled. I told Rosenberg he had done well. Not by a word or a look did I reveal the bitterness and rage devouring me.

Why did I not go to Sonya, who believed in me and who, with her fighting spirit, would have helped me so much? She was waiting for me to speak. When I remained silent I saw a shadow of disappointment fall over her face. I could not speak. I must have been a boy still, with a boy's foolish shame.

Rehearsals began. Spivakovsky and Rosenberg explored the role. At such and such a moment the great Kozelsky had done thus and so. The great Lavinsky had taken the monologue in this fashion, the mighty Sonnenthal in that. And Spivakovsky demonstrated to Rosenberg the different ways these renowned artists had played the part.

I watched him with scorn, for with his best abilities I saw he would create nothing new. There would be a bit of Lavinsky, a little Kozelsky, a touch of Sonnenthal, but very little Spivakovsky. And though I envied him that he had seen these artists, I fiercely embraced my own provincial isolation. "Wait!" I told myself. "If ever I play it, it will be *my* Acosta! Mine, and no one else's!"

Young as I was in my art, I already felt it was not only wrong but pitiful for an actor to deck himself out in another's feathers, to play his role like a beggar grinding out an old tune on an organ. The gifted artist will always play a part differently than anyone else, will always give it another nuance. Why? Because he lives it through in himself, in his temperament, in his life experience, and it is not possible for any man to reproduce the temperament, the life experience, of another. No matter how excellent the copy, it will impress only the gallery. The true connoisseur will always see the bloodless, cold mechanism of such a portrayal. No! Better to fail with something of your own than to succeed with the most brilliant imitation! This has been my belief from my earliest years in the theater. It has never changed.

To go back to Uriel. Since Spivakovsky was to have the lead I might at least have been given the sympathetic role of the honorable Santos. But no—that role, too, went to another. And I, the juvenile lead of the company, must play the dried-up sixty-year-old philosopher Da Sylva! Bad, would you say? Yes, very bad. But how does the saying go? When God has decided, a way will be found. It was destined that I, and only I, was to play Uriel—and that this play, this role, would make me famous.

The Portuguese philosopher Uriel da Costa (1585–1640) is one of the great scholars—and great heretics—of Jewish history. The play, by the German dramatist Karl Gutzkow, is set in the early seventeenth century, with the Spanish Inquisition still at its height.

Acosta, raised as a Catholic, has always known he was a Jew. His family were *Marranos,** Jews who professed Christianity but secretly continued to practice their own faith.

In 1619, fearing their secret had been discovered, this family sought refuge from the Inquisition in Holland. Here, with great joy, they could live openly as Jews. But Uriel's growing belief in the Copernican theory that the earth moved around the sun aroused anger in the congregation. Because he stubbornly held to this belief he was charged with heresy and was placed "in *herem,*" that is, under "the great ban"—excommunication.

* The word *marrano,* or "pig," was an insult aimed at all Jews, but particularly at "hidden Jews," who were especially hated.

The play revolves around the hero's conflict between reason and faith. Cast out of the congregation, his family ruined and in disgrace, Acosta agrees to undergo the "return to Judaism," a medieval ritual designed to break both body and spirit. Under this ordeal, he recants his heresy.

But in his heart Uriel still believes in the truth of what he has renounced, and his nature is such that he cannot keep silent. Repeating Galileo's famous "And still it moves!" he recants his recantation.

There is now no hope of return. Forced to choose between his passion for scientific truth and the Judaism that is his soul, he resolves the conflict, and ends the play, with his suicide.

The first Yiddish performance took place at the Odessa Mariinsky in 1882. Abba Schoengold scored a triumph as Acosta, and the role remained for decades the supreme test of the Yiddish actor.

The critic and director Harold Clurman, who saw Adler in the role, wrote: "When, as Uriel Acosta, he raised the banner of free thought in epic loftiness, I was transported, and a little frightened. The man's *size*—I do not refer to his physique—imposed a sense of peril. Grandeur always inspires a certain shudder at life's immeasurable mystery and might."*

It was early fall, getting close to the holidays. We put on old plays and rehearsed *Acosta.* The weather turned bad, with continual rains and storms. The audience dwindled, and money ran low. As if all this weren't enough, thieves broke into the theater, stole our costumes and, what was worse, our winter coats. The women wept, the men walked around steeped in gloom. Only Rosenberg was undaunted. "Dirt!" he declared scornfully. "As soon as we put on *Acosta* we will all have more money than we can spend!"

The rehearsals came to an end. Rosenberg put up a poster splashed across with the words HERR JACOB SPIVAKOVSKY AS URIEL.

My jealous nature burned. I could not bear to see Spivakovsky's name on the poster. But three days later Rosenberg walked into our hotel room, and I saw immediately that he was not himself. He came in too quietly; his nose was three times longer than usual, his face dark, upset. He showed me a letter in Russian from Spivakovsky. He

* Introduction to Lulla Rosenfeld, *Bright Star of Exile* (T. Crowell, 1977).

sends greetings to his colleagues. He is weary of our wandering life. He asks our forgiveness. He has gone away.

In the time we had been together Spivakovsky had several times gone off in this fashion. But now it was serious. We had to put *Uriel* on in three days.

Sonya rose to her feet. "No tragedy!" she said with energy. "Yakob will play it. As well as Spivakovsky, and perhaps better!"

At these words my heart gave a lurch. Springing up I said in the sharpest tones, "No! I have studied Da Sylva. I will play nothing else."

Rosenberg began to plead with me. "Be reasonable, Yankele," he begged. "A misfortune has befallen us. We are robbed as in a pogrom. We have lost our costumes, our winter clothes. We do not hear from Cheikel. There is still no permit from Warsaw. We have only one hope—the new play. If it is a success, all will be well. If not, we will still have enough to pay our debts and get back to Odessa." He added with a certain bafflement, "Why don't you want to play it? If I had your face, your figure, your head of hair, I would play it."

"Throw away your fears, Yakob!" Sonya exclaimed. "Do you think I have not seen your bitterness and pain? Spivakovsky lies! He is not weary of our wandering life, but fears to stand on the stage with an actor greater than himself!" And she ended with a strong outburst. "My Yakob, my Uriel! God will help! We have three days. We will work, we will study rigorously, and you will be victorious!"

Rosenberg's eyes filled with tears. "*Spasibo*, thank you, Sonichka," he said gratefully. "You have softened his heart. He will do it!" And all his trouble forgotten, he ran off to change the posters.

I was already praying for a miracle that would prevent me from playing Uriel.

The high holidays were upon us. Pious Jews of Lodz shivered in the synagogue, confessed their sins, and took the measure of their lives. And my soul, I too, shivered in these Days of Awe.

We opened between *Sliches,* Confession, and Yom Kippur—Atonement. In that short interval I would have three rehearsals to prepare me for Uriel, at that time the highest ambition of our stage, the role that would decide my fate in the theater.

On the night before the first rehearsal I lay in my bed awake. In my mind I was already on the stage, and I went through the role, scene by scene. I came to the great monologue:

When you are driven from this good land you will know pain, thirst, hunger, cold. Do you think I will remain here under the perfumed flowering branches of Spain? No! I am a Jew, and I will remain a Jew.

I was so deep in this moment, I lived through it so sharply, that I actually heard a thunder of applause. Suddenly a voice said, "Yakob, why are you screaming?" It was Sonya, waking me. Apparently I had little by little slipped into a dream, and in my sleep declaimed the monologue. I lay awake after that, and did not close my eyes again.

When I was a child my grandfather, Reb Avremele, would take me to early prayers on the high holidays. I did not like to get up before dawn and go through the cold windy streets to the synagogue, but I felt the deep importance of it, and did it willingly. Everything was so strange at that hour. The buildings cast such long dark shadows along the street. The crowds hurrying beside us to the *schul* were so silent, so intent. One heard only the rustle of their clothing and perhaps now and again a low word of greeting. Everything was awesome, everything more mysterious than in the familiar daytime world.

Once, as we were hurrying in this way to the *schul,* I saw a star appear. The star before dawn. I stopped in wonderment, gazing. "Yankele, why do you stop?" the *zayde* called. "It is only the morning star."

Many times since then, when I am up very late, or awaken very early, I have seen that star. Always it brings back those dark streets, those dark houses, those unforgotten nights of *Sliches.* Again I feel that atmosphere around me. Again I breathe that magic air.

And that same "soul-shiver" of Confession, of *Sliches,* I felt as I saw the star that morning, the morning of the first rehearsal.

"Help me, God," I silently prayed. "Do not let me be shamed."

I was the first one on the stage that morning. Sonya and the others came later. Sonya joked with me. "Other Uriels grow pale only at the end," she said, "but my Uriel is white as a ghost before he begins."

At my first lines I silenced the prompter. His voice interfered with my illusion that I was, in truth, Uriel. Everyone understood my fear and respected it.

The rehearsal was marked by one notable occurrence. At a certain point Uriel's two brothers, now poor and ragged, but still full of Portuguese pride, lead their blind mother to him to reproach him for his heresy. The role of the mother was played by Keni Liptzin. Yes, the same Keni Liptzin who now lies abandoned, alone, gazing out at the lake of Central Park and fighting with weakening, sinking powers, for her life. But then she was young, beautiful, our gay companion and comrade. And when Rosenberg decided on *Acosta* she threw herself into the project with all the fire and enthusiasm of her passionate nature.

Now, in her desire to help, she had devised a surprise. At this first rehearsal she came before me in full costume and makeup, a gray wig covering her head, her face pale and wrinkled, a black mantle over her shoulders—a noble, tragic figure. And this picture had such a violent effect on me that I blurted out, "Mama! Mama!" and burst into a storm of tears.

Poor Keni! What frightful moments you are living through now. And how happy you were at that rehearsal when your idea had just the effect on me that you had hoped!

As Jews go to Kol Nidre, so the actors came to the first performance of *Acosta*. The audience, too, came with the same sense of solemn holiday. But what an audience! There were so many carriages outside you would think the Victoria Theater was the opera house! The greatest Jews of the city, the wealthiest manufacturers, had come. They came in cloaks with huge fur collars, in high silk hats. And in the parquet they sat in frock coats, white vests, white gloves, and the ladies beside them in gowns fit for a ball.

The house was growing more and more packed at every moment. Backstage the huge hum of the audience could already be heard. The tension of the actors reached a height. This was the first day in my actor's life that I was playing a historic figure, and seeing myself in the beautiful black costume, I decided, not without a thrill, that I looked the part.

At the last minute Rosenberg came into my dressing room. He was dressed as one of the rabbis in a long coat and a yarmulke, but with a great clanking sword at his side and another in his hand. This he offered me. "Yankele," he said. "Wear it! It will give you equality with your fanatic oppressors." And he showed me how useful a sword could be on the stage, how you could lean on it, take poses with it. "Remember, Yankele, remember the battle of Plevna!" he exclaimed with rising excitement. "Yes, I saw you there, sword in hand, and knew you were riding to victory!"

In spite of myself, a shiver went through me. To this day I don't know whether that unforgettable scoundrel was making fun of me or meant it.

I did not wear the sword. I judged it would be wrong.

The first act went fairly well, but ended in a bad fiasco. The curtain falls on Uriel's words, "Truth will come even from under the earth and justice fall from the heavens." I uttered the line thoughtfully, seriously, quietly, as was proper for a great philosopher, Spinoza's teacher. But the curtain fell on dead silence, and coming off the stage I heard Rosenberg's angry sigh. My sincerity had done me no favor. The actors, too, walked off with bent heads like punished children. If I had thundered out that last speech I would have been cheered to the rafters, and they too would have shared in the applause and bows. I admit I was sorry for them, for in those days when we hungered, applause was often our only reward. Not like today, when we don't care about the applause, as long as we get the money.

In the second act a great deal depended on Sonya. She was a strong favorite in Lodz, and her entrance as Judith was warmly received. The clever Sonya did not have to be told what was needed. With her first lines she picked up the tempo. Instantly the public felt the difference. The scene came to life. The dialogue began to crack like rifle fire. Our fears left us, our ambition awoke. The audience was with us, and we were full of confidence again.

Sonya closed this act with a stormy monologue. Revealing her own Judaism, she comes to Uriel with the words, "And we both love one great God!" I took her in my arms and with triumph and joy, cried, "My Judith! Mine! Mine! Mine!" The curtain fell on our embrace. It rose and fell again and again. Twenty curtain calls after a second act! And at each curtain call we felt the enthusiasm of the public, their gratitude and love.

Backstage joy mounted to a celebration. "Success!" Rosenberg shouted. And beside himself with pleasure, he cried, "Knock out the third act, Yankele! There you can shake Spivakovsky out of your elbow!"

In this act the great synagogue scene takes place. Acosta, in a white robe, mounts the steps of the high altar to recant his heresy and go through the return to Judaism. The scene was going well. I was playing with true feeling. I *felt* the audience, knew they were with me. I came to the climactic moment when Uriel adjures the congregation to punish him for his sin. "And I lay myself here on the threshold," he cries, "that all may trample me!" And with this he casts himself from the high altar to the ground.

Now I had practiced this fall many times, and was sure I would do it well. But at rehearsal the altar had been lower by several steps, and the ground beneath had been covered with straw. If I had taken this into account, all might have gone well. But that night I was so carried away by my speech that I took no care at all, but simply flung myself, face down, from the altar to the ground. I heard a roar from the audience—a roar like that of a lion—saw myself lying in a pool of blood, and with one last thought spinning in my brain—"If I live I must learn to fall better"—fainted.

How long I lay in that condition I do not know, but when I opened my eyes a whole crowd was around me. Actors, ladies in décolleté, and a gentleman in a frock coat taking my pulse. The ladies were do-gooders who, seeing from the front rows that a misfortune had taken place on the stage, came to help with their moans and sighs. The gentleman in the frock coat was a doctor from the audience.

I gazed from one face to the other. The actors were white as ghosts. Sonya, drenched in tears, was exclaiming like a lost child, "Doctor! Will he ever play again?"

"Even tonight!" came the cheerful reply. "A little courage, a glass of cognac, and he is as good as ever."

From this I understood that the world was still a world, and that an eternity had not passed since my fall, but at most twenty minutes, at that time no more than a lengthy entr'acte.

Rosenberg, looking me over, said, "If you are not dead after this you'll live forever!" He was between laughter and tears. "Well, Yankele," he said, "shall I tell them there has been an accident, or do we go on?"

"We go on," I answered. I called for a mirror and a little alcohol, washed my wounds, put on a fresh beard, set my costume to rights, and gave the call: "Curtain up!"

Behind the scenes the waltz of Acosta's wedding. By now everyone in the theater knew what had happened, and when I made my entrance the whole audience rose as one man and gave me an ovation. I delivered my first line and was surprised by a second ovation. A rumor had spread that the fall had knocked out all my teeth! Hearing me speak gave the public a thrill.

The play came to an end, and the final curtain fell. Countless curtain calls. Applause and bravos from the public. Rosenberg with streaming eyes called from the wings, "Yankele, I blessed you the first time you went on the stage, and now I bless you again!"

We played Acosta for many weeks and one night in the midst of the recantation scene, I was startled to hear a noise backstage like thunder. A Polish troupe, I later learned, were rehearsing in a room over the stage. One of them, with time to kill, came down to have a laugh at the Yiddish actors. He was so transfixed by what he saw that he called out, "Quick! You must see this!" The noise I heard was all the troupe members' feet running down the iron staircase. I marked the event off as a red-letter day in my life.

But how says our King Solomon? *A moment after greatness, the fall.* A good thing we do not believe it, or our poor bit of happiness would not be enjoyed!

GLORY — AND THE AFTERMATH

Who was my equal after my historic fall in Lodz, when I loomed like a giant over my whole theater family? Could it enter my head in that night that the dark days of Kremenchuk were about to engulf me? But misfortune was never far in those early, unsure times.

As always the trouble began with poverty. A long time before *Acosta* we had done badly, and even *Acosta* could not be played forever in Lodz. Sooner than we thought possible, we had empty pockets and a forest of debts.

We felt the change soonest at the inn where we lodged. The owner had always been a pleasant man, respectful in his manner. Now he turned hard and angry, came into our room without knocking, barking out, "Well? How long? It can't go on much further!" And what he did not say in words we felt all the more in the miserable cold of our rooms. It was already November, but we still got no heat. The actors coughed, caught cold in the freezing Polish winter.

Poverty was not the worst of it. We all shared that, and could deal with it. Worse than hunger and cold, a falseness was in the air. Envy and intrigue were at work.

I knew soon after *Acosta* that something was wrong. The actors talked in undertones, they had secrets. I shrugged it off. In the theater world these little intrigues are not rare. Soon, I told myself, we will go on to Warsaw. There, in the great city with its great Yiddish public, we will make a living, and all the nonsense will be forgotten.

The truth, when I discovered it, was like lightning out of a clear sky. The troupe was not going to Warsaw. They were going south again, to the town of Zhitomer. But wait! The company will now be smaller by four members. Who are the four? Rosenberg, Liptzin,

Sonya, and myself. Short and sweet, we are free to go, they can manage without us.

After the success of *Acosta* we could hardly believe our ears. Yet it was true. Everyone was buying Polish hats, Polish cloaks with hoods, warm gloves, getting ready to leave.

It was Spivakovsky who had brought about the change. He was returning to the troupe. But not alone. He was bringing with him a new director, rich in rubles, and these two, between them, were taking over the company. Since they now have a new rich director, why do they need Rosenberg? Since this new director also happens to be an actor, what need of Adler? Without me, of course, they could not hold Sonya. As for our protégée and friend, Keni Liptzin, they can dispense with her too.

The new director? It turns out I know him. His name is Hartenstein. A young man from Galicia with long hair and short brains, half educated in Vienna, and half an actor.

You will ask how had this Hartenstein, an absolute nobody, acquired money enough to take over the troupe? How had he, a Galician, gotten a permit for southern Russia, something our own directors could not do? A simple answer. The governor of Zhitomer was in love with a beautiful Jewish girl. The beauty had an ugly sister. Hartenstein married her. In this way he gained a dowry of a thousand rubles, and the goodwill of the governor.

Rosenberg found a way, but only for himself. Somehow he scratched some money together, from where I don't know, and made ready to leave for Odessa. "How is this?" I said, confronting him. "We have always been comrades, brothers. Now you leave us, desert us?"

Rosenberg could not meet my eyes. "Forgive me," he said hastily. "I must go to my family. If things go well in Odessa I will send help."

What could I say? I knew Rosenberg's devotion to his parents and sisters, knew he would commit crimes to keep them from want.

He left for Odessa. Two days later the actors also left, first for Warsaw, to meet up with Hartenstein, then on to Zhitomer, where they had a permit to play. Sonya, Keni Liptzin, and I remained in Lodz—alone.

But to say alone is hardly enough. We were in a strange city, without a troupe, without money, and with not one friend to whom we could turn.

Sonya came up with a plan. The three hundred fifty rubles that got the troupe out of Nezhin. The money had never been repaid. Now, Sonya said, I must follow the actors to Warsaw, seek out Hartenstein, and demand that the company return this money.

Much as I doubted the outcome, it was still our only hope. Sonya found money for the trip—probably she pawned something—and I left for Warsaw. I was not joyful as I boarded the train. I was going to collect a debt from an actor—much like saying I was on the way to my grave.

Hartenstein, I found, was staying at the best hotel in Warsaw. I waited for him in a lordly room crowded with people, all full of deepest respect for the "Herr Direktor."

At last a door opens. He appears. A white, classic, effeminate face, actorish hair to his shoulders, diamonds in his watch. He surveys us, seats himself at a kingly desk littered with cigars, cigarettes, banknotes, and photographs of girls. There, after dealing with a number of visitors, he turned his attention to me. "Ah yes, Adler," he threw out carelessly, "I believe I have done you an injury."

At this my hands began to shiver. His condescending tone, the insulting familiarity of that "Adler," gave me an overpowering desire to answer as I used to in the old days of the Moldovanka. I lunged forward in a rage, repeating, *"Adler? Adler?"*

Fortunately, Spivakovsky was present. Also a certain Herr Manyevich, a play agent and a friend of Sonya's. Both of them intervened, and between them managed to smooth things over. Spivakovsky, who knew why I had come, explained the situation to Hartenstein. Manyevich also put in a word, and in the course of all this the insult was passed over.

Hartenstein, I discovered, was not mean in money matters. As soon as he understood the facts he called over some of his people and gave them orders to pay me in full. This was such a relief I forgave him everything.

I immediately sent a telegram to Sonya reading, "Have money. Come to Warsaw with Liptzin. We leave tomorrow for Odessa."

The women arrived that night. Hartenstein and Spivakovsky retired to their splendid suite upstairs. We three found ourselves a hole somewhere in the depths of the hotel and went to bed without supper.

In the morning we joined the others in time to see them make an excellent breakfast. More than the food I envied Hartenstein's coat. A magnificent coat with a checked silk lining, a huge satin collar, and on top of that, a fur. And my own coat so shabby! "Ech," I told myself, "never mind! Let me only get back to Odessa, and all will yet come right." I was waiting from moment to moment for the money. Finally I was told we would receive it at the railway station.

At the station the three of us stood at a distance from everyone else and waited. At last Hartenstein sent over a messenger with two railway tickets. Both were only as far as Berdichev. At this I felt an actual stab at the heart. "What is this?" I said. "Where is the money?"

It was too much. I went up to the group around Hartenstein, and Sonya was there before me. "You people without shame!" she flung out with burning scorn. "You dress yourselves in silks and velvets and laugh at all pity and decency! We will forget that you stole our troupe from us, we will forget that you left us stranded and penniless. Give us at least our money and let us go home. What good are your two tickets? We have to take with us an unhappy woman with a broken heart who followed what she thought was a noble, intelligent profession and has been deceived and fooled to the point of suicide!" And here, unable to go on, Sonya broke down entirely.

Her words were not without effect, for Hartenstein was ashamed, and his whole tone changed. He gave us to understand that he also was not the happiest of men, and had paid a heavy price for his good fortune. He asked us to be patient. The messenger with the money had not come to Warsaw, but would meet the troupe without fail at Berdichev. There everyone would be paid, ourselves included.

The end of it was we took the train to Berdichev with the others. Hartenstein and his group traveled first class like lords, ate, drank, spared themselves nothing. We traveled in a third-class carriage feeling as though we were going to our burial. Keni Liptzin looked out the window the whole way and wept. The troupe was going to Zhitomer, the town of her birth. It was ten years since she had visited her mother's grave.

The smaller actors, those of no standing, traveled in our carriage but held themselves at a distance. Perhaps they felt guilty. Only Herr Manyevich concerned himself with our situation. At every stop this kind man brought us food and tea from the station buffet. Between stops he continually stuck his head in at our door, giving us sometimes a smile, sometimes a sigh, always showing his sympathy. The last few times I noticed that the good man had something new to impart. And, in fact, as we were nearing Berdichev, he came in with a shout of "*Mazel tov!*," shook each of our hands in turn, and all but fell on our necks. It seemed that, owing to his efforts, we were all engaged again. Hartenstein had finally consented. We were going on to Zhitomer with the troupe.

At this news Keni Liptzin promptly fainted. We thought she was overcome by joy but as soon as we brought her to, she began tearing her hair and banging her head against the wall. "To Odessa, to Odessa!" she screamed. "Not Zhitomer! Better suicide!" She had run away as a girl from a marriage arranged by her stepmother. She felt unworthy to see the father she had disgraced, unworthy to visit her mother's grave.

We talked to her, tried to calm her. We said we would hide her in some quiet hotel, seek out her father, speak to him, soften him, tell him she had been fooled, deceived, that it was not her fault. In time she grew a little calmer and found some courage.

But what are human plans? In an instant they fall away like a house of cards. Passengers bound for Zhitomer had to get out at Berdichev and travel the rest of the way by coach. We had no sooner descended into the station than Liptzin came face-to-face with the man she feared most. The postmaster's stagecoach had been sent for us from Zhitomer. Her father was the driver.

Of all the scenes this great artist was to play in her long and wonderful career, this was the bitterest, the most painful. The coachman, a burly, black-bearded giant, seemed dazed. She stood before him, silent, her body swaying like a weak branch. The rest of us stood aside, frightened at how the matter would end. The coachman's big hands trembled. A heavy sigh escaped him. His honest face worked. Suddenly a terrible outbreak. "Daughter!" he called hoarsely. "Unhappy little orphan!" Enough! The great heart of the ordinary man of the people had opened. It was over. She fell on his breast wailing, "Father, forgive me! I was young! I didn't understand!"

We had to help her, still weeping, into the coach. The driver climbed to his high seat and whipped up his horses. A gray autumn night. A gray moon. Sad little stars.

"Zhitomer!" the driver called. A sob came from the coach.

ZHITOMER — ODESSA — THE FINAL BLOW

In Zhitomer our theater was always packed—on the outside! Although we racked our brains we could not understand it. On our way to the theater every night we saw a whole city of Jews going with us. The street outside the theater was black with people. But inside—half empty!

In time we penetrated this mystery. Zhitomer was a very Jewish city. Jews like the sands of the sea. Wherever you looked—a Jew. But the Zhitomer Jews were not like those of other cities. Especially the young people were different. They all dressed in the latest style, they all had handsome little walking sticks, rings on their fingers, watches with gold chains. And they walked about so carefully, so importantly, these young people, never hurrying, never pushing, never shoving.

We finally learned the secret of the "Zhitomer manner." The entire youth of this city were living on percent. Every young man was a whole banking house dealing in notes and interest. Boys barely past Bar Mitzvah were collecting interest. And their parents took pride in it! One lady, I remember, pointed out her youngest to me, saying with motherly pride, "You see? Still a child! And how much, beloved son, have you already earned on interest?" "Eight hundred rubles," the infant replied.

Here lay the mystery of our half-empty theaters. These Zhitomer Jews, who from childhood knew the value of a *groschen,* had found a new way to go to the theater. The whole family went but on one ticket.

It was quite simple. Tzippe sat half an act, went out with her ticket, and sent in Zelda. Zelda sent in Berel. Berel sent in Shmerel. Each one told the other what was happening on the stage, and so the whole family saw the play.

You can easily understand that from such audiences no great profit came to us. In addition, the theater belonged to a Russian troupe who took up most of the nights and let us perform only a few times a week.

Hartenstein ignored everything. His ambition was to play, to take the leading roles, and to be the director. He put his trust in the governor, or, rather, in the governor's mistress, Hartenstein's wife's sister, But from such management the troupe soon stood on the brink of bankruptcy.

One day Hartenstein's father arrived from Galicia. The old man had sunk some heavy thousands into this venture, and had come to examine the books. We actors, not aware of how far things had gone, were talking together inside the theater entrance. Suddenly through the glass doors we saw the old man come out on the street weeping, tearing his white hair, and screaming, "Ruined! Ruined!"

With a shock, the real state of affairs broke in on us. We turned to each other, frightened, one question in all eyes. What now?

We thought we had found a quiet corner where we could hold our own, perform, make a bit of a livelihood. Now suddenly no more quiet corner. Move on!

For me personally the whole thing left a bad aftertaste. I had lowered myself, played under a man small as an actor and small as a human being. And what had I gained? The stale fish was swallowed, and still there was hunger!

Sonya, who was nearing her time, went back to Odessa to have our child in the home of my parents. I remained alone to swim as I could.

We were saved by a Dr. Berenstock. This much-respected man arranged a meeting in his home, a sort of consultation. Several wealthy Jews were present, men of standing in the city. Also some young people, students, intellectuals. The advice finally was that we take the theater ourselves for a few nights of benefits. I was assured by these friends that the evenings would be successful.

I decided on three benefits. The first for myself, the second for our two remaining actresses (with Sonya and Liptzin both out of the troupe, only two remained). The third would be for the rest of the company, fourteen persons in all. For my own benefit I announced *Acosta*.

Never underestimate the Jewish soul! Not long ago, I believe I spoke not very kindly of the Zhitomer Jews. Let me now take back those words. This time there were no crowds around a half-empty theater. The whole city was inside, every ticket was sold, and at the final curtain the stage was drowned in flowers.

The whole evening would, in fact, have gone off perfectly if, in my desire for success, I had not drawn in some of the Russian actors. The famous artist Borisov took part, and also a Mademoiselle Kislova, a young actress who greatly admired our theater. This talented girl, with a beautiful ringing voice and a fiery temperament, made a speech that almost landed us all in Siberia. She spoke first of our talent and dedication. Then she went on about what it meant for a people to have a theater, and how it was for them to appreciate and support that theater. Then, being a sincere person who cared nothing for politics and pandered to no one, she began to heap reproaches on the Zhitomer audience for their coldness, their lack of fervor. "Why are you so dry, why are you such mathematicians?" she scolded. "Art cannot exist without a childlike trust, a childlike belief!"

Bankers and wealthy men in the audience stirred restlessly, but the students in the gallery broke into salvo after salvo of hot applause. The whole thing was taking on the air of a political demonstration, and the police chief at the back of the hall called out for the actress to bring her address to an end.

But no power on earth could now stop the impassioned young speaker. Now it was not the Jewish audience, but Russian society she blamed. And she poured equal scorn on her own colleagues, the Russian actors. The Russians sent up a stormy protest, a tumult broke out in the theater, and the police chief came up onto the stage, shouting for the curtain to come down.

The situation was bad. Hartenstein's influence with the governor extended only to himself; and we were playing these benefits without an official permit. We went home that night in consternation at the turn things had taken.

There was a hearing next morning in the governor's chancellery. The Russian actor Philipovsky was present, and told me he would speak for us. Mademoiselle Kislova arrived with her parents, her brothers and sisters. And openly before everyone, this remarkable girl presented me to her family, showering me with praise meanwhile as an artist and a human being.

Why draw it out? The whole affair began to take on the tone of a family gathering, and a little later, of an actual comedy. The governor apologized for not coming to our performances, which, in fact, had never been officially allowed by his buildings minister. But he was clearly well disposed toward us, and finally, unbending like a lord, he asked us to sing "something Yiddish."

My colleagues and I exchanged a resigned look. "Children," I said softly, "the great lord says sing—and sing we must!" I chose Gold-faden's irresistible "The Rabbi Bids Us Be Merry." The troupe sang it with a will. The governor's wife and children came in. Russian offi-cers came in. The servants crowded into the doorway. It was truly "theater."

The governor was well entertained. He gave us a gift of fifty rubles, and carried away by enthusiasm, exclaimed, "Play as much as you like! On my responsibility!"

"I hear you, Highness!" the police chief cried. And with a low bow before Kislova and another before the troupe, he asked our forgiveness.

Once the benefits had been played, the troupe broke up, and I remained in Zhitomer alone. In my heart a stormy reckoning was taking place. What was I doing, I asked myself, in this world of false colors and meaningless tumult? What future did it hold for me? I was almost thirty, soon to be a father, and still I had no sign of a home. And though I had won some honor, how soon it had been drowned in tears and despair! Enough! It was time to make an end. A stern revision was needed in my life. I would throw off these theatri-cal rags, root out of my soul the sound of the applause, and go back! To Odessa! To work, to business! I will bow my head before Uncle Arke and begin to live like a man who is a husband and the father of a family.

And yet, something held me back. Poor actor's soul! Poor Yiddish theater! You are an unfortunate, a loved hunchback. Those who take shelter under your coat can never be straight again. Though we may curse you, we cannot leave you.

For all my resolution, one thought gave me no rest. For three years I had wandered in the cave of the Witch in the clown's rags of Shmen-drick, and what did I really know of my trade? Who can tell what may happen in this life of ours? If someday I should return to the Yid-dish stage, let me at least not be so ignorant. Let me know at least something of the craft, the ABCs of theater art.

It so happened that here in Zhitomer, with my career at its lowest ebb, I had become acquainted with two famous Russian actors, Borisov and Philipovsky. These two artists had become my friends. They encouraged me in every way, and had offered to share with me the secrets of their craft.

These two men, character actors widely known in Russia, had several times "guest starred" in the theaters of Moscow and St. Petersburg. Borisov had played in St. Petersburg before the tsar. Yet these two celebrated artists always returned to Zhitomer, not because they lacked other opportunities, but because it was their theatrical home.

The theater of that time was not centralized as it is today. Every town had its playhouse, and an audience passionately loyal to its favorites. Well-known artists often lived out their whole professional lives in these small cities, where they had full say over everything in their theater and were loved as nowhere else. The artistic level of these provincial companies was often high. In Zhitomer, to judge by Adler, both production and acting were superb.

The friendship of these two actors, to say nothing of the passionate advocacy of Miss Kislova, shows the independence such people enjoyed even under the brutal reign of Alexander III. Borisov lent the prestige of his presence to Adler's benefit; Philipovsky, of his own accord, spoke to the governor on his behalf. Both freely gave their time and energy inducting this altogether obscure Yiddish player into the mysteries of their art.

Adler, for his part, never forgot what they taught him. The productions he later staged in America, productions one critic would describe as "little short of a miracle," came directly out of the weeks he lingered with these friends.

For six more weeks I remained in Zhitomer. Night after night I visited my Russian friends. And night after night, willingly, beautifully, they taught me. How to mix colors so as to get different effects. How to make lines, and how to make wrinkles. How to make the face look full, how to make it appear sunken and thin. How to alter the figure by means of costume. The magic effects of light and shadow. All the secrets of their great art, of what it means to really put a play on the stage.

Working with these actors I felt shame for my own theater. Makeup with us? Slops of color, slapped-on powder, a Purim masquerade! It was artistry with the Russians, a great accomplishment. The Russian actors could make themselves taller, shorter, fatter, thinner. They could change their noses, their eyes, their chins—the entire face! And their voices and speech they could also change. Both men worked from a palette like that of a painter, and their dressing rooms were like the atelier of a painter, with pots of every color lined up on their dressing tables. And with these colors they could remake their faces—more, rebuild them as with sculpture!

And with us? A few pieces of colored chalk. Burnt matches for the dark lines, a bottle of glue for the beard. Our costumes a joke. A few wigs, the same ones over and over. The Russians wore costly silks and velvets on the stage. They had magnificent wigs of every period. They paid their scenic artists as highly as their greatest stars, imported French landscape painters for their outdoor scenes, took endless pains with every prop, every detail, so that the whole stage lived, a thing wonderful to the eye.

Only after I had learned and mastered all this did I part with Borisov and Philipovsky and the many other friends I had made in this city. Last of all I parted with Keni Liptzin. Then back to work, to business. Enough wandering! Enough years lost in the cave of the Witch in the motley of Shmendrick.

Firmly resolved to forget theater, to return, as it were, to the right path, I came back to my native city.

I found Sonya in the home of my parents, a new Sonya in white clothes, a tiny morsel of humanity at her side. This was our little daughter Rivka (Rebecca), a child not fated to be with us long.

My sister was now a young Fräulein of eighteen, tall as her mother and beautiful as a picture. She welcomed me with a joy that had in it a certain sympathy. In my mother's embrace I also noticed something of tact. I had come back after three years, and what had I achieved?

Uncle Arke was older, more gray than I remembered, but with all the old spirit and heart. No sooner in the house was he than ten- and five-ruble notes lay under my Sonya's snow-white pillow.

Uncle Arke did not touch on my situation on this first visit, but as he was leaving he took my hand with an affectionate smile and said, "Well, Yankele? Was it worth it? How long to drag yourself over half a world? And what have you had from all that? Enough, Yankele! Enough wandering, enough seeking miracles from the skies. Now you are, with God's help, a father, so become a human being!"

And so I went out to become a human being. I visited my old haunts, looked up good friends of other days—lawyers, notaries for whom I had worked. These friends, I felt, would surely have a place for me. At least, I thought, they would speak for me, recommend me for some good position. I was mistaken. Like a shadow wherever I went, my "bad name," the name of "actor" followed me. My friends thought of me now as a merrymaker, a sort of clown. They asked for a song, a dance.

Hard for the actor to turn businessman. The way back is barred. To tell the truth, I missed it all, the hurrying to the theater at night, the tumult, the sound of the overture. Nothing else had any real interest for me. It was the same with Sonya. She, the strong one, said nothing, but it was as though a light had gone out in her soul. At night when she thought I was asleep, I heard her restless sighs.

My uncle's advice, my parents' concern, my own resolutions, all had led to nothing. There was no way back to my old life. I began to sniff around the theater again.

I looked up the actors I knew, went to see plays. How could I stay away? In that winter of 1882 Odessa was the hub and center of the whole Yiddish theater world. Osip Lerner was at the Mariinsky with *La Juive* and *Uriel Acosta.* Goldfaden's masterpiece, *Shulamith,* was at the Remesleni. Both companies were performing nightly to packed houses, and all Odessa was boiling over with excitement about two actors, the comedian Mogulesko, already famous throughout the Jewish world, and the dramatic star, Abba Schoengold.

Schoengold, a Romanian Jew, was the god of the Yiddish public, the god, indeed, of all who saw him on the stage. I first caught sight of him standing at the door of the Mariinsky Theater, and I can say without exaggeration that he was the handsomest man in the world. Tall. Blue eyes. Golden hair. An Apollo. He was wearing a coat of sable and over it had thrown a black cloak. To this day I remember the color of that cloak, and against it, his white and exquisite hand. I stopped at the sight of him, and not only I, but everyone stopped, asking each other who this man could be.

I confess I greatly envied this actor, whom Russian critics were comparing to Possart and Salvini. He was especially admired in *Uriel Acosta,* which he was the first to play. Yet for all his success he was charming, easygoing, without conceit. We drew closer, and a friendship grew up between us that would never be broken. Indeed, it would one day be strengthened by an even closer tie.*

* In 1911 Joseph Schoengold, Abba Schoengold's son, married Frances Adler, the first child of Jacob and Sara Adler.

In the winter of 1882 I also met the famous comedian Siegmund Mogulesko. Although he had not yet attained the full genius of his American years, Mogulesko was already idolized. With *Acosta* and *La Juive,* Lerner had opened the door to the European drama. Who knows what this gifted man might have accomplished if not for the dark and tragic turn his life was to take.

In 1882 Lerner was a known personality in our world, one of our strongest fighters for the Jewish world. If anyone had told me this man would end his life an apostate and an enemy, I would have hurled the words back as a slanderous lie.

Lerner and I had talked on several occasions, but in the meantime I received another offer. This came from Sheikevitch. The well-known novelist had now turned playwright and had a troupe of his own. He had returned to Odessa just then from a tour of nearby towns. We met, we talked. His wife, Sonya, who managed all of his arrangements, liked me on sight and cast me as the lover in his play *The Bloody Adieu.*

But my stay in Odessa was short. As soon as Sonya recovered from childbed I put together a troupe of my own, and with Fishkind, Keni Liptzin, our infant daughter, and the wet nurse, went back on the road.

We were traveling from town to town and doing well when—suddenly—Rosenberg! The two of us joined forces, and together we toured Rostov, Taganrog, and various Lithuanian cities.

In Dünaburg (now called Dvinsk)* Rosenberg took fire with the old dream. Petersburg! "What do you say, Yankele?" he asked. "Shall we make a try at the capital? See the spot where Alexander fell?"

Rosenberg did not like to waste time with long thinking. He got together with our old entrepreneur, Cheikel Bain. Cheikel put in a few hundred and we were off, smoking cigars and traveling first class by special express.

We stopped off for a few performances at Riga, and had good business there at the Lithuanian Club. Meanwhile I drew up a petition and sent it off to the Petersburg authorities.

While we waited for the permit, we played. It was holiday time. Money came in. Again there was a life for us. Everyone was happy, everyone free of care—when the final ax fell: By edict of the tsar,

---

* In present-day Latvia.

Yiddish theater was forbidden throughout the length and breadth of Russia.

The Russian newspapers were full of the news, the Russian and German troupes glad to be rid of a galling competition.

Again, like death itself, the bitter question—what now?

On May 3, 1882, Alexander III officially appointed a High Commission for the Revision of Current Laws Regulating the Jews. The notorious so-called "temporary rules" went into effect soon after.

Hundreds of Jews had by this time left the country, and emigration had already become the burning question of the day. A wealthy few feared it as a sign of disloyalty. Jewish revolutionaries also opposed it, believing Jews should stay in Russia and fight. Ordinary people who do not live by theories saved themselves as best they could, and fled.

The edict against Yiddish theater came out on August 7, 1883. This was the law that would send Adler's troupe into exile. The other troupes hung on for a time, but one by one they eventually gave up and left.

Although the High Commission sat for six years without producing evidence that the Jews had worked harm to the people or the state, they were denied due process under the law, driven out of their trades and professions, their land confiscated, their schools shut down, societies banned, and their press outlawed.

The worst fate fell on those who lived illegally in the central cities. They were ruthlessly expelled, and when they fled to the rural communes, they were driven out again. Within a few years ten thousand of these people would be wandering destitute over the land. Masses of them went over into Galicia, drawn by a false rumor that the French would take them in. Famine and plague broke out in their camps. The governor-general in St. Petersburg forbade collections for them, and money that had been donated to aid them was returned.

A letter from Leo Nikolayevich Tolstoy, rough in tone, practically ordered the tsar to stop his criminal persecution of this people, but we know of no other voice raised on their behalf.

It is possible that no one else dared. In these first years of the new regime every trace of the father's reforms were torn down and demolished by the son. Liberal influence had been rooted out of the judicial system. The universities lay under the domination of the church.

Spies and informers proliferated. The press was gagged, and in the mounting fear all discussion of public affairs grew silent. These were the years when Tolstoy's home was under police surveillance, Maxim Gorky was a fugitive. The eighties had begun, that melancholy decade when Russia's artists and intellectuals felt that all hope was lost. Arbitrary police power terrorized the land. Floggings and executions were common events. The new tsar had set the clock back to the days of Nicholas the Flogger.

Time, however, unlike the clock, goes only forward. Alexander III would end a prisoner in his own palace, his country moving inevitably toward revolution.

Our Last Piece of Russian Earth

Three Yiddish troupes existed at that time in Russia. Our own, and those of Goldfaden and Sheikevitch in Odessa. The edict struck all of us down.

For us in Riga it was as though the very thread of our lives had snapped. It was a long time before we could come out of our paralyzed state, look around, try to find a way out.

Our first idea was to send someone to St. Petersburg. We soon gave up the idea. Our first frightened inquiries brought the inescapable truth. No way around the edict. It was steel and iron—the law.

Nothing remained then but to leave Russia entirely. But where were we to go? Romania? If the great Goldfaden had fled there as from a plague, what chance had we, tiny atoms that we were? From Galicia we had such news that not even a lunatic would go there in his dreams. America? We could not form a picture of a place so distant and so vast. And money for such a journey?

Only one possibility remained, one ray of light in the darkness around us, one piece of earth still visible above the flood. London. At that time people spoke of London as a little later they spoke of America. But could we survive there? Would Yiddish theater be possible? Could we play, earn our bread? Questions there were in plenty, but answers hard to find.

Rosenberg and Cheikel worked out a plan. Riga was a port. Boats from London came in every day. We would go to the dock and wait for such a boat. Among the passengers there was sure to be a Jew. We would question him, and he would tell us what we wanted to know.

Well and good. We go to the dock, God helps, and we sight our Jew. But he was somehow a peculiar person, not young, not old, not old-fashioned, not worldly, his beard half shorn, his Yiddish so mixed with foreign words we could hardly understand him. Nevertheless, we surrounded him, showered him with questions, and carried him off with us—carried him off, that is, to Cheikel Bain.

Cheikel had been with us for three years now. What he lived through in that time is a part of the history of the Yiddish theater that will never be written down. Who interests himself in such unimportant people as Cheikel Bain?

The little Odessa businessman had come to us with a stammer and a cough. In his three years with the troupe, both had gotten worse. Riga killed him. When he heard of the edict we thought his heart would stop. He took to his bed and did not get up again.

Because of his illness we took a room for him outside the city. A good room, on the ground floor with no stair for him to climb. But the room had one drawback. The court outside belonged to a poultry dealer, and all day long it was loud with the cackling of turkeys, hens, and geese. If you dared open a door or a window you let in the noise of the whole feathered tribe.

But we have our Jew, and we bring him to Cheikel. We get him a chair, Cheikel sits up in bed, we stand around him, and the questions begin. Are there many Jews in London? What kind of Jews are they? Are they the kind that will want to see theater? Can actors make a living there?

But the stranger's Yiddish was so horribly mixed with English it was impossible to make out anything he said. Cheikel began to stammer and cough in his impatience. "Reb Jew, are you a Jew?" he finally broke out, exasperated. "Speak so we can understand you!"

But our Jew was beginning to pull a very long face. His eyes rolled fearfully, taking in our shaven faces, our sporty-elegant clothes. "Listen to me, young people!" he said in a hollow voice, "London is a city with terrible laws. In London they hang you if you steal even a bagel!"

"You—you Englishman!" Cheikel shouted, beside himself. "We are actors, a devil on your father's father! We are not going to London to steal. Out of my house! Out!" And rising from his bed, he drove the stranger out the door, letting in such a cackle and a crowing that the man ran for his life.

We knew as little about London as before. But what remained was—we were going! And that put a new soul into us.

Once again we took ourselves over the city, knocking on strange doors, whispering, tapping. But ships' companies, it seemed, have an unpleasant habit; they like to be paid. We were by this time full-fledged paupers. And Cheikel, who had always found money for us from under the earth, could not help us now.

At last, by long trying, we found a German Jew, a man, we were told, who had connections with shipping companies and could arrange ship's passage. Since our condition could not be hidden, we told him the truth. We are actors, we said. The edict of the government has stranded us as in a shipwreck. We are going to a strange country, our only baggage our art and the few plays we possess, our only hope that among our own people we will not fail.

The German Jew was skeptical. He did not seem to believe we were really actors, as we said. We assured him it was true. We were ready to perform for him on the spot. But he seemed to be more convinced, and after thinking a little he told us to come back in a few days, when he might have something for us.

Eventually, through the German Jew, we got passage to Hamburg on a cattle boat. But with two conditions. We had to provide our own food for the journey. And every other night we had to entertain the captain and the ship's officers. The second condition was easy enough; the trouble was with the first. To provide our own food was not at all to our liking. But we were in no position to bargain, and agreed to everything.

Happiest of all was Cheikel. He had always favored the idea of London. He was eagerly looking forward to the trip, and was convinced to the last that the sea air on the voyage would cure him.

Poor Cheikel. Not destined to go with us to London. Not destined to share our fortunes there. One dark night we get word that our journey will be minus one passenger. Cheikel is no longer among the living.

He died there among the chickens and the geese, and in the morning we came to mourn him. He was laid out on the ground and we stood around him and wept. Through all the years of our wandering he had been a father to us all. And what worse omen now than his death just before our departure!

His wife and brother came from Odessa, and his wife wailed over his body. "Died in a strange land, my Cheikel!" she wept. "No wife, no child, no brother, no sister!" And every time the door opened to admit new mourners, turkeys, hens, and geese also entered. Rosenberg, reciting the prayer for the dead, continually broke off to whisper, "Yankele, chase away the rooster before it alights on the body."

May God not punish us. Actors are also no more than human. In spite of our grief we laughed hysterically.

Bitter laughter. Can it be anything but a comedy—when actors die?

We had hardly mourned our entrepreneur and brought him to Jewish burial when suddenly Yisrol Gradner appeared. He had come to Riga with his wife, he heard we were leaving the country, and he rained in on us out of the blue. "Forgive me, children," he cried. "I sinned against you in the past. But is this a time to bring up old debts when our actor's bread is being snatched from our mouths? You know me of old. You know what we can do, my wife and I. Take us with you."

I was overjoyed. Gradner, the great singer, the great actor! His wife a marvelous prima donna. Old friends, besides, from the Odessa days! Without hesitation I gave him my hand and said, "You are with us!"

But when Rosenberg heard this he flew into a terrible rage. "Again Yisrolik Gradner?" he cried. "Again the bird of the ill omen who never brought us anything but misfortune?" And he swore that if Gradner came to London we could count him out.

The whole cast argued with him, begged, pleaded. Nothing helped. He could not abide the Lithuanian. He insisted Gradner was bad luck. He knew that with such a star in the troupe he would be overshadowed, and he would not budge. It was Gradner or him, and I had to choose.

But leave me alone? Certainly not! He gave me no peace night or day, but ran after me through the streets demanding justice.

One day as we were arguing the matter at the Riga harbor, Rosenberg suddenly said, "Wait! Let us rely on people! Do you see that Jew over there with the sack on his back? He will be our judge." And going up to a stranger entirely immersed in his own affairs, Rosenberg took him familiarly by the arm as only Rosenberg could, and said, "Come along with me, uncle. We need you to judge a case."

The stranger, wary, not sure what he was getting into, nevertheless let himself be steered in our direction. Rosenberg, holding him by his lapel, pointed to me and said, "Look at this man, uncle! He and I grew up in one town, learned from the same rabbi, danced together at strange weddings, and dragged ourselves side by side over half Russia. We are actors. Theater folk. Now we are forbidden to play and are leaving the country. Comes between us a stranger, a Litvak, a bird of ill omen, and wants to steal my friend from me. I will not go if the stranger comes with us." Having summed up his case, Rosenberg released his hold on the man and said, "Now I am going to buy myself a cigar. While I am gone, consider and decide. With whom should my friend go? With me, his brother, or with the Litvak?"

Certain of success, Rosenberg darted across the way, bought a cigar at a kiosk, and quickly returned. The stranger, freed from his grasp, studied first his back as he left, then his face as he returned. Next he carefully perused my face. "Young man!" he finally said, pointing to Rosenberg. "Go with him! With this man here." And shouldering his sack, he went his way. Rosenberg fell into my arms, weeping for joy.

And for all that, it was with Gradner that I sailed, and not with Rosenberg. My mind, my practical brain, told me I had done well. In my heart I knew better. The deed cannot be undone. It must stand, a blot and a stain on my youth. Yet what could I do? Rosenberg would not give in. In that great, cold, unknown world of London I already guessed how bitter would be the fight to survive. I knew that with Gradner there was a chance, and with Rosenberg I would go under. And beyond London that other image rose. Bathed in unimaginable colors, the land beyond the sea where there was no king and no tsar, where men lived in freedom. I had made my decision, and I held to it. Rosenberg went back with a broken heart to southern Russia. I sailed with the Gradners for London.

Before we left, a few of us put together what money we had and bought a stone for Cheikel Bain. We came together one last time at his grave and were washed in our own tears. "Farewell, Cheikel," Rosenberg cried. "We will see each other again in a better, truer world." Then, as the law commands, we pulled up grass, threw it behind us, and weeping aloud, left the cemetery.

We took ship on a cold November day. No one came to see us off, no one was there to shed a tear, to wave a last good-bye. God knows we had little reason to love our country, the country that had crushed our hopes, stifled our art. Yet how it ached in us, this parting. How the tears burned as we saw its shores recede.

Adieu, Russia. Adieu, my youth.

Adler's memoirs break off here, and would be resumed only after an interval of six years. The last entry in the *Varheit* appeared on February

25, 1919. The paper had failed, and three days later published its final issue.

Because of a quarrel with the Hebrew Actors Union, Adler played the entire winter of 1919–20 at the Pavilion Theater in London. He took with him as part of his troupe his wife and leading lady, Sara Adler, and two of their daughters: Frances, the eldest, and Stella, a girl not out of her teens.

The season in London was a triumph with capacity houses at every performance and many people waiting two days outside the theater for tickets.

But strains were also mounting. Adler was getting older, the demands he made on himself were beginning to tell on his health. In the summer of 1920, while vacationing with his family in upstate New York he had a sudden attack of dizziness and lost consciousness. He had suffered a paralytic stroke.

After a number of months in a sanitarium, Adler came back to the big apartment on Riverside Drive that was now his home. Once a year a benefit was organized for him. These widely advertised "Final Appearances" provided him with an income, but his active career in the theater was over.

In 1925 he received an offer from his old friend the Socialist leader Louis Miller. Miller was making another try at newspaper publishing. Adler's memoirs had been a successful feature in the old paper, and Miller wanted to go on with the series in the new one.

The stroke had paralyzed one side of Adler's body, but his mind and speech had not been affected. Three times a week Joel Entin, the critic and journalist, came to the apartment on Riverside Drive and took down Adler's recollections of London and New York.

The first issue of the *New Varheit* came out on March 14, 1925, with Adler's photograph on the front page and the first entry of his memoirs prominently featured.

Now under the title *My Life,* he picked up the story where he had left it—in the year 1883, when he and his actors, at the end of the long voyage from Riga, came into London harbor.

OUR THEATER IN EXILE

Great London! City of millions! City of Sir Henry Irving, of Garrick, of Shakespeare! Do you know who is now at your portals and will soon be treading your stones? Do you know what strange language will now sound forth from your majestic stage? Do you know, great London, how much poverty and hunger we incoming children of the muse will live through on your gray old streets, how many nights we will pass without rest or sleep, how often we will stand beside your historic Thames, mingling our tears in its greenish waters?

No—London is eternal. One more dark corner in so much darkness. A few more lost children among so many lonely and lost. Great London knows nothing of them. Neither can it know, and neither can it care.

At the end of November 1883, our ship came into London harbor. No one expected us, no one knew we were coming, no one was there to greet us. The great world city swallowed us up as it had so many others, without a ripple. We took ourselves out over the streets, doubly wanderers—actors and Jews.

Great London with its deep-throated roar lay all around us. The onward-rushing crowds, the shouts, the confusion—the giant world city seemed not only indifferent, but as though it would annihilate us with its indifference. And though the human being can never know what is in store for him, a premonition that something here did not bode well for us struck, snakelike, at the heart.

All through the voyage on the sea one name had been on our lips, a name scribbled for us on a card by kind people in Riga. All of us, from the greatest stars to the lowliest player, knew that name, and my little two-year-old daughter, Rivka, if she could speak, would have

known it too. The district was Whitechapel, the street Mansion
Street, and on this Mansion Street a Jew by the name of Sonnenschein
had a restaurant. Sonnenschein was a Romanian who had seen Yiddish
theater in Bucharest. And to this Sonnenschein we knew we must go.

Kind fate gave us a clear cold day, not one of those fogs where out
of nowhere total night descends and people stand paralyzed and lost
until finally torches appear in the streets and lights come on in the
windows. We had luck. The London policeman in his cape was a gentleman accustomed to the human wreckage coming off these boats.
With a word of German, a word of Yiddish, and our card—we had not
a wraith of English among us—he grasped what was needed. With his
help a boy was found who, for a shilling, was willing to take us to
Mansion Street.

We had gone only a little way from the docks when a notable
group came into view—individuals in whom an acute eye would per-
ceive not a little of both the comic and the tragic. The men, clean-
shaven, young, several of them with tall hats and walking sticks, the
women, also young, even better looking and better dressed—one or
two even with a piece of jewelry. And still the pauper peeped out from
under the masquerade! On one a turned-out shoe, on another a cuff
less white than virgin snow. Here a patch. There a tatter. Who were
they? What were they doing near the docks? I never knew, but after
forty years I still recall them as among my first impressions of London.

After walking a way with our baggage, we boarded a tram. This
carried us into the East End, where we dismounted and continued our
journey on foot.

You must know that in London there is a West End and an East End.
The West End is for those happy mortals sent into the world with a
kiss. The East End is for the others. Here live the poor, the small, the
shamed, those whom fate, seeing how bent and shrunken they are as
they creep through the gates of life, spat in their face for good measure.

In this East End is one corner where the poor, in addition to the
spittle, are sent through the gate with a kick, a blow, and their hats
shoved over their eyes. In this corner with the holy name
Whitechapel, a piece of Israel existed. There we would have to sink or
swim, survive or go under, find bread or, if we could not—find death.

The further we penetrated into this Whitechapel, the more our hearts
sank. Was this London? Never in Russia, never later in the worst

slums of New York, were we to see such poverty as in the London of the 1880s. Hunched-over houses with lopsided roofs and lopsided walls, houses black with age and old as though they carried the years of Methuselah on their backs. Narrow twisting alleys. Dark little shops full of crazy, useless goods. At the corners women in ragged shawls shivering with the cold. And the men pushing their barrows through the streets going about their work without grace, without joy, all of them bent, waxen-faced, old—old as though they had never had a childhood, but had come out of their mothers already gray and old.

Our journey ended at what seemed a poor lodging house with a tavern or restaurant on the ground floor. Just outside this establishment an enormous man in a long apron was stirring a kettle from which came the aroma of frying fish. This person, round as a barrel and with pale, runny, fishy eyes, was none other than the Sonnenschein whose name we had pored over a thousand times on the ocean.

This Sonnenschein, known to Whitechapel as "Velvel Fish," had a partner as thin as he was fat and called, for some reason, Chaim the Demon. From these two men we had our first meal in London. After resting a little in the rooms upstairs, we came together to take counsel with each other. Where to turn? Where to find help?

Our main hope in London rested on the very revered and famous Rabbi Adler with whom, by good fortune, I had a family connection. A distant connection to be sure, but still the great chief rabbi was of our family. My grandfather had often told me as a child that the Adlers had come originally from Germany, and that the German-born chief rabbi of London was, in fact, my great-uncle. Learning I was about to leave for England, my father had sent me a Hebrew letter presenting me to this illustrious relative.

The following day, then, armed with this document, and wearing my high hat and best coat, I called at the great rabbi's home. I went alone and fairly certain of success, for in all my experience I had never gone to anyone for help and not received it. This shows that in my appearance, my dress, my demeanor, was something that called out respect.

The very renowned Rabbi Adler had performed the duties of his office for over thirty years, and was a man respected in the Christian community as well as his own. Men in high places often called on the Jewish leader when they needed help with the urgent problems of the day, and the rabbi, among his other accomplishments, was among the founders of the National Society for the Prevention of Cruelty and Better Protection of Children—a task on which he had labored with Sir Benjamin Waugh, Herbert Spencer, and the Cardinal Archbishop of Winchester.

The chief rabbi has a place, in fact, among the great reformers of the Victorian era, and the Jewish Institute stands in London today on the East End thoroughfare of Adler Street.

It was to the Crosby Square residence of this important man that his young relative, just arrived in London, came in hopes of finding help.

The very revered Dr. Hillel Nissim Adler, highest religious authority not only of London Jews but of all Orthodox Jews throughout Great Britain and the Empire, was at that time a man in his eighties. Although he was still vigorous and with unimpaired faculties, his duties were so many and so arduous that his congregation found it needful to give him an assistant. This was none other than his son, Dr. Herman Marcus Adler, a man in the full strength of his fortieth year. Though the younger rabbi had his own congregation in the fashionable suburb of Bayswater, he was mostly to be found in his father's company. Thus, on my first visit I met both father and son.

The old man received me in the official manner typical of men who are occupied with serious community affairs. But his greeting was not entirely without friendliness, and even sweetness. And when he heard I was of his family, and had brought a letter from my father in Hebrew, he became truly warm, presented me to his son, begged me to be seated, and sent for refreshments.

The conversation took place in German, which the two rabbis, both from Hannover, spoke very well. I ate a few morsels out of politeness and exchanged some words with the younger man while his father looked deeply into my father's letter. The more he read, the more relaxed he became. Occasionally something brought a smile to the old yellowed face. Once or twice he raised his head and cast a soft look in my direction as if asking if this was indeed a lost little branch of the great Adler tree. At last, apparently satisfied, he folded the letter, made polite inquiries about my father and mother, expressed regret for the death of my grandfather, and coming down to brass tacks, asked what I was doing in London and in what way he could be of help.

At just this crucial point, however, the smile on the rabbi's lips disappeared. An actor? An actor who played in the "jargon"? In *Yiddish?* Though he did not actually say it, every line and wrinkle of the eighty-year-old face told me I had lost him. For all my wonderful *zayde,* for all the beautiful Hebrew letter from my father, I saw I had become nothing in his eyes but a blot on the proud name of Adler.

Many times in Russia when the troupe fell into straits, I had gone for help to the rabbi of some small town. I was always received with tolerance, even friendship. But I saw no such kindly forbearance in the face of my famous relative. His head, which until now had moved up and down with such approval, now moved forbiddingly from side to side. He still smiled, but now with disbelief, mistrust, even mockery—as one smiles at the impudent lie of a child one does not intend at that moment to punish and correct. The very way he had pronounced the word *Yiddish*—with such a twist of the mouth—told me our beloved language held no honored place in his heart. And I had come to spread this "jargon" further? To popularize it? Worse, to do so in public where, God forbid, strangers might come to jeer and make a mockery of our people? In the eyes of both rabbis I saw anxiety and fear.

Yet the great chief rabbi remained polite. He suggested the matter might be taken up at some future time. He assured me I would be welcome should I call again. He did not forget to send greetings to my worthy wife.

I left the house stunned by my defeat. This powerful man, whose influence extended even to the great Christian world, could have saved us, it seemed to me, with a wave of his hand. Instead he had turned his back and left us to our fate. This to people in a strange land, people stranded as in a shipwreck!

Later in life, when I became more familiar with the deeply religious type of German Jew, I came to a better understanding of the Yiddish archbishop of London. The great rabbi, one of the Frankfurter Orthodoxy, pious and rigid as one can hardly imagine, could not but hate and fear a Yiddish theater. Little as he knew of it, he understood it must somehow touch things with a less than sacrosanct hand, that a scene must sometimes take place in which there would be a prayer, a blessing, that an engagement or a wedding would be represented not

with the sacred purpose for which it was intended, but as a mere theatrical spectacle. Such a God-fearing Jew could not endure so much as
a blessing on the stage, for such a blessing would be given *in vain,* and
according to the great Oral Law, this is not permitted.

Lastly, such a sternly pious German-born rabbi wants the Jew to
keep his Jewishness in two places: his home and his temple. He must
not show it to the outside world for fear the Gentiles will get the idea
that Jewish life is, in any respect whatsoever, like their own.

Above all, the London rabbi was aware that the enemies of Israel
are always about, ready to criticize, to mock. And where would they
have a better opportunity than in a Yiddish theater?

All this I understood in my later years. At the time I was still
young and more superficial in my understanding of Jewishness, and
so the rabbi's attitude seemed to me very heartless, and I left his home
broken and bitter.

I was to call again on the chief rabbi, but on my second visit the
old man did not receive me cordially, and soon withdrew his presence
entirely. His son, too, spoke little of my situation, but talked the
whole time of family lineage and the Adler family *viches* (religious or
scholarly prestige). Apparently the doctor felt nothing could interest
me more, for he took from somewhere an old book and began grub-
bing through the pages, reading out great-grandfathers and great-
grandmothers, his eyes shining with excitement, and all this in
such detail that I almost forgot my trouble in the effort to hide my
laughter.

Suddenly he looked up with an angry face and said, "You are no
longer of the *kohanim*!" He had discovered, it seems, that some great-
great-grandfather of mine had broken his holiness by marrying a
widow. "Such a sin remains unto the tenth generation," Dr. Adler
informed me. I took this misfortune with some philosophy. The sight
of this little man, so wrapped up in the importance of *viches* struck me
as so comic that I have always wanted to reproduce it on the stage.
When I had the Dewey Theater a few years ago I described the scene
to a playwright with the idea he might include it in a play. Nothing
came of it. The play remained unwritten, and the portrait of Dr. Herman Marcus Adler was never presented on our stage.

All the same, family lineage is no small thing. Just before I left
London, when things were very bad with me, my illustrious uncle
gave me, of his charity, as much as thirty pounds.

Adler, turned away from the home of his famous uncle, did not fully understand the political nature of his uncle's problem. The chief rabbi, coming from Germany to London, had found a score of hostile, quarreling congregations. Only after years of effort had he succeeded in welding them into one United Synagogue. Even now the alliance was an uneasy one.

The Jews of the West End, many by now English-born, had little in common with the immigrants of Whitechapel, who made no effort to Anglicize themselves. And the human avalanche now pouring into London, refugees fleeing from the Russian temporary rules of 1882, did little to bring the two groups closer.

The Yiddish spoken by the East Enders had from the beginning been a sore spot, a "jargon" that cultivated men and women felt could only separate those who spoke it from the rest of the nation. Rabbi Adler, chief defender of the Orthodox faith against the encroachments of Reform, still hoped to wean the Jews of the East End away from this divisive language. The great aim, the great battle of this serious man's life, was unity. He was the last man in the world who would have given help or support to a Yiddish theater in London.

My visit to my aristocratic uncle left me with a very heavy heart. The troupe were putting all their hopes on my connection with the great chief rabbi, and his cold answer could only be felt as a terrible blow.

But you must not think we lost our courage. Once we understood we could expect no help from that quarter, we were determined to find it elsewhere. Someone in the troupe—I don't remember who—proposed we appeal to the wealthy Jews of the West End. And for a time, I recall, we all considered this as a possibility, at least a hope. People of that kind, we reasoned, more worldly and less pious than the chief rabbi, might support a Yiddish theater.

In the end our help came from humbler circles. It came, as it had in Russia, from small Jewish businessmen, from poor intellectuals, writers, and journalists, though God knows how little influence they had in those days, and how they struggled.

But while we waited, the most surprising intelligence came from our landlord, Sonnenschein. Though he could not tell us how it got there or who had brought it, the Yiddish theater, strange to say, had apparently found its way to London before us! Sonnenschein himself had once taken part in a Yiddish play, and his partner, "Chaim the Demon," acquired his peculiar nickname playing "an imp" in a Whitechapel one-acter. Both our landlords, and others too, assured us that at that very moment Yiddish actors were performing here in London!

The Surprising London
"Dramatic Clubs"

The mysterious players of Whitechapel, we soon discovered, were simply young people who had seen Yiddish theater in Russia or Romania, and fired by a longing for the stage, had formed little amateur groups in their native towns and cities. Finding each other now in London, they again began putting on plays of one kind or another, rehearsing and performing after a hard day's work in a factory or shop.

These young people did not play in theaters. There was no money and no public for that. They gave their performances in club rooms. These could be rented for a few shillings and were also free of the regulations and fire laws governing a theater or a public hall. Performances in these rooms were allowed, provided they were "private"—that is, given for the entertainment of club members only and, of course, with no admission fee.

These, however, were hard conditions for the young amateurs. No matter how modest the venture, some outlay is always entailed. The room itself had to be paid for. The actors inevitably incurred certain expenses. Needless to say, all who came were admitted, and money also changed hands. What could not pass over the table could always pass beneath it, and the shilling not taken on one side of the door could always be collected on the other.

A meeting was soon arranged for us with two of these young would-be actors. Solomon Manne, born in Galicia, and Annie Eisenberg of Kraków, Poland, had met each other in a London dramatic club. Falling in love, they had married here in London. This young couple, who would both be part of my theater for the next forty years, led us to the amateur clubs of London.

Here is a "word picture" of a club on Prescott Street, the very hall, as it happened, where we would make our own first London appearance.

The room itself was somewhat long, lit by gas, and drab as a stall of horses. At the far end a raised platform was concealed by a dingy curtain. This was the stage. To the right and left along the wall were several rows of benches. These had been placed lengthwise, to show this was a club, not a theater. A large wooden table surrounded by chairs took up the center of the floor. This was reserved for the president and his committee.

We had come early and found some twenty or thirty people drifting about, some looking for seats, some calling to each other across the room, others talking, gossiping, flirting, relating incidents of their day at work, or criticizing the actors. A thick haze of smoke from cigars and pipes rose to the ceiling, and the noise was so great that nobody could be heard without shouting.

After a long wait the president and his committee filed out from behind the wings and, with some pomp, took their seats. The president gave a rap of his gavel, silencing the noise, which, however, immediately broke out again. At length he gave three loud raps, a signal to both actors and audience that the play was about to begin. The musicians struck up a bit of a tune, the curtain was drawn to one side, actors appeared, spoke lines, sang, danced, all without interrupting the hubbub in the hall, which at times rose so loud as to drown out the voices on the stage. Clearly the audience had come more for warmth and company than for the play, which, to tell the truth, was very weak.

We would have been glad enough even of Prescott Street, but we could see no way. We could not play without scenery, without costumes. We had to live ourselves. Such was our situation that even this poor room was beyond our reach. God knows how we would have fared in London altogether or what our fate might have been, if not for those who held out their hands to us and saved us.

In Sonnenschein's restaurant in Mansion Street we met a young journalist named Rabinovitch, a coworker on an anarchist weekly that came out, I believe, on Fridays. This Rabinovitch wrote articles for his paper, wrote potboilers, wrote novelettes, translations, worked night and day, and was still so poor it broke your heart to look at him. But he was young and handsome, and he took his poverty lightly without being depressed by it.

Finding a sympathetic soul, we did not hide our condition or our need for help. And since we were thinking at that time of the rich Jews of the West End, we asked this kind young man if he could not do something for us with these people. He said with a smile that he had no influence in that part of London, but that he might be able to help a bit all the same.

Rabinovitch was our first London friend. He introduced us to people, talked about us everywhere, and when things looked really bad, always gave us a word of courage. "Never mind, dear ones!" Rabinovitch would say at these dark moments. "Your sun, too, will rise. You will see that the Jewish people will one day recognize and honor you."

It goes without saying that he never failed to put in a word for us in his anarchist weekly. Whether this had any effect I do not know. Even years later, when the Jewish labor movement in London grew larger and more important, this paper still came out under the words "Appearing When Possible."

But it was not only idealists like Rabinovitch who came to our aid. Hardhearted usurers, men who in everyday life were coarse, hard materialists, found for us a buried spark in their soul. And if some of them took interest on their loans to us, it was still on more lenient terms than to others. They had a weakness for us, a certain respect.

One of our first benefactors was Lewis, son-in-law of our innkeeper. A simple soul, entirely uneducated. But learning who we were, he took up our cause, became our "patriot" and good brother. And immediately we felt that here in London was a heart that beat for us, eyes that looked on us with warmth—and we had courage again.

A small agent called Gutman also helped. Closemouthed, badly dressed, neither a friendly nor a pleasant man, he gave us money, caring little for his interest, simply out of friendship for people playing Yiddish theater.

When we began to play and I needed costumes I would go to a man called Posover whom I had known in Odessa. In London Posover sold cigarettes and lent money on percentage. He never refused me, though his only guarantee was my word and his profit, light as a feather. I don't know how he was with others. We remembered him as a good man.

But our greatest help in London came from a person little known to the theater world today. This was Herman Fiedler, a man in an entirely different category than others mentioned here. A relative of Sonya's, Fiedler became not only a friend, but an indispensable part of our theater family. He led the orchestra, gave help as a play consultant, and even filled in from time to time as stage manager. Most important, he possessed an inexhaustible supply of plays, some of them his own, others he had rewritten or adapted. I believe we sometimes gave him a few shillings for one of his plays. Mostly he got no more than a simple "Thank you"—often no more than a smile.

Other more simple souls helped in their own way. Our innkeeper, Leavenworth, gave us lodging week after week on credit. Sonnenschein never pressed us for the meals we took in his restaurant. I remember a Jew called Shloime—we knew him by no other name—a simple laborer, tall, broad-boned, red-haired, with a little red beard. He was our messenger, our courier, fetched, carried, and never asked for pay. I think of him now as one of the good things of a bad time.

It was men like these who started the mill of our theater and made it run. In that London desert where we hungered and thirsted, they gave us our first cup of water, our first crust of bread. Their warmth and devotion in those cold days and nights kept us alive, made us feel that even here, in great cold London, we were not alone.

Our mood lifted. We took heart, we grew lively, gay, threw off our fears, took the Prescott Street Club, and began to rehearse.

How We Played in London

At the end of December 1883, we newly arrived actors gave our first performance on the London Yiddish stage. I cannot say it was a gala occasion. The street outside was not beleaguered with carriages. Police were not needed to restrain the public excitement. We played on a stage not much bigger than a grave, and the whole jostling, pushing, noisy crowd, including children, came to about 150 persons.

We had advertised as well as we could, mostly in and around our restaurant and hotel. Actually, it was no small thing to have on one stage—one heaven—such stars as Yisrol and Annetta Gradner, Sonya Michelson, and me, but the sensation failed to bring in a larger audience. And perhaps it was better they did not come, for if they had, heaven knows where we would have put them.

We opened with *Der Bel Tchuve,** by Sheikevitch, a play not unlike many others of this period. A banker, Samuel Beinholz, marries for the second time. The new wife, ruthless and ambitious, prevails on him to leave the Jewish faith, and plots against his daughter, whose youth and happiness arouse her jealousy. Seeing her finally for what she is, the banker returns, broken and penitent, to Judaism.

In Russia I had played Rafael Weinglas, the lover role, but here in London changes had to be made.[†] I played Beinholz, the infatuated banker, Sonya was the ruthless, ambitious wife, Annetta Gradner the plotted-against daughter, and Gradner, our star comedian, played the heroic lover who defeats the plot of the villainess, clears the daughter's name, and marries her.

It was a good debut. We knew from the beginning that the audi-

---

* *The Penitent,* or, more accurately, *"he who returns to Judaism."*
[†] Gradner, the greater star, took the starring role.

ence was ours, and we played, as the saying is, "with flutes and violins." At the final curtain the audience responded with true enthusiasm, and there was even a review in a Yiddish weekly.

The reader must know, however, that it was not I, but the two singing stars who captured the public that night, Annetta with her plaintive, beautiful voice, and Gradner, who gave a fine performance in a serious role, and whose songs were encored over and over in a tumult of applause.

In our next play, *Shulamith,* the honors, once again, went to the Gradners. Annetta created a storm in the leading role, and Gradner overturned worlds as the comic, mischievous Tzingatan. I, again, had to come on in the uninteresting role of the father.

For my third London appearance I put aside the plays I had brought from Russia, and chose instead something Herman Fiedler had given me, a piece called *The Odessa Beggar.* Where Fiedler had gotten it I do not know. I believe there was a play about a ragpicker on the French stage. In the Russian theater also they had a play on this subject. Maybe Fiedler put them together. To tell the truth, I never bothered to ask. Maybe that is how it should be. An actor is not a historian or a keeper of literary archives. Give him a play, a role, he's satisfied.

A piece of perhaps no great literary value, and with not too nice a subject as regards family life. But the role gave so much room for ability, for variation, for the art of mime—in short, I decided this was an excellent, a truly theatrical, play.

The Odessa Beggar was Herman Fiedler's adaptation of Felix Pyat's *Ragpicker of Paris,* a play that took Paris by storm on the eve of the 1848 revolution. It had been pirated many times, and versions had already been seen in Russia, in America, and in 1864, at the Surrey Theatre in London. Fiedler had simply translated it, turned Pyat's famous Ragpicker into a Jew, and transposed the action from Paris to Odessa.

It was a story, you understand, about rich and poor, virtue in rags, villainy in satins. A foul deed long ago in high places. A mother murdered, her innocent babe abandoned and left to die on the street. A lonely pauper, a beggar who finds the child and raises her as his own.

Jacob Adler in
The Odessa
Beggar,
London, 1884

As in the Talmud, she "eats his bread and sleeps in his arms." Come the rich, the powerful, who trick the Beggar, make him drunk, and steal from him his only treasure, his one ewe lamb. Broken, robbed of the only creature he has ever loved, the Beggar cries out for justice in a bitter speech against the rich and mighty of the earth.

I knew from the first that the part belonged to me. As the Beggar I sat on the ground, smoked my pipe, and philosophized as I went through the rubbish in my basket. A torn glove comes out of the basket—the Beggar improvises a story of women, fine ladies. A bottle without a cork—he conjures up a young man gone to the dogs. A torn scrap of newspaper—a political sensation forgotten long ago. Last, he fishes up a corset cover. This he turns every which way without being able to understand or find a use for it. This scene, with its long perplexed pauses, brought great laughter from the audience. In another scene, the Beggar, looking for a place to hide, crawls into his own basket. The trick of making myself small and disappearing into the basket and growing tall again as I came out of it created a sensational effect. The drunk scene and the Beggar's bitter outcry against the rich brought out another side of my talent—that of the tragicomedian and character actor.

In a word, I felt so at home in this role, so free in my gestures, that

*Jacob Adler
as Uriel
Acosta*

my hands seemed no longer hands but wings. The audience went out of their senses. They laughed, howled, stamped, thundered, broke the roof, all but climbed the walls to the ceiling in their joy.

This play was my first success in London, and it remained in my repertoire for the greater part of thirty years—one of my best.

Two months later, when I played *Acosta,* we had an audience of five hundred—like two thousand today. We took a good theater, the Holborn, and invited the Jewish aristocrats of the West End. I remember a wealthy Londoner by the name of Posner, and Dr. Herman Marcus

Adler, the chief rabbi's son, came to the opening, and brought a Rothschild with him.

I was nervous before *Acosta,* but only until I made my entrance. As soon as I came onstage, as soon as I had the boards under my feet, the strength of a lion, the energy of demons, came into me. I knew I would play as never before, knew my spirit would open and my very soul would play. I spoke the monologue with power, believed my words, lived through the tragic situation of my Uriel. With him I loved, hated, suffered, was bent, broke, bowed my head, became a slave—and only in the depths of the soul the inward tears, the hidden wounds. I was torn by doubt, and the audience felt my pain. I flamed, and they caught my fire. The same with my Sonya as Judith, and if she received less applause, it was only because her part was smaller. A storm in the theater at every sharp speech, every strong movement, every passionate clash of will.

And I fell beautifully! Not as I had fallen in Lodz, but lightly, gracefully, receiving not even a scratch. And just as easily and lightly I sprang to my feet again. At the final curtain we were overwhelmed by the applause. Many in the audience could not leave until they had expressed their happiness, their gratitude. Dr. Herman Adler came backstage with compliments, and because of this the old man, the chief rabbi, also honored us with his presence.

But why draw it out? The play caused a stir in the press, and even in the English press. More important, Whitechapel rang with it! My name was established.

OUR LONDON PARADISE,
AND HOW THE SERPENT CAME

In Paradise Adam and Eve knew not of sin. They lived at peace with the beasts, lived on roots and flowers, and were refreshed by the sight of their own beautiful forms in the mirror of the lakes. They lived under God's protection; could anything be better?

But man is bad from the time he is born, corrupted even in the belly of his mother. Came greed, came curiosity, came slyness, big eyes, ambition, hatred—came, in a word, the serpent. This, as we know, led to the parting, the separation from paradise, and death.

A small paradise there was for us actors in the Yiddish theater clubs of the eighties. We hungered a little, true, got our small pittance with care and pain, woes paid for in the end by frail women and helpless children. (In those four years I lost first my little daughter, my three-year-old Rivka, and afterward my wife, my Sonya.) We played for a tiny audience, on a stage the size of a cadaver, but we played and played well, with pleasure, with a drunkenness of happiness.

We all lived together in one corner, this one a flight above, this one a flight below, meeting every night after the play at Moishe Kibins's restaurant, or Sonnenschein's. And though we were divided into peasants and aristocrats, great stars who live by art alone, and humble "supers," who did their part after a hard day's work in a factory, still our life together had the heartfelt warmth of the commune.

When Saturday and Sunday came and we played, we felt it was for our friends, for an audience that took us into their hearts, gave us their soul, lived in what they saw on the stage so that play and audience—art and life—came together as one.

Perhaps it was only a poor little paradise, but still it was a paradise. And though others may feel I sing its praises like the well-known worm in horseradish, rejoicing because he knows nothing better, let him remember that without this poor stage, without this dark Whitechapel, there would have been no Solomon Kaus, no Elisha ben Avuya, no "Dovid Moishele" in the *Yiddish King Lear.* *

Those years in London seem to me now like some great group painting in a museum or art gallery. Look close, you see only stains. Move farther off, figures appear against a background, but still unclear, unrelated. Move farther still, and now, from afar, everything comes together. The painter's vision is before you—the whole panorama, the whole great hymn of life.

How could I have understood those London years, bewildered as we were, struggling as we were? What was London for me then? In a good mood, a place to play, to eke out a living, to cultivate sometimes worthy, sometimes less worthy acquaintances. In a bad mood, nothing more than a hodgepodge of little insects all struggling in the same swamp. Only now, looking back through the veil of time, do I know how to value those years for the growth and development of our stage.

In spite of poverty and hardship we did not waste away or pine in our little London corner. On the contrary, we grew as strong as Samson's locks! I felt in myself that my talent every day grew stronger, deeper, more sure, more powerful. And who knows? In time our material problems might have improved, and the Yiddish theater might have grown to maturity in London—if not for the serpent, if not for jealousy over parts, plays, *genre.* And between whom should the serpent come if not between Gradner and myself, the two most popular stars!

Naturally, each of us had his supporters, his patriots. The smaller planets take sides. The thing spreads. In the end the troupe splits up, Gradnerists on one side, Adlerists on the other.

The division between me and Gradner is easy enough to understand. The Yiddish theater was born in comic characters, in comic antics, in song and dance. It was born with *Shmendrick,* with *The Two Kuni Lemels,* with *Hotzmach,* roles that gave Gradner, Mogulesko, and Zuckerman their fame. Later we had Goldfaden's *Shulamith* and *Bar*

---

* These characters were among Adler's most important roles in America. They were well known to his readers, many of whom had seen him perform them more than once. See commentary at end of chapter.

Kochba, plays that lifted the theater to a new and better level. But though it was no longer a comic dance, it was still a dance, still the light musical theater of Goldfaden.

But to live forever with jest and song, even when they become more rarefied, was hardly my idea. And so, between Gradner and me an ideological struggle arose, a basic disagreement over the principles of our art. On top of this there was a wrangle, pure and simple, over parts. Was it *Shulamith?* He and Annetta are at the top of the poster, Annetta as the prima donna, Gradner as the lively, mischievous Tzingatan. I had to come out "in Fortinbras's suite," as the Russian actors say, in the uninteresting role of the father. But wait! Is it *The Odessa Beggar?* Ah, then I am cock of the walk, the Gradners insignificant little chicks, almost invisible!

It was the same in *La Juive.* As the Jew, Eleazar, I had such situations to bring out, such scenes to play, such tones to take, and all so strong, so basic, so deep, while Gradner, even in the great role of the Cardinal, still had less to do than I.

In *Esther of En Gadi,* the two of us had a duel scene. During the first performance I accidentally touched him under the arm. Nothing serious, God be thanked. He felt only a pinprick, but getting out of his costume he noticed a few drops of blood. A trifle. We joked about it. Later we wounded each other worse. With dry sarcastic words. And these thrusts were exchanged not only behind the scenes but even on the stage!

In such a case the one with the most skill at improvisation comes out the winner. At such tricks I was an old hand. I would improvise a remark my rival understood all too well. Beside himself with anger, he answered in kind, and between us such a curtain scene developed as the playwright never dreamed of.

These verbal contests did not end in London. For a short time in New York the late David Kessler, Thomashefsky, and I all played together. One night some difference between us came up, and on the stage the three of us fired word arrows at each other. One, for anger, took a plate from a shelf and smashed it. Fine! Got rid of his anger, and made a good effect. "Aha!" says the other, "you break plates?" He breaks half a dozen plates. The third broke all the plates. Curtain. The three stars stand glaring at each other, three angry swollen Holland roosters, ready to spring.

Nothing is worse than a quarrel between actors. Ordinary people can keep their distance, but our world is the stage, and though dynasties crumble and thrones fall, we still must rub against each other. For Gradner there was no escape but the grave or America. The grave was too cold, America too far. Gradner went to Paris. But not so fast! First he broke away, founded a club of his own. He stole my actors, I stole his. So we practiced on each other, and neither of us licked honey or drew health from it.

Gradner did not stay long in Paris, he had no success and had to come back. We played together again, but in London, too, his luck ran out. Only a few years before the first and greatest of our actors, he was already dwindling, going downhill. He was terrified of falling into penury, and this fear drove him into speculation on the London Exchange. Where he got the money, no one knew. In his desperation he found it. He lay on the Bourse all day and at night hurried in to play. Naturally, he lost.

In those days they had a custom on the London Bourse; it may still exist. The one who lost that day had flour flung at him like a bridegroom. The poor rabbit ran, and they ran after, whitening him again. Poor Gradner ran in one night, white as a miller.

Solomon Kaus (*Shloime Chuchem*), a semihistorical work, was drawn by Gordin from a French source. The events take place in the France of Louis XIII, and the all-powerful Cardinal Richelieu, the dominant figure of the period, takes part in the play as a character.

The plot is loosely based on the life of an obscure Jew who lived in the Paris of the seventeenth century. This man, Solomon Kaus, apparently believed he could build a machine run by water power, an idea predating by two hundred years the invention of the steam engine. Born before his time, the inventor was believed by no one, and in the Jewish community was laughingly known as Shloime Chuchem, "Solomon the Wise," the mocking nickname that is the play's Yiddish title.

In the Gordin play the inventor falls into the hands of Sherbelieu, an adventurer with a place in the councils of the Cardinal as a spy. This man sees at once that a fortune can be made from the Jew's invention, and sets about getting his own hands on it.

Through his connection with the Cardinal, Sherbelieu brings Kaus together with a certain Lord Worcester. Kaus is hoping for financial help from the Englishman, but after looking over his plans for the machine, Worcester wants to buy the rights to the whole idea. Kaus refuses. These plans are his most treasured possession, his "child." He will not part with them at any price.

Worcester leaves, disappointed, and Sherbelieu, in a rage at being balked, tells the Cardinal the Jew is a spy in the pay of the Hapsburgs, Richelieu's greatest enemies. Kaus is charged with treason and is interrogated, but Richelieu, hearing his claims for his machine, decides he is deranged and has him confined to a madhouse.

The hearing before Richelieu is the historic episode of the play.

Kaus is imprisoned among lunatics, but gets word he will soon be set at liberty. His wife arrives, together with Sherbelieu and Lord Worcester, who now offers an even higher price for his plans. This time, at the entreaties of his wife, Kaus agrees to part with the plans.

Sherbelieu, still posing as his friend, suggests that he will keep the money until Kaus is released. The money once in his hands, he decamps, and Kaus, robbed of his life's work, now discovers that the order for his release was a forgery. At this blow his reason deserts him. A madman in the eyes of the world, he has at last truly gone mad.

In the final act his wife appears before the Cardinal, where she reveals Sherbelieu's treachery and makes a moving plea for justice. A letter from Worcester, describing the success of Kaus's invention, proves the truth of her story. The villain Sherbelieu is led away in manacles, and the Cardinal orders Kaus released and brought before him.

But Kaus is now hopelessly insane. A terrible scene takes place, and ends only when the madman's heart gives way. His wife falls on his lifeless body, and the play ends as the Cardinal, with a pang of conscience, realizes his own part in this miscarriage of justice.

The critic Henry Tyrell describes the play as a romantic-historic work easily bearing comparison to the best of its kind on the English stage. A more lengthy appraisal appeared in the *New York Dramatic Mirror* (July 7, 1906). (*Uriel Acosta* and the melodrama *Broken Hearts,* by Z. Libin, were written up in the same review. Though the critic acknowledges that Adler "towered" as *Uriel Acosta,* he dismisses the play as a "conventional drama that, in its wanderings, one day got lost in the ghetto." He is even harsher with the Libin melodrama, though again, he notes the "remarkable acting" of Sara Adler as the heroine.)

Although the *Mirror* reviewer did not conceal his dislike for what he calls the "religious and emotional proclivities of the Hebrew drama," we have the following review of *Solomon Kaus:*

It may be the sight of so much really profound tragic acting within the past ten days has destroyed the analytical equilibrium of this critic; however, if he be not suffering from chronic ecstasy faith may be placed in his honest statement that in all his years as a theatregoer he has seldom seen a histrionic exhibition equal to the performance of Jacob Adler as Solomon Kaus. In fact, the impersonation will remain imprinted on his mind with very few tragic portrayals, he has seen.

Until confined to the lunatic asylum Adler played the part as an intellectual dreamer, self-possessed, assured of his powers, his dignity heightened by his emotional restraint. It was performed, in fact, almost as a "straight part," though tinged with dramatic heroism. The culmination of the third act was infinitely more stupendous after this quiet, normal beginning. As he read the order for his release and saw the falsity of it, a wonderful thing transpired. There was in those first moments scarcely a vestige of demonstration, yet, so to speak, one could see the light of understanding fade from his eyes. Then came the delirium, and the pity of it.

Though the last act was enough to agonize the soul of an Egyptian sphinx, it was, artistically speaking, always within bounds. Adler's insanity in this act surpasses the power of description. Now he sits on the floor in an idiotic stupor, now he starts to his feet and hurls curses at the Cardinal with the wild fury of a dangerous maniac. His wife, at the height of this scene, dies of a broken heart; Kaus himself gasps out his last breath after one of these frenzied outbursts.

The death of Kaus was horrible. Even more horrible than the death of Henry Irving in *Louis XI*. Nevertheless, it somehow belongs to the same class. May God send us all happier endings!

After reviewing three Yiddish plays in a row the critic closes with what reads like a devout plea for help! He has come from a Broadway where other plays reviewed that week include the Clyde Fitch comedy *A Square Deal,* the musical *M'amzelle Champagne,* advertised as "A Bubble in Two Bottles," and a new production of *Uncle Tom's Cabin.*

Aside from classical revivals and Shakespeare productions, the American theater was devoting itself almost exclusively to light popular entertainment. Though Hutchins Hapgood of New York's *Globe,* a man deeply sympathetic to the whole downtown scene, recoils at the ending of some of the stronger Yiddish plays, he admits that the relentless realism of the Yiddish theater was often a relief after the pervasive triviality on Broadway.

It cannot be denied, however, that the Yiddish theater too often sinned on the side of sensationalism, or that Adler, who understood better than most the power of restraint, seldom missed a chance for a spectacular effect. In the third act of *Solomon Kaus,* the inventor, obsessed with the power he alone knows, gives way to madness with the wild cry, "Solomon Kaus now rides his fiery steed!" On this line Adler executed a leap that carried him to the brink, and almost over the brink, of the footlights. It never failed to bring a gasp from the audience, a moment of electrifying "theater" in an otherwise realistic, albeit heightened, performance.

In Jacob Gordin's *Elisha ben Avuya* we hear the unmistakable voice of the Haskala. If *Uriel Acosta* was a call for Reason and Enlightenment, Gordin now claims for the Jew the right to freedom, beauty, and art.

The play is set in the early Christian era and, as in *Acosta,* the hero is a heretic.

Elisha ben Abuyah, a renowned *tanna* (teacher of the Oral Law) of the second century A.D., fell away from Jewish teaching under the influence of Greek philosophy.

This heretical hero is very attractive in Gordin's hands. Elisha's every word rings with deeply felt Jewish irony and wisdom. Boundlessly generous, he is ready to give all he has to a friend. And though, like Gordin, he is an atheist, he believes in the genius of his people, and thinks of himself as, unalterably, a Jew.

Although he has turned away from Jewish dogma, Elisha will have no part in the Christian idea, now growing among the people, that this earth is a vale of tears with joy possible only in heaven. He loves life, surrounds himself with Greek statues, reads Homer, entertains Roman aristocrats, and allows his young daughter to adorn herself and live for pleasure. And he thinks himself no less a Jew for taking into his life all that is beautiful in the world around him.

Like Timon of Athens, Elisha is undone by what is best in his nature—his generosity. He is tricked out of his fortune, is betrayed by his Roman friends, and is condemned by his own people. His wife leaves him. His daughter runs off with a Roman soldier. Of all those once around him only Toivye Avyoini, "Toivye the Poor Man," is still his friend.

Faithful to a wife who gave him neither joy nor understanding, Elisha denied himself the love of Beata, the Fallen Woman who once offered him her life. Beata has turned Christian and renounced all happiness in this world.

Toivye Avyoini brings back Elisha's daughter, but too late. Elisha has already taken poison. He dies haunted by a prophetic vision of terrible Jewish suffering. The rabbis cast him off as a sinner who will not come to eternal life, but his disciple, Rabbi Meier, "cries to the heavens" that Elisha was a great Jew who will live forever.

His daughter weeps over his body. Beata goes her way to a nunnery. And the curtain falls with church bells tolling the coming of Christianity.

The play was a failure when Adler first produced it. "Put it on after my death and you will have a success of it," Gordin told him. The dying playwright gave him good advice. After Gordin's death, in 1911, *Elisha* ran for a year.

The Fallen Woman, Beata, was played by Sara Adler. Mogulesko played Toivye Avyoini, and Frances Adler, now nineteen years old and part of her father's company, played Elisha's willful runaway daughter, Naumi. Ten years later this role passed to her younger sister, Stella Adler, who named her own daughter after the much-loved Naumi of the play.

The role of Elisha was written for Adler, and no other actor ever attempted it.

WHAT WE LEARNED IN LONDON

How shall I describe the clubs of London? They were like amoebas, those microscopic creatures studied by the naturalists. Tiny, blind, insignificant, they separate, split, split again—yet live on. And every little part gives birth again and splits into new parts!

I have already told how Gradner and I quarreled, how he broke away and formed his own club. But our clubs were not the only ones. A thousand clubs! Wherever you looked, clubs, splits, shouting, quarrels, and before you knew it—a new club! They were a training ground for our acting recruits, the chief source of our theatrical merchandise. For without them where would we have gotten our actors?

In the theaters of Europe and America this problem does not exist. These theaters have schools where they train their people. We had no such schools, and still do not have them. But if the Yiddish theater was destined to go through its infancy in Russia, and in America grow to manhood and success, we can say with truth that London was its school. A poor and narrow school, perhaps, but there we learned and there we grew.

Take my own case. When I arrived in London I was all but unknown. I had mastered and been accounted good in two or three roles, successes I owed mostly to my youth, my looks, and the appeal of a daring Odessa boy. I left London with a long row of roles in my repertoire, a tragedian who could lift an audience of hundreds to heights of emotion. And now I did not recite my roles, did not declaim them, did not get through them with poses and heroic positions, but played so that it could be called playing! And to what do I owe all this but to the clubs of London!

Earliest known photograph of Keni Liptzin, Russia, 1879

I cannot say it was a good life. A life of fear. We were always in danger from the municipal authorities. And even worse was the stick held over our heads by the Orthodox community. Our first audiences were Russian immigrants, people like ourselves. Later came the London Jews—so rigid, so pious! We were always afraid they would report us, and had to give in to their every caprice. On Friday night we did not dare to play—you would think our actors' faces were an insult to the high heavens! And on Saturday afternoon, when they finally allowed it, we were forbidden to light a fire on the stage or smoke a cigarette, even when the scene demanded it! We had to watch every move, every word, or in the middle of the play there would be a scandal.

It is a story still told by London actors, that the revered Rabbi Adler not only took an interest in my production of *Uriel Acosta,* but even gave it his personal assistance! With his own venerable rabbinical hand, the chief rabbi gave me a paper ram's horn to be blown in the synagogue scene. The God-fearing rabbi would not allow a real ram's horn—one that had actually grown on the head of a ram—to be played in a mere theatrical spectacle, a thing performed for money on a stage. In its place he gave me a replica made of cardboard.

The cardboard ram's horn looked remarkably like the real thing, but it had one defect—it could not be blown.

For two years we performed in the clubs, performed in places little better suited to theater than a stable or a stall, on stages so small we could hardly turn about, much less make the heroic movements required by our parts in those days. And even in those conditions we achieved effects that astounded the audience, and already we had actors who would be among the best on our stage in America.

Keni Liptzin, for example. Little more than a beginner when she came from Russia, in London she achieved heights of dramatic art. I don't say she was yet at the level of her Medea—just as I was not yet a Doctor Goldenweiser or a Yiddish King Lear. But even then she showed outstanding talent, and there were plays we could not do without her.

When death took my wife, my Sonya, it was Liptzin who replaced her as our first tragedienne. She grew with every role, and it is London we must thank for her Mirele Efros, for *Shochita,* for all the marvelous portrayals of her later career.

Liptzin rose to stardom in America in the 1900s. She made her mark originally in the Finkel-Kessler company, but afterward rented her own theater and played independently.

Although entirely uneducated, she produced plays by Ibsen, Hugo, Andreev, and other European masters. Her Medea astonished the profession—a performance, Abraham Cahan tells us, that "scorched the boards of the stage."

Her most famous plays, however, were *Shochita* and *Mirele Efros,* both by Gordin. In *Shochita* (a word denoting the kosher slaughter of animals), Liptzin played a frightened young girl married off by her parents to a wealthy butcher, an angry man with a mistress and three grown children by a former wife.

The girl is afraid of her shouting, overbearing husband and feels a growing horror of the ritual animal slaughter that is part of his trade. Pregnant, with no escape from her life with him, increasingly obsessed with the horror of slaughter, she goes mad. As her husband lies behind a curtained alcove in a drunken sleep, she kills him with the ritual slaughter knife.

The play was Gordin's attack on marriages made by parents. Hutchins Hapgood, who describes the play in his book *The Spirit of the Ghetto,* points out that it is the pitiful young girl who is symbolically "slaughtered" in this marriage.

Mirele Efros was Gordin's portrait of a type well known to a Yiddish audience. The all-powerful matriarch, the support and mainstay of her family, was drawn directly from nineteenth-century Russian life, where a learned man spent his days in the study of the Torah while his wife took on the practical problems of the house and, like as not, had to be the breadwinner too.

The character of the dominant woman, stronger and more ruthless than the male, appears as early as 1825. Solomon Ettinger's Serkele rules her house with an iron hand and ruthlessly enforces her will on everyone around her. The type appears again in the early Goldfaden comedy *Auntie Sosya,* crops up again in his *Breindele Cossack,* and finds a twentieth-century echo in the Bessie Berger of Clifford Odets's *Awake and Sing.*

The mother figure loomed large in the Yiddish theater for fifty years, sometimes seen negatively, sometimes as the fount of all compassion and forgiveness, but always as a force operating *outside* the moral code. In *Mirele Efros,* Gordin presents her for the first time as the *ethical* head of her home.

Widowed early in life, Mirele took over her husband's bankrupt business after his death. Through hard work, astute judgment, and honorable dealing she paid off his debts, turned the business into a success, and now, having amassed a fortune, is regarded by the whole community as a very great personage indeed.

Now in her sixtieth year, eccentric, accustomed to instant obedience, Liptzin's portrayal brought out the character's inborn authority, her penetrating intellect, intractable will, and at the core of it all, her care and provision for everyone around her.

Mirele is challenged by the wife of her son. The angry young Shaindl fights this powerful mother, and finally tells her openly that it is time she stepped down, gave over the business to her son, and gave him his inheritance, money she has kept too long for her own use.

Mirele has always concealed the bankruptcy that her dead husband left her to deal with. Now, her honesty questioned, she reveals it. But since her son's feelings are divided, and in the end he stands with his wife, Mirele gives him the keys to the safe that holds her fortune, and with it, sole possession of both the business and the house she no longer feels is her home.

She finds refuge with her faithful steward, Kalman, working first as his assistant, later as his partner. And in these reduced circumstances she remains as unbending and autocratic as before.

After a ten-year rift a much-chastened Shaindl comes to ask for a truce. All has not gone well with Shaindl's marriage. The young wife fought for the rights of her husband. But the husband, freed from a dominating mother, was pushed aside by his wife. It was she who took control, ran the business, and enjoyed the power she had really desired for herself. The business had gone downhill in her hands, and together with a good part of their material wealth the young wife has lost her husband's love.

Her husband has never forgiven her for driving his mother from her home. Now, with her son approaching his thirteenth birthday, Shaindl asks Mirele to come back to her rightful place, or at least to be present at her grandson's Bar Mitzvah.

The request is refused. Mirele, unbending and without compromise, had vowed never again to set foot in her son's house, and will not break that vow. But alone with her faithful Kalman, she breaks down, seeing herself at last as nothing but a heartbroken old woman.

It is the young boy himself who is determined to see the grandmother of whom he has heard so much. Although his parents tell him it is hopeless, he is certain that if he can speak to her face-to-face, she will not refuse to be with him on this great day of his life. And on the day of his Bar Mitzvah, he secretly goes off, determined to bring her back with him.

At home the guests have arrived and all is ready for the celebration, but the son of the house cannot be found. Concern grows to alarm, but turns to joy as the boy appears in the doorway, his grandmother at his side. Mirele is welcomed back into her home, all feuds and quarrels are forgotten, and the play comes to a happy end with song, dance, and celebration as the son of the house comes of age.

Probably the best loved of all Gordin's plays, *Mirele Efros* was performed by every leading Yiddish actress, including Esther Rouchel Kaminska, an artist of great talent and power, who visited New York in 1912. Kaminska was acclaimed for her Mirele, but Abraham Cahan, comparing the two performances, preferred Liptzin's interpretation to the more realistic portrayal by the Polish actress. "Liptzin's pride, her humor, her shrewdness, came not from Lithuania, but from Shakespeare," Cahan wrote. "She was not proud like an ordinary woman, but like a Lear. She did not go about the stage like a rich housewife of Grodno or Berdichev, but like a queen. In the mechanical means that help a melodramatic performance, Liptzin was more expert than Kaminska. Melodrama was the core of her Mirele Efros, but whatever one may say about the faults of her playing, her Mirele Efros was an outstanding interpretation of the Yiddish stage."

The son, torn between his love for his mother and his passion for his wife, was played by David Kessler. Morris Moskovitch, a rising star of this era, played Kalman the steward. Mrs. Dinah Feinman, married for some years to Jacob Adler, played the rebellious young Shaindl.

But it was not only Keni Liptzin who grew and developed in London. Max Rosenthal, today one of our best character actors, one of our most intelligent directors, began in London as Gradner's student. From the beginning there was something special, quiet, beautifully modest in this actor's work. In his early years he played lovers, and when I left for America in 1889 I took him with me as my juvenile lead.

Max Radkinson, known to the stage as Rudolph Marks, was another child of the London clubs. He played a great part in the New York of the nineties as a playwright, a writer of songs, and a comedian who for a time rivaled the great Mogulesko. One of our few intellectuals, he left the stage some years ago. We see him only rarely at a banquet or a benefit, his story one of the sadder ones of our history.

The same is true of Israel Weinblatt, one of our most intelligent actors, one of the few who could speak of worldly things. He could discuss character, he cut photographs from magazines and newspapers, used these photographs for his character makeup. I thought he would have a great career. The New York audience never appreciated him; he left the stage and became a farmer.

The career of Dinah Shtettin (now Mrs. Siegmund Feinman) also began in London. Daughter of a strict Jewish home, she had hardly a notion of theater when she came to us. We taught her, and she learned. When I put on Gordin's *Siberia* at the Union Theatre in New York I gave her the tragicomic role of the villain's daughter, Fanya. She played it wonderfully, with a lightness and gaiety that masked the tragedy beneath. A new kind of soubrette.

Who among my readers has not heard of Anna Held? For decades the world was at her feet. Legends and love stories gathered around her name. She was as famous as Lillian Russell a generation back, or today the movie queen Lillian Gish. Would anybody believe today that this Anna Held made her first stage appearance in a Whitechapel club? Yet it is true. We in London knew her only as "Hannale," a poor Polish girl whose parents had wandered from Warsaw to Paris in search of bread. As a child their daughter sold flowers on the Paris streets.

At eighteen her mother and father had died, and she came over to London. I had a club at that time on Mansfield Street. She sang first in the chorus, but very soon I coached her to sing the role of Shulamith. And in that Goldfaden operetta she was first billed as Miss Anna Held.

After a year or so with us in Mansfield Street, Anna Held left for an engagement in Paris. When the Paris company failed, she joined up with a French vaudeville troupe, going on with them to Berlin and then doubling back to Paris and London again. Everywhere she went she created a sensation, and as the whole world knows, she was soon one of the most famous vaudeville artists of her day.

Having been raised in France, she had bewitching manners. There was such coquetry in her glance, she pronounced each word so charmingly and looked at you so graciously, moving her clear white fingers as she spoke, that truly, it was hard to withstand her enchantment. She was quite intelligent, too, and altogether not a bad person, only somewhat frivolous and light-minded.

Anna Held died not long ago, a deathbed convert to the Catholic faith. She has been criticized for this in certain circles. But we in London remember her only as a sweet, friendly, competent Jewish girl who knew Yiddish well and who sang and danced in our theater.

Anna Held and Max Rosenthal left for Paris together, engaged by Goldfaden, who had a company there. The troupe did well, but failed when the cashier ran away with the money. Goldfaden went through a period of great poverty after this. He fell ill in Paris, spat blood, but later, apparently cured, went on to Lemberg (Lvov). In that city he seems to have fallen into actual want.

Max Rosenthal went back to London when the Paris company failed. Anna Held, of course, went on to her extraordinary international career and her famous association with Florenz Ziegfeld.

Adler paid a backstage visit to the enchanting French star on one occasion in New York, but she sent word from her dressing room that

*Anna Held in her first
appearance on the stage,
in* Shulamith, *in London
at the Mansfield Street
Club,* 1885

*Anna Held, when she
had become an inter-
nationally famous
Ziegfeld star,
ca.* 1900

she could not see him. Throughout her career, this actress carefully concealed her past from the public.

These were some of the actors who rose from the ranks in London. Their talents were perhaps not fully developed, my direction also not as one accepts it today. The Yiddish theater has since then freed itself of much of its childishness, its ignorance, its unliterary bent. But can London ever be forgotten? The fire of those days! The daring! The naïve striving for the highest! From where did we get the strength? It was a time of pioneers, and those pioneers worked wonders.

THE GREAT NEW CLUB
ON PRINCE'S STREET

In November of 1885, exactly two years after our arrival in London, my star rose. Not in the American way, God forbid! No hundreds did my new fortunes bring me. My weekly earnings rose to three pounds ten—about sixteen dollars in American money—and on this I had to live with my wife and child. Don't forget I was an actor too, and the artistic soul is worth more than a spit in the gutter. One must look like somebody, with a high hat at least, and a cane. A bit of fun is also needed now and then. I can't say I was a very brilliant star in those days—I was in fact a good bit befogged and clouded over. But a star I was nonetheless!

To rise so high in the world, one must have luck. I had the luck to find favor in the eyes of the wealthy and pious London butcher, Mr. David Smith. A simple, old-fashioned Jew, this Mr. Smith, but how great his love for our theater! He thrilled with every role I played, overcome with joy at each performance. And so great was his "patriotism" that he built for me, at Number 3, Prince's Street,* the famous Prince's Street Club.

Here we had such phenomenal success that we played every night except Friday. This we still could not do because of the Orthodox London Jews. Even when we, the actors, no longer feared them, Smith, the Jewish butcher, had no courage to defy them.

According to the recent American fashion for intimate playhouses, the new club could be thought of as a small theater. We had a large and fairly comfortable stage, a gallery as well as a parterre, and a hall that could seat three hundred. Although by today's standards the building itself was poor and primitive (by city ordinance it still had to

* Later Princelet Street, London E1.

be built as a club), it was nevertheless the greatest Yiddish theater club ever seen in London, and in every way a new, even a revolutionary, development.

With a bigger audience and bigger profits, a remarkable idea began to circulate, an idea that not only great stars, but even ordinary actors, should receive a salary. No wonder there were suddenly more actors! From too few, there were all at once too many!

But it was not only with amateurs and beginners that we now filled our ranks. Every great star of the Yiddish stage played with us in Prince's Street! Every troupe, every actor on his way to Paris or to America, stopped over in London for a performance, a "guest appearance," to use the plain American word, a job that would cover expenses before they moved on.

Very varied and different were the people carried to us on this wandering theatrical stream. They ranged from the great Mogulesko to actors who had not even a name, whose naked word you had to take that they were actors at all. We had learned authorities on dramaturgy like Professor Hurvitz and people who could not spell out a word of Yiddish or anything else. Some attached themselves to us and remained. Others, after a short stay, went on to America. But great or small they came, thin, pale, depressed, this one in a battered high hat, this one in a soiled cravat, and all with a hunger—God help us! And though all of them put up a front and tried to look big, it was clear they had come touring, but had fled for their lives as from a fire!

Mogulesko came, I believe, in 1886, and with him, haughty and standoffish as ever, Maurice (Moishe) Finkel. A tragic figure in our history, Finkel. One of the first pioneers, an excellent artist, a good director, for many years a power in our theater world, until in 1904 he put an end to his career and his life with a bullet in his brain.

Maurice Heine came, and with him Sara Levitzkaya, who would later be my wife. The public needs no introduction to Sara Adler, the world-renowned tragedienne, the romantic heroine of Tolstoy's *Resurrection,* the star of Gordin's *Homeless.* Brought up in a half-Russian environment, she spoke no Yiddish at that time, but came out before the curtain and sang Russian songs. And that is how I knew her in London.*

The learned Dr. Ben Zion stayed a time among us, and for a time

* Sara Levitzkaya became Maurice Heine's wife in Russia, but later divorced him. She and Adler were married in America in 1891.

*Maurice Heine, Sara
Adler's first husband,
Russia*

*Sara Heine (later Sara
Adler), London*

we also had Professor Halevy-Hurvitz. This was the well-known play-wright who would be the king of the Yiddish theater for many years, and even today his plays are done from time to time.

Hurvitz, a Romanian, had not come to Russia at all. He wandered in different lands, involved himself in various undertakings, and then moved on, often leaving, it is said, not altogether pleasant memories behind him. Be that as it may, we London actors were happy to have him. He was a widely read man who understood theater, and we had few enough of his sort in those days. He gave us many of his plays—*The Gypsy Girl, The Wisdom of Solomon, The Polish Boy*. For all his learn-ing he was not proud, and behaved with us like a colleague. He even played a small part now and then when, as sometimes happens, some-one fell out of the cast. And he played it well too.

Kessler came, a big name now, from Romania. He was not so changed since I had seen him last. A tall, broad-boned man, a bit on the proud side, perhaps, but a good fellow. Clapped you on the shoul-der when he liked you, and wrung your hand.

Schoengold came with Clara, his wife, both of them friends from the Odessa days. Schoengold in his time was the handsomest man in the Yiddish theater. I remember when I first caught sight of him in Odessa I was spellbound by his beauty. Fate brought us together again in London. And with what appetite and joy he and Clara and I played together! In America, too, we lived our lives together, lived on the stage, where one lives more in a half hour than in life in a year.

Schoengold, one of the best actors I ever played with, had for some reason developed a mania for adding to his costume. No matter what he was playing, he would put on a plume, a feather, a cape, a scarf. He had a special weakness for medals. I remember when he played *Bar Kochba* in London, he was so covered with tin he looked like a man in armor.

But who was *not* in London in those years! Everyone was there! Yankele Katzman, whose career had begun in Russia with my own. My old friend and rival, Spivakovsky. Laiser Zuckerman, whose danc-ing had captivated me in Odessa. And all of us played together in Smith's theater on Prince's Street, and played there "with fire and flame."

By 1886, as the reader can see, our situation had considerably improved. Our circle of friends and acquaintances was growing wider. We came a bit to ourselves, ventured out now and then, saw something of London. We could go to the English theater from time to time, and perhaps learn something there. I myself often went to see Wilson Barrett, then the most famous actor on the London stage.

Altogether, things were looking up. Our theater was doing well, the general mood was gay. Every night after the play we got together at Moishe Kibins's restaurant in Whitechapel. And there the nights went merrily, for it was known that if you wanted a good word, a joke, a pretty story, or perhaps a song or two, this was the place.

Actors are energized after their performance, and in urgent need of food, company, and amusement. They have always had some special coffee-house, café, or restaurant where they get together after the play, often staying on into the small hours of the morning. The restaurant of their friend and "patriot," Moishe Kibins, was apparently the favorite spot of the actors in Prince's Street, but other places in Whitechapel also catered to this special clientele.

In the New York of the nineties, a number of these meeting places became famous because of the Broadway actors who congregated there. For the Yiddish actors downtown the most notable spots were Zeitlin's and the Café Monopol. The Café Royal, the most famous of them all, opened in 1910 and remained a New York landmark until it closed its doors in the 1950s.

My patron and friend, David Smith, often took part in these gay evenings at Moishe Kibins's. Herr Smith loved me very much. He loved my jokes and stories as much as my playing. And if jokes and stories gave out, any little kibitz was also good coin. I loved to make him laugh and sometimes allowed myself a practical joke. He took even this in good part, and truly, it was a pleasure to hear the healthy laughter of the man.

We also had a "patriot" called Stone, a cigar merchant, a solid sixty-year-old Russian Jew. All day this Stone gave out the bitterness of cigars and smoke to the world, but in the evening, especially a theater evening, he came to us to forget the smoke and fog of his life. But he did not only take, this Stone. He also gave. Sometimes he paid for the whole table, as much as a pound. More important, he often said something worth hearing. An intelligent man, Stone, and his words had a meaning and a worth.

I must not forget our restaurateur, Moishe Kibins. A plain man of the people, but also with a spark of something fine, something of the heart. Because he loved theater, he loved us too. We were his *kohanim,* his holiest. This he showed not only with applause in the theater, but also in his tact with the actor down on his luck. Nobody knew better how to look the other way when an actor with empty pockets walked out without paying. In our first sad days in America we theater folk met few with the understanding, the true fineness, of this humble Londoner.

THE LADDER OF WORDS

Except for 1887, when I spent several months in America, I lived in London almost seven years. How in London I grew, how, with me, our theater grew—grew in its *soul*—and how, in the same moral sense, our audience grew.

How did we grow, you ask? Through plays. Workmen climb on ladders. Sailors climb on ropes. Actors climb on words. On plays.

I have spoken of my success in *Uriel Acosta*. The climax of this play comes with Uriel's recantation in the synagogue. Here Uriel gives up his fight, confesses to heresy, and breaking, accepts humiliation and punishment. In this scene, I reached the high point of my performance.

This was new. Usually an actor wins the public with *activity,* a scene of burning anger, a moment when he shows his strength. To call up a storm in the audience with *silence,* with *submission*—this demands a higher level of understanding in the audience as well as a higher level of art in the actor. To the credit of our audience in London and later, in New York, it was just this passivity, this *hidden* feeling, that gave me my finest moments in this play.

But our London stage, sad to say, could not always remain on those heights. The theater is a mill that must go. If there is no wheat, corn is also food. As I have related, our first play in London was *The Penitent,* by the novelist Sheikevitch. A month or two later I put on another piece by the same author. This was *Trefnyak (The Impure One).*

We have only to compare this play with those on our stage today to see the remarkable progress the Yiddish theater has made over the years. *Trefnyak* would seem very strange to us now, and its success in London tells us a good deal about those early times!

The content of the play is pure melodrama. Intrigue and fanaticism ruin a fine family. Dena loves the modern enlightened Erwald, but her parents want her to marry the village rabbi, a hunchback with six children by a former wife. The lovers elope to Petersburg. They marry, have a son, and are happy. But the fanatic father sends an informer who plots against Erwald, and has him sent to prison.

Husband and wife lose each other. Erwald, released, goes back to his native Denmark, believing Dena and her son are dead. Years pass. Because the son, Marcus, is a modern boy, the fanatic village congregation labels him "impure" (*tref*), and has him sent away as a soldier. He is saved by Erwald, his father, who is now the Danish consul to St. Petersburg. Mother, father, and son are reunited. The villains, of course, are punished and sent away in chains.

So here we have a melodrama with all the dramatic trimmings. Nothing so crude as this can be found in Goldfaden. Although Goldfaden is of the same time and school, although he often portrays the old-fashioned Jew as an angry fanatic, he never gives us characters so far from life, so coarse and exaggerated. On the other hand, the humor in Sheikevitch is more believable. There are two comic characters in *Trefnyak:* Shepsl the Matchmaker and Limping Avremel. The audience laughed at them, yet they behave like human beings and do not climb the bare walls.

Trefnyak did not belong to the red-letter days of my career, but betweenwhiles, it served to fill out the emptiness and poorness of our repertoire. The play was a success, and I had a success in it. Our audience was small. The clubs held no more than a hundred. Even Prince's Street, built for me later, held no more than three hundred. We had to continually give the audience something new.

A higher step for me on the London ladder was *Doctor Almasaro,* a play, like *Shulamith* and *Bar Kochba,* belonging to Goldfaden's best period. A historic operetta, *Doctor Almasaro* is written entirely in rhymed couplets. Annetta Gradner, as the daughter, did most of the singing, but I played the title role, and sang the most famous song. And what Jew of the older generation does not remember that song!

> "Lost, alone, driven from his home,
> Punished for his sin,
> He wanders the world, God's outcast child,
> With all lands closed to him.
> Useless to weep, useless to moan,
> The answer is always No!

You cannot enter. The way is barred.
You are a Jew? Go further! Go."

I was not an outstanding singer. Still, I did well in this song. I stressed the rhythm, gave it life with gesture and movement, brought out the sadness of the words. Almasaro sings it in prison, and naturally, I wore chains. True, the text does not mention these bracelets, but we actors know what we are doing. A Jew in prison in the old Spanish days without chains? It would be like a wedding without musicians! Everyone knows that chains make a terrific impression, and bring out all the tragedy of the situation. In short, what I could not sing I *acted*—and not without effect.

In contrast to the highly "Germanized" plays of this era, everyone in *Doctor Almasaro* speaks a clear, simple Yiddish. Not only the Jews in the play, but also the Christians. Not only Almasaro and his daughter, but also the governor of Palermo, the grande dame Isabella, the two court beauties, Elvira and Mariana, the disguised Jew, Alonzo, the bandits, and even the soldiers of the guard. Only occasionally, for the sake of a rhyme, does Goldfaden sin and bring in a German word.

The play, however, gives few opportunities to the actor. There are no strong monologues, no powerful situations. Only one scene allows for fire, temperament, power. Here the daughter of the governor of Palermo is dying, stricken with a mysterious illness. The great Almasaro can cure her, but the governor fears him. He sees in the Jew his natural enemy, and the more so because he has in the past done Almasaro harm. "Revenge! Revenge!" he exclaims fearfully. "Well I know that revenge is in your heart!"

To this I replied in a tone that reflected the historic strength of the Jew, together with the high responsibility of the doctor, the healer:

"My heart is one you cannot understand,
    I battle with an enemy far stronger
        and more grand.
    For know, that while I live on earth
    And while I still draw breath,
    My mission here to heal the sick,
    My adversary—Death!"

I cannot say I was at my best in *Almasaro*. In general, the play lacks dramatic conflict. Yet I always played it with success and with powerful effect. At the time this surprised me, and only after years have I come to understand it. The great historic physician was an awesome figure in my eyes, something of majesty in every wrinkle of his old face, every hair of his Moses-like beard. I felt as I played him that under the calm of his demeanor lay a giant power, a power he has sworn never to use unless all else has failed. And this sense of majesty, of power, despite the faults of my performance, I was able to convey and make the audience feel.

Though I could not know it, Almasaro was destined to be a model—perhaps a weak, still half-amateurish model—but nonetheless the first attempt, the prototype, the mold into which was poured what I call the "Grand Jew," a figure I was to portray in later years and that has given my life in the theater its greatest meaning.

One other London success must be mentioned here, a success written in red outstanding letters in the chronicles of my life. This was *Moishele Soldat* (*Young Soldier Moishele*), also sometimes called *The Russian Soldier.* When I think of the plays that lifted my name in London, *Moishele Soldat* is one of the first that comes to mind.

It is an old play, probably dating back to the 1840s, and written in the generous spirit of the German liberal movement—there was a flood of such plays after Schiller. The author is no longer known, but the Yiddish adaptation was done by none other than my friend Gradner, who gave me the play in London. And very fine it was on his part to give me a role in which I could show my powers. In no play, not even *The Odessa Beggar,* did I have such success as in *Moishele Soldat.*

From a literary standpoint the piece is no better than *Trefnyak.* But it has scenes, action, surprises. You can do something with it!

Here is the content. Manya, a poor girl working as a servant in the home of Julius Waldman and secretly in love with him, discovers that on a trip to Paris, Waldman, forgetting his promise to her, has married another woman. Waldman's father, learning that Manya is pregnant, angrily drives her out of the house. Before leaving, she says to him, "Tiger in human form! I swear by the holiness of nature* that your son Julius is the father of my child!"

---

* Apparently an echo from the French revolution, when "nature" was officially crowned as the Deity.

In my copy of the play (I still possess it), these words are crossed out. Above them in pencil is written: "I swear by the holiness of my *Jewish wedding vows* that your son Julius *is my husband!*"

From this we see that in the original play the love of Manya and Julius Waldman was unsanctified, and their son, in the eyes of the world, was a bastard. For our Jewish audience this had to be changed.

Taking the play in hand, I began to direct it. In those days this meant one thing—melodrama. Sad moments were introduced by sad quiet music, and sometimes this continued throughout the scene. Manya, driven out by Waldman's father, remains alone on the stage. The music steals in as she begins her monologue: "Where shall I go? Lost and dark the way for me."

Melodrama (now called incidental music) accompanied the play in every theater of this period. Though now banished from the stage, this musical accompaniment is still accepted in motion pictures, and was not dropped even when the sound film came in.

In the 1920s when Yiddish critics demanded a stricter realism, melodrama was frowned on. Actors like Kessler abandoned it. Adler, who needed music to stir his emotions, never gave it up.

Moishele the Soldier, the son of Manya and Julius Waldman, shows himself twenty years later. Home from the army, happy he will see his mother again, he finds her in a desperate situation. Because she became ill, Manya has lost her work in a *kretchma*. Penniless and threatened with eviction, she is dying of hunger.

To save her, Moishele goes out on the street to beg. Here he encounters Julius Waldman, back from abroad and now a widower. Seeing a rich man, Moishele accosts him and demands money. When Waldman refuses, he tries to take the money by force, ready to kill for it if need be. A struggle takes place, police appear, and it ends with Moishele's arrest.

In prison he learns that the man he attacked is his father, Julius Waldman, who betrayed his mother in her youth. As soon as he is released Moishele seeks out Waldman, determined to avenge her. But out of a scene of revenge and murder comes instead a scene of compassion and recognition. Waldman realizes that he loves his son, and takes back the mother.

The play was strong and there were scenes that could really be played. The third-act monologue, for instance. Moishele counts over the coins he was given on the street, relating the story of each: "These two kopeks from a rich man for telling him my sad tale. One kopek from a lady who got out of her carriage to admire the landscape. Half a kopek from a merchant with a thick belly. And this *whole gulden* from a tired, half-starving worker!"

I made a great play of this scene, laying out my coins with broad gestures, and taking on the voice, the face, the character of the people I described so that the audience could see them, hear them, almost feel they were on the stage with me. The undercurrent of social protest in this monologue always worked powerfully on a Yiddish audience.

Moishele Soldat was a milestone in my career. It laid the path for my success in London, and it would be my trump card in America.

All these plays, some of them worthy, others less so, prepared the way for what may be called an epoch in the Yiddish theater. I refer to the heroic epoch of Schiller,* which would endure on our stage for some twenty-five years, and which I began in London with his masterpiece, *The Robbers.*

Whatever the reason, the great Schiller seems to have as many "patriots" among us Jews as in his own German public. I do not know why this is so. I believe it must go back to the time of Moses Mendelssohn and his Enlightenment, for ever since then a weakness for German culture has somehow stuck to the Jewish intellectual.

This is Adler's only reference to the faraway "German Socrates" whose influence, more than any other, shaped his life and his theater.

Moses Mendelssohn, the giant figure who changed Jewish history, was born in the ghetto of Dessau, seventy miles southwest of Berlin, in 1729. Because of a malformation of the spine (caused by scoliosis) he was taught at home in his early years, but at sixteen he had shown so marked an aptitude for learning that he was sent to Berlin to continue his studies under the renowned Hebrew scholar, Moses ben Israel Samocz.

* Friedrich Schiller (1759–1805).

This teacher led him to Maimonides* and the merging of Greek and Hebrew thought that flowered in twelfth-century Spain. In the seventeenth century the rise of mysticism and Cabala had brought with it a hostility to secular learning, and in Mendelssohn's day Maimonides was looked on as a heretic. But the idea that faith and reason could exist side by side had a profound effect on him and remained one of the central ideas of his life and work.

It was a concept, as it happened, that fell in well with the mood of the time. In the 1750s all Europe was ringing with the name of Voltaire, and the hub and center of the German Enlightenment was Berlin.

To be part of this ferment, Mendelssohn had to master French, Latin, Greek, and, most important, a faultless German. Young scholars taught him these languages. He prepared himself further by a course of reading that took in classic literature, the sciences, philosophy, and history, as well as the many burning social and political questions of the day. He also held regular talks with the rector of a Protestant church, an act that shows the remarkable range and independence of that still youthful mind.

His first philosophic essays, published in his twenties, gave him immediate entry to the most advanced circles of the city. The massive philosophic works that followed, together with his immense scholarship, his essays on literature, his reflections on both religious and temporal themes, soon gave him the leading position among his peers that he held until his death.

Mendelssohn owed his rise not only to his prestige as a philosopher, but also, we are told, to an extraordinary personal magnetism. Afflicted with a physical infirmity, an unconverted Jew, he had cordial relations all his life with some of the most eminent men of his time. For years he carried on a voluminous correspondence with Immanuel Kant. The liberal Prussian minister of education continually complains in his affectionate letters that he does not have enough of his company. His friendship with the poet and playwright Gotthold Lessing was never broken while both men lived. And there were scientists, scholars, philosophers, and statesmen, too, who not only admired, but defended the "gentle son of Mendel" in the troubles of his later life.

Mendelssohn, loved for the mildness of his character, could speak with fire about the wrongs to his people. In 1871, with the help and

---

* Greek name of Moses ben Maimon (1135–1204), the foremost intellectual figure of medieval Judaism.

collaboration of Christian Wilhelm von Dohm, a man of affairs high in the Prussian cabinet, he prepared a formal treatise, "On the Civil Improvement of the Jews," a document drawing attention to harsh laws against the Jews of Alsace and acts of violence against them in that region. The document was signed by Dohm and another high official, while Mendelssohn's name remained in the background.

The treatise came under the eye of the liberal Joseph II of Austria, who called on his cabinet for comments. The result of this inquiry was the famous Patent of Tolerance, an edict issued first in Vienna and Prague, and the following year to the whole of the Austro-Hungarian Empire.

Among other liberal reforms, the Patent of Tolerance mandated that Jewish children be instructed in the sciences, arts, and crafts. Their parents had the choice of placing them in government schools, or in Jewish schools that would have the same academic status. Textbooks would omit everything offensive to the Jewish faith.

There was jubilation in the Jewish community. Jewish scholars, fired by the Enlightenment, prepared to take teaching posts. Mendelssohn remained cool, feeling conversion was the motive. It was not reform he wanted for his people, but emancipation—freedom from a ghetto existence and the rigidly controlled religious life that limited their outlook, sapped their capacity for action, and isolated them from the world.

To achieve this end he approached the rabbinate directly, asking them of their own will to relinquish their strongest power—the right of excommunication.

Calling this long-held right an abuse of religious authority, and citing the case of a man placed "in *herem*" (i.e., excommunicated), Mendelssohn wrote: "The ban excludes him from the society of his coreligionists, degrades him in their eyes, injures him in his means of a livelihood, and may even lead to acts of hatred against him."

Though fierce debate must have raged over the question, Mendelssohn's prestige was great, and the ban was voluntarily halted by the rabbinate. The state, which had sanctioned the practice, now intervened with laws against it, and with this the medieval ritual was effectively ended.

A blow had been struck for Jewish liberation, but Mendelssohn had given offense to many, and in ultra-Orthodox circles he remains a questionable figure even today. Though his Jewish faith was the core of his being, he refused to place it above other faiths, asserting the validity of *all* religions. "In order to serve the Omnipresent Shepherd it is not necessary for all sheep to graze in one pasture," he wrote. "Judaism is best for us, best for our generation, best for certain times and circumstances."

This view, to some, went a long way toward apostasy, and there were those who did not forgive him.

Ultimately, he came under attack from both Christians and Jews. Since he had admitted the validity of Christianity, a Lutheran minister by the name of Lavater publicly challenged him to embrace that faith or, failing that, to admit its superiority to his own. The long-drawn-out polemics that followed, forcing him repeatedly to defend his Judaism, embittered Mendelssohn's life, affected his health, and had a part in bringing on the illness that caused his death.

He died in 1786 at the age of fifty-seven. He had proved that a Jew could take a leading place in the European world, contribute to its culture, and still remain a Jew. But this achievement had been sustained by a delicate balance that had its perils. Six of Mendelssohn's eight children converted after his death to the Protestant or Roman Catholic faith.* Mendelssohn himself was forced to fight bitterly—a thing not in his nature—in the relentless public polemics of what he called "the Lavater affair." He had hoped to end the prejudice against his people, and in this great aim of his life he failed. But he made the first great step in the separation of Synagogue and State. He opened a path from Judaism to the outside world, paving the way for the liberating force of the Haskala. And every generation that succeeded his still walks in his footsteps.

---

* Felix Mendelssohn, a grand-nephew, belonged to this Christian branch of the family.

SCHILLER: AN EPOCH IN OUR THEATER

I can say that except for Shakespeare, no European dramatist has achieved such a place on our stage as Schiller. Goethe, for example, is unknown to the Yiddish public to this day. Molière, god of the French, also unknown. Ibsen and Hauptmann were only with greatest trouble pushed onto our boards by our intellectuals, and often their plays met with difficulty, even resentment. Schiller, on the other hand, came into our theater without a struggle, from the first a wildly popular favorite.

And let me ask, is there a drop of appreciation for this in that ungrateful, anti-Semitic nation? So much as a drop of recognition that for generations now we have loved their classic, their adored favorite, their Schiller? And the great Friedrich himself, the thinker, the historian, doesn't he, too, give us Jews a dig, a barb, every chance he gets? And in spite of it, we believed in him! For it was not the intellectuals who fought for him in London, but we ourselves, the actors! And we fought like a storm, like a flood. Young and inexperienced as we were, we knew our audience. And knowing them, we dared undertake that difficult and ambitious play still known to the Yiddish public as *The Robbers of Schiller.* *

For you must know that with us this play was never referred to as *The Robbers,* but always as *The Robbers of Schiller,* as though Schiller were the town from which the robbers came! The mistake was probably made in some first translation in Poland or Galicia. It was never corrected, and for thousands of Yiddish playgoers, it apparently never will be.

It was, of course, our charming Courland intellectual, Herman Fiedler, my orchestra leader and friend, who prepared the play for us.

* Schiller's *Die Räuber.*

Most likely, it was also his idea to do it. Once we had it in hand we set to work to "adapt" it—that is, make it more suitable for our stage and audience.

First of all, a good deal had to be cut. Our Whitechapel Jews could not leave the theater at three in the morning; they had to get up next day and go to work. Next, the many mythological names and references in the text had to be politely escorted out of it. Our Jews, not being of the same "shtetl" as these Greek gods and godlings, would feel no special need to make their acquaintance. A number of deeply Christian speeches were also allowed to take their departure. Respectful as they are of the Christian Torah, our audience would not care to have so much of it in their own theater.

With a shorter and more suitable version, we went into rehearsal and opened. We were sure of a success, and we were not mistaken. The audience caught fire from the first performance.

The Yiddish public would in later years thrill to Shakespeare. Then how would they not respond to the playwright who, they say, begins where Shakespeare leaves off! The great Schiller, the thinker and historian, was, God forbid, no plagiarist, but Shakespeare was his school, and he learned from him with a passion that still smokes on the page.

This is particularly evident in *The Robbers*. Except for the nineteenth-century ideas, the whole play moves with the unmistakable sweep and line of Shakespeare. It can be said that when Schiller wrote it, he was drunk on Shakespeare! For one thing, there is full measure with nothing held back. Five long acts, all crammed with characters and bursting with action. At every moment the situation changes, at every turn something new happens— today we could easily make two plays of it!

The characters, too, play on all the strings of Shakespeare's harp. The devoted old Danilo is the blood brother of the friar in *Romeo and Juliet*. In the hero, Karl Moore, we find not a little of Hamlet's high philosophy. Amalia, with her deathless love, is Juliet's sister—and how strikingly the wicked Franz resembles Richard the Third!

But how dense and alive they are, these characters, how broad and fundamental! Take Karl Moore. A nobly born knight in the wonderful guise of a robber chieftain, a great soul who turns his back on the corruption of his own world, takes his stand with the poor, steals from the true "robbers" and gives back the spoils to the robbed. And then his monologues! So daring, so magnificent! And with what keen appreciation the Yiddish audience drank in the *almost socialist criticism of society* in these monologues!

Such characters, such elements, must take—I believe will always take—any audience. Then how much more a *Yiddish* audience, and one so young and naïve as ours in the London of the 1880s.

I opened in the role of the villain, Franz Moore. For many reasons this was the part I wanted. It would have been no great feat for the handsome Adler to play the handsome, noble Karl Moore. Let me show a real feat, I told myself, and appear instead as the wicked, repellent Franz.

It has always been one of my ambitions to win the audience not in a "grateful" role, as we call it, but precisely in an "ungrateful" role, that of a scoundrel, a godless villain like Franz Moore. I have always enjoyed playing men of mind—men with eyes that look cleverly, even knavishly, on the world around them, men who can analyze and dissect their enemy, plumb his depths, find his weaknesses, play on all his strings! At every moment a new idea comes to him, at every instant he sees another stratagem, another way to outdo his enemy. And he enjoys the fertility of his own brain, enjoys the power it gives him, the harm it can do!

I found a particular pleasure in the cynical monologues Schiller gives his villain. "What? He is my brother? He came out of the same oven as I? And for this I must hold him holy? What? He is my father? He is my flesh and blood, he gave me life? And for this I must hold him holy? Was he thinking of me when he did this deed? Did he know me at the time? Was I in his thoughts at the time?"

Most powerful of all is the villain's last night. Here he lives through the fall from self-belief, the awakening of conscience, the fear of death. And at the last there is his defiance, his turning away from God. *"I cannot confess, God. All is dark. I will not confess. Such a triumph over me I will not give heaven!"* In that one scene there is a world to play.

After appearing many times in the role of Franz, I changed over to the role of Karl. Truly, it is hard to say which is the better part. If Karl does not have his wicked brother's passion, he has spiritual beauty. If he has not Franz's infernal brilliance, he has a Hamletlike philosophy. If he has not his storm and rage, he has a beautiful sadness. And then he is so great a hero, so daring a nature, a tamer of men whom the desperate robbers obey with greatest fear and deepest love.

Take the close of the second act. A message is sent to the outlaws, a word that if they give up Karl Moore, the sentence hanging over them will be lifted. Karl agitates among them to do as they say, to give him up. His arguments grow stronger and stronger, until, won over by his greatness, the bandits tear the paper to pieces. "Now, comrades, we are truly one!" Karl shouts in his joy. "There is an army in my fist! Death or freedom! At least, let them not take one of us alive!" With drawn swords, they follow him out.

For an actor, this one scene is worth everything.

In 1886, when we were already in Prince's Street, I had the happiness of playing both roles. Since the two brothers never meet in the play, I had time between scenes to change my makeup and costume and come on in the other character. For an actor this was truly a Herculean task. In one night to play two such parts! Just to throw myself from one into the other cost me whole rivers of sweat. But the satisfaction of it! The achievement!

The Robbers was a great rung for me on the London ladder. I climbed it step by step, over good plays and bad. Over *The Penitent,* over *Trefnyak,* over *Moishele Soldat, Acosta, La Juive, The Odessa Beggar,* and Schiller's *The Robbers.* One step higher with every rung, until, when I came to America in 1889, I was already known by the proud name of *"Nesher Hagodel"** and was an actor famous throughout the Yiddish theatrical world.

---

* "The Great Eagle." The sobriquet, by which he was known throughout his life, was a play on his name, Adler, which in German means "eagle."

From Joy to Deepest Night

Things in London might have arranged themselves. As I have related, my life as an actor was going well. My playing was appreciated. *The Robbers,* for example, caused a furor among the London Jews. And when I played Karl Moore or Franz, to say nothing of when I played both, I felt as though wings were lifting me into the clouds—such happy sensations as are experienced only in our innocent young dreams.

As for my Sonya, she, the gentle, the quiet one, said nothing, but after these performances I felt in the power of her kiss that she loved me more than ever before—more even than when she consented to be my wife and gave herself to me, body and soul.

Then all was well, was it not? What had we to fear? As the sun mounts higher and higher in the heavens, who thinks of the night? Yet, silent and unnoticed, night was coming.

Death was coming. In the winter of 1886 our Rivka, our three-year-old daughter, was taken from us.

And what was her sin that she deserved death? Why did it have to be? Was she needed as a sacrifice on the altar of Yiddish theater art? What does such a little bird know of beauty, art, ideals? Why must it be children who pay for our happiness with their gentle lives?

Ach, the London poverty, the bitter poverty of the Yiddish actor of the eighties! It was the fate of our little Rivka, our Nunia, as we sometimes called her, to be dragged over the sea in a cattle boat and to be brought into the darkness of Whitechapel and our pauperish actors' existence. In Russia my mother or my sister would have looked after her. In London, whom did we have? There was no money for a woman, a nurse. The poor mother had to take her every night through the snowy, windy streets to the theater—how else were we to live? Somewhere under the hellish stage the child had to be left while father and mother went to entertain the public. And after the performance, to wake her again, drag her again through the raw, bitter London night. Is it any wonder that in the cold damp rooms over Moishe Kibins's restaurant the pale, quiet, affectionate child took sick, coughed, choked, grew worse . . .

"Croup," the English doctor told us. "The child has croup."

Night after night we sat beside her, listening with dread to the heavy cough, the heavy uneven breathing, and reading in her eyes each time she woke, the childish bewilderment and pain. With fear in our hearts we kept watch, hearing always closer the flapping of the heavy black wings of death.

Mother and father sat together, but looked away when their eyes met. It was fear that did not let us look into each other's eyes. Worse than fear, the other thought—that it was our fault, that we had driven our child to death, that, strong grown creatures as we were, we had not saved such a fragile little butterfly.

The hours drew out, and the child slowly sank. The fever went up, the cough grew worse, more and more her throat was choked by the disease. She began to be delirious, confused. Oh, those moments when we saw her light fading, those moments when we saw our child die.

Deep in the night I bent over her whispering in Yiddish, "*Rivkale, die derkennst mich?* Do you know me?" In a clear voice and in English, she answered, "Yes, Papa."

Those were her last words. We did not hear her voice again.

I am old now, ach, how old! How much have I not lived through since then! But I still hear those two words as I heard them that night, with the same desolation, the same animal pain.

The curtain came down on the first chapter of my life in Riga. In the year 1886 it closed on the second.

In that year, on Tisha Bov, day of sorrow and penitence, my Sonya died.

On the threshold of that spring and summer she had borne me a son. We were happy. We hoped the firstborn son would console us for our other child, the little daughter we had lost.

Some force in the universe denied us that joy. The delicate woman, already weakened by her confinement, fell ill with an infection. The sickness grew worse, and they took her away to the London hospital, a Christian hospital in Whitechapel. There, day by day, she slowly sank.

I was allowed to visit her freely and stay as long as I wished. Probably the doctors already knew it was hopeless. It may be they pitied me too, seeing how desperate I was, how my life hung by a thread.

I did not know the truth of her condition, but I saw for myself that she grew no better. Every day she was more silent, more sad. Every day her beautiful eyes looked more deeply, more piercingly, into mine. She, the clever one, at last the despondent one, knew she was dying, knew she was leaving in the stormy seas of life two children—one barely a month old, the other, for all his thirty-one years, also a helpless child.

Hours and days I sat beside her, listening to her sighs, although with her last strength she tried to stifle them. "Come closer, Yasha," she whispered. I bent toward her. She took my head in her hot damp hands and with feverish strength, drew it down until her lips pressed a kiss on my forehead. That kiss. It was a kiss from eternity, from the grave, from hell itself!

Tired, she sank back. Her eyes closed. She fell into a dream. I gazed at her pale sunken cheeks, her hair that fell like two raven wings on the snowy white pillow. I could no longer master myself. I wept. She opened her eyes and with a frightened look, seized my hand. "*Nye platye, Yasha,*" she said. "*Nye platye! Golubchik moi! Dorogoi!*"*

And still it was she, the same Sonya, the same Fräulein Oberlander who had come into my life together with the new Yiddish theater. The same Sonya who lifted me out of the empty worthless existence I had known until then. It seemed only yesterday that the two of us rehearsed *Uriel Acosta* together, and she taught me to believe in myself. "Courage, Yakob!" she had said. "Courage! We will be victorious!"

And that unforgettable trip by sleigh to Kremenchuk when Rosenberg had cooked up a hell of lies between us. We went in separate sleds, I like a wild wolf, drunk with jealousy and pain, ready with one blow to kill her, myself, and the whole world. And when she came to my room and asked forgiveness, I, out of wildness and young actor-ish bravado, called her a terrible name and drove her away.

But soon enough I was on my knees before her. She embraced me, she forgave me. We were happy. She said she would be my wife, she put her life in my hands. And what did I give her in return? I took her from the Odessa she loved, from the glorious streets, the glorious sea, took her from her home, from her parents, from her whole beautiful life. And for what? To bring her to this desolate Whitechapel—to die.

---

* "Don't cry, Yasha! Don't cry, my dear one, my darling."

She, who rose like a sun in my life, is it possible I will lose her, that my sun will be no more? Is it possible that I will have to live out the rest of my days without her? It cannot be so, I told myself. I will not allow it to be so!

One of those small things never forgotten, one of those trifles for which the human being never forgives himself, took me from the hospital for several hours. While I was gone, my Sonya died.

Did she look for me before the light faded? Did she call my name with her last breath? She did. I am sure of it. But the indifferent eye of an English nurse took her last look. Her dying words fell on the ears of a stranger. When I returned they told me it was over. Touching her, tearing at her, trying to wake, to revive her, I saw that she was dead.

No—then I was no actor. And perhaps, if you will, it was never acting, and the last cry of Naphtali Hertz in Gordin's *The Stranger* was only the echo, dragged out of my memory, my soul, of the cry I gave that day.

I fell to the ground, beat my head against it, bellowed like an animal, tore at my flesh, tore at my hands, struggled like a man who has taken a poison that has driven him mad. "Sonya!" I cried out, "Sonya, my So-o-nya!"

They took me, led me, dragged me away from her corpse.

In the days that followed my friends were afraid for me. They were right. I was determined not to live, not to live without Sonya. But soon I was quiet. Too quiet. A lethargy came over me.

That was how it was when we buried her, and I threw the first spadeful of earth on her coffin. That was how it was when, for our infant son, I said Kaddish over her grave.

In the early nineties I had a play by Gordin called *The Russian Jew in America.* It is a play I have always loved, reading into it much that was autobiographical of Gordin's life and also my own.

As Gordin originally wrote the play, the Russian Jew does not die but lives on, an old, broken, disappointed man. Later, for an evening in honor of the Frei Volk's Buhne,* he wrote an epilogue that showed the death of the Russian Jew.

* The Free People's Theater, a young theatrical group started by Gordin in New York City.

The Russian Jew dies, and dying, has a vision, a hallucination. Broken pictures of Russia come before him. Pictures of America too, of his life there. And he dies in the strange land, quietly singing, "Ech, Moscow, my Moscow! City of cities! Streets of gold!"

I played this epilogue with such tearing inner feeling that my wife, Sara Adler, became fearful I would cause some injury to my heart, long since a broken, damaged thing. And just as in London poor Gradner used to call from the wings to his sick Annetta, fearful she would injure her health, so Sara Adler stood behind the paper wall of the Windsor Theatre, and I heard her repeated warning, "Adle-e-r! Adle-e-r!," reminding me over and over to control my emotions.

In the strange land, like the Russian Jew, my Sonya died. Like him she was buried in the alien earth, far from the Russia she loved.

Years later, having won much recognition in America, I came back, great man that I was, to London. There I went to Sonya Oberlander's grave, stretched out my length on the earth that covered it, bit the grass that grew there, and quietly, for a long time, wept.

If these were not memoirs, if they were instead a day-to-day journal, a record of events as they spun themselves out, the reader would surely feel from the last chapter that I could not survive the blow of Sonya's death. And it is true that without Sonya I felt my life had no value. All those close to me knew this was so, all those who knew us well, and knew how we had lived together.

Plays—theater—the words had lost their meaning. A thick forest of memories surrounded and enclosed me. I saw her everywhere—as she was when we first met—in the time of our fevered wanderings over the face of Russia—in our moments of greatest happiness and joy—last of all in the days when, side by side, we toiled together over the sandy hills of life's sorrow and pain.

Hours together I sat alone, listening only to these inner voices, lost in the pictures that rose up before me as out of some deep underground chasm.

And from thinking only of the past and comparing it to the present, a deep, fixed melancholy came over me. All this *was*, I told myself, but is no more. Vanished. Flown away. Nothing can bring it back, no power on earth can deliver it again into your grasp. And how beautiful it was, and how delicate!

Days and weeks went by in this way, how many I do not know. Then, suddenly, a change! My longing for solitude and silence gave way to a raging need to be up and about, to do something, anything, but not to be still. To be still meant I accepted what had happened, accepted Sonya's death. And this thought drove me out like a storm into the boiling tumult of the London streets. It did not matter if my feet took me through the lordly streets of the London rich, or to those terrible lanes and byways where the squalor and crime of the city lie naked to the light of day—to move on was all that mattered. Hurrying, never resting, seeking without knowing what I sought, I would find my way at last under the bridge to the river. There I talked with someone unseen, asked questions, nodded at the answers, stared down into the watery depths where I seemed to see my own grave, and in my heart only one longing—death.

And in this ceaseless rush and hurry, in this senseless roaming over the city, lay my survival. The storm of pain began to subside. The wound began to heal.

We have an old Jewish saying, "What the earth covers the heart forgets." Does it mean that we who live on the earth forget those who lie beneath it? No—the very opposite is true. We forget those we love never! We remember them more often than a thousand things that soon fall out of our consciousness. But with time the remembering changes. Little by little the ache grows weaker, the sorrow milder, until what is left is only an inner longing, deep, quiet, almost sweet.

Turgenev has a story to which he gives the title "Grief." A young man, deceived by an intrigue, suddenly kills his beloved. Afterward he tears his hair, weeps, goes half mad over what he has done. Yet in a short time this same man finds he is breathing the sun-filled air with joy, and drinking in, like a cup of fresh water, the beautiful world around him. And this not because he did not love her, or was not true, or did not care, but simply because it was his nature to live.

Apparently I was like that young man. Too strongly through all my being, life sang its song. I was thirty-one years old, and it was not nature to die.

My grief did not leave me. Long after, a rush of tears on my lashes as I thought of the past. But the eye itself, wide open again, was taking in with a renewed interest and curiosity the world around it.

I began to make the best of my situation. My boy, my Abram, had to have care. Whether I had the means or not, I took a nurse for him.

My theater had to go on; plays had to be done. And since Sonya, our first tragedienne, was no more, another had to take her place. That other was Keni Liptzin, whose rise thus began with the death of her best and dearest friend.

And afterward—long, long afterward—I fell into a life—well, much like the life before my marriage. It was a life, looking back on it now, that I do not remember with pride—a life, much as I want to be openhearted, about which I must leave out many details. The English have an expression. A man, they say, must "sow his wild oats." They feel, it seems, that the sins of youth, even when far from harmless or innocent, must be accepted, since they are inevitable.

My time of "wild oats" was not over. I was still young when I was swept up into the whirlwind of events I must now describe.

A Storm in Whitechapel

Never since I began these pages have I felt such dread as at this moment. How shall I speak of this episode, the happiest, yet the most terrible I have known. How can I make clear all that happened, all that did not happen? And will it ever be understood? This is the tragedy of our life, that between us stands an unseen but indestructible division. Never can one human being know what takes place in the soul of another. Never. Never.

Is it possible now to unravel the tangled threads of that far-off time? We live in a world with a fixed moral code, a measure applied dogmatically to all circumstances, all situations. A bass voice from above calls down, saying, This is right and this is wrong. This is good and this is bad. And then—the secret is not only mine; it also belongs to another—the one who gave me so much happiness—the one to whom I am still so grateful—the one who, in her great love, forgave me so much.

Jenny Kaiser ("Jennya"), a young actress who played in Adler's theater in London, is not mentioned by name in his memoirs. Their son, Charles Adler, was born in London in 1886.

If I have a regret it is that, in the years we were together, truly two souls that were one, I did not observe her more closely. For break my head as I will, to this day I do not understand her. To comprehend a nature so full of contrasts and contradictions I would have to borrow the talent of a Gorky, to wander, like him, throughout the length and breadth of Mother Russia, finding there the women depicted only by this author, women ruled by no law but their free, unfettered instincts.

I met her soon after we came to London, possibly through another actor, possibly through my wife, who knew her for a time as a neighbor. Through the mutual accommodations of the poor, lending and borrowing, I believe an acquaintance sprang up between them hardly noticed by myself.

Where we actually came together I cannot say exactly. Most likely it was in some theatrical café or restaurant, places where encounters of this kind were not rare.

Here is the way such things happened in our small actors' world. Sitting late in these surroundings, you feel hanging over you a pair of pleading, passionate young eyes. You are drawn by their magic, charmed by their wonder and admiration. You answer with a friendly smile, a deferential nod, and take pleasure in the happiness you have given this young heart.

You see her again. Her glance this time is shy, uncertain. You take courage and give her a greeting. And so, over time the ice of strangeness melts and two human beings stand face-to-face.

She was very young when I met her, sixteen or seventeen at most, but fully developed, as is often the case with Jewish daughters of the people, especially those in whom there is a trace of Eastern blood. A figure somewhat under medium height and rounded. Eyes of deep black on a white matte background. Hair very dark, setting off an unflawed complexion. A child of London's Whitechapel, there born and raised. The poor dwelling, the street, the shop, the simple relatives that brought her up, these were her world.

Of the so-called higher ideals she knew almost nothing, of Judaism little more than superstition and fear, of English education only what remained of a few years in the lower forms of a Whitechapel public school. She spoke Yiddish well, though with a strong English accent, and Yiddish theater was her greatest joy. Watching the sad scenes of a play, this girl found pleasure in weeping whole cups of tears, with never a thought that she might injure those beautiful eyes!

Ethical principles, moral standards—for her such ideas did not exist. She was truthful, she was honorable, not because she had been taught to be so, but because it was her nature to be open, because in her character there was nothing of slyness, cleverness, shrewdness,

Jennya Kaiser

guile. She was good, she was generous, not out of any ideal of behavior, not even out of love of humanity. Her goodness was simple good-heartedness. She was as good as one who says, "You want something of me? Here! Take it! I don't need it. It doesn't trouble me."

With such a character you can imagine how little she withheld from me, whom she worshiped as an actor, and wildly, hot-bloodedly, loved. From the first steps of our acquaintance, without coquetry, without feminine tricks, her whole free, open behavior said, "Here I am. Take me."

And I came to love her too. Many feelings were in this love, from those the world thinks of as the coarsest to those they call the highest and most refined. I loved her as one loves a beautiful, blooming young woman. I loved her as a good comrade, a good brother. I loved her because she was not ashamed of our love and let the whole world see it. I loved her goodness, her daily motherly concern for me. I loved her simple frankness, her honesty never masked by a hair. I loved the stream of life that rushed from her. With every drop of my being, I loved her.

The bond between us lasted long, a wellspring for both of us of both joy and pain. I struggled continually with my doubts, asking myself whether or not I should bind my life to hers. It seemed to me she was not serious, that there was something inconsistent in her. I did not understand her need for freedom, and from the first I knew the taste of jealousy.

She also doubted. Strange to say, much as she loved me she did not want to marry me. She did not want to lose her freedom. Most remarkable of all, she had the idea that if I married her I would stop loving her! At bottom, she probably feared the future, knowing my nature, my unquiet temperament. And in truth, it had been a source of much adversity in my life.

And so the thing drew itself out, in happiness and disquiet, months and years of both happiness and uncertainty. And meanwhile, weak vessel that I was, another came into my life. A person of a different kind and from a very different background. And a cry went up that there must be a marriage.

I was caught between two fires. The situation was becoming a scandal. The whole theater colony was talking. London, out of nothing at all, became a place too hot to hold me. I withdrew for a time from this burning circle, but the storm raged on. The side that was more determined did not rest, and in the end a date was set for the wedding.

As the day drew near her brothers came to her. "Go to the wedding and make a scandal," her brothers said. "If you don't go, we will! We will break his bones! We will kill him!"

"Take one step," she said, "and I will throw myself into the river!" And this she said in such a way that they believed her.

"Then go to him," they said. "Or we will do it."

"Very well," she said, "I will go to him."

She came on the day of the wedding. People in the house had been warned, and the door was locked against her. She stood outside and knocked until they opened it. And I, on the stage a Karl Moore who destroyed castles and slaughtered armies, turned out in life to be no such hero. The house had an attic, and the groom, in high hat, frock coat, and white gloves, climbed up there and hid. She stood on the stair below, and the balcony scene of *Romeo and Juliet* began—but a little the other way, Romeo above and Juliet below.

"Adler, come down," she called.

"I am afraid," I answered.

"What are you afraid of?"

"You will do me some harm."

"Come down. I will do you no harm."

"Swear it!"

"I swear it by my dead father!"

I came down the stair. We looked at each other, fell into each other's arms, wept. In the rooms inside musicians were playing, young people dancing. In the end she went her way.

The wedding ceremony began. They circle the groom seven times. The rabbi intones the seven prayers. Bride and groom sip the blessed wine. The goblet is smashed. *Mazel tov!* Man and wife!

THE TRAGEDY IN PRINCE'S STREET

In the fall of 1888 I received an emissary from America in the person of a Mr. Mandelkern. This man, later an important mediator in and around the Yiddish theater, arrived with a contract, a sum of money, an advance, all in hopes of bringing me and my troupe to America.

Mandelkern's functions in the Yiddish theater were not yet clearly defined, but the actors in New York already spoke of him as a man who could get things done. A man, it was said, who could "put a wall together with another wall, and make money out of both."

He was to remain Adler's friend and, at a critical point, was instrumental in bringing him to New York, where his American career was launched.

Mandelkern was not our first visitor from the other side of the Atlantic. As the Yiddish theater took hold in America, managers there began looking to London for actors. They came to our clubs, looked over what we had, sometimes went back empty-handed, sometimes took back a star at a bargain rate for the newly opened New York Yiddish theater market.

Mandelkern, however, had not come from either of the New York companies. He was acting for two Chicago men, a certain Drozdovitch and Rosengarten, two well-to-do tailors, both interested in Yiddish theater, mostly as a business venture, but also, I believe, out of a patriotic love for the Jewish word. They had heard about me from actors in New York. Also, I gathered, from a company of amateurs in Chicago.* Since these men knew my theater in London was not covering me with gold, they were sure I would accept their offer without delay. In fact, they had already rushed a notice to the Yiddish press saying I was on my way, and would overturn worlds when I arrived.

As the devil would have it, the whole thing fell through. For one thing, I was not eager to leave London at the moment. My theater was beginning to pick up again. I had a public that loved me, and that I loved. And why should I deny it—here in London I outshone all others, the star of stars, while in America I would face strong competition. And while I have no great fear of rivalry on the stage, I admit it is not a thing I have ever hotly pursued.

In the end more practical considerations decided matters. After Sonya's death my theater remained closed a long time. To open it again I had to borrow heavily. Because of this, the advance Mandelkern gave me soon disappeared in the welter of my debts. To bring my troupe to America I needed more money in hand. And a second advance Mandelkern was either unwilling or unable to give.

It was our good fortune that the troupe of Mogulesko and Moishe Finkel were in London. They had just left Russia, they had more vivid memories of conditions there, made fewer demands than I, bargained less, did not waste time with long thinking, but promptly accepted Mandelkern's offer and sailed with him for America.

Only one good thing came of all this. I had gotten from Mandelkern the address of the tailor Drozdovitch in Chicago. This I carefully hid on the chance it might be of use someday.

For the rest, I did not greatly care. I stayed on in London the better part of that year. And I might have stayed longer if not for a catastrophe in the Prince's Street Club, a catastrophe that echoed throughout the English press, cost many innocent lives, and ended, for years to come, all Yiddish theater in London.

The tragic events that rocked Whitechapel, and brought my London career to a close, took place in the winter of 1887. I do not recall what we were playing that night. It must have been a popular piece, the kind that "drew," for we had a full house. The orchestra and, even

* It was the still obscure Boris Thomashefsky, playing in Chicago with a group of amateurs, who told the Chicago tailors about the famous Adler in London.

more, the cheaper gallery, were packed to the doors with men, women, and, as usual, children.

Some scene in the play that night apparently called for a fire on the stage—an effect we created with a chemical called Bengal Fire or some other theater trick. During this scene a slight mishap must have occurred, perhaps a thread of smoke on the stage, or a spark somewhere. In itself this is not dangerous. What gave it fatal importance was that someone in the gallery saw it, gave way to panic, and sent out over the theater that most terrible of all words: "Fire!"

What followed was the scene played out whenever men and women cease to be rational beings and give way to blind animal panic—that scene which, as often as it has been played, can never be described. In one instant inhuman screams filled the theater. And then it began. A rushing, a pushing, a squeezing, a blind animal struggle to get out of the trap. A devil's mix of terror, agony, noble self-sacrifice against demonic egotism, and everyone for himself! In a word, a wild rout. A hell. All terrors loosed from their hiding places, all devils breaking free of their chains.

We on the stage were struck by the full force of the panic. *They* were the actors now, we their helpless, terrified audience. The horror of death was in us all. Only the consciousness of my responsibility as director forced me to control my fear. Coming down to the edge of the stage, I shouted with all my strength, "There is no fire. There is no danger. Go back to your seats. Nothing has happened. You are all safe!"

For an instant the racing, boiling Gehenna was stilled. I controlled it with my eyes like a snake charmer, a basilisk. But only for an instant. One voice—and at such a moment only one is needed—shouted with frenzy, "He is lying! Fire! Fire! Fire!"

And again it began. The racing, pushing, wrangling, struggling. In the gallery a woman was already preparing to leap over the railing into the pit. She had thrown her coat over, she was astride the railing. I became desperate. I became coarse and cursed her. "You will fall and be killed, devil take you!" I shouted. My words, my curses, useless. She leaped over the railing, and to the screams of fear below were added her screams of pain. Another woman was already climbing after her, skirts lifted, legs bared. I tried to appeal to her shame, her wifely modesty. "Not fine!" I cried. "A Jewish daughter with naked legs!" But at such a time even the deeply rooted instinct of human sexual decency is forgotten. She leaped, was injured in her fall, and her screams of agony were added to the chaos below. Another leap over the railing. Still another. More screams. More agony. And a renewed pushing and struggling, the strong against the weak, the young against the old—three hundred human beings falling over each other, clutching each other, trampling each other . . . Merciful God, when a man has lived through such a thing, has he not been punished enough for his sins?

The police and fire wagons came too late. It was over. We counted the victims. Seventeen suffocated, trampled-out lives, most of them women, two of them children. Seventeen dwellers of the London ghetto. They had wanted a little make-believe joy and sorrow to drive away the bitter winter night. A little happiness they had asked. For money. For a price.

David Smith and I were both called in and questioned, but we were soon allowed to leave. How were we to blame? The authorities did not even close the club.

But the dread event brought its own consequences. A horror had seized the Whitechapel Jews and they would not go near the theater. Nothing helped. No special program. No special announcement. Yiddish theater in London was over—played out.

The misfortune of the false fire at the Prince's Street Club befell us in the middle of winter. Naturally, we moved heaven and earth to get the theater going again. It was useless. Our appeals to the public, our attempts to make them see reason—all to no avail. There had been, in fact, no fire and no danger to anyone. But talk to the trees and the stones! An almost religious fear had seized the whole of Whitechapel.

Naturally, a few people still came, friends who did not desert us. But what could we have from so few? At the best of times the nightly intake had been no more than forty dollars. How much could we take in now? Not even water for the kasha! No matter what we put in, the theater stayed so cold, dark, and empty you could hunt wolves in the gallery.

Again, as in Riga, the bitter question: What now? And as in Riga, the same answer: "Wanderer, go farther!"

In our troupe we always had one actor who was a bit of a scholar. This specialist could always be depended on to find, buried in his memory, some passage in the five Books of Moses that he could apply to the case in question and expound with Talmudic reasoning. This learned actor addressed me as follows: " '*And Yankev waited in Canaan.*' Time to go on to the next reading: '*And Yankev set out on the road.*' "

To set out on the road was fine, but where should we go? Russia was finished, fenced off, no return there possible. Romania and Galicia, also out of the question. From these lands no help could be expected. France? Ah, that was another matter! France, or better said, Paris, pulled us like a magnet. The magic of the gay, terrifically famous world city fascinated and enticed us. In a word, the obsession of Paris! We knew that Jews were already there, and Jews of our own kind, too, Russian, Romanian, and Galician immigrants. These wanderers had already found a haven, an oasis around the Place Montmartre known to Yiddish comedians as "the hangout." In that tiny corner, we knew, a thread of Yiddish theater existed.

I threw off the dangerous fantasy. I had the example of the Gradners, who had rushed off to Paris and as quickly returned, sad and disappointed, their noses down. Paris, I knew, was a grave. I could see only one open way, one open gate—America.

From America we had already received joyful tidings. Maybe too joyful. Experts ourselves in the art of bragging, we had long discounted half the great good fortune reported by our colleagues in that land. But even with half discounted, the other half remained! And one sign we had that erased every doubt: Of all the actors who had gone to America, none had ever returned.

With America more and more on my mind, I searched out again the address I had hidden away, the address of the Chicago tailor, Drozdovitch. But why do we need Chicago—a city, I had heard, full of devils and thieves! As concerned Yiddish theater in Chicago, there were only confused, uncertain rumors, while in New York two real companies were playing—the troupe of Maurice Heine at the Oriental Theatre, and Mogulesko and Finkel at the Roumania Opera House. In both these theaters were actors I had played with, worked with, hungered with—old friends, I was certain, who would not let us fall. In any case, since the path to Chicago led through New York, why not stop a few days and see what the fates would bring?

I rolled up my sleeves and wrote three letters. The first to Drozdovitch in Chicago, the other two to my colleagues in New York, telling them we were on our way, and asking them to meet us at the boat.

Everything, of course, turned on the question of money. My brother-in-law, Alexander Oberlander, had come to London at the time of Sonya's illness. His wife and children had joined him, and the whole family was sailing. Keni and our prompter, Volodya Liptzin, together with most of my London troupe, would be passengers. I was also taking our music conductor, Herman Fiedler. Ship's passage had to be found for all these people, and money was nonexistent. Those who had saved anything, a ring, a necklace, thought themselves fortunate. Most of us had nothing.

We began searching out old friends, some "patriot," some admirer who had helped before, or who owed us perhaps for a bygone favor. From all this we managed to scratch together enough for one or two farewell performances, but not enough for such a journey.

Now I recalled my highly placed relative, the great Rabbi Adler of London. He had not entirely cast me out, and his son had come to see *Uriel Acosta*. The son had brought a Rothschild with him. In spite of his coldness to our theater I could not believe the great chief rabbi would not help if things were really bad with me. Once again I called on him.

On this occasion the old man was surprisingly cordial. I soon guessed the reason. From my first words the rabbi grasped the all-important fact: I was taking myself and my theater out of London. Short and sweet, he gave me thirty pounds (about $150 in American money) and in the friendliest manner, accompanied me to his door.

The gift was hardly lordly, but it would be enough to get me and my actors across the Atlantic.

LAST DAYS IN LONDON

Before we left for America I married again. My second wife was Dinah Shtettin, an actress mentioned earlier in these annals. The daughter of a strict Orthodox family, she was drawn to our circles by nothing but her love for the stage. A girl of sixteen, petite, charming, vivacious, she came to us much as Miss Damby comes to Kean in the famous Dumas play, asking only to give herself heart and soul to the theater, and share its uncertain destiny.

Dinah Shtettin, mother of my talented daughter Celia Adler, was born in London, the child of parents from a village in Poland. Her mother was dead, her father a *shammos** in a small Whitechapel synagogue. If not for the Yiddish theater, she would most likely never have risen above the surface of an ordinary Jewish life. The London clubs lifted her high over her environment, and made her into a serious actress who for many years served and brought honor to the Yiddish theater.

She began in the chorus of Gradner's club but quickly rose there to small parts. There was a constant migration of actors between his club and mine. When the Gradners left for Paris this young actress came into my troupe. She grew and developed, and before long I was able to trust her with longer and more difficult parts.

I knew her only slightly when she was with Gradner. Now, thrown together, we drew closer. She, like others, marveled at my playing. I was charmed by her devotion to the theater and by a talent that blossomed like a flower in early spring. We fell in love, and the love grew always.

Did we think of marriage? Hard to say after so many years. Cer-

* A lay post like that of a beadle.

tainly not seriously. I was careless, irresponsible, a little wild and loose as always. She was young, fresh, full of gaiety—the gaiety of a girl who still knows nothing of life, wants to know nothing, and gives never a thought to the future.

Very different was the attitude of her father, the pious old-fashioned Jew. It was entirely against old Shtettin's wish and without his approval that his daughter had taken up this life in the theater. He did not think much of actors in general, and by the looks of it, had no great opinion of me, either. It did not overwhelm him that my name was on all lips, my portrait in the window of so many Whitechapel photographers. He was not impressed that I numbered among my friends the rich and pious David Smith. Nor was he overawed by my connection with the great Rabbi Adler, chief cleric though he was over all Orthodox congregations throughout the empire of Her Majesty, Queen Victoria. To old Shtettin all that mattered not a pin. He was not sure of my trustworthiness, he doubted my character, my substance, my reality. Altogether, he was not happy to see his daughter's destiny linked so closely with mine.

But when the father saw that our relationship had already gone far, that I would seek his daughter out, see her often, walk with her, and all this with no mention of an engagement, his feelings took an entirely different turn. He began to storm, and to protest in sharpest terms that the situation could not go on. And now a new chapter began! Marriage! "Let it be a divorce tomorrow, but a marriage there must be!" the old man angrily repeated. And from these words alone one can see the opinion he had of me and the great good fortune he foresaw for his daughter under my protection!

Old Shtettin had his way. His daughter obeyed him, and before we left for America the wedding took place. My young wife was to join me in America only after I had tested the ground and made sure a life there would be possible. For the time being, she was to remain in London.

As the day of our departure grew near a wild gaiety broke out among the actors. Laughter, a feeling of irresponsibility, and among the men especially, an outbreak of tricks and horseplay. All this suited me well enough, and I played a series of practical jokes that kept everyone's spirits soaring.

Under it all my mood was somber. I did not want to leave London.

Dinah Shtettin Adler (later Dinah Fein-man), London

I had my two graves there in the Jewish cemetery, my memories that bound me to the place. My heart misgave me about the step we were taking. We were coming unbidden to a strange land, with who knows what welcome awaiting.

We sailed at the end of February, a few weeks before Purim. I don't even remember the name of the boat. We were good paupers again, leaving London as penniless as we had come. This time, it is true, we did not have cattle as our fellow passengers, did not have to entertain the captain and his officers. But all through the tumult and commotion as we cast off anchor, that other voyage from Riga was in my thoughts. How different it was this time! Then I had had my Sonya, the friend who was everything to me, my protector, my guide who showed me the way. Now I had no one. In this serious life moment, I was alone. Only the boy was left to me, Sonya's two-year-old Abram, a child who never left my side.

We traveled in steerage along with hundreds of others. But it was not so bad on the boat. A word, a jest—when you are with your own people you do not lose hope, you do not altogether despair.

The great day finally dawned. Land. The voyage was over. America.

Passengers of that time disembarked at Castle Garden on the Battery, where the Aquarium now stands. Few difficulties were made in those early days. We were simply registered and allowed to leave.

But the loneliness! God, what loneliness! No one had come to meet us. No one at all. We sat down, waited, hoped. We went outside, onto the lawn, onto the grass, looked in every direction, hoping every moment for one face we knew, one voice not the voice of a stranger. Nobody. Of all the Yiddish actors on the Bowery, not one had found it needful to give a *sholem aleichem* to forlorn colleagues washed up on a strange, friendless shore. And this although in both theaters were people I knew well—some I had even reckoned as friends.

For this behavior there can be only one explanation—the dire poverty of the Yiddish theater in New York. There was no business, and everyone was bitter at heart. The stars, I suppose, thought of me as an extra burden they would have to carry. The smaller actors knew that swimming along with the big fish was a whole shoal of little fish. They probably feared that with our coming their poor little fishpond on the Bowery would grow even more crowded and muddy.

Whatever the reason for their absence, we knew well enough what it meant. We decided then and there we would not stay one night in New York, would not even look at the two theaters there. We would go straight on to Chicago. And let them know what we thought of them!

CHICAGO DAYS — THE TROUPE SPLITS

We got to Chicago, by luck on Purim. I looked up the tailor Drozdovitch, and our whole troupe sat that night at his holiday table. Over the haman cakes and the wine, the two of us talked business. The outcome was a decision not to wait for Passover, but immediately to take a theater and begin to play.

Since he was short of money for the venture, Drozdovitch had to go about the city looking for partners. Within days these were found, and we opened at the Madison, a theater in the heart of Chicago's Jewish quarter.

I put on plays we had done in London: *Acosta, Almasaro, A Madman for Love* by Bezelinsky. We did well at first, but at the end of the holidays things began to fall on the buttered side. The Chicago audience was very small, and once they had seen these plays, we had nothing new to give them.

How does the Russian saying go? "Where it is tight, there it will burst." Business went down, and soon there was little on the plate for anyone. Though Liptzin and I received hardly more than the others, we were blamed for the general misfortune. Bitterness began. Anger began. In the end the actors declared a strike—the first strike, if I am not mistaken, of Yiddish actors in America.

Was the strike justified? Hard to say. We had gone through worse in London, and still held together. I believe something in the American air carried these seeds. Labor unrest was breaking out in every part of the country, and though the Jewish labor movement was still in its swaddling clothes, there were continual strikes in the Jewish streets of both Chicago and New York. My actors caught the fever. Half of them walked out, gave their performances in a neighboring hall, and conducted their affairs of state without me.

One can easily imagine what came of all this. In the cramped little

Jewish quarter of Chicago, where not even one theater could stand on its feet, two were now competing. And do you know what competition meant in those days? It took the lowest form imaginable. Competition meant lies, accusations. It meant couplets insulting our rivals sung before the audience in the middle of the play. It meant speeches praising your own troupe and throwing mud at the merchandise of the other. Our competitors plastered the whole quarter with posters and leaflets against us. And to claim we did not use the same ammunition would not be true.

If both sides did not go to even greater lengths it was because slander costs money, money neither of us had. What could be the end of it? We tormented each other a little longer, each driven by his need, and naturally, both fell. Finished, Yiddish theater in Chicago. We both went under.

The actors in both troupes scattered. One got work as a messenger for a telegraph company, another as a coachman, or cabman, as they were called in those days before automobiles. Some went into factories and sweatshops. Others fell back on the usual resource of the impoverished Yiddish actor—a small poor restaurant or boardinghouse in the Jewish quarter.

And I, the mighty star? What did I do? I, in all my greatness, enjoyed to the full my hunger. With my aristocratic manners, my artistic habits, could I think of finding work? And if I had wanted work—and I did not—would anyone have given me work? And so I went nicely and tastefully hungry, and with me hungered my two-year-old Abram, Sonya's boy.

Since I seldom had anyone with whom I could leave the child, I had to take him with me through the hot Chicago streets. I was looking for friends, "patriots," people with whom I could talk of opening the theater again. Since these people had to be found wherever they were, I dragged myself about the city every day, and the boy with me. I have a long pair of legs and strode, but a two-year-old soon has to be carried. So I lifted him up, and with this little live package in my arms, plodded on. To go on foot was all we could do, for often I had not even money enough for carfare.

On one of those days I had to see a man who lived at the other end of Chicago. Chicago is vast beyond imagining. Well, walking with the boy we came to a candy stand. What does a child know? He asks! And I, always a dreamer lost in my thoughts, took out my entire capital—six cents—and bought him what he wanted. My little Abie munched and was happy, and I realized too late that I had left myself without a penny and would have to cross the whole city of Chicago on foot.

At least we got something to eat at the end of that day. There were times I dragged myself from one house to the other late into the night, and went hungry at the end of it. Not that these people did not offer me food. Of course they did. I was offered food in every house, but in every house, I refused it. For all my heroics on the stage, you see, I was in certain ways very shy. I did not want these people to know I was hungry. I was ashamed of it. So I waved away everything they offered me, pretended I was full and needed nothing.

I had only one corner I could call my own in those Chicago days, one place where my boy could get a little rest, where I could open my heart in quiet talk to a friend and remember how things used to be. Masha, Alexander Oberlander's wife, had, one way or another, managed to open a little restaurant. Evenings, while she prepared for her customers, I stayed beside her, talked, reminisced, and meanwhile rolled up my sleeves, chopped livers, chopped cutlets, helped with the dishes and made myself useful.

The summer came to an end with no change. Things were still hopeless, and I could see nothing but to pack up and try my luck in New York. I got the troupe together and we talked it over. Yes, the strike, the rivalry, was over. Bitter poverty had brought us together again.

The actors did not want to go to New York. They had no money for the trip and no reason to go. Still, there was bitterness that I was leaving. They felt betrayed, deserted. And while I could see no help for them or myself if I stayed, I knew they were stranded and in a pitiful case. In the end I pledged myself to organize a performance for them before I left. This they accepted.

I pawned a ring—the only thing I had left of any value. With this I got the few pennies needed for the hall, the posters, a few musicians, and the rest of it. Before I left we gave the performance, and the proceeds were divided among my stranded colleagues.

Oberlander and his wife stayed on in Chicago. Of all the actors that came with me from London, only Keni Liptzin was still at my side, the only one left to me now of the old days.

There were two Yiddish theaters in New York at that time, the Oriental Theatre and the Roumania Opera House, both in a desperate competition for actors. Liptzin got her chance at the Roumania Opera

House, and made an immediate sensation in Mosenthal's *Deborah*. She had won her place, but no one was running after me. At the Roumania Opera House, where Kessler reigned, I was not needed. I would have gone in with Maurice Heine at the Oriental, but Silberman, his leading man, had full say over casting, and I could not come to terms with him about my roles.

I spent some time looking at the sky between the tall buildings of New York and finally realized it was time to go.

This, officially, was the reason I went back to Europe. The real reason only I knew, and I relate it here for the first time. In those years I was still a widower. My Sonya was no more, and I had not yet married Dinah Shtettin. In London I had left someone to whom I was closely bound—someone I loved. The thought of this "someone," of whom I have written in a previous chapter, pulled me back as with a rope. I longed for her, and went back to London.

Clearly, the facts have been altered here, probably more as a sop to convention than in hopes of deceiving anyone. Everyone knew Adler had married a second time in London. His memoirs make public his wedding there to Dinah Shtettin and will later relate that she came to America, where their daughter was born. What remains is his confession that he went back to London with his thoughts on Jennya Kaiser.

What happened between them there has never been disclosed. Apparently some hope he had was not realized, for although Yiddish theater had picked up again in London, he left very soon for Warsaw.

He remained in that city for two years, receiving great acclaim. When he returned to London in 1889 he had become too famous to be ignored. He found both Heine and Mogulesko waiting to take him back to America.

NEW YORK

I FAIL IN *THE ODESSA BEGGAR* BUT TRIUMPH AS MOISHELE SOLDAT

I returned to America in the spring of 1889. A different arrival this time, and with a very different welcome. This time I came with pomp and parade. If my chariot was not hung with flags and trophies of my triumphs in Europe, it was greeted on every side by posters screaming in huge letters that the "new Salvini," the "great eagle" of the Yiddish stage, had flown to the shores of America.

The Oriental was closed now, its days as a theater over. I made my debut at Poole's, a house on Eighth Street near Broadway.* And what would I choose for my first appearance but *The Odessa Beggar,* a play that broke the walls of Jericho in London.

I opened Passover week to a packed house. The curtain rose. The play began. I delivered my most famous monologues, took my Beggar through his best situations. I heard no laughter. I heard no applause. The audience was cold as ice, and scene after scene went by in a deathly silence. *The Beggar,* a triumph in London, had fallen through completely in New York.

Adler was hissed by the audience that night, and the German manager of Poole's ran out before the curtain to say he had been deceived by a bad third-rate actor. There were whispers in the cast, too, that the London

---

* This theater had been leased to Heine by John Poole, an actor who also wrote sketches for Tony Pastor.

star was "not for New York." Only Mrs. Sara Heine, who had played his daughter, came up to Adler and, in the presence of all, spoke some words of recognition and praise.

Since things were bad, and my debut had failed to "take," I dug down into my theatrical baggage for whatever else it might hold. I came up with my second jewel of great price, and later that Passover week, appeared before the New York Jews in the role of Moishele Soldat.

How shall I describe it? The public shouted until they were hoarse, stamped until the columns shook.

Why this success after the failure of the *Beggar*? Is *Moishele Soldat* a better play? Is it more interesting? Does it give the leading actor more room for variety, more scope? Not at all. *The Beggar* is a tragicomedy, a play where in the most tragic moment, lips twist into a smile, where the audience laughs, but with eyes still wet with tears. This type of theater piece, this genre, was entirely new to the New York audience. They had laughed at comedies, wept over tragedies. The mixture of both in one play they did not understand. Not knowing whether they were to laugh or to cry, they sat the whole night in silence.

Moishele Soldat, on the other hand, is melodrama through and through. A few little comic moments before the plot develops and the main characters come on. The scenes that follow are full of tragedy, high drama, and tears. This the audience understood!

My own success I attribute above all to my youth and my appearance. I was handsome, and my soldier's uniform made me handsomer. I was by nature fiery, and since Moishele is full of youthful impatience and heroism, I could use this trait to advantage in the role.

We must remember also that Moishele is a hero, and the world loves heroes, onstage and off. His mother dying of hunger, he goes out to get money for her and does not care how he gets it. Refused money for his mother, he is ready to kill for her. Learning she was betrayed, he goes instantly to avenge her. And added to all this, the play has truly melodramatic moments—monologues and speeches that I delivered with all the force of my strong and moving dramatism.

A week later I had another success—I admit a more worthy success—in *Uriel Acosta*. This was truly *my* play, a play of literary and dramatic substance, a play with a tragic conflict, with scenes that climbed—in a word, a play that has to be played! *Acosta* and *La Juive* had been the crown of my success in London, and until 1891, when I met Jacob Gordin, these two plays would be the foundation of my career in America. In these two plays I felt strong, secure, felt I was creating something. I can say that these two plays brought out my talent as a tragedian.

Given something better, the New York audience proved they had both mind and soul. *Acosta* was greeted by applause that mounted to the rafters.

With my position now more assured, I sent to London for my wife. She came to America, and we took up our life together. All went well, and for a long time it seemed her father had done me an injustice, that he was wrong not to trust me with the happiness of his daughter. My wife and I loved each other, lived together well. Why not? She was clever, talented, honorable, true. A child was born to us here in America, my talented daughter Celia. The birth of our child gave a new joy to our marriage. My wife and I shared another spiritual bond in our devotion to the Yiddish theater.

And yet, as the women say, it was not to be. The great new life in America swallowed us. The giant kettle of intrigue began to bubble and cook. We parted. The old father's heart had not fooled him.

Among us Jews, people who divorce do not see each other again, do not speak together, do not come together under the same roof. And in general, I believe, a divorce ends with bad feeling on both sides. Dinah and I were the exception. We parted without hate, without bitterness, and so it remained to the end.

The child, of course, was a link that held us together. In those early days in New York my path was not covered with roses. There were troubles in the theater, complications of every kind. It was a comfort to me in those days to visit with the child, play with her, and as far as my limited means allowed, help the mother in her often distressed circumstances.

But the mother's life soon took a better turn. She married the well-known artist Siegmund Feinman. They had a good life. Their marriage was a happy one. We all remained friends and often played together.

The "difficulties and complications" began soon after Adler's first success at Poole's. Heine had agreed to a partnership on his performances, but as they continued to draw big houses, he began to regret the loss of half these profits.

Tensions between the two men rose, and in the spring of 1890 a quarrel broke out. Adler, holding up the curtain, insisted on the terms of their agreement. Heine held his ground. As they argued the curtain suddenly went up, and Adler saw another actor come onstage in his role. He had no alternative but to quit the premises.

After brooding a few days he wrote to Boris Thomashefsky. This young man was no longer an unknown quantity; he was creating what would later be "the road" for the Yiddish actor. His troupe had already played Philadelphia, Washington, Baltimore, Pittsburgh, Boston, and Chicago, the first of the Yiddish actors to appear in those cities. Mogulesko and Kessler had both guest-starred under his management, and both had toured with him in the summer months.

Thomashefsky wasted no time, but came immediately to New York. He found Adler at the Occidental Hotel at Broadway and Broome Street. Young Mrs. Adler had just given birth, and the room was crowded with visitors. "It broke my heart," Thomashefsky writes, "to see the great Adler with his great clever eyes living in this rundown hotel. He sat and joked, his majestic form in a torn jacket, his feet thrust into out-of-shape slippers. He kept everyone laughing, but I could see that under it all he had a bitter heart.

"Mrs. Adler finally said with a sigh, 'Yakobsche, what's the use of these jokes? Mr. Thomashefsky has come here on business.' Adler put on a high hat and a handsome coat and took me to a Jewish restaurant on Canal Street. He wanted to play *Uriel Acosta* in Philadelphia. The two of us got along well, and soon came to an agreement."*

Thomashefsky's following in Philadelphia was small, but he wanted to make a splash with Adler. He took a good theater, the Standard on South Street, and was excited at the opening to see people in evening dress in the audience.

Adler had a triumph in *Acosta*. Ladies threw flowers to him from the boxes, and young people waited outside afterward and gave him an ovation at the stage door.

After a week the troupe moved to Dramatic Hall, where they continued to have good audiences. Philadelphia was a wide-open city at that time, and there were gay parties for the actors every night.

---

* Boris Thomashefsky, *My Life*. New York: Trio Press, 1937. (In Yiddish.)

All this was causing a good deal of comment in New York. Sara Heine had come to Philadelphia as Adler's leading lady. This fact was much talked about, and the Philadelphia performances were cut short by the unannounced arrival of Adler's wife. Adler had to leave town to prevent a scandal, and Mrs. Heine was forced to retreat to an out-of-the-way hotel. She remained there in seclusion. She had broken with her husband and was resolved, come what may, that she would not go back to him.

Thomashefsky's troupe, losing its two stars, would have disbanded for the summer, but a letter came from Adler, who was now in Chicago. He had not succeeded in getting a theater there, but wrote that Chicago was a good city for Yiddish actors, and for Thomashefsky to "take Sonya and come." The two of them took the train the following day.

Once in Chicago, the capable Thomashefsky organized everything. He got a good theater, the Halstead, and sent for his troupe, and they played in Chicago all summer. The playwright Hurvitz joined them, and they had a success with his new play, *The Johnstown Flood.* *

They were looking forward to a good season when two visitors arrived—Henken, manager of Poole's, and Adler's old London friend, Mandelkern. The big news from New York was Heine, who had pulled off a major coup. He had taken the Thalia, a theater where the great German Sonnenthal had lately played. The Germans in the quarter were moving uptown, it was becoming a Jewish neighborhood. With Heine's troupe at the Thalia, Poole's was standing empty. Henken and Mandelkern wanted Adler to come in.

Thomashefsky argued that they were doing well in Chicago, but Adler, he says, wanted only to compete with the actors who had driven him off the stage in New York. Adler left with Henken and Mandelkern.

Thomashefsky went on without him, but his successes in Chicago no longer gave him pleasure. He felt he was lost in a backwater, began to feel he may have gone far astray in his art, and longed to be with the greats of New York.

New York, in fact, was buzzing with activity. Adler, beginning to assemble a cast for the coming season, found that the opening of a third

---

* *The Johnstown Flood,* written by the socialist Hurvitz, is the only known play on this disaster, which killed 2,200 people in one night and wiped out an American town. While the event was given huge publicity, the names of Frick, Mellon, and Carnegie, the three tycoons responsible, were never mentioned in the press.

Yiddish theater was an exciting event for everyone. Kessler and Mogulesko, dissatisfied with Heine's terms, went in with him, and with these great stars, Adler had the strongest of the New York companies. He had sweeping plans in mind, and prepared for the new season feeling that everything was at last going his way.

MY GREAT MOMENT COMES —
I MEET JACOB GORDIN

In 1891 I formed a company of my own and took over the Union Theatre on Broadway and Eighth Street (formerly Poole's). I opened the season with *Samson the Great* by Zolotkev, and followed with *La Juive* and then *Quo Vadis* by Sinckievich, all three from the standard European repertoire. It was time, I felt, that our theater touched on the deeper sides of life, time that plays of a more serious character found a place on our stage.

In this task—the task of deepening our theater, of, so to speak, "tragicizing" it—I had to stand alone. Those who have grown into the old way, those to whom the old represents not only a material but a spiritual income, must oppose the man who brings the new. This is the fate of the innovator, the reformer.

I was weak as a singer. I had not a good voice nor, I confess it, a very good ear. But is this why I turned from the operetta to purely dramatic plays? I think not. Though I could not take first place as a singer I could have done so as a dancer. For a dancer I was, and perhaps the best in the theater world of that time. Only a few years ago, in Gordin's *Tree of Knowledge*, I performed the dance of Moses Stoller with a true, fresh, lively rhythm. But from my earliest years I have leaned toward those plays where the actor works not with his feet, but with his voice, face, eyes; not with jests and comic antics, but with the principles of art; not to amuse the public with tumbling and *salto mortales,* but to awaken in them and in himself the deepest and most powerful emotions.

Like everyone else, I had heard of Jacob Gordin. I knew he was a socialist, a follower of Tolstoy, and a writer whose stories of Jewish life under the tsarist terror were making a stir in our literary circles.

Because he could not support his family by his newspaper work, Philip Krantz, the London-born editor of the *Arbeiter Zeitung*,* had advised him to try his hand at a play for the Yiddish theater.

It was this Philip Krantz who brought us together.

Jacob Gordin, the man who would revolutionize the Yiddish theater, had been in turn a journalist, a writer, a farmer, a worker in the Odessa shipyards, and an actor in a traveling Russian company. Born in 1853, the son of a well-to-do merchant of the Ukraine, he soon came under police suspicion as the head of a "Spiritual Biblical Brotherhood," an organization denying the hereafter, denying the existence of God, opposed to circumcision and marriage, and demanding that the Scriptures be interpreted in the light of moral, rather than religious, ideas.

The brotherhood, fiercely attacked in the Yiddish press, was dissolved in the repressions that followed the tsar's assassination. Gordin emerges next as unofficial editor of the *Yelizavetgrad News* and the leader of a "Tolstoyan circle," giving Bible readings to the peasants in the light of Tolstoy's ideas. The circle was disbanded by the police, and Gordin, in imminent danger of arrest, left the country and came to America.

Although he and Adler were both moving through southern Russia in the 1880s, they did not meet until 1891, when both were in New York.

Gordin and I met in a wine cellar on the East Side where the Russian-Yiddish intellectuals often gathered in those days. As usual, I spoke of my great need for better dramatic material. I had brought with me a German play of some kind. I offered this to Gordin, saying, "Here is a ready-made subject. Perhaps you can do something with it for the Yiddish theater."

With a fine gesture, Gordin refused it. "If I write a play for you," he said, "it will be a *Yiddish* play, not a German play with Yiddish names."

* *The Workers' Newspaper,* later issued as *The Jewish Daily Forward.*

After some talk we came to an understanding, and before we parted Gordin said he would have a first act for me in three weeks.

The play by Gordin was a risk, but a risk that Adler had to take. In spite of his personal success in *Samson* and *La Juive,* the Union Theatre was in danger of failure. A new personality had come on the scene, a star who had taken the East Side public by storm. Moishe Finkel, losing Kessler and in urgent need of a leading man, had sent for Boris Thomashefsky. This young unknown had stepped into Kessler's role in the Hurvitz operetta *David ben Jesse* and had created an overnight sensation.

It was soon clear, moreover, that the handsome new star was on the scene to stay. His operettas at the National Theatre ran for months, whereas Heine at the Thalia had to change his program every week. Kessler, who had been the king of these spectacles, was directly affected. Adler suffered even more. He had to take the better plays off the boards and put on the old operettas.

Thomashefsky did not conceal his satisfaction at these triumphs. "The Yiddish theatre of that day stood on Hurvitz and Lateiner," he declares. "To look like a star an actor had to wear slashed doublets, satin cloaks, golden crowns. Everyone had to do it, there was no other way. Kessler wore a hat with a feather, bare feet, and a shirt with red silk patches. Adler, to outdo him, wore a hat with three feathers, a naked throat, a spangled throw over his shoulders, and to make it more realistic, he put on chains, bracelets, and long Turkish earrings.

"I showed the two of them I could play that game! I put on a crown, a sword, chains, bracelets, silk hose in three colors, and three cloaks instead of one! If they had lightning I had thunder. If they shot arrows, I stabbed with daggers. If Kessler sang the Evening Prayer, I sang Kaddish. If Adler came in on a horse, I came in with three horses and a golden chariot. And believe me, next to me the two of them looked like ordinary soldiers of the line!"*

None of the elaborate operettas of this time have survived, but in their day they were considered the only way a theater could bring in the public. For the most part they were roughly based on events from Jewish history, were furnished with largely borrowed music, and relied heavily on sensational effects and nationalistic speeches. They had to be

* Boris Thomashefsky, *My Life.*

Jacob Mikhailovich Gordin, New York, 1892

Jacob Adler in A Sailor in Distress, *by Rudolph Marks; the actress may be Sara Adler.*

turned out with lightning speed, for Hurvitz and Lateiner, deadly rivals, often wrote on the same subject, and in their efforts to get ahead of one another, they often threw overboard not only historical fact, but every vestige of sense.

Cahan writes: "It sometimes happened that on opening night a play was not ready, an act or so still unwritten. 'Put it on,' Hurvitz would say. 'We will see.' And instead of a third act Hurvitz would come out dressed as a Sultan and talk any kind of high-sounding nonsense that came into his mind. A minute before the curtain went up Hurvitz would say to Feinman or Weinblatt, 'Whatever I say, nod your head.' Hurvitz is the Sultan, Weinblatt the Prime Minister. The Sultan speaks. The Minister nods his head. And the public took it!"

Attacks of this kind did a great deal to weaken the prestige of Hurvitz and Lateiner. But their power was also threatened at this time by certain actors who were taking a central position by the sheer force of their talent.

Reviews of the day continually refer to extraordinary acting moments. Cahan tells us that when Adler came out as Samson with his jawbone, the audience sat paralyzed, afraid Samson would destroy the world with his terrible strength. Keni Liptzin, playing a double role in Morris Rosenfeld's *Rachel and Leah,* amazed the poet-playwright Rosenfeld with her "hair-raising transition from heavenly beauty to devilish laughter."

Kessler, who loathed the operetta, once begged for a "bit" usually given an extra, an ancient Hebrew warrior who silently follows a group of soldiers across the stage and exits after them—nothing more. Leon Blank, a fellow actor, tells us the entire cast watched him, hypnotized. "We saw the old soldier, ready to die for his flag," Blank writes. "And such was Kessler's magic that we saw all the others too! We saw that one had been a hero, that another had been a coward. We saw how they had fought around him, how they had died around him! And the audience understood! They saw the greatness of it! A crash of applause on Kessler's exit. He was happier that night than I have ever seen him. And truly, it was one of his finest moments."

The critic Rothblum wrote, "In those years when the entire repertoire consisted of foolish operettas and comedies, a repertoire without a subject, without even a decent language—even then a moment of artistry, a lightning flash of talent, would hold the simple audience transfixed and astonish those intellectuals who now and then fell into a Yiddish theatre."

But if the situation was beginning to shift and change, there was as yet little outward sign of it. Adler had just produced *Judith and Holofernes, Titus Andronicus, or the Second Destruction of the Temple,* and finally, *Hymie in America,* the last a comedy by Rudolph Marks, in which he played Jake. He went to the meeting with Gordin feeling that only a miracle could save him.

Gordin was the miracle.

Gordin had promised me a first act in three weeks. He came to the theater one week later, bringing all four acts of a finished manuscript. He had written the play *Siberia* in one unbroken wave of inspiration, feeling, he said, "like a scribe at work on the holy Torah."

An item in a Russian newspaper had provided him his plot! The hero, an innocent man accused of a crime, has been sentenced to Siberian exile. On the way the prisoner escapes. He joins his family in another part of Russia, changes his name, and begins a new life. He has prospered and is a respected member of the community, when a rival, jealous of his success, discovers his secret and betrays him to the police. Torn from his family the innocent man goes out again into lifelong exile.

The actors at the Union Theatre listened to the play in a gloomy silence. There were no nationalistic speeches, no music. The setting was drab, modern. The characters spoke in simple ordinary language. They felt the audience would never accept it.

I put it on over the objections of the cast. I believed in it.

We opened on December 3, 1891. I knew from the first that a giant step had been taken, a step from which there was no turning back. I played the hero, Reuben Kahn, Kessler played the fanatical villain, Mogulesko the faithful servant. We played together harmoniously, with spirit, with true and powerful feeling.

That was the beginning of Jacob Gordin, and the beginning of the new Yankev Adler.

Probably out of consideration for his colleagues, Adler passes over the storms that rocked this production. The actors at the Union Theatre did not like *Siberia* or its author. Some of them, who knew about Gordin's

Boris Thomashef-sky in the operetta The Hungarian Singer *(Photograph courtesy of the Yivo Institute)*

"Spiritual Biblical Brotherhood," even looked on him as an anti-Semite. Tensions during the rehearsal period exploded when Mogulesko inserted a section of the opera *Hernani* into the second act. Gordin rose in the audience shouting that he would not allow it. Kessler sided with Mogulesko; others joined. Adler, the only one defending Gordin, was shouted down, and Gordin left the theater and did not come to his opening.

The first performance narrowly escaped disaster. The audience, seeing ordinary people on the stage speaking ordinary language like their own, grew more and more restless. Halfway through the second act laughter was heard followed by hisses. When the curtain fell, Adler, in despair, came out before the audience. His presence produced a silence, and in a voice shaken by emotion he addressed them in a historic appeal. "Believe me, *gospoda,*" he concluded, "if you would open your hearts, if you would open your mind and your understanding, you would not laugh at this play by the great Russian writer Jacob Mikhailovich Gordin, but would give it your most earnest attention."

His speech brought applause from a certain part of the audience, and according to Leon Blank, because of this the rest of the play went better. "The scene where Adler begged Kessler not to betray him made a strong impression," Blank writes. "And when Mogulesko, playing the servant, came to the line, 'Master, we are parting,' he burst into real tears and could not go on. And the great artist played the scene in such a way that the whole audience wept with him."

Because of this the actors apologized to Gordin. He came to the second performance and was given a warm ovation from a house filled with his friends.

We could play *Siberia* only a few nights. The press supported it, but the public did not come. *Two Worlds,* a second play by Gordin, had an even shorter run. When I announced *The Yiddish King Lear,* the whole cast predicted failure. They swore the play would never "take," that the audience would die of boredom. They begged me not to play an ordinary old Jew in a long coat and a yarmulke. But I stood there steel and iron, all because of a song I remembered in my youth—a song about an old father turned away by his children. Why had that song impressed me so deeply, I asked myself, why had grown men wept every time they heard it? And in spite of the opposition of the cast I put on *The Yiddish King Lear,* which was then and still remains the greatest success of the Yiddish theater.

The new play opened with a greatly reduced cast. Kessler and Mogulesko had left the company, convinced that Adler was committing suicide. A number of others also deserted. He had to bring over actors from Europe and even take in some amateurs.

But the Union Theatre had gained an important leading lady. Sara Heine, now divorced and married to Adler, made her first appearance as his wife in the play that was to change the history of their theater.

"The complaints of the cast soon died away," Sara wrote. "It was clear from the first rehearsal that Adler was going to do something extraordinary with this part. Everyone caught the spirit. And if any of us clung to the old bad way, striving for cheap laughter, cheap effects, it only reminded us all the more how great was the change taking place before our eyes."

The scene curtain of Gordin's *Lear* rose on the Purim feast of his Yiddish merchant-king. We see the great David Moishele, patriarch and ruler of his family, surrounded forty strong by his family, friends, and retainers—truly a little "court."

Sara wrote: "I have in my time witnessed ovations for great artists. In Odessa especially, these demonstrations could rise to remarkable heights. Adler's Yiddish 'king' seated at the head of his holiday table created such a moment. From the orchestra to the gallery, the theatre crashed! His part had 'taken' before he spoke a word.

"And this was nothing to the scenes that came later! He was not an actor that night, but a force. All of us played with inspiration, but the great figure that night Gordin had given to Adler, and the triumph was his own."*

Ten years later, when New York critics began taking an interest in these theaters on the Bowery, this review appeared in *Theatre Magazine:*

> The "Lear" of Jacob Adler is not Shakespeare's *King Lear* at all, but a modernized Russian-Hebrew comedy of manners, into which the old patriarch and his three daughters are transported in all their emotional picturesqueness and with surpassing dramatic effect. It is a poignant drama of domestic life, vividly true in its portrayal of contemporaneous middle-class Jewish characters and custom under the Russian monarchy, but world-appealing in its broad passion, tenderness, irony and intensely human flashes of fun. No finer acting has ever been seen in New York than Adler's gradual transition from the high estate of the Hebrew father distributing his bounty in the opening scenes to the quavering blind beggar of later developments.†

---

* "My Life: The Life of Sara Adler," *Jewish Daily Forward,* October 20, 1938.
† *Theatre Magazine,* November 2, 1901, p. 18.

Jacob Adler in
The Yiddish
King Lear

With the success of *Lear,* the small Union Theatre could no longer hold the audience. Adler joined forces with Finkel at the National, and from there moved both companies to the Windsor, a house with 1,500 seats. The whole population of the Lower East Side had embraced the Yiddish theater as their own.

Hurvitz and Lateiner, embattled allies now, fought on together at the National, but their stranglehold on the theater was broken. The success of *Der Vilder Mensch (The Wild Man)* signaled the end of their era.

Adler's portrayal of this grotesque child, his terrifying innocence, his flashes of insight, his mad dreams of power, have been described as an example of the intense realism of the Yiddish theater. The *New York*

Times recalled this performance as a "deeply tragic and unblushing clinical study of mental and moral degeneracy."*

Written for Adler, *The Wild Man* was pirated by actors for decades. A version was even written where the father repents, the family is saved, and the "Wild Man" is cured of his illness. Franz Kafka saw this bastardized version in 1910 and has noted some of the wild excesses of this production. He remarks on the "obviously great powers" of the playwright.†

After the success of *The Wild Man* every star followed the new trend. Kessler, Liptzin, the new idol, Bertha Kalich—everyone clamored for Gordin. He was the man of the hour, the voice of a new Yiddish theater.

It was in this era, the New York of the nineties, that we had our first great popular audiences—those lusty, unruly, noisy, madly devoted audiences of a time now past. Looking back from the present to those years I ask myself, where are they now, those "saints of the gallery," those boys and girls who once lived, flourished, made a racket, clapped, stamped, whistled, hooted, wept, and laughed, filling our theater with such fire and such joy? Where now? Where? Withered away, grown old, run out, dwindled, died. Yes, dead as the mastodon, the young "patriot" of those days, his bones buried in the cold depths of earth, and no heirs left to take his place. His high post in the gallery is empty, and the gallery is empty, too, cold and dark with wind blowing between the benches. No wonder it rots away and disappears!

In the Yiddish theater today we see order, decorum, politeness. Respectable people sit, finely dressed, finely fed, those who have forgotten youth. But high in the gallery, holding to the sides of his seat, the young "patriot" sat, and high was his enthusiasm. No two dollars could you ask of him, no dollar fifty. Ten or fifteen cents was all he could pay, and if we needed extras, we put him on the stage in a long coat and a crepe hair beard, and afterward he went up to the gallery and saw the rest of the five-act play for nothing.

The poor boy, by day a baster for a tailor, an errand boy on Orchard or Rivington Street, was by night the king, the soul of our

---

* Editorial on Adler's death, *New York Times,* April 1, 1926.
† Franz Kafka, *Diaries 1910–1913,* New York: Schocken Books, 1971, pp. 111–14.

Jacob Adler in
The Wild Man,
1893

theater. Without binoculars he saw the stage better than any critic. And no lady infatuated with a matinee idol ever followed more breathlessly every move and turn of her idol, every transition, every rise and fall of his voice, every gesture, every cadence!

When we were good, how broad and proud his happiness, his triumph. He was more than an onlooker. He *believed* what he saw on the stage, gave himself to it, lived it with his whole heart, his whole soul. And we, the actors, felt his love like a great wave from the gallery to the stage. And because of that oneness, that warmth, we knew we had conquered, knew the audience was with us. And we had the courage to go on, to achieve even more, to strive even higher.

And if the gallery was silent, the applause lifeless, we knew the play was wrong, a failure, and we must give another. The love of the gallery was our life. We needed it as water is needed by fish, as air is needed by all that breathes.

I recall that once, at the opening of the season, Gordin made a speech that insulted the gallery. *They struck!* They did not laugh at the comic scenes, did not weep when it was sad, and, when it was over, did not even move their hands. How dismal the whole performance after that! How spoiled for everyone the holiday opening of the season! Heavy and sad the curtain came down, and we actors left the theater that night as though we were already buried.

It was in London they first showed themselves, those never-to-be-forgotten boys and girls, deeply committed and ready for battle. Later we had them in New York, in Argentina, wherever we played. But always they came of the poorer classes. It was from these "folk masses" that we drew our strength. They were the soul, the flame, of our theater.

"Classicismus"

Somewhere in the middle nineties, the classics became popular with the Yiddish audience. This began with Shakespeare's *Hamlet,* which my colleague Boris Thomashefsky first presented. Later Bertha Kalich also played in it. After *Hamlet,* naturally, came *Othello,* where I gave one of my finest interpretations as Iago. And after Shakespeare, which playwright more logical than the one who, they say, "begins where Shakespeare leaves off"—Schiller!

Since the women were not yet the stars in our theater, we did not touch such plays as *Maria Stuart* or *Die Jungfrau von Orleans (The Maid of Orleans)*. But we had *Don Carlos, Kabale und Liebe (Intrigue and Love),* and other Schiller tragedies.

The Robbers, of course, was done on every Yiddish stage in America, and performed by every actor with God in his heart or a hope of stardom in his head. And I must admit that if this actor, however small, possessed even a spark of talent, the play always meant a holiday in the theater, a rush to the box office and a storm in the gallery. I myself performed it hundreds of times in New York with my German-Jewish colleague, Morris Morrison, as the noble Karl Moore and me as his wicked brother, Franz.

As I have already related, this was the role I had chosen in London. Apparently I knew even then that in my artistic territory I had a strong fortress in intellect. Roles of this kind have always drawn me strongly as an actor. I have often played them, and almost always with success. With pleasure and joy I played Lessing's noble *Nathan the Wise,* the learned Protassoff in Gorky's *Children of the Sun,* the genius Ben Zion in Gordin's *Der Metureff.* And with triumph and joy I have played such brilliant villains as Shakespeare's Iago, Shakespeare's Richard the Third, and Schiller's Franz Moore.

Today, of course, Schiller is altogether dead on our stage. Why this is so I cannot say, but since the death of Morris Morrison in 1910 this playwright has been cut off from us as with a knife.

An echo, however, remains. My readers will in all likelihood recall Gordin's *Zelig Itzik, the Fiddler,* a play I put on in the late nineties, my blooming time in America. The piece went for months, and remained in the repertoire for decades, and even today we quietly put it on now and then. I will speak of this play when I come to that wonderful period. Here it is enough to say that this capricious, foolish, poetic, musical, gossipy old Yiddish fiddler was one of the shining diamonds of my crown. It was a tragicomic role, much like Kobrin's Mina or Gordin's Wild Man. Comedy together with tragedy was the secret of my success in *Zelig Itzik.*

And from where, this play? Schiller! It is Gordin's free adaptation of Schiller's delicate, romantic *Intrigue and Love.* A last echo of the great German dramatist whose epoch I began on our stage in the London of the eighties.

Though Gordin's influence undoubtedly led the way to the "classic era," it was a success of Thomashefsky's that triggered it. "Better" theater had triumphed, but an inexhaustible appetite for *all* Yiddish theater had been created. In this new, prosperous era the old thrillers and musicals had their attractions too, and their violently partisan "patriots."

With *Alexander, Crown Prince of Jerusalem,* Thomashefsky had one of the greatest hits in Yiddish theater history. Women fainted when the handsome star made his entrance. The box office of the Thalia was besieged with people fighting for tickets, and for month after month the whole East Side wanted nothing else.

Adler, playing at a theater across the street, every night saw half his public disappear into the other house. Something had to be done, and one night he announced that he and Kessler would put on the greatest tragedy ever written, Shakespeare's *Othello.* And Adler added that Othello was not a little "princeling of Jerusalem," but a part that only an actor could play.

Within ten minutes Thomashefsky heard about his speech. Stung, he came out before his own audience and announced that he would play Hamlet.

*Jacob Adler
as Zelig Itzik
the Fiddler*

Both plays were put into production, and to everyone's surprise, both had success. The Yiddish public loved Shakespeare! In a theater continually in need of plays this suggested vast possibilities, and in the next years a flood of such standbys as *Trilby, Camille,* and *The Two Orphans* was staged, together with works by Ibsen, Strindberg, Hauptmann, Shaw, Hugo, Sardou, Scribe, Andreyev—some of these names hardly known to the Broadway of that time.

Three plays mentioned here, Lessing's *Nathan the Wise,* Gorky's *Children of the Sun,* and Gordin's *Der Metureff,* may throw some light on the range and scope of this period in the Yiddish theater.

Nathan the Wise, Gotthold Lessing's remarkable plea for religious tolerance, brings together Muslim, Christian, and Jew in a vision giving honor to all three. Written in 1779, it takes place during the Third Crusade, at a time when twelfth-century Jerusalem is under the sultanate of the famous Saladin.

The play opens with Nathan, a wealthy Jew just returned from war-besieged regions to Jerusalem. In his absence, Nathan learns, his house had caught fire and his daughter had all but perished in the flames. The girl was rescued by a Knight Templar, a young Christian who rushed into the burning house and carried her to safety.

This Knight Templar* who saved his daughter, Nathan learns, is allowed to roam the city in freedom because the sultan found in him a striking resemblance to a long-lost and much beloved brother.

Nathan seeks out the Knight Templar, but the young knight will accept neither gratitude nor reward. Despising both Muslim and Jew, he roughly reminds Nathan there can be no friendship between their peoples.

Nathan, always mild, points out that neither he nor the Knight Templar has chosen his people. "What then is a people?" Nathan asks. "Are Christian and Jew more Christian and Jew than they are men? Ah, had I found in you one to whom it sufficed to be called Man!" Too generous to resist this plea, the young man becomes Nathan's friend.

The idea of a religion transcending division occurs again in a later scene. Saladin has summoned the wealthy Jew, hoping to fill his depleted treasury. But Saladin, representing the great Muslim traditions of clemency, hospitality, and honor, soon drops talk of money and instead challenges this man, famed for his wisdom, to say what law, what faith, has satisfied him best.

"Sultan, I am a Jew," is Nathan's reply.

"A Muslim I!" Saladin returns. "Of the three faiths, one only can be true."

Nathan answers with Lessing's much-discussed story of the three rings. A father (Nathan tells the Sultan) possesses a ring that has the divine property of giving its wearer grace in the eyes of both God and men. Having three sons whom he loves equally, the father has two imitations made, and in this way can give the ring to all three sons. But after the father's death a quarrel breaks out, each son claiming that he alone possesses the true ring. The matter comes to judgment, and the judge pronounces this verdict: Each of the brothers must strive with the others to brighten the world with deeds of unselfish love. When they have all performed these deeds, and when ten thousand years have passed, a greater, wiser Judge than he will say which of the brothers possesses the true ring.

Nathan ends the tale saying, "Are you that greater, wiser Judge, Saladin?"

---

* The Poor Knights of Christ, members of the Knights of the Temple of Solomon, one of three great religious-military orders of the twelfth century, were under vows of chastity, poverty, and obedience. They were sent into the Holy Land to check the advance of Islam, protect Christian pilgrims, and "fight with a pure heart for the Supreme King."

Saladin (grasping his hand): "Nathan! The ten thousand years have not yet passed. Not mine the Judgment throne!"

As the play develops, we learn that the Sultan's lost brother married a European woman, a Christian. The Knight Templar is the son of this marriage, and is therefore both Christian and Muslim by birth.

Nathan's daughter is also revealed as a child of Christian parents, entrusted to Nathan in her infancy. She and the Knight Templar were born of the same mother, and the young man who hoped to make her his bride embraces her instead as his sister.

Nathan falls into great danger from the Christian patriarch of Jerusalem when the Christian origin of his daughter comes to light. His daughter saves him from death by pleading his cause with Saladin. And since this daughter can love no father but Nathan, the play ends with all three faiths united as a family.

Moses Mendelssohn hailed the play as a masterpiece, declaring that Lessing had spoken for him in every line, but the playwright found few other defenders. He was accused of insulting Christianity, friends cut him dead on the street, and a story got about that he had taken a bribe of ten thousand ducats from the Amsterdam Jews. He died in his fifty-second year, a man vexed all his life by poverty who had known only one happy year with an adored wife who died in childbirth.

The play, translated into a dozen languages, survived as a classic and was performed for years by leading German and Russian actors.

The role is generally regarded as among Adler's greatest. It was, in fact, his performance in this play and in *Uriel Acosta* that awoke the theatrical ambitions of the young Harold Clurman, the fiery critic and director who would one day revolutionize our own theater.

Although the bulk of the Yiddish audience was deeply Orthodox, we know of no opposition to *Nathan the Wise*. The public accepted Lessing's strange universalist Jew as they accepted the free love of Gordin's *Sappho*, as they later would accept Portia in *The Merchant of Venice*, and even the detestable Jessica.

Dazzled by the world's great minds, they seem to have simply taken in much that was new, carried away, like any audience, by the thrill of the play itself.

Maxim Gorky wrote *Children of the Sun* during the abortive Russian revolution of 1905, a moment when hunger, mass unemployment, and defeat in the Russo-Japanese War led to a crisis hailed by Socialists throughout the world as the end of the tsarist regime. A quarter of a million men had responded to a general strike that shut down mines, oil fields, railways, and ports, paralyzing the country. Mutinies broke out throughout the navy. Moscow was the scene of armed insurrection, and a *soviet* ("workers' council") was organized in St. Petersburg with Leon Trotsky as its vice chairman.

Gorky, in the forefront of the struggle, was put under arrest and imprisoned in St. Petersburg's Peter and Paul Fortress. Gorky had been thrown into prison before, but this time an international outcry led to the release of the world-famous writer. He left the fortress on February 2, 1905, taking with him the first draft of *Children of the Sun.* He had written it at white heat in eight days.

The action takes place in 1862, a time when a cholera epidemic led to riots in certain towns along the Volga. But this device fooled no one. The play was clearly inspired by the events of 1905 and was condemned by the censor as an incendiary tract calling for revolution. The ban, however, was soon withdrawn. The authorities feared it would mobilize just the kind of public demonstration they wished to avoid. Gorky himself, it is said, had written a letter suggesting this outcome.

The play was first performed in the theater of Vera Komisarzhevskaya, an actress noted for her political courage at this tumultuous and dangerous time. Differences between Gorky and Nemirovich-Danchenko were eventually cleared up, and the play had its premiere at the Moscow Art Theater on October 24, 1905, with the celebrated Kachalov as Professor Protassoff, and Olga Knipper as the sick, distraught, but prophetic Lisa.

The opening took place in an atmosphere of public tension. A close friend of Kachalov's, a revolutionary, had been shot down on the street by the police. There were rumors that the Cossack Black Hundreds planned to stop the performance by an attack on the theater.

There was no trouble during the first scenes, but in the third act, at the first offstage sound of an approaching mob, panic broke out. Half the audience rushed for the exits. Others surged toward the stage to protect the actors. Calm was restored only when Kachalov assured everyone he had been in danger only in his character of Protassoff.

The "children of the sun" in this Gorky play are Russia's intellectuals, a privileged elite, lofty-minded, idealistic, but blind to the gathering fury of the oppressed and brutalized masses around them. While the fantasies of the distraught Lisa repeatedly hint at social tragedy to come, the general tone is surprisingly light, and the leading character, Protassoff, is humorously drawn.

Unworldly, well-meaning, engrossed only in his experiments, Protassoff is comically oblivious to everything around him. He fails to understand that a hysterical woman has fallen madly in love with him. He is blind to the growing alienation of his wife, who is on the verge of leaving him. He cannot bring himself to be hard on the terrifying Yegor, a wife beater and drunkard, but a clever fellow who understands what Protassoff needs for his experiments. Pursued by a murderous mob, he indignantly "shoos" them away like a swarm of gnats. He fails to understand the situation even when felled by a revolver shot. Only when he speaks of his work, of a world set free by science from soul-killing drudgery, does Protassoff rise to the stature of visionary and idealist.

His fellow writers felt Gorky had lampooned the intelligentsia with his absurdly unworldly professor. Gorky himself felt the play called on artists and intellectuals to ally themselves with the working masses. It was, in fact, this writer's lifelong conviction that only such an alliance could bring beauty and freedom to those in society's "lower depths," allowing them, too, to take their place as "children of the sun."

The play was produced by Max Reinhardt in January of 1906 at his Kleines Theater in Berlin. But by then the 1905 revolution was over, the tsar had reasserted his authority, and Gorky himself had fled Russia.

During this exile Gorky wrote six plays, two novels, and a part of his autobiography and traveled to several countries. In 1912 he came to America, hoping to raise money for the Bolshevik party, and to influence the American government not to support the tsarist regime. His mission was icily received. He was ignored by American officials, and society turned its back, outraged by his relations with Maria Andreeva, the woman he regarded as his wife.

But if Gorky got a cold reception in these upper regions of the New York social world, his arrival was a great event to the Yiddish intelligentsia downtown. The actors were thrilled. Most of them were deeply sympathetic to the revolutionary movement in Russia, though only a few had taken active part in it.

In the year 1912, Alla Nazimova and her husband, Paul Orleneff, gave Russian-language performances every Sunday at Adler's theater on Eighth Street and Fourth Avenue. We know Gorky saw these actors in a Russian performance of Chekhov's *The Cherry Orchard;* he shared a box with Jacob Adler, Sara Adler, and Jacob Gordin. It was probably then, or soon after Gorky left America, that *Children of the Sun* reached the Yiddish stage.

The role of Protassoff was something of a challenge for Adler. A Russian intellectual who was also a country gentleman—and in a comedic vein! Apparently the play did well, since Adler mentions it among his successes. Socialist sympathy was high in a good part of his audience, and such people must have been thrilled by *Children of the Sun.* There were excellent character parts for others in the cast. The main role demanded only a gift for light comedy, a fund of personal charm, and the ability to convey high intellectual passion—all well within Adler's range. And although the play did not remain in the permanent repertoire, it apparently scored a decided hit in Adler's theater.

While the masterpieces of Europe could now be presented on the Yiddish stage, Gordin's plays, concerned with the great questions of Jewish life, had more meaning to this audience than any other.

Metureff (*The Worthless*), a study of provincial bigotry and fear, takes place in the 1880s in Soroka, a small factory town in the Ukraine—a time and place still vivid in immigrant memory.

In the Jewish community of this town, a world of narrow religious beliefs and quarreling commercial interests, Gordin places Ben Zion Garber, a man of genius lost and misunderstood in an environment that ultimately destroys him.

The son of a rich but illiterate factory owner, Ben Zion Garber has grown to manhood the butt of continual derision and anger. This son of a rich father does not behave like anyone else. He constantly reads and tries to educate himself, walks about lost in his thoughts, tells the truth no matter what comes of it, and in spite of anger and blows will take no part in his father's underhanded schemes against his business rivals.

In money-minded Soroka such a man can be regarded only as a *metureff*—a term of contempt for a hopeless misfit of use to no one.

The close of the first act reveals that this misused son is feeling the pain of a secret love. Lisa Rosenberg, daughter of a rival Soroka merchant, has come home from abroad the wiser for the loss of her illusions. The young physician Lisa loved, expecting a more handsome dowry, has withdrawn his offer of marriage, preferring to court a richer bride. Now Lisa's father, facing bankruptcy, has prevailed on her to marry Garber's coarse but successful older son, a man who boasts he is rich enough to take her without a dowry.

With marriage for a woman obligatory, and no other suitor likely, the twenty-year-old Lisa has accepted her fate. She hardly cares about the rest of her life and indifferently shrugs off the thought of her affianced husband with the revealing words, "In time, they say, one can get used to the devil himself!"

Lisa is drawn to the original young Ben Zion. She prefers him a thousand times to his older brother, and even has a thought of running off with him—a thought of escape. The impulse passes. Lisa has learned the value of position, safety, the respect of the world. Ben Zion is too unformed, too young. She finds his idealism childish, his insistence on truth naïve. In the end she laughs at him as a dreamer, a "little provincial Yiddish Hamlet." Their scene together ends with Ben Zion in despair, Lisa more moved than she is willing to admit.

After her marriage to Ben Zion's brother a quarrel breaks out between Ben Zion and his father, and Ben Zion leaves the house. He is taken in by Yisrol Yakob and his wife, a poor aunt and uncle who have always understood and befriended him.

In this poor home Ben Zion receives great news. Certain scientific observations he submitted to an Odessa newspaper have been accepted for publication. This is the first recognition he has ever known—a great moment in his life. With a new belief in himself he determines to go on with his studies and perhaps achieve something.

The idea of perpetual motion (a popular nineteenth-century concept) has seized his imagination. He envisions a machine needing no fuel, its action continually renewed by its own movement. Such a machine, he believes, would release a vast new source of power. Lisa's brother, an engineer, laughs at this idea as a dream, but Ben Zion, gazing at the stars, muses, "There is everlasting motion there. Why not here?"

Ben Zion is now earning his keep as a watchmaker, a trade he has learned from his uncle. But he gives every spare moment to his machine, convinced he is on the brink of a great discovery.

This strange machine, however, is arousing more and more fear in the Jewish community. There are whispers that Ben Zion is a freethinker, an atheist, even a friend of the devil.

His behavior does nothing to dispel the growing hostility. He interferes on the street with a husband beating his wife, and is beaten by both. He protests publicly that poor children are neglected and mistreated in the town Talmud Torah (Hebrew school). He writes to the newspapers, exposing unhygienic conditions in Soroka factories, his father's factory included. He does not seem to care whom he injures in his relentless demand for justice and truth. His uncle warns him that there is talk of driving him from the town, even some kind of plot against him, but Ben Zion hears it with mocking laughter. Grown bitter and gloomy, he takes a dark pleasure in having the whole world against him.

In spite of his uncle's warning he remains unguarded and alone, working at the almost completed machine. He is deep in his last calculations when Lisa appears at his door.

She has been sent to tell him his father is gravely ill. His mother is hoping that Lisa, if no one else, can prevail on Ben Zion to come and ask his father's forgiveness before he dies.

Ben Zion is not sure, between himself and his father, who should ask forgiveness of the other. But he promises to do as his mother has asked.

Lisa and Ben Zion have seen each other only at a distance for two years, and Lisa is now the mother of a child. She is nervous to find they are alone.

Ben Zion reminds her that she once called him a provincial Hamlet, but adds that she herself is a kind of Ophelia. "Shakespeare's Ophelia drowns herself," Ben Zion says. "This Ophelia marries my brother."

Lisa replies that Shakespeare's Ophelia was luckier. "She drowned in clear pure water and died only once, while this Ophelia dies every day in the filthy mire of a swamp."

Their conversation has gone too far and Lisa prepares to go. But at the door she pauses, saying she has made her choices, and will carry her responsibilities to the end, but Ben Zion must know that she loved him from the beginning, and will love him all her life.

She has brought back feelings that Ben Zion has made himself forget, and he responds with a violent despair, asking why she comes now, when she has no right to come, when it is too late, when happiness is no longer possible.

As the frightened Lisa tries to calm him, a fanatical townsman appears at the open window. Pronouncing Ben Zion's machine the work of the devil, its destruction the greatest *mitzva* (good deed), he steals it from its place. Lisa and Ben Zion are startled by a shout of many voices outside the window followed by a great crash as the machine is shattered against the ground.

The final act takes place in the home of Ben Zion's father. Old Garber is growing weaker every day but will not take to his bed or see a doctor, and is stubbornly refusing to produce his will. His older son is afraid he has left no will at all, in which case Ben Zion will inherit half his fortune. Ben Zion comes in on this quarrel. He is calm, but pale and obviously close to breakdown. He is carrying a suitcase. Finding a number of townsmen present he tells them there is no need to drive him from the town, since he is leaving it, never to return.

From these men, who regard him as a deadly enemy, Ben Zion learns that his brother gave a cowardly consent to the destruction of his machine. He hears it with indifference, answering only that the everlasting motion of the universe cannot be stopped by his brother or anyone else. He then asks his father's forgiveness for any hurt or harm he may have given. Having kept this promise to Lisa and his mother, he opens the suitcase, draws from it a revolver, and in the presence of all, discharges it into his heart.

His father now vainly tries to show him the will in which, after all, he was left his rightful share. His brother, cold with fear, feels he will be blamed for his suicide. Lisa, in an impassioned speech, declares they have all killed him with their fear of the truth, their bigotry, their hatred. And his mother, together with the old aunt and uncle, weep over his body as the curtain falls.

Although clearly there is a "message" here, the playwright in Gordin is always stronger than the teacher and propagandist, and *Metureff*, like all his work, is written on an emotional level that rises at times to moments of intense lyric beauty.

Nevertheless, the playwright leaves no doubt as to where he stands. This is shown most clearly in his "negative" characters. The father is redeemed by a moment of remorse in the final scene, but the egotism and greed of the brother is unrelieved, as is the empty pretentiousness of Lisa's father, the "enlightened" Rosenberg.

By contrast, Ben Zion emerges as not only a genius but a saint. "Not for nothing were you named Ben Zion!" (son of your people), the old uncle exclaims, reflecting Gordin's view that to fulfill his mission, the Jew must be the world's conscience. And in fact Ben Zion, the freethinker and atheist, is presented throughout the play as more truly a Jew than all his pious enemies.

Lisa—lost, tragically alone—is the play's most complex character. Her two scenes with Ben Zion, both essentially love scenes, can be compared to the best in modern literature. Her unexpected entrance in the third act is masterfully written for maximum dramatic impact. In her one scene with her husband, the fiercely feminist playwright gives us a shattering glimpse of her marriage—a woman of character and intellect chained for life to a man of coarse appetites, an empty egotist.

Sara Adler, who had excelled as the ill-educated, ill-behaved wife in

Gordin's *The True Power,* gave another star-caliber performance as the strong-minded, cultivated Lisa.

Adler is remembered for his agonized confession of love at the close of the first act, and for the moment when the young Ben Zion learns that his article will be published. Stella Adler recalls that as her father walked up and down reading and rereading the great letter from Odessa, he created an extraordinary illusion that he was growing, gaining in actual physical size.

As Ben Zion, who comes to believe in himself, Adler relived the great turning point of his own life. He loved this role above all others, and speaks of it as his best.

His greatest challenge, however, was still to come.

How I Saw the Role of Shylock and How I Played It

In the course of my long career I have played almost every kind of Jew. I have played simple Jews, Jews who were poets and dreamers, Jews who were clowns, fools, unfortunates, *schlimazls*. In all of them, I had joy. But true happiness, the proud happiness of the creative artist, I knew when it was given me to create the Jew of high intellect, proud convictions, and grand character.

I am neither a philosopher nor a historian—far from it—but my understanding of the Jew in history is as follows: He is a patriarch, a higher being, a man who has within him the gathered strength of generations. A certain grandeur, the triumph of long patience, intellect, and character, has been imparted to him by the sufferings and traditions that have been his teachers. Not only can he go through life, he is *rooted* in life and has grown strong in it. All this must be seen in his face, his glance, his dress. Weighty and proud his walk, calm and conclusive his speech, a man of richest personal and national experience, a man who sees life through the glasses of eternity.

So I saw him, so I had joy in him. So I played him as Goldfaden's Almasaro, as Lessing's Nathan the Wise, as Gordin's Yiddish King Lear. And so I played him as Shylock. My pride in him reached those who saw it. And this was our mutual triumph.

The first great sympathetic portrayal of Shakespeare's Jew was that of Edmund Kean in 1847. Before him the role was played by a comedian as a repulsive clown or, alternatively, as a monster of unrelieved evil. Kean chose it simply as a part in which his slight stature would not tell against him.

The illegitimate son of a part-time actress and prostitute, Kean had won some recognition in London as a child prodigy, but he ran away in a year or so after a quarrel with his mother about money. He spent the next ten years on the provincial acting circuit, and got his chance in London only because the Drury Lane Theatre, in the lordly hands of Richard Brinsley Sheridan, had been overspent to the point of bankruptcy. A dozen London stars had failed to save it, someone had seen Kean in the provinces and recommended him, and in the growing atmosphere of imminent collapse and disaster, even an unknown strolling player was allowed on the stage.

Kean went to his performance that night thinking of suicide. A torrential rain was falling, he had no money for a hansom cab, and had to walk from his lodging house to the theater carrying his costume in a bundle under his arm.

In a half-empty theater and with his scenes barely rehearsed, that first tremendous human Shylock has come down in history as the greatest theatrical event of the century. The audience was galvanized by Kean's first electrifying line. After that he was repeatedly interrupted by acclamations from the house. He went home that night a famous man.

Every actor after Kean has given some measure of sympathy to the role. Booth, the exception, could see nothing but a villain in Shakespeare's Jew, but Booth is not remembered for his Shylock. His father, Brutus Junius Booth (who claimed a modicum of Jewish blood), gave a patriarchal dignity to the part. The British-born American actor Richard Mansfield wrung from it all the sympathy he could get. Sir Henry Irving went furthest of all in justifying Shylock. A martyr, almost a saint, Irving's aristocratic Shylock was driven to cruelty only by the greater cruelty of the Christian world around him.

Adler made his first attempt at Shakespeare's Jew in 1901 at the People's Theatre on the Bowery. His Solomon Kaus and Yiddish Lear had already attracted notice in the American press. *Theatre* magazine came out with an article on the "Bowery Garrick"; he was compared to such actors as Booth, Irving, and Edwin Forrest. Articles, interviews, and photographs followed in other theatrical publications. Broadway actors came down, drawn by reports of a powerful and original performance. His name, in fact, was taking on a certain prominence, even a certain eminence, in the larger theatrical world.

In the winter of 1903 this actor received a remarkable offer. The

Jacob Adler in The Merchant of Venice; *Shylock's entrance over the Rialto Bridge.*
The American Theatre, 1903.

producer, Arthur Hopkins, wanted to bring Adler's Shylock to Broadway. The production, as Hopkins planned it, would have an American cast. Adler would speak his lines in Yiddish.

Given the surprisingly international tone of that time, the idea was not without validity. A dozen French, German, and Italian playhouses existed in New York. Sophisticated people went to the Théâtre Comique or saw an Italian play at Vercelli's Grand Central, much as they now go to see a French or Italian movie. European stars came over regularly, their language no barrier to success. Even mixed languages had been accepted. Tommaso Salvini had toured the country with a cast of American actors. Cocquelin had made an American tour with success. Hopkins felt the thing could be done; Adler was less sure. Broadway was a great opportunity, but an even greater risk. No doubt he thought the matter over carefully, but Hopkins made his offer twice, and twice Adler refused it. He did not want to play for strangers, did not want to leave his own public.

According to his children, it was the persuasions of a friend that led to his appearance on Broadway. This friend, an embattled Zionist named Dorf, thought Adler a match for any actor living or dead. Waving away such names as Edwin Booth and Sir Henry Irving, the ironical Dorf pressed his friend with a jest: "Adler, you owe it to the Gentiles!" and the burning Zionist added with a fierce cry, "Let them see how a JEW plays Shylock!"

Dorf's words apparently made the difference. Adler sent word to Hopkins that he was ready to talk.

In the two years he had played the role his ideas had gone through certain changes. He began with the villain Shakespeare wrote, relying only on the playwright's great lines to justify him. Over time this gave way to a Shylock of high morality, a man whose better nature was overcome only by a passion for revenge.

In the end Adler's whole life experience went against the image of a bloodthirsty Jew. Justification was thrown aside. It was total exoneration he wanted.

To vindicate Shylock, *pride* rather than revenge would be his motive. This Shylock would want to terrify and humiliate his enemy, but at the supreme moment, Antonio's life in his hands, he would refuse the murderous pound of flesh. To quote Adler in an interview in *Theatre* magazine, "His *scorn* would be the only cut, the only wound, Antonio would suffer."

In this interview, with Henry Tyrell, Adler presents a view of the play in which the characters of Shylock and Antonio are interestingly reversed:

> Shylock, rich enough to forgo the interest on his three thousand ducats for the purely moral satisfaction of his revenge, such a Shylock, I say, would be richly dressed and proud of mien rather than the poor cringing figure time has made familiar. Antonio, on the other hand, is far from the chivalrous gentleman he is made to appear. He has insulted and spit on the Jew, yet comes with hypocritical politeness to borrow money of him. Instead of the legal interest on his loan he binds himself to a preposterous forfeit he obviously never expects to pay, and in fact, never does pay. The two men are confronted in a supposed court of justice, a court packed with Antonio's friends, the judge openly committed to Antonio's cause, the prosecuting attorney a masquerading girl soon to be the bride of his bosom friend, and Shylock alone against them all without counsel, without advocate, with nothing on his side but the law.
>
> The verdict, of course, goes against him. A quibble reverses the case, Antonio and the court divide the spoils between them and— *exit Shylock.* That's the end of him as far as Shakespeare's stage direction goes. But having bought so dearly the right to his contempt for his Christian enemies, would he not walk out of that courtroom head erect, the very apotheosis of defiant hatred and scorn? That is the way I see Shylock, and that is how I have played him.*

At the People's Theatre Adler's innovation was accepted without question. A murderous Jew lusting for blood would have aroused only the scorn of an audience that still remembered the pogroms of Russia.

A number of American critics have lingered with interest on the "racial" aspect of Adler's performance, but in the main they were impressed by its strength. It was not a "softened" Shylock he brought to the stage, but the proud, vengeful figure who towers in every scene above the unreal Venetians of the play, the ambiguous, overwhelmingly human figure about whom even Shakespeare seems to have had mixed feelings.

---

* "Jacob Adler—The Bowery Garrick," *Theatre* magazine, November 1902, p. 18.

Above all, Adler's was the most deeply *Yiddish* Shylock. A glance at his portrait in the role will make this clear. In the gesture, the eyes, the whole bearing, one instantly recognizes the Jewish mind-set, the Jewish personality. We find no attempt at this in the portraits of other actors, even the greatest. Though the Jew is unmistakable in every line Shakespeare gives him, it is surprising how far these actors strayed, how alien their whole idea, from the Jew of any type.

Adler went a long way in this regard. The first chilling dialogue about the "merry bond" ends with Antonio's lighthearted words as he leaves the stage. Edwin Booth, we are told, turned on his departing enemy a look so malign that the audience shuddered. Sir Beerbohm Tree spat after him with almost comic effect. Adler, releasing the rage he had felt throughout the scene, hurled a Yiddish malediction at Antonio's back.

The curtain of the balcony scene falls on Jessica's elopement with Lorenzo, leaving us to imagine what came next. Sir Henry Irving was the first to supply the scene Shakespeare failed to write: Shylock's return to find that his daughter had eloped with a Christian.

The addition of anything to the play would be unthinkable in our time, but in Irving's day there was less reverence for the playwright. The actor was still supreme, and no star after Irving dreamed of leaving out a moment so effective.

Irving went up to the door of his house, and with telling effect, knocked, knocked, and knocked again, as the curtain fell. Sir Beerbohm Tree ran up and down uttering cries of grief and throwing ashes on his head. Adler crossed the stage in a profound silence, opened his door with a great key, and from within called his daughter, first in a low voice, sure of a reply, again with mounting fear, and at last with a *"Jess-i-ca"* that shook the walls—the terrible cry of a father betrayed.

After a silence he sank onto a bench, uttering, all but inaudibly, the distinctive Yiddish moan of pain. The curtain fell on the sound of ripping cloth. His child is dead. The Jew rends his garment.

Kean left the courtroom a broken man, Mansfield with a hint to the audience of imminent suicide, Irving with a mob outside howling for his blood—a shattering effect. Adler left the stage scornful, proud—a symbol of his people.

This was the portrayal that would be tested in a series of out-of-town performances before the play opened in New York.

It was at the Philadelphia Academy of Music in the year 1903 that I first appeared before an American audience as Shylock, speaking my lines in Yiddish with an American cast.

What would the world say about this, I asked myself. How would they accept a Yiddish actor in the role made famous by Booth, Novalis, and Irving? An actor from New York's Lower East Side on an American stage? Our Yiddish language side by side with Shakespeare's immortal English?

All that night after the performance I waited in Greene's Hotel on Chestnut Street. My family and close friends had come from New York. My two attorneys, my American director, my agents—everyone waited with me for daylight and the first reviews. Morning came at last. The reviews are before us. In every paper critics proclaimed my achievement, in review after review, my creation of Shakespeare's great character was lauded.

Great God, I had done it! It was true. Never did happy lover greet his love as I greeted that day. With joy, with champagne, with the embraces of those dear to me. Sleep? Who thought of such a thing? Does a newborn babe know weariness?

Already telegrams were arriving from near and far, messages from well-known artists, from Christians and from Jews. And I knew that from this moment the news would be carried over the country, carried, actually, over the world.

Only once before in my life had I lived through such a night followed by such a morning. That was in my first youth, when my rival, Spivakovsky, had replaced me in my best role—that of Guberman in *Breindele Cossack*. I could not bear to watch the performance, and paced up and down in an outside corridor. Suddenly I heard a great rush of applause. Spivakovsky had made his entrance. I had an attack of hysterics; Sonya's brother had to take me home and get me to bed.

At midnight Rosenberg, Sonya, and Spivakovsky came from the theater. And Spivakovsky himself told me he had failed as Guberman, failed completely. I sat up at this news, already cured.

All through that night these good friends waited with me for daylight and the first reviews. Morning came. I ran down myself for the papers, and read with my own eyes the blessed news that Spivakovsky had failed. I rejoiced in his failure, and he, the generous youth, rejoiced with me!

Terrible nights followed by wonderful mornings. The first morning that of a naïve boy making his first unsure steps in the theater. The second that of a man who had traveled half the world and already tasted all that life had to offer.

The first morning in the morning of my life. The second, only a little before its night.

Philadelphia, always one of "Adler's cities," received him as a distinguished artist. His appearance was heralded in the press as the most interesting and important event of the waning season. He opened at the Academy of Music, in itself a mark of prestige. A number of prominent people, among them Mayor Weaver, Judge Sulzberger, and Congressman McCreary, were present, and by all accounts, the well-filled hall rang with ovations after every act.

Though Adler would be given his due by many critics, Philadelphia was unquestionably the great affirmation of his life. In this remarkable city, as in no other, his Shylock was unreservedly accepted.* Every review, without exception, is filled with praise.

Philadelphia Inquirer: "With the memory of Booth still undimmed and the conceptions of Irving and other of our foremost tragedians still fresh in memory, it may perhaps be considered an exaggeration to say the Shylock of Jacob P. Adler is the greatest ever seen on the American stage. But there were veteran theatergoers and Shakespearean students at the Academy of Music last night who unhesitatingly expressed that view."

Public Ledger: "The sympathy of the audience was with the Jew from first to last, and it was all so logical and consistent that it seemed as though this must have been the great poet's thought in writing the play. . . . [Adler's language] did not grotesquely obtrude on Shakespeare's immortal English as many had feared, but seemed, as uttered by this actor, replete with gentle cadences and harmonies."

Evening Bulletin: "As an actor Adler must stand among the great. His Shylock alone would place him there, for it is a remarkable impersonation, the work of a genius."

---

* Because of its special Quaker history, this city escaped the racial and religious intolerance endemic throughout the country.

After a short and successful tour of Boston and Washington, the play opened at the American Theatre in New York on May 24, 1903. Once again the theater was packed with an enthusiastic audience, and according to all accounts there were numerous curtain calls after every act.

There were superlatives for Adler from New York critics.

Theatre magazine: "A striking and original conception, wrought out not only of careful study, but above all from a racial sympathy, an instinctive appreciation of the deeper motives of this profound and complex character."

New York Herald: "That rare dramatic experience on Broadway, the coincidence of a great play and a great actor."

Evening Journal: "He played the character in a way never seen on the American stage and defying imitation. . . . Shylock revealed as the Jew of the Ages."

Daily Mirror: "An artistic and dignified representation, whether or not it was 'the Jew that Shakespeare drew.' "

Other voices are more critical.

New York Times: "Since in his artistic sense he eschewed the Hebrew prophet of modern sentimentality and stuck to the Shylock of Shakespeare—and the Ghetto—his performance remains ambiguous and without theatric force."

Commercial Advertiser (later the *Evening Globe*): "A performance markedly uneven, due apparently to his desire to avoid exaggeration. He is sometimes too restrained, and as a result, the more offensive traits in Shylock are modified until they are no longer striking."

New York Sun: "The actor's countrymen predominated in the audience, but before long the Americans in the house were ready and willing to applaud him just as vociferously."

Other papers refer mostly to the novelty of the occasion. Almost all admit that the actor "scored" and held the audience from first to last, in spite of the language barrier.

There is some surprising comment on his "unsympathetic" interpretation. Opinion over the years had swung so far the other way that Adler's angry Shylock was seen by some as a "negative" portrayal.

But if New York gave this Shylock only a mixed press, it won the unqualified enthusiasm of Adler's fellow actors. John Drew came backstage one night with red roses for Jacob Adler. Frank Gilmore, later president of Actors' Equity, was another visitor. Leo Dietrichstein, a reigning star of the period, spoke of Adler as the equal of Booth and Salvini. And in the coming years this actor would number among his friends and admirers such theatrical lights as John Barrymore, Richard Bennett, David Belasco, Ruth Chatterton, Lenore Ulric, and a host of others.

The Merchant was revived for a limited engagement at Proctor's Fifty-Eighth Street Theatre in 1905, the production under the management of the George C. Fawcett Company, and with Frank Gilmore as Antonio.

There was talk of another Broadway appearance for Adler in *Uriel Acosta* or *Solomon Kaus,* but these plans did not materialize. Adler had been received with honor on a world stage. He had been compared to the greatest by men who had seen the greatest. He had done it as a Jew, and in his own language. It was enough. He went back to his own stage.*

In the summer of 1903, his theatrical engagements concluded, Adler left for Europe. News of the Kishinev pogrom had just reached the world, and he intended to bring his family back with him to America. He sailed on the *Kaiser Wilhelm der Grosse* and then took the train from Germany into Russia. He crossed the Russian border by bribing border officials; there was, in fact, no other way to enter.

He found his sister married and with a brood of children, all in a state of excitement about their famous uncle from America. But there were sadder changes. His father, the genial Feivel Abramovich, was no more, and his mother was now entirely blind.

Hessye had grown strangely silent these days, but her will was as strong as ever. She had lived her life in Russia and intended to die there. She would not change her decision, and when the time came for parting she and her son both knew it was their last embrace.

Twenty-three years later, in 1926, Adler would recall that visit to Odessa, and would record in his memoirs a last encounter there with the great friend of his youth.

---

* Shylock and the Yiddish King Lear were ultimately Adler's definitive roles, the plays presented at the great yearly benefits in his honor. In later performances of *The Merchant,* his children were part of his cast, Frances Adler as Portia, her younger sister Stella as Nerissa, Julia Adler as Jessica, and Luther, youngest of the clan, as Lancelot Gobbo.

My Last Sight of Rosenberg

A winter day, cold and windy. My armchair at the window looks out over the Hudson and Riverside Drive. The river is frozen as far as the eye can see, the thick gray fields of ice cut through here and there with long greenish cracks, showing that here the water had struggled with its icy enemy. On the eastern shore the land was low and flat, but in the west, sharp and bold, the thickly wooded Palisades rise to the sky, a mountain on a mountain, a tower on a tower, a long mighty fortressed wall.

Am I not in Moscow? Is it not the icebound Moscow River stretched out there before me? And that wall, so gray, so high, is it not the Kremlin of barbaric days that protected the Winter Palace from the oncoming Tatar hordes? Russia! My thoughts carry me back, and pictures of the past mix and mingle in my mind. The assassination of Alexander II. The ascension to the throne of Alexander III. The suffocating reaction that followed, the edict against our theater that sent our hopes, our very lives, crashing in ruins around us.

In Riga, saddest city of my actor's life, the edict struck us down. There we lost our beloved Cheikel Bain. And there too, I parted with Rosenberg, parted with him forever, as an actor and as a man.

It fell to me in Riga to choose between the two "Yisrols"—Gradner and Rosenberg—and it was Gradner I chose. Because we were hungry, and had to have bread. Because we were drowning, and had to save ourselves. Gradner was the better actor, the more versatile actor. Even in faraway London his great name might be known. And Gradner also brought with him his beautiful wife, an actress who played so well, and sang with such moving effect. My reasons were good. I was right to save the troupe, I was right to save myself. But Rosenberg, old friend—where was pity?

After Riga, I was to see him only once again. Soon after, I heard of his death.

But before the grave closes on him forever, let me set down who and what Rosenberg was, what he meant in my life, and how the last scene between us was played out.

Rosenberg was in every way the most remarkable, the most interesting man I have known. After all my years on earth, and in the two halves of the world where I have lived my life, I can finally say he was the most intelligent, the most interesting.

I was still a naïve boy when we met. He was a man who knew people, knew the world, and had mostly seen the bad side of both. I was seventeen. He was in his forties. I came of a known, respected family. His people were entirely obscure. I made my way in the world by honorable work. He lived a hole-and-corner existence on the thin edge of the law. In appearance, too, we were opposites, I tall, slender, handsome, he stooped, clumsy, not attractive in his person. We were winter and summer! But somehow our very differences brought us closer. I was dazzled by his worldly experience. He probably liked my youthful liveliness. I put myself in his hands, and he taught me everything. All the ways of life. Both the open ways and the hidden, the good and the bad.

When the Russo-Turkish War broke out in 1877, Rosenberg left for Romania. He met Goldfaden there, got the knack of theater from him, stole some of his plays, and came back to Odessa a theater man. Finding me home from the army, he made me into an actor. That was when our lives became truly entwined.

It was twenty years after we parted that our paths crossed again. In the summer of 1903, having finished the season in New York, I sailed for Europe on the *Kaiser Wilhelm der Grosse,* and from Germany took the train across the Russian border. In Odessa the two of us came face to face again.

It happened in this way. Going through the street one night my eye was drawn to a remarkable figure—a beggar with a stick, his beard wildly overgrown, a wild idiotic look in his vacant, bulging eyes, and one trembling hand stretched out to those passing. I took all this in with one sharp look and instantly called out, "Rosenberg!"

He peered at me uncertainly, and at last muttered, "Ah, so it is you, Yankele!"

I tried to speak to him, but it was useless. He was half paralyzed, his tongue lamed, his thoughts confused. But a look of intelligence slowly came over his face. "So you've done all right over there in America, Yankele," he murmured with a knowing look. "Well, then, share with a brother, eh?"

I pulled out everything I had, Russian rubles and American dollars together. But for some reason at just this point Rosenberg changed his mind. Backing away with an uneasy laugh, he said, "Up to your old tricks, eh, Yankele? Stage money!" And with that he suddenly made off.

I ran after him shouting for him to wait, shouting that these were American dollars, that they were worth more than his Russian rubles. But sick and paralyzed as he was, he still had his old quickness. I lost him in a maze of streets, and though I looked for a long time I did not find him again. I gave up finally, still shouting his name and weeping aloud, my dollars and rubles falling to the ground around me.

It was our last meeting, and that was such a meeting that better it never had been. I have carried it the rest of my life like a leaden weight on my heart.

When I returned to America a letter came telling me Rosenberg had been taken to the Odessa hospital. Soon after, word came of his death.

In the fall of 1903 Adler opened at the People's Theatre. He had leased the house in a partnership with Thomashefsky, but with a proviso in their contract that they were never to play on the same night.

The season began badly. Adler had just come back from Russia. He was exhausted and ill, and on many of the nights he should have played, the house remained dark. At last he asked Thomashefsky to release him from his contract. Word spread that Adler was leaving the stage.

Thomashefsky had always talked him out of these moods, but this time the situation seemed serious. After consulting with his manager, Thomashefsky drew up a paper offering Adler $10,000 contingent on Adler's agreement not to appear again in New York.

This document was a bad mistake. Adler stopped talking to Thomashefsky, began to perform regularly again, and, in his anger, announced as his next production a play not one other actor would have dared: *The Power of Darkness,* by Leo Tolstoy.

Although Gordin offered to write the translation in Yiddish, Adler, ignoring him, took on this task himself. His relations with Gordin had noticeably cooled. Possibly he felt that this friend should have prevented the offer of money that had so bitterly offended him.

Thomashefsky, living at that time in the same building as Adler, writes, "For some reason Adler and I were not talking just then, but from my dining room across the court I could see the room where he worked. Late at night I saw him, writing, erasing, going over the text again and again, his whole soul in Tolstoy's great work."

The subtitle of *The Power of Darkness* is a peasant proverb: "Once the claw is caught the whole bird is lost." Nikita, the peasant hero, lives a merry life, takes women at his pleasure, seduces a young girl, abandons her, marries a handsome widow, falls into an affair with her stepdaughter, gets her with child, and thus is drawn, step by step, into the crime that destroys him—the murder of the newborn infant. Nikita was played by Adler. Anisya, the wife who drives him to murder the child, was played with blood-chilling conviction by Sara Adler. The wedding of the third act, with its spectacular peasant dance, brought ovations, and at the end of the play—Nikita's confession and surrender to the police—the audience rose to its feet in a roar of tribute.

The production was acclaimed as a picture of peasant life equaled only on the Russian stage. Gordin came to the opening, sent flowers afterward, and acknowledged that the whole cast had played like artists. Thomashefsky came backstage with tears in his eyes. And for once the whole profession rejoiced in a triumph they took as their own.

"There was joy in the box office," Thomashefsky writes, "but an entirely different joy than was felt for other plays. An entirely different audience came. Not the kind of customers we were used to. Not the girls and pretty little women who ran to my performances. The Russian-Yiddish intelligentsia came!"

If we discount a short-lived attempt at *Resurrection* that had practically been laughed off the Broadway stage, Adler's *Power of Darkness* can be considered the first Tolstoy play presented in America. The greatest writer of the age was all but unknown here as a dramatist, and in general, not widely appreciated in this optimistic American era.

The review by Henry Tyrell in *Theatre* magazine reflects this negative attitude as well as the critic's continued admiration of Adler and his theater:

Tolstoy's sombre drama, *The Power of Darkness,* was presented recently on the Bowery by the Yiddish Artists Company, Mr.

Jacob Adler being seen in the role of Nikita. Gloomy and depressing as is this masterpiece of Slavonic art, the play was admirably performed, and the stage direction little short of a miracle. Would that some of our managers—and actors too, for that matter—made the pilgrimage downtown to receive lessons from this gifted actor who is unquestionably one of the great players of our time. If Adler could perform in English in a Broadway theatre he would be idolized. Unfortunately, he is not sufficiently versed in the vernacular, yet, for that matter, neither are Bernhardt, Duse or Salvini, in whose class Adler belongs.*

The Power of Darkness was followed by *Resurrection,* adapted from the Tolstoy novel by Gordin. The production, remarkable in itself, must also be noted for Sara Adler's electrifying Katyusha.

With her portrayal of Tolstoy's peasant heroine, Sara rose to the starring position she would hold for the next fifty years. The simplicity and grandeur of her performance, her transition from peasant girl to prostitute, the scene of her spiritual "rise from the dead"—all this was achieved with the restraint and artistry that were uniquely her own.

Sara followed *Resurrection* with another major performance, in *The Homeless* (*Un a Haim*), a play by Gordin centering on a tragedy in an immigrant family of that day. Here Sara played Mrs. Bathsheba Rifkin, a simple housewife who loses her husband to a woman of progressive ideas, a woman of the new era.

Knowing all her life only family and home, lost in an American world she does not understand, the wife has a breakdown. After two years in a mental institution, she comes home to a house where she no longer has a place. Her husband cannot give up the other woman. Her son shrinks away from her embrace. The boy is afraid of her.

Outside the tenement window, snow is falling and Mrs. Rifkin's thoughts go back to the home she had in Russia. Her illness is coming over her again, and she believes that other first home will still be there for her. She does not see herself now as a pitiful, deceived wife, but as the primal mother, the foundation of all life, who cannot be robbed of her great place. Neighbors call for help, but when the ambulance comes for her, Mrs. Rifkin has become a child again, circling, gliding, repeating over and over with joy that she is going home. The young American

---

* *Theatre* magazine, November 1903, p. 8.

Sara Adler in The Homeless, *by Jacob Gordin*

Sara Adler in Tolstoy's Resurrection, *act 3*

*The Grand Theatre
(built for Adler),
at Canal Street and
the Bowery, 1910*

David Kessler in
Yankel the Smith,
by Jacob Gordin

doctor is compassionate and tells her he will take her there. And circling, gliding, repeating with joy, "I'm going home—I'm going home," Mrs. Bathsheba Rifkin dances away as the curtain falls.

Keni Liptzin produced her own rival version of Tolstoy's *Resurrection*. But even this ambitious star never followed Sara Adler as the simple Jewish housewife of Jacob Gordin's *The Homeless*.

Thomashefsky and Adler were friends again, but their partnership was drawing to a close. In 1904 the Grand Theatre on the corner of the Bowery and Canal Street was built for Adler—the first house built specifically as a Yiddish theater.

The Grand and the Thalia theaters would be the scene of Adler's activity for a number of years, but by 1912 most of the troupe were moving to Second Avenue, a street without derelicts and with no elevated tracks overhead.

The Yiddish theater was coming into its best, most prosperous years. The great stars were playing nightly to large, excited audiences, new actors and playwrights were coming to the fore. Stock companies had sprung up in half a dozen cities, and in a few more years the "road" for the Yiddish actor would reach from Canada to California.

With the formation of the Hebrew Actors Union in 1899 every actor was assured of a decent wage, but the big stars were now living high. When Adler "guest-starred" on the road these days, he received a thousand dollars a performance. He and Sara moved from St. Mark's Place to a four-story brownstone at 31 East Seventy-second Street, a house with ample room for their growing family, and with the amenities of an elevator and a garden. Sara furnished her sitting room in the style of Louis Quatorze, with Aubusson carpets and satin wallpaper, and every spring went to Paris to have her gowns made by Worth.

The Thomashefskys also spent freely. They had a twelve-room home on Bedford Avenue in Brooklyn, a bungalow at the sea, and another twenty acres in Hunter, New York, where the actor built an open-air theater he called Thomashefsky's Paradise Gardens. Each of the three Thomashefsky boys had his own Arabian horse, and the star's dressing room was fitted with lamps of every color, marble statuettes, blue tapestries, and gold-framed mirrors.

Creatively, too, this is remembered as the Golden Age. Adler no longer had a monopoly on "good" theater. The volcanic David Kessler matched and outmatched him in certain roles. Mogulesko was still at the height of his powers. Thomashefsky, all his ambition roused, did outstanding work in the plays of immigrant life by Leon Kobrin.

Poster for Midway, *by M. Schorr, starring Bertha Kalich*

Bertha Kalich in Monna Vanna, *by Maurice Maeterlinck*

Max Rosenthal and Sabina Weinblatt in Damaged Goods, *by the French feminist Eugène Brieux*

According to Jacob Ben-Ami, Thomashefsky in these character parts was only a little under Kessler and Adler.

The women, too, were coming into their own. Bertha Kalich, famous for her "women of the world," was at her best in roles like Zaza, Fedora, Gordin's Sappho, and the Magda of Sudermann's *Heimat* (*Homeland*). After a few years in America this actress spoke an English of such purity that Harrison Grey Fiske was able to star her on Broadway, most notably in Maeterlinck's *Monna Vanna*.

Keni Liptzin had her own theater and produced plays by Hugo, Daudet, Hauptmann, and Andreyev, and as Gordin's Mirele Efros created a type so unique and original as to set a standard for every actress who followed her.

Sara, now an independent star, leased the Novelty Theatre in Brooklyn and held it for several years, producing plays by Ibsen, Shaw, and the French feminist Eugène Brieux. When Randolph Schildkraut, in Vienna, quarreled with Max Reinhardt, Sara brought him to America to play the husband in her production of Gordin's *Kreutzer Sonata.* Jacob Ben-Ami, a member of the famed Vilna Troupe in Europe, also made his first American appearance in this production. The boy and girl in the play were enacted by Stella and Luther Adler, youngest of the Adler brood.

A number of critics were now taking these theaters on the Bowery very seriously. Lincoln Steffens, then a reporter on the *Globe,* was a frequent visitor, and in the opinion of this journalist and critic, the Yiddish theater downtown was the best in New York. Hutchins Hapgood, the brother of Norman Hapgood, the editor of *Collier's Weekly,* was another early visitor. Hapgood, charmed by the whole downtown scene, took up residence there for eight years, finding in these crowded slum streets a spiritual unity and an intellectual excitement otherwise missing in American life. His book, *The Spirit of the Ghetto,* is a remarkable study of the working masses of the quarter, as well as the poets, philosophers, dreamers, journalists, actors, and playwrights who made up its intellectual life. He devotes several chapters to the Yiddish theater, and his comments on Gordin, Adler, Kessler, Mogulesko, Hurvitz, and others make fascinating reading.

As often happens, men like Steffens and Hapgood, far to the left of the mainstream, made a path that critics like S. J. Kaufman, George Jean Nathan, and later, Stark Young would eventually follow.

But the theater was reaching this high point in a scene already changing. In the years between 1905 and 1908 more than half a million

Sara Adler and her two youngest children, Stella (far left) and Luther,
in Gordin's Kreutzer Sonata

immigrants came through Ellis Island. These people, survivors of persecution and bloody pogroms, wanted a theater that amused them. Music
halls sprang up, with cafés where customers sat at tables and could buy
drinks while the performers on the stage entertained them. Many of
these music hall performers became great popular stars, and a pitched
battle began between the music halls and the theaters. Yiddish managers began looking for any sensation that would bring the public back,
and melodramas were staged in this era that outdid the worst of the old
Bowery thrillers.

In 1909, while Gordin's last play, *Dementia Americana,* failed,
Lateiner had the hit of the season with *The Jewish Heart.* Thomashefsky
followed the trend with *Minke the Servant Girl,* and then had a sensational forty-week run with *Pintale Yid,* by Seiffert. Both were comedies
of the old type.

"At the People's Theatre Kalisch and Kessler were playing Gordin,"
Bessie Thomashefsky writes. "Well, they had made their reputations

Left to right: A. Schrage, Jacob Adler, Sara Adler, Frances Adler, Joseph Schoengold. The title of the play and the year are unknown.

Left to right: David Kessler, Jenny Goldstein, Malvina Lobe, in The Jewish Heart, *by Joseph Lateiner*

with Gordin, so who could blame them? But at the Thalia Thomashef-sky and I were making fortunes. Very soon they began envying our big houses, threw away the art, threw away Gordin, and began delivering the goods to the great almighty Public."

Bessie's cynical gibe hits the mark. Kessler was forced to succumb. Others followed. Even Adler had to give in every now and then and put on a tearjerker. There was no other way to keep the theater going.

The actors took this downward trend as a thing they could neither control nor change. But for Adler this avalanche of *shund* (trash) seemed to be burying everything he had given his life to build.

SHMENDRICK, MY MEPHISTOPHELES

The reader will forgive me if my story takes on a certain sadness, for I confess that my beloved Yiddish theater has brought me some regret as well as joy. There are men today, for example, who go out on the road with Gordin's finest plays. They do not pay for these plays, and this is money that belongs to Gordin's estate, money his family badly needs. Worse, these people alter the plays, cut them to pieces, corrupt them, coarsen them. What does the provincial public know? The public comes, sees a travesty of theater, and turns away in disgust. And later, when the real actors come, there is no getting the audience back.

Gazing at the situation today, my thoughts go back to that memorable evening of my youth when I first saw the play all the world was talking about—*Shmendrick.* For you must know that this clown, this side-splitting Shmendrick, has brought more than a drop of sorrow into my life. I did not love him. I could not love him. Yet he clung to me, and there was no shaking him off.

My first encounter with him, it may be remembered, caused me both sorrow and shame, leaving a memory far from pleasant. Yet I ran many times after that to see *Shmendrick*—it may be I had a weakness for cheap, coarse plays. Mostly, however, I ran to see my young friend, Yankele Katzman, whom I loved as one loves a sweetheart. In spite of everything, I laughed at his antics. I was his best audience.

Later Katzman left the troupe. I saw him no more. A new actor played Shmendrick—an actor who interested me very little. Yet from Shmendrick himself there was no escaping. The audience wanted him. He could not be rooted out of the repertoire.

Years passed. I became my own master, director, and head of my own troupe. Still Shmendrick was with me. *Parnosse!** that same bitter Shmendrick was our livelihood. He brought money into the troupe, money we could not be without.

I last saw the play a few years ago in 1912 at Kessler's Second Avenue Theatre. A memorial performance on the anniversary of Goldfaden's death. The evening was arranged by the Hebrew Actors Union, and I, with my white hairs and sixty years on my shoulders, sat in the box, an honored guest.

No, that night I did not laugh; I was closer to weeping. In the theater the same deafening uproar, the same coarse empty laughter as in the Remesleni Club thirty-five years ago. On the stage, too, no change. The same clownish costumes, the same empty jokes, but worse now—mixed with the slang of Canal Street. And I asked myself with bitterness, Why *Shmendrick?* Goldfaden has written better things. And if, as it seems, it must be *Shmendrick,* could it not have been treated as a historical fact, a period piece, the first weak step of a still undeveloped theater?

A few years ago, at the Strand in London, I saw a company of French actors in a memorial performance in honor of Molière, father of the French theater. Molière was also a writer—more, he was himself a comedian. But what a difference! The play was *Le Malade imaginaire,* Molière's last play, one of his best and most serious—a play that has in it much of the tragedy of his own life. And the production! A miracle! Just as it was in Molière's time. The same scenery, the same atmosphere.

And here on Second Avenue? Triviality and vulgarity, both on the stage and in the audience. And this at a memorial, a *yuhrzeit!* I gritted my teeth. I called on the ghosts of Aristophanes, of Shakespeare, of Lope de Vega. I wept and swallowed my own tears. "Shmendrick, clown!" my soul shrieked. "Coarse Yiddish Mephistopheles! Have pity on my white hairs! Leave me!" And I cursed the fate that bound me to him, and the actors who had made a memorial a senseless antic holiday.

Yet even as I cursed and condemned, the tears rose. For my whole life, my whole past, was before me on that stage. All the lost days, all the lost years—I saw them again, knew them again. Again I heard the voice of Goldfaden: "The Jew is asleep. We must win him with a song as we awaken him." And high and great the dead dramatist rose in my

---

* Money to live on.

eyes. I bowed my head before him. I took back every hard thought, every hard word I had ever spoken about him or his theater.

And I embraced my unlucky little life's companion. I kissed away his foolish tears. Shmendrick! Poor weak first step of our Yiddish theater! Poor as you are, you are dear to me. I thank you, brother, for the laughter you gave us. I thank you for the happiness you gave us. Yes, with tears in my eyes I thank you, Shmendrick—my beloved— my own.

While the Yiddish theater had begun with Shmendrick, and Shmendrick would never be driven out, he would not forever entirely dominate the stage. As the era of "art alone" had lasted only a time, the reign of unadulterated *shund* would also run its course. The craze for music halls subsided. The new immigrants developed an appreciation of better things. Though vaudeville would from now on remain a popular, lucrative part of Yiddish entertainment, it ceased to be the all-devouring threat.

Ultimately, of course, both tastes had to be served. As in every theater, including our own, both the best and the worst, "art" and *shund* would alike find their audience. A balance was restored. Better plays became profitable again. And though Gordin died in 1910, it is his voice that will pervade this era to its end.

Though the theater downtown was largely outside the interest or knowledge of the great American public, Adler nonetheless was by now an actor of international reputation, and in the fall of 1911 several New York papers carried news that the Tolstoy estate had given him first American rights to the posthumous Tolstoy play, *The Living Corpse.*

This recently discovered play was creating a sensation at the two imperial theaters in Moscow and St. Petersburg, and was now keenly awaited in Berlin and at the Hofburg Theater in Vienna, with unprecedentedly heavy bookings reported in both cities. A translation from the Russian original was published in the Sunday *New York Times* of November 1, 1911, and another appeared in the theatrical magazine *The Call.*

All this was creating extreme interest in theatrical circles, and Adler's premiere on November 3 drew such an array of celebrities that one New York paper described the event as the sensation of the season!

The play, an early work and in a different vein from Tolstoy's later writings, is concerned chiefly with his central character, Fedya Protosov. A Russian of the upper class, Protosov is tormented by a conviction that his wife has never truly chosen between him and another man, Karenin. Since his own existence seems to him without use or purpose, and he feels he is standing between his wife and her happiness, he resolves on suicide.

In a startling scene, Protosov tries to end his life, but lacks the courage to pull the trigger. Failed at suicide, he decides to disappear, to become, in effect, a "living corpse."

As actually happened with Tolstoy's older brother, Protosov falls in with gypsies and finds solace in the love of a gypsy singer. Eventually he wanders off and, possessed of neither money, profession, nor skill of any kind, sinks lower and lower.

The turn of the drama comes when this supposed "corpse" is revealed as a hoax, the man is not dead, and Protosov's wife, now married to the other man, is brought up on a charge of bigamy. Barely recognizable, a wreck of his former self, Protosov appears in court to plead that his wife knew nothing of his existence and is therefore innocent of the charge against her. Finding that she must either give up her present husband or face Siberian exile, he frees her of the bigamy charge by shooting himself.

Protosov's character, his impatience with cant and pretense, his rebellion against the coldly correct world around him, give the play its intense appeal. His wife, drawn by these qualities but also needing the colder, more conventional Karenin, has continually veered emotionally between them, and at the end of the play hysterically tells Karenin she hates him and has always loved Protosov.

The Yiddish press was divided. Critics found Adler's performance wanting, the character not realized. The playwright Kobrin, who wrote the Yiddish translation, was enthralled by Adler's performance: "Not one loud cry! How softly and dreamily he told his drinking companions the story of how he became a 'living corpse.' With every move, every turn, you saw the Russian aristocrat! And in the courtroom when he saw his wife, how he looked at her, how his eyes begged her to forgive him. What a world of soul was in this mute play! Even his suicide did not break the quiet of his performance. Silent as a shadow he took himself off, and then—offstage—the shot!"

Though American reviews still have a tendency to shy away from the grimness of Russian realism, time had brought a certain acceptance.

Sheet music for the gypsy music in act 2 of Tolstoy's The Living Corpse,
with photos of Tolstoy (top center) and Sara and Jacob Adler

The *New York Times* warns us to expect "no touches of lightness in the action or dialogue," but concedes that "a wealth of characterization makes up for it." The *New York Dramatic Mirror* comments on Adler's "courage" in presenting this somber drama, noting that while the Yiddish theater cannot be held to the scenic standards of Broadway, the Bowery can present tragedy with insight and dignity.

> Throughout Fedya Protosov's fall from revelry to penury, Mr. Adler kept burning that spark of nobility that would end his pitiful existence. His love for his wife he subtly but vividly declared in raving at the magistrate, "Why do you intrude into other people's lives? There are three of us—I, he, and—she." The pause before the last pronoun and the change of intonation, told the whole story.
>
> Although a pistol figures in the dramatic personae, the tragedy never flared into melodrama. It was played by the entire cast with too much gravity and sincerity. Mrs. Adler particularly, met the serious situation with a sensibility nonetheless effective in that it did not indulge in hyperbole.*

Adler regarded Protosov as one of his greatest roles, and played it throughout his acting career.[†] The gypsy Masha, who sings the haunting gypsy music of the second act, was played over time by a number of actresses. Julia Adler, superior, in her father's judgment, to all others, played it in his later life.

With a national audience across the country, the Yiddish theater was growing every year. By the time America entered the war there would be twenty-two Yiddish theaters in New York alone, not counting two houses that showed Yiddish vaudeville. News of this downtown theater world, with its business deals, lawsuits, partnerships, and mergers, often found its way these days into the theatrical pages of the town. Reviews were frequent. Critics were interested in the strong plays, the

---

* *New York Dramatic Mirror,* November 15, 1911.
[†] Renamed *Redemption,* the play was produced on Broadway by Arthur Hopkins in 1919, with John Barrymore in the starring role. A revival some years later starred Jacob Ben Ami, an actor with a distinguished career on both the Yiddish and American stage. Ben Ami is remembered for his remarkable acting in the failed suicide scene. A German production of the play was brought to Broadway in the early thirties by the visiting star Alexander Moissi.

huge emotional responses of the audience. Adler, in particular, with his white hair and tall silk hat, was now a well-known figure, the incidents of his theatrical, and even his personal, life apt to be rehearsed in the press. In fact, the downtown theater—with its successes, failures, "patriots," and personalities—had been accepted as a colorful part of the New York scene.

Time, however, was bringing inevitable changes. Gordin died in 1910, Abba Schoengold soon after. The stage lost Mogulesko in 1914, and Keni Liptzin two years later. In 1920, David Kessler collapsed at a rehearsal in Brooklyn. He went on that night in spite of a doctor's warning and was taken, unconscious, to the hospital immediately after. An operation was performed the following morning, but Kessler died the same day.

Of the old guard only Adler, Sara Adler, and Bertha Kalich were still performing. But in the summer of 1920, after a triumphant season in London, Adler suffered the stroke that ended his career.

LAST APPEARANCES

After a number of months in an upstate sanitarium, Adler was enough improved to go back to the apartment on Riverside Drive that was now his home. On good days he could get across the room unsupported and raise his afflicted arm to the level of his shoulder. On bad days he stayed in his room or dreamed away the hours at a window looking out on the river. A man was engaged who read to him and once a day, weather permitting, took him out along the drive in a wheelchair.

Most of his children were still living at home, and the big apartment was full of their comings and goings.

After Adler's mother's death, the whole brood of pretty "Russian cousins" had come to America and were always in the house. Frances, Adler's married daughter, brought his grandchildren, Pearl and Lulla, every weekend. Visitors came to see him, actors, admirers. The house was full of life and gaiety, but the sick man dreamed away most of his days at his window overlooking the river.

He had never saved his money, and when expenses grew too pressing a benefit was planned, a grand last performance that would take care of the mounting financial problems caused by his illness. A number of people were active in organizing this event, prominent among them his daughter Frances Adler, who rounded up the roster of Broadway stars who took part and did more than anyone to make the evening a success.

The benefit took place on January 15, 1922, under the auspices of a committee that included Abraham L. Erlanger, Morris Gest, Edgar and Archie Selwyn, Lee and J. J. Shubert, Arthur Hopkins, Marcus Loew,

*Jacob Adler and six of his nine
children, left to right: Luther, Stella,
Julia, Jay, Frances, and Abe*

*One of Adler's Russian-born nieces,
whose stage name was Francine
Larrimore*

*Luther, Jacob, and Stella Adler,
Pine Hill, New York, 1920*

and David Belasco. The whole of the American theater had united to honor an actor now recognized by all.

Advertised as the "final appearance on any stage of Jacob P. Adler," the performance took place at the Manhattan Opera House to a sold-out house and with a dazzling array of Broadway personalities appearing in tribute. Telegrams of congratulation came from Dr. Stephen S. Wise, Justice Otto Rosalsky, Adolph Lewisohn, and the labor leader Joseph Barondess. Al Jolson sang. Will Rogers performed his famous rope act. Giovanni Martinelli came from the Metropolitan Opera to sing the popular wartime hit "Pack Up Your Troubles." Lionel Atwill performed an act of Sacha Guitry's *Deburau*. Other lights of the vaudeville and legitimate stage included Richard Bennett, David Belasco, Emily Stevens, Belle Baker, Frank Craven, Lenore Ulric, Robert Warwick, Leo Dietrichstein, and other glittering names of that moment.

The program opened, as announced, with the first act of *The Yiddish King Lear.* Since this takes place entirely around the festive table of Gordin's merchant-king, Adler could remain seated throughout. The tributes went on after that until one in the morning, and the audience went home happy.

The benefit raised $15,000, a success that prompted the series of "Positively Last and Final Appearances" that provided the paralyzed man with his only income.

The second of the "farewell performances" took place in 1923 at the Metropolitan Opera House in Philadelphia. Once again Adler appeared in the first act of *Lear.* Since Broadway stars were not available here, his son-in-law, Joseph Schoengold, an actor with the requisite dramatic power, took over his role for the remaining acts of the play.

In 1924 Adler's condition improved, and he decided to attempt Gordin's *The Stranger,* one of his great successes. Since the role called on him to portray a sick and broken man, he felt it would not be beyond his powers to perform all four acts.

He was advertised first in Toledo, Ohio, and according to the *Toledo Blade,* ten thousand people came to the theater for tickets. Police were called out, but the crowd remained orderly, and no incident is reported.

The Stranger was inspired by the narrative poem "Enoch Arden," Tennyson's tale of a man for many years believed dead, who comes home to find that his wife has married again and his children have another father. Gordin had adapted this plot to Jewish life, but included, at a

Jacob Adler's last role, in The Stranger, *by Jacob Gordin*

critical moment in the play, a passage from the Tennyson poem.* The hero of the play, Naphtali Hertz, has been missing for six years in the Russo-Turkish War. His wife believes he is alive, but is finally persuaded, for the sake of her children, to marry again. The missing man, of course, is still alive, and after years of searching, has learned that his wife, now remarried, is living and prospering in America. Broken, old, unrecognizable, he follows to claim his wife, his children, and his home.

The entire first and most of the second act both lead up to this dramatic "return," giving Adler an entrance that has been called the greatest moment of all Yiddish theater. But in Toledo, when the moment came and he flung open the door, such an emotion broke out in the theater, there were such tears, such shouts of his name, that he broke down, weeping aloud, and the curtain had to be lowered.

Nevertheless, on May 12, 1924, at Kessler's Second Avenue Theatre, *The Stranger* was again performed. Several reporters covered the event. We learn from the *Morning World* that the audience "wept unashamedly" as Adler made his entrance, crossing the stage afterward on a stick, that although he had only a short scene after his entrance, he was called out eighteen times when the curtain fell, that he struggled visibly through the rest of the play, gave his last cry "magnificently," and then sank back, exhausted.

He wept afterward in his dressing room, and Sara could not console him. "You made them cry as they never cried before," Sara said.

"But it was not my art that made them cry," he answered.

He rarely left his home in these years, but in 1923, when Stanislavsky came to New York with the Moscow Art Theater, Adler insisted on paying his respects. Luther and Julia accompanied him, but when they arrived at the hotel, Adler was too ill to leave the automobile, and a message was sent up with his apology. They were about to drive off when Stanislavsky hurried out of the hotel in his bathrobe and slippers, distressed that the sick man had come. They exchanged a few words in Russian in the car, and embraced. Adler wept, and Stanislavsky wept with him.

His children were grown now, and finding careers in the American theater. Luther Adler got the coveted role of Laurette Taylor's son in

---

* Gordin often drew elements of his plays from the world of dramatic literature, but always acknowledged his source. In the first act of Gordin's *Lear,* for instance, the story of Shakespeare's play is recounted to the Jewish merchant as a warning.

Humoresque in 1923. Stella was on Broadway in 1922's *The World We Live In* by Karel and Josef Čapek. Julia was starred by Belasco in the 1922 comedy *Rosa Machree.* Abe was a well-known Broadway manager. And "Fanya," prettiest of the "little Russian cousins," was now Francine Larrimore, a rising star on Broadway and soon to be the hero-ine of such legendary successes as *Chicago, Brief Moment,* and *Let Us Be Gay.*

Yiddish actors were also turning to the American stage. Muni Weisenfreund, now Paul Muni, electrified Broadway audiences as the young criminal of *Four Walls.* Ludwig Satz scored a hit with *Potash and Perlmutter,* a comedy about the coat and suit business. Joseph Schoen-gold, who had inherited his father's talent and voice, won acclaim in Sigmund Romberg's operetta *The Magic Melody.*

Downtown the big popular performers were Jennie Goldstein, Molly Picon, Aaron Lebedeff, Menashe Skulnick, Nellie Kasman. But Maurice Schwartz was looming as a big force, his Yiddish Art Theatre bringing in a new idea, a new era. The great comedies of Sholem Alei-chem belong to this period, as does Solomon Ansky's Cabalistic play *The Dybbuk.* American critics were charmed by the fascinating world of the shtetl, intrigued by David Pinski's *Forgotten Corner,* captivated by Peretz Hirshbein's idyllic rural *Green Fields.* Adler was downplayed. Gordin was forgotten. The "world Jew" of the Haskala was no longer in style. But Schwartz's impressive productions were bringing a much-needed infusion of life to the Yiddish stage. In 1922 Congress passed the Immigration Act, which halted the flood of incoming immigrants who had supported it. American-born boys and girls were drawn to the great movie palaces on Broadway. They had no interest in Yiddish plays and Yiddish actors. The language itself was dying.

In 1925 publication of Adler's serialized memoirs was cut short. Louis Miller's *New Varheit* had closed its doors in less than five months. The last entry of Adler's memoirs was published on July 18, 1925. And he himself had less than a year to live.

On February 12 — Avrom Lincoln's birthday — I reached my sev-entieth year. I am now at the time, the poet tells us, when the soldiers, the hands, begin to tremble, and the watchmen, the feet, begin to falter. The sun is growing darker. Clouds begin to cover the moon. What was deepest, most satisfying, most beautiful in my rich life is every day fading.

My dressing room I see once a year, at most twice, that dressing room where I have lived the best and truest part of my life. My public, too, I see seldom, that public with whom I have grappled fifty years like a gladiator in the time of Rome—a battle that begins on their side with coldness and indifference, on mine with fever and disquiet—the battle that, again and again, *I must win!* But if victory should be achieved, if my Antoninus yields and is conquered, if the barrier between us falls away and disappears—then how joyfully we draw close to each other, how dear we are then to each other, and how grateful!

Now I am far from my public, and as an artist, I am alone. Of all the companions, all the pioneers, who together with me laid the foundations of our stage, only I remain.

Where are they now, my true ones of yesterday? Where is Goldfaden, my rabbi, my father, the teacher who taught me my art? Where is my young companion, Mogulesko? Where is Gordin, the wise man, the sincere, the writer in whose plays my talent unfolded like the petals of the rose? Where is Keni Liptzin? Fate brought us together in a faraway Russian town, but in this great city of the New World we were not parted. Where is Kessler, my eternal colleague? Yes, we were competitors, but how deeply—better than anyone else—each of us loved and understood the talent of the other! Where are they all? Where? The black Kassaman has laid them all away, and left me here alone, the last of my generation.

Old and lonely though I am, I have my memories of the Yiddish theater, memories I must set down while my strength holds out and my imagination can still give them form and color. For the story cannot be told in records and documents. Only dipped in blood and lit with the tears of a living witness, can the world understand how with our blood, with our nerves, with the tears of our sleepless nights, we built the theater that stands today as a testament to our people.

I must give it over, I must set it down, for it belongs to a future generation, part of their life, their culture, their history.

Adler died in the week of Passover, on March 31, 1926. A sudden collapse. A flow of blood from the mouth. It was over in less than a minute.

The funeral procession of Jacob P. Adler, April 2, 1926

There were eulogies and articles in the cities he had played. An editorial in the *New York Sun* traced the history of his acting career. An editorial in the *New York Times* declared that with his passing the heroic age of the Yiddish theater had died.

For twenty-four hours before the funeral the body lay in state at the Hebrew Actors Club at 31 East Seventh Street. The portraits of Avrom Goldfaden and Jacob Gordin looked down from the black-draped wall above him, but Adler now lay simply an Orthodox Jew, the yarmulke on his head, the striped Jewish *tallith tefillim* over his body.

Early on April 1 the long lines of mourners began filing slowly past the open coffin, and by eleven o'clock the crowds outside had grown so dense that the doors were closed to all but the family and members of the union.

By the morning of April 2, fifty to one hundred thousand people had poured into the streets in what the *New York Times* described as a demonstration on the Lower East Side seldom equaled in the history of New York.

A squad of twenty-four mounted police and one hundred patrol-men had been stationed along the avenue. Buttons were sold bearing Adler's picture and the words WE MOURN OUR LOSS. Store windows displayed his black-draped photograph. Many stores were closed during the two hours of the funeral procession.

Wails were heard and the crowd surged forward as the coffin was brought out of union headquarters. Many people broke through the lines, and twelve policemen had to march abreast, clearing a path as the pallbearers carried the coffin to Kessler's Second Avenue Theatre, where the services were held.

Inside the theater an audience of three thousand listened silently as Abraham Cahan, the editor of the *Jewish Daily Forward,* giving the principal address, spoke of Adler's death as the end of the great triumvirate that included David Kessler and Siegmund Mogulesko. Speeches followed from Boris Thomashefsky, from Samuel Tobias, who had played with Adler in Odessa, from the playwright Leon Kobrin, the labor leader Joseph Barondess, and from Moishe Katz of the *Jewish World,* Dr. Alexander Mukdoiny, drama critic of the *Jewish Morning Journal,* and Dr. Samuel Margoshess, editor of *The Day.* The Elmoleh Rachamim, the prayer asking mercy for the dead, was sung by the cantor, Yossele Rosenblatt.

Outside the theater police were able to keep an area cleared as the family and mourners emerged, but once the procession got under way the huge crowd, occupying every inch of space from Fourth to Houston streets, fell in behind the cortege, following it east to the Bowery, past the People's Theatre, the National Theatre, the Grand Theatre, past Grand Street, past Forsythe Street, where thousands more watched from tenement windows, fire escapes, and roofs, and on to Delancey Street, where the procession entered the Williamsburg Bridge. Every girder of the bridge was hung with men watching silently to see the hearse go by, and hundreds more stood watch at the burial grounds of Mount Carmel, where Jacob Adler, his journey over, was finally laid to rest.

He left us a legacy in that veteran band of actors known to the whole theatrical world as "the Adlers." Irreverent, magnetic, each of them with a character and a view of life that clashed with the others', they were held together by their theatrical heritage, and by something in the look, the speech, the whole persona, that identified them instantly as members of this family.

In 1928, two years after their father's death, these brothers and sisters performed together in one of his great successes, *The Wild Man,* by Jacob Gordin. All the Adlers performed in this play, and the family might have formed a permanent company—but individual careers called them. They went their separate ways.

Luther and Stella joined forces with the struggling, newly formed Group Theatre. Jay went on the road with the Broadway hit *Blind Alley.* Celia was carving out her place in the emerging Yiddish Art Theatre movement. The others took work as it came, sometimes in the Yiddish, sometimes the American, theater.

One way or another the Adler family made it through the shoals of the thirties. But as the Depression deepened, and both on Broadway and Second Avenue theater after theater closed its doors, their children were growing up in a world where the opportunities of the past were dwindling. Some of these younger people made their way in fields other than the theater. One or two, knowing no other life, hung on, believing times would change and their chance would come.

Pearlie Schoengold, first and most loved of the grandchildren,* was led onto the stage by her grandfather at the age of two. When Stella Adler left the cast of *The Wild Man,* the seventeen-year-old Pearlie was sent on the stage to replace her. She gave a shaky, uncertain performance, but thrilled the audience with a flood of emotion in her all-important curtain scene. She had earned her place in the family.

When the Adlers disbanded, in 1932, an offer came to Pearlie from the Boston Repertory. She played a season of Shakespeare in Boston, but came home to find that jobs were scarce. She joined the Theatre Collective, one of a score of semiprofessional groups and workshops, all strongly left in tendency, that sprang up in New York at that time.

She did some excellent character parts for the Group Theatre in the next years, notably in their London production of *Golden Boy* and in the Paul Green–Kurt Weill musical *Johnny Johnson.* She had a leading role opposite Donald Moffat in an interesting production of Pirandello's *Henry the Fourth,* played with Buster Keaton in a season of summer stock, and was offered parts now and then both on and off Broadway. She did not look for work, did not make the rounds of agents and producers that are the curse of the American actor; her career took second place to a stormy personal life. She was known in the profession as a strong actress, and though she did not seek them, from time to time there were parts for her.

* Daughter of Frances Adler and Joseph Schoengold, later known as Pearl Pearson.

Seated, left to right: Stella Adler, Joseph Schoengold, Sara Adler. Standing, left to right: Luther, Julia, Abe, Frances, Charles, and Jay Adler.

Left to right: Frances Adler, Joseph Schoengold, Stella Adler, in The Wild Man, 1928

Left to right: Julia, Jay, Luther, Charles, and Abe Adler, in The Wild Man, 1928

Luther and Stella Adler in Success Story, *a Group Theatre production,* 1935

Celia Adler and Paul Muni in the Ben Hecht pageant A Flag Is Born

Maurice Carnovsky, Charles Niemeyer, Elia Kazan, Art Smith, Roman Bohnen, Luther Adler, and Robert Louis in Golden Boy

Sara Adler

Jacob P. Adler

In her later years she had an important place in Stella Adler's prestigious acting school. She was possessed of exceptional beauty and a great natural talent, and she might have gone far had she desired to do so.

Allen Adler, grandson of Jacob Adler and Sonya Oberlander, made it through the lean years as best he could. He ran a little movie house, lost it again, produced a road show of Ben Hecht's *Front Page,* tried his hand at a play, wrote an interesting novel, and after a two-year stint in the army had a fling at Hollywood in the fifties. His movie, *Forbidden Planet,* is now a classic. But his career ran aground in the political carnage of the Hollywood hearings, and the studio did not renew his contract. Like Jacob, the son of Luther Adler and Sylvia Sidney, he died before his time. The gifts of both these young men were too soon lost to the world.

Sara Adler lived to the age of ninety-one, and in her seventies performed all four acts of Jacob Gordin's *Homeless,* a production she herself cast, staged, and directed. There was still magic in the way she moved. And the portrayal that never strayed from realism still had the power and beauty she had given the role when she was young.

When she had passed her eightieth year a Diamond Jubilee was organized in her honor. Testimonials were given from the stage, a number of celebrities spoke, and Sara performed the great third act of Tolstoy's *Resurrection.* Actors who were present on the occasion never forgot the performance.

She died in 1953 surrounded by her family and in full possession of her faculties. She had survived her husband by twenty-five years.

Some members of this family rose to stardom and fame. Others had less success. Among themselves these differences did not exist. They were all of the theater. They knew its shabby side and they knew its great side. They had their place in their own eyes—it did not change with their place in the eyes of the world.

They are remembered for their fire, their laughter, their arrogant pride in their tradition. They have left some imprint of that tradition—some imprint of that excellence—on our theater and on our time.

INDEX

Page numbers in *italics* refer to illustrations.

A NOTE ON THE TYPE

The text of this book was set in Garamond No. 3. It is not a true copy of any of the designs of Claude Garamond (ca. 1480–1561), but an adaptation of his types, which set the European standard for two centuries. It probably owes as much to the designs of Jean Jannon, a Protestant printer working in Sedan in the early seventeenth century, who had worked with Garamond's romans earlier, in Paris, but who was denied their use because of Catholic censorship. Jannon's matrices came into the possession of the Imprimerie nationale, where they were thought to be by Garamond himself, and were so described when the Imprimerie revived the type in 1900. This particular version is based on an adaptation by Morris Fuller Benton.

Composed by North Market Street Graphics,
Lancaster, Pennsylvania

Printed and bound by Quebecor Printing,
Fairfield, Pennsylvania

Designed by Iris Weinstein